AFRICA AND FRANCE

Postcolonial Cultures, Migration, and Racism

DOMINIC THOMAS

INDIANA UNIVERSITY PRESS

Bloomington and Indianapolis

This book is a publication of

Indiana University Press
601 North Morton Street
Bloomington, Indiana 47404-3797 USA

iupress.indiana.edu

Telephone orders 800-842-6796
Fax orders 812-855-7931

⊜ The paper used in this publication meets the minimum requirements of the American National Standard for Information Sciences—Permanence of Paper for Printed Library Materials, ANSI Z39.48-1992.

Manufactured in the United States of America

Library of Congress Cataloging-in-Publication Data

Thomas, Dominic Richard David.
Africa and France : postcolonial cultures, migration, and racism / Dominic Thomas.
p. cm. — (African expressive cultures)
Includes bibliographical references and index.
ISBN 978-0-253-00669-1 (cloth : alk. paper)
ISBN 978-0-253-00670-7 (pbk. : alk. paper)
ISBN 978-0-253-00703-2 (eb)
1. Africans—Cultural assimilation—France. 2. France—Race relations. 3. National characteristics, French. 4. Multiculturalism—France. 5. Racism—France. 6. Africa—Emigration and immigration—France. 7. France—Emigration and immigration—Africa. 8. Postcolonialism—France. I. Title.
DC34.5.A37T48 2013
305.896'044—dc23 2012036060

1 2 3 4 5 17 16 15 14 13

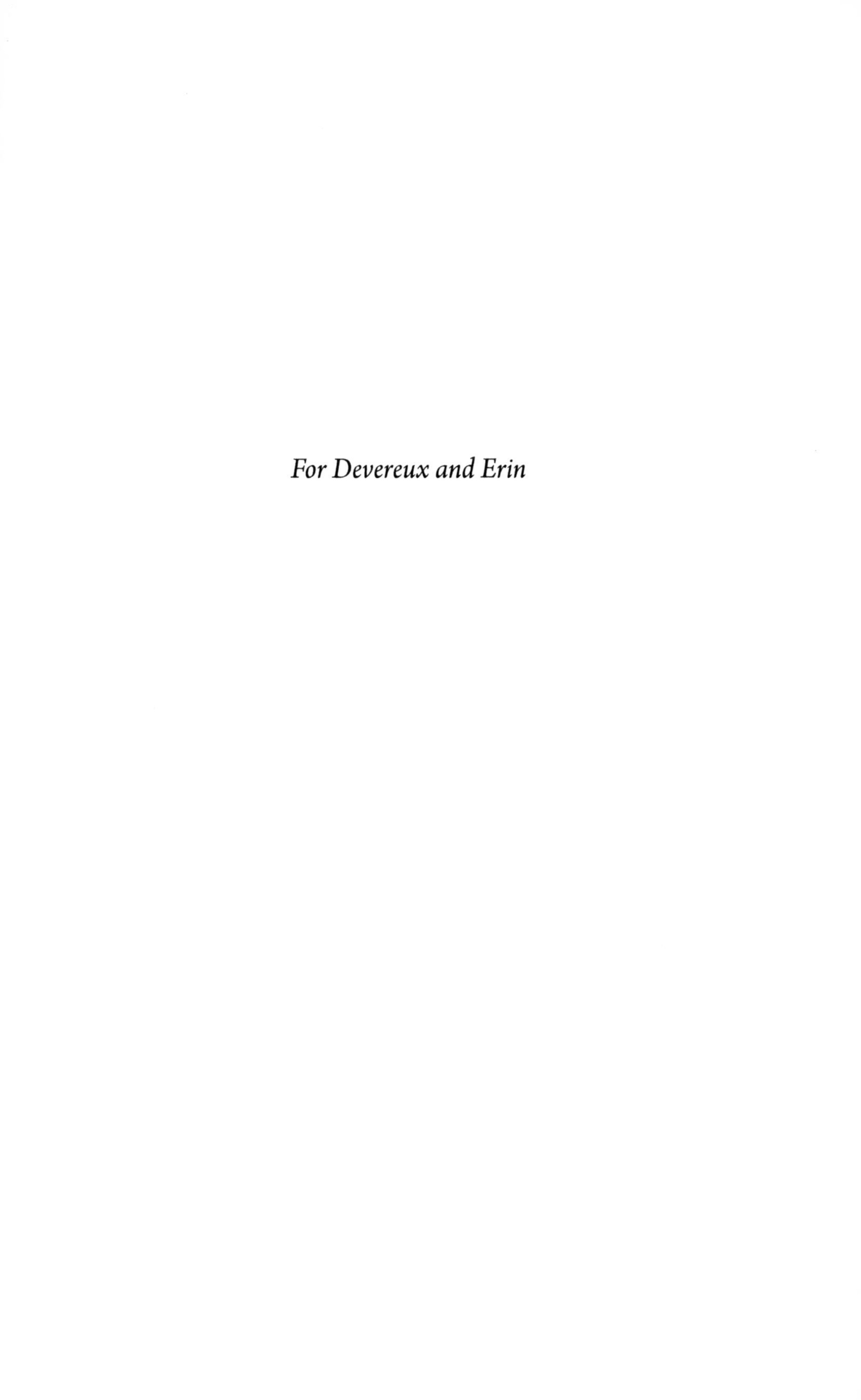

For Devereux and Erin

Having authority over our own story, and the means to tell it, is the most potent weapon that any of us are able to utilize against the corrupt vision of the far right.

—Caryl Phillips, *Color Me English* (2011)

The question is not "Who is French, but rather what is a human being?"

—J.-M. G. Le Clézio, "Universalism and Multiculturalism" (2009)

CONTENTS

ACKNOWLEDGMENTS

I am deeply appreciative of the generosity of colleagues and friends who have helped me—through their research, questioning, and thought-provoking ideas—improve my understanding of the various concepts, issues and questions explored in this book. My greatest debt of gratitude is to Dee Mortensen, Senior Sponsoring Editor at Indiana University Press, for her unyielding support and indispensable insights, and also to Sarah Jacobi, Assistant Sponsoring Editor, for her encouragement and editorial help.

Earlier versions of several chapters were previously published in edited books and international journals, including *Radical Philosophy, Yale French Studies, African and Black Diaspora, French Forum, Australian Journal of French Studies, Transnational French Studies* (Liverpool UP), *Sites: Contemporary French and Francophone Cultures, Black France-France noire* (Duke UP), *European Studies: An Interdisciplinary Series in European Culture, History and Politics, Bulletin of Francophone Postcolonial Studies, French Cultural Studies,* and *Expressions Maghrébines.* They are reproduced here with kind permission.

AFRICA AND FRANCE

Introduction

FRANCE AND THE NEW WORLD ORDER

Why is it that at a time when the globalization of financial markets,
cultural flows, and the melting pot of populations have engendered
greater unification of the world, France, and by extension Europe, remain
reluctant to think critically about the postcolony, namely the history
of its presence in the world and the history of the presence
of the world in France, before, during, and after Empire?

—*Achille Mbembe*[1]

an is di same ole cain and able sindrome
far more hainshent dan di fall of Rome
but in di new word hawdah a atrocity
is a brand new langwidge a barbarity

—*Linton Kwesi Johnson*[2]

On November 21, 2009, the front page of the French daily newspaper *Le Monde* included an entry—"Albert Camus au Panthéon?" (Albert Camus at the Pantheon?)—by the well-known political cartoonist Plantu. This image highlighted the complexity of former president Nicolas Sarkozy's ambition of moving Camus' remains to the great Panthéon mausoleum. In the cartoon, Sarkozy is standing behind a podium bearing a French flag and inscribed with the wording "Sarko-Malraux," and singing "Entre ici l'étranger" (Come in foreigner/outsider). This is an obvious reference to Camus' most well-known novel *L'Étranger* (1942). Indeed the cartoon reinforces an association further by the presence of a winged and airborne Camus holding a copy of his novel, the recognizable structure of the Panthéon in the background, and a police officer ordering a black man with the familiar "tu" ("Toi, tu rentres ici!" [Hey you, this way!]) to get in to a police vehicle. Only too evident is the allusion to Sarkozy's numerous attempts at instrumentalizing immigration since 2007 through the creation of a Ministry of Immigration, Integration, National Identity and Co-Development, highly publicized arrest and deportation statistics, and controversial *National Identity Debate.* Here, Plantu points to Sarkozy's calculated gesture of embracing a cultural icon such as Camus, cautiously selecting, privileging, and memorializing components of a complicated colonial history of Algerian-French contact (and thereby appealing to electoral constituencies among *pied-noir* communities). The insertion of Camus into these contemporary political debates emerges as particularly opportunistic when one considers equally meritorious figures; what becomes clear though is both the acceptability of the *Algerian* Camus juxtaposed here with undesirable immigrants, and simultaneously with an author such as Jean-Paul Sartre whose presence in the Panthéon remains unimaginable at this moment in history, not least as a result of his anti-colonialism.[3]

There are of course numerous precursors to this latest debate concerning the pantheonization of historical figures, most notably as far as the commemoration and status of Black figures are concerned, including Félix Éboué (the colonial administrator), Louis Delgrès (a mulatto leader in the struggle against the restoration of slavery in 1802), and Toussaint Louverture (who played a key role in the struggle for Haitian independence).[4] Further illustration is the petition launched in 2007, "Pour la panthéonisation d'Olympe de Gouges (eighteenth-century French author and anti-slavery activist) et Solitude (a slave who fought alongside Delgrès against the restoration of slavery)."[5] Associating André Malraux with these matters proves to be significant in multiple ways; his own remains were, after all, moved to the Panthéon in 1996. As Herman Lebovics has argued, "The great man in the Panthéon has become one of the most frequently invoked markers of the glory days of the French nation and French culture."[6] French cultural and political institutions have, historically, enjoyed symbiotic connections, precisely because of Malraux's appointment by President de Gaulle as the inaugural Minister of Cultural Affairs (today the Ministry of Culture and Communication), a position he held from 1959 to 1969.[7] Numerous events were planned in 2009 to celebrate the fiftieth anniversary of this ministry, and half a century later, the Ministry of Culture and Communication remains committed to the promotion and development of France's archeological, architectural, archival, and museological patrimony, and continues to occupy a central role in national politics, fostering Gaullist notions of "grandeur" but also in supporting a policy of international "rayonnement" (radiance). Prominent appointees have included Jack Lang (1981–86 and 1988–93), the catalyst behind the ambitious architectural projects known as the "grands travaux" that transformed the Parisian landscape (the Institut du Monde Arabe, the Musée d'Orsay, and Opéra Bastille); Jacques Toubon (1993–95), the forceful advocate and protectionist of the French language; and more recently Frédéric Mitterrand (former President Mitterrand's nephew), a no less controversial figure.

During Sarkozy's presidency (2007–2012), policies included a broad range of interconnected and interaligned operations between various ministries.[8] Historically, articulation between these ministries played a central role in sponsoring imperial ambitions overseas, in supporting the establishment of museums in which to display the acquired spoils and glorious symbols of geopolitical power, and in mobilizing public support for expansionist ventures. In turn, decolonization has entailed an interrogation of the relationship between former colonial powers and colonized subjects, alongside the various claims and demands that have been made by ethnic minorities and immigrants insisting upon improved representation in the genealogies of European nation-states. Today, for example, the Ministry of the Interior, Overseas Department and Territories, Local Authorities and Immigration also shares responsibility for "memory/remembrance, patrimony and archives."[9] Museological practices are subject to greater scrutiny in light of these political and social transformations, and a comparative transhistorical and transcolonial analysis of European museums stands to improve the contextualization of these experiences and legacies. In addition to the refurbishment and restructuring of colonial era museums, new spaces have also been inaugurated, thereby further highlighting the importance of museums in postcolonial Europe, as well as the significance of incorporating the perspective of postcolonial European populations into these museums.

Foremost among Sarkozy's initiatives was a concern with French history and French national identity; in other words, with the preservation of "patrimony" and with a definition of "memory." Not surprisingly, Sarkozy actively pursued a project to open a French history museum. Indeed, several cultural and social projects have come to fruition in France in recent years. Most noteworthy is the opening in 2006 of the Quai Branly Museum (MQB, *Musée du Quai Branly*, a museum that has centralized French holdings in the arts of Africa, Oceania, Asia, and the Americas) and in 2007 of the National Center for the History of Immigration (CNHI, *Cité nationale de l'histoire de l'immigration*). The CNHI is located at the Porte Dorée in eastern Paris in the building that had formerly accommodated the Musée d'arts africains et océaniens (MAAO), a site with a fascinating transcolonial history since it was initially created in 1931 to house the Musée permanent des colonies.[10] Of course, when one considers the complex practices utilized to display human subjects (in human zoos, for example) *and* objects during the colonial era, and subsequently the manner in which these have been updated during the postcolonial era, then the connections to the Panthéon *as* a museum space that narrates the multiple chapters of a *national* history become in and of themselves all the more compelling.[11]

The Quai Branly Museum is an inheritance from the Jacques Chirac era and presidency, and Sarkozy's own interpretation of colonial history signaled his discomfort with this presence. In fact, Sarkozy's focus on historical revisionism yielded instances of disquieting nationalistic fervor. Today, globalization and French cultural and national identity have emerged as central concerns in national politics; the authorities have argued that uncontrolled immigration, as well as certain *symbols* (Islam, polygamy, headscarves, veils, Burqas, and so on), serve as indicators of the widespread erosion to the fabric of French society, while observers have evoked a different kind of *crisis* of French identity, pointing to France's failure at negotiating the demands, exigencies, and realities of the new world order.

When Brice Hortefeux was appointed to head the new Ministry of Immigration, Integration, National Identity and Co-Development in 2007, he devoted his attention to regulating immigration and, building on France's presidency of the European Union (E.U.) from July 1, 2008, to December 31, 2008, successfully lobbied for policy standardizing through the *E.U. Pact on Migration and Asylum*. However, his successor Éric Besson elected to amplify concerns with national identity when he took office in 2009 by launching a debate on the following question: "Qu'est ce qu'être Français aujourd'hui?" (What does it mean to be French today?)[12] Whereas the CNHI was conceived around the idea that "Leur histoire est notre histoire" (Their history is our history)—whereby the "est" (is) encouraged constitutive and inclusive notions of *Frenchness*—Besson's imperatives and priorities instead placed this verb under pressure leading one to hear the word as the conjunction "et" (and), pointing to separate and tangential histories in which hierarchies, different forms of belonging, citizenship, and adherence were foregrounded.[13] This fragile relationship between twenty-first-century cultural, economic, political, and social aspirations and the past/history have framed governmental policy-making and museological developments. To this end, President Sarkozy commissioned a report—the

Lemoine report on the "Maison de l'histoire de France" (2008)—that would seek to outline what a museum of French history might look like—a project therefore diametrically opposed in its aims and aspirations to the presentation of French history at the CNHI.[14]

Christopher L. Miller has shown us how, "The history of Africanist discourse is that of a continuing series of questions imposed on Africa, questions that preordain certain answers while ruling others out. . . . One can assert with assurance that the relationship between Europe and Africa has continually been represented as simply North over South, light over dark, white over black: as an unmediated pairing of opposites."[15] Analogous conclusions are to be found in pioneering research, in works such as Catherine Coquery-Vidrovitch's *La Découverte de l'Afrique* (1965), William B. Cohen's *The French Encounter with Africans: White Response to Blacks, 1530–1880* (1980), and Valentin Y. Mudimbe's *The Idea of Africa* (1994).[16] But how have twenty-first-century geopolitical alignments altered these alignments and configuration? How has "the presence of strangers, aliens, and blacks and the distinctive dynamics of Europe's imperial history . . . combined to shape its cultural and political habits and institutions?"[17] Examining processes of commemoration, reflections on national identity, government speeches, film, literature, and new museological approaches will invariably assist in the process of accounting for and then reckoning with these entangled histories.

As the Nobel laureate, Turkish novelist Orhan Pamuk has lucidly written, "Anyone remotely interested in the politics of civilization will be aware that museums are the repositories of those things from which Western Civilization derives its wealth of knowledge, allowing it to rule the world, and likewise when the true collector, on whose efforts these museums depend, gathers together his first objects, he almost never asks himself what will be the ultimate fate of his hoard."[18]

Chapters 1 and 2, respectively, examine the Quai Branly Museum and the National Center for the History of Immigration. These museums, MQB and CNHI, opened at a time of political transition, and the conflicting interests of foregrounding non-Western artistic and cultural heritages and humanizing the migratory experience (in state-sponsored public institutions) have been at odds with the government's objectives of redefining immigration policy. These issues are of course connected to the focus of chapter 3 in which immigration and national identity are explored. The long history of African-French relations, as confirmed by the archival holdings and permanent collections of the MQB and CNHI, tend to be obfuscated in policy-making. However, closer scrutiny of immigration history serves to complicate French and European debates on identity and singularity.

As Edward W. Said so eloquently showed us in his book *Culture and Imperialism,*

> The world has changed since Conrad and Dickens in ways that have surprised, and often alarmed, metropolitan Europeans and Americans, who now confront large non-white immigrant populations in their midst, and face an impressive roster of newly empowered voices asking for their narratives to be heard. The point of my book is that such populations and voices have been there for some time, thanks to the globalized process set in motion by modern imperialism; to ignore or otherwise discount the overlapping experience of Westerners and Orientals, the interdependence of cultural terrains in which colonizer and colonizer co-existed and battled each other through projections as well as rival geographies, narratives, and histories, is to miss what is essential about the world in the past century.[19]

Immigration and national identity have been central issues in French politics for decades now. But this question has become all the more complex given that to talk about France today necessarily means to talk about Europe, and to talk about Europe is also to talk about the longer historical experience overseas. This realization informs Paul Gilroy's argument, whereby, "The racisms of Europe's colonial and imperial phase preceded the appearance of migrants inside the European citadel. It was racism, not diversity, that made their arrival into a problem" ("Foreword: Migrancy, Culture, and a New Map of Europe," xxi). Political leaders recognized the benefits to national interests of harmonizing European imperial ambitions in Africa, and this awareness provided the rationale for the 1884–1885 Berlin Congress. Such historical forerunners to more recent transcolonial developments in E.U. policy making and to schemes such as the European Neighborhood Policy (ENP) and partnership treaties with African countries are hard to ignore.

"Africans were citizens of the French Union according to the 1946 Constitution and in theory at least free to circulate on French territory," Pap Ndiaye has reminded us, and "Independence did nothing to alter this relationship given the bilateral agreements that were signed between African countries and France. French industry needed labor, . . . and in those days it was easy to enter France, even illegally, to find work and then to put one's papers in order after the fact. But a decisive change occurred in 1974 when the borders were closed off to work-related immigration from non-European countries."[20] France is not of course alone when it comes to considering how it is addressing the question of belonging and identity. In fact, repeated expressions of racism and xenophobia have placed the founding concepts of the E.U. under pressure. Immigration today has come to concern *both* facets of the term, namely, the control of external factors (migration, border control, security) *and* the internal dynamic of ethnic and race relations, integration, and multiculturalism.

The "immigration" and "co-development" components that came under the Ministry of Immigration, Integration, National Identity and Co-Development's list of responsibilities between 2007 and 2010 (when it was officially closed down) specifically concerned the bilateral aspects of population movements between Africa and Europe. Chapter 4 is thus strategically located to examine the European and French *Africa policy,* Sarkozy's official speeches (and the responses to these) delivered on the African continent (in Brazzaville, Cape Town, Cotonou, Dakar, Kinshasa, and Tangiers) and what they tell us about how he conceived of Africa and Africans *and* how this in turn informed the treatment of African immigrants in France, and the lingering problem of neocolonialism known as *Françafrique.*

By the end of the nineteenth century, the British and the French shared the ambiguous prestige of wielding the most powerful empires and colonies. Their respective projects varied considerably in terms of geographic spheres of influence, and naturally so did the cultural strategies deployed. Any consideration of the legacy of these historical encounters must necessarily acknowledge these factors, particularly when it comes to analyzing the nature of cross-cultural influence. Nicolas Bancel, Pascal Blanchard, and Françoise Vergès have shown that "France and Africa share a common history, expressed jointly by the role France has played for centuries in Africa north and south of the Sahara, and by the more recent presence in the Hexagon of Africans who have, in turn, through their actions, their work, their thinking, had a concrete impact on the course of French history."[21] In this regard, the French context is all the more complicated given the concerted effort made by the colonial authorities in shaping policy through a *civilizing mission* determined to establish cultural prototypes in France *overseas.* Some fifty years have now elapsed since the official end of the French colonial presence in most of francophone sub-Saharan Africa, yet the failure of the French authorities to address and reconcile this colonial legacy with the challenges of globalization, immigration policy, and minority politics is striking. To accurately contextualize the landscape of postcolonial writing in France, its particularities and specificities, necessarily entails reflection on the transition from the colonial to the postcolonial and a consideration of the dynamics of race relations. But this is also a pan-European phenomenon, because "every European power contributed to the expansion of Europe's borders overseas. Every European power is experiencing today the 'return of empire' on their soil" (Bancel, Blanchard, and Vergès, *La République coloniale,* 161).

Chapter 5 endeavors to improve the contextualization of the cultural, political, and social dynamics of twentieth- and early twenty-first-century (post) colonial societies through a consideration of imperial discourse and the emergence of decolonizing imperatives in film. Initially, the French colonial authorities endeavored to restrict African access to this mode of expression, but gradually African and diasporic filmmakers succeeded in bypassing limitations and in developing an autonomous corpus of works. From the 1950s onward, the Parisian metropolis provided a privileged topographic space for African film production (with films such as *Afrique-sur-Seine, Paris c'est joli,* and *Les princes noirs de Saint-Germain-des-Prés*). Since at least the 1970s, Africa and African-centered films have successfully evaded simple categorization, and the degree of interpenetration has been reflected in films featuring African populations in Africa, in the diasporic communities of France and Europe, among ethnic minorities and immigrant populations, as well as asylum seekers and refugees. These films therefore provide us with important antecedents to current (re)formulations of African/European/French relations, but also directly engage with, deconstruct, and demystify the kinds of longstanding fantasies and reductive representations of Africa and Africans circulating and recycled in official governmental speeches. The films considered, from 1955 to 2011, reveal a significant diversification of the topographic spaces in which films are made, thereby announcing an expansion and decentralization of the parameters of French-language film production itself. This is a phenomenon that has also been accompanied by a thematic evolution that has reflected shifts in the political and social concerns of immigrant populations. As with government policy, concerned as it is with migrants and immigrants, films (by Med Hondo, Idrissa Ouedraogo, José Zeka Laplaine, Jean-Marie Teno, Alain Gomis, Rachid Bouchareb, Jean-François Rivet, Abdellatif Kechiche, Mathieu Kassovitz, Moussa Sene Absa, and so forth) also engage with this dual component, offering challenging insights through their engagement with the evidentiary mode and the plight of transnational migrants.

In chapter 6 our attention shifts to the fascinating case of writer Marie NDiaye (of African descent, the daughter of a white French woman and black Senegalese father), who was awarded the prestigious Prix Goncourt for her novel *Trois femmes puissantes* on the very day (November 2, 2009) on which

Éric Besson launched the *National Identity Debate.*[22] Several months earlier, NDiaye had been critical in an interview of Sarkozy's immigration policies, and when these comments came to the attention of Éric Raoult (the mayor of Raincy and UMP deputy for the Department of Seine-Saint-Denis), he took it upon himself to attack NDiaye on the grounds that the "[w]inners of this prize must uphold national cohesion and the image of our country."[23] Such claims for patriotic flag-brandishing bring to mind one of the most well-known posters of French colonial propaganda, namely Éric Castel's *Trois couleurs, un drapeau, un Empire* (Three colors, one flag, one Empire, 1941), a tri-colored allegory, in which the three *races* are superimposed under French rule over the French flag.[24] Having said this, this controversy has made it possible to think about a broad range of questions pertaining to racial classification in France, and by disentangling the knotted intersection of government, media, and cultural discourses to complicate discussions on national identity and the subject of "World Literature in French."

In chapter 7 we examine the increasing attention accorded to notions such as *Eurafrica* and the *Euro-Mediterranean.* Economic, political, and social asymmetries that account for transitions in migratory patterns within countries and continents and beyond strict nation(continent)al borders remain of crucial importance, and recourse to the *global south* as a category has made it possible to circumscribe those disadvantaged regions from which emigration is most significant, while also highlighting the unidirectionality of human mobility toward those economically prosperous geographic zones in the E.U. Naturally, these migratory routes and patterns inscribe themselves alongside a multiplicity of other twenty-first-century transnational networks. Indeed, if migration has emerged as a key geometric coordinate of globalization today, then so too has the concern with *controlling* the planetary circulation of human beings, particularly when it comes to the African continent. Political leaders recognized the benefits to national interests of harmonizing European imperial ambitions in Africa, and this awareness continues to inform more recent transcolonial developments in the E.U. Perhaps not surprisingly, a number of writers—French, Italian, Spanish, Moroccan, and so on (including Alain Mabanckou, Abdourahman Waberi, Tahar Ben Jelloun, Laurent Gaudé, Mahi Binebine, Salim Jay, J. R. Essomba, Abasse Ndione, and Laïla Lalami), have turned their attention to these realities, thereby introducing new forms of political commitment, and narrating the latest biographical chapter in the history of African-European relations. These pioneering works engage with globalization while themselves being globalized and raising consciousness with regard to these important facets of twenty-first-century globalization. We find ourselves, therefore, evaluating the role of literature in documenting and recording these circumstances, and ultimately assessing and determining the effectiveness of literature in humanizing individual and collective experience.

Whereas chapter 7 was organized around the Mediterranean, underlining the globalized nature of migratory dynamics, chapter 8 is located at the opposite end of the Schengen space, namely in Sangatte in northeast France where the Red Cross set up a refugee camp in 1998 to welcome Afghan, Iranian, Iraqi, Kurdish, and Kosovan refugees seeking passage across the English Channel to the United Kingdom. Although French authorities officially closed down the Red Cross Center in 2002, refugees kept arriving and sought shelter in the neighboring woods, an area that became known as the "jungle." The refugee crisis in Sangatte thus served to expose an unintended consequence of harsher migration policy, shortcomings in the coordination and harmonization of E.U. policy, while also emphasizing the tenuous relationship between governmental authorities determined to control and regulate migration and those individuals and groups concerned with human rights. The consideration of literature (such as Olivier Adam's novel *A l'abri de rien*), films (Jean-Pierre Améris' *Maman est folle* and Philippe Lioret's *Welcome*), and theatre (Ariane Mnouchkine's *Le dernier caravansérail*) provide the opportunity to juxtapose artistic creation and anthropological, political, and sociological research on camps, detention centers, holding areas, and humanitarian organizations, with a new vocabulary geared toward circumscribing and defining new forms of contact and existence.[25] The acceleration of exchanges and circulation have become defining characteristics of society today, and as such, difficulties associated with these new forms of human mobility are now intrinsic to the very nature of population movement.[26] Questions pertaining to plurilingualism and pluriculturalism find themselves inextricably linked to immigration policy, and as one investigates the vocabulary employed by officials, the language of conventions, treaties, and pacts, a new *grammar of migration* comes into evidence whose referentiality, signifying power, and linguistic coding can also highlight forms of intolerance, a kind of "phobic democracy."[27]

Belonging and solidarity are of course central questions today as we ponder what it really means to be *European*. Some have suggested greater integration while others have advocated for a "lock down of the Schengen space," or even promoted an "illusory quest for common roots."[28] But how do these questions apply to internal European populations, to the descendants of immigrants? In chapter 9, we consider the works of writers and filmmakers who for the most part were born *in* France, yet who find themselves at the periphery because they live in the urban housing projects known as *banlieues.* This new generation seeks to represent the cultural, economic, political, and social circumstances in the *other France,* challenging dominant views and perceptions, and inscribing themselves in a long postcolonial tradition of cultural production and political activism. In 2007, a group of artists, filmmakers, rappers, and writers got together and formed a collective and published a manifesto—"quifaitlafrance"—and explained their motivations in the following terms: "*Because* this country, our country, has all it needs to become exemplary again, as long as it accepts itself as it is rather than as it was."[29] Chapter 9 therefore assesses the emergence of *banlieue* writing in general and more specifically through close readings of Faïza Guène's novels and short-films. This makes it possible to formulate a perspective on the shifting cultural, political, and social circumstances of ethnic minorities in France, conditions that have produced, Achille Mbembe maintains, "a new phase of state racism [that] began within the context of globalization, the establishment of the European Union, and above all the war on terror. In that context, the risk is that the *banlieues* will become one of the designated targets of authoritarian populist movements, whose increasing power in the last quarter of the twentieth century has been observed in all European democracies."[30]

The concluding chapter applies these considerations to the publication in 2007 of another manifesto, namely "Pour une 'littérature-monde' en français" (Toward a World Literature in French), one that rendered all of these questions additionally intriguing.[31] We have become accustomed, in the English-speaking world at least, to the various usages and registers of the term "postcolonial." But in France, where colonialism itself remains a highly contested and politicized subject, *postcolonial studies* occupy a precarious position (particularly in the fields of French studies and history) and are often denigrated in intellectual debates and associated with broader social mechanisms pertaining to various memory wars, the politics of reparation, and disparate claims for social rehabilitation. In recent years, various scholars (such as Nicolas Bancel, Pascal Blanchard, Jean-Marc Moura, Françoise Vergès, and Catherine Coquery-Vidrovitch) have endeavored to redress this imbalance, underscoring the need to bring "France's colonial past to the forefront of national thinking and historiography, in order to produce perspectives that make postcolonial situations intelligible."[32] This is of course essential, since, "[i]n this proliferation of commemorations, tributes, inaugurations, monuments, museums, and public spaces, the boundaries separating history, remembrance, and propaganda have been obscured."[33] During the 1980s and 1990s similar forms of resistance were in evidence in institutions of higher education in the United Kingdom and United States where, by contrast with France, the field of francophone studies is today an integral component of French studies. Such advances are the product of writings in French, but within a global framework that includes the Caribbean, sub-Saharan Africa, France, Indochina, the Maghreb, Mauritius, and Quebec, as well as authors writing in French from European countries that were not colonial territories.

Thus, the publication of *two* manifestos in the same year underscores the pronounced sentiment that the French authorities are not adequately representative of the diverse aspirations and claims of significant segments of the population. In claiming that "[t]he emergence of a consciously affirmed, transnational world-literature in the French language, open to the world, signs the death certificate of so-called *francophonie*. . . . With the center placed on an equal plane with other centers, we're witnessing the birth of a new constellation, in which language freed from its exclusive pact with the nation, free from every other power hereafter but the powers of poetry and the imaginary, will have no other frontiers but those of the spirit" ("Toward a World Literature in French," 56, translation altered). The signatories of the manifesto clearly had in mind a *different* kind of Europe and France than the one currently defined by government policy orientation and bounded by such initiatives as the *National Identity Debate.* To this end, the publication in 2010 by the "littérature-monde" group of a second anthology, *Je est un autre: Pour une identité-monde* (one that included some of the original signatories but was also augmented),[34] confronted the *National Identity Debate* and exhibited signs of a more inclusive and incorporative understanding of social exclusion and marginality. These measures must be understood alongside countless examples of social protest and racial advocacy, expressing a desire to see France and Europe open up and renounce the kinds of nostalgic interpretations of history that have shaped current debates on immigration and national identity.

We thus find ourselves at a crossroads where competing, contrasting ideas intersect when it comes to determining how France and Europe should strategically position themselves in the twenty-first-century. "Why is it," Achille Mbembe asked in this introduction's opening epigraph, "that at a time when the globalization of financial markets, cultural flows, and the melting pot of populations have engendered greater unification of the world, France, and by extension Europe, remain reluctant to think critically about the postcolony, namely the history of its presence in the world and the history of the presence of the world in France, before, during, and after Empire?" Through an extensive range of interconnected documents and materials—films, government reports, juridical documents, museums, newspapers, novels, official decrees, plays, policy briefs, and presidential and ministerial speeches—*Africa and France: Postcolonial Cultures, Migration, and Racism* attempts to answer this challenging question. Certainly, now that we are in a position to evaluate the first decade of the twenty-first century and the presidencies of Jacques Chirac and Nicolas Sarkozy, our conclusions point to the lingering omnipresence of empire in French society. Indeed, the specter of French colonial history continues to haunt the national psyche, inserting itself into concerns pertaining to diversity and multiculturalism, identity, education, religious tolerance, and of course immigration policy. These observations serve to further highlight the importance of confronting this colonial legacy, in order to achieve a more comprehensive understanding of French society today, but primarily so as to *locate* and *address* emerging challenges affecting Franco-African and Eurafrican relations according to the rapidly metamorphosing architecture of twenty-first-century geopolitical realities.

1

Museology and Globalization

THE QUAI BRANLY MUSEUM

Almost nothing displayed in museums
was made to be seen in them.

—*Susan Vogel*[1]

The history of European nation-building and identity formation is inextricably connected with complex display practices in which the lines of demarcation between human and material entities have become indistinct, yielding as a consequence an apparatus of signifiers relating to objectivity and subjectivity that require examination and scrutiny.[2] The study of exhibition sites in Europe during both the colonial and postcolonial eras provides an opportunity to engage in comparative historical analysis and to improve the contextualization of the official and public discourse they have triggered. Europe and other regions of the world are symbiotically linked through a long history of contact informed by slavery, colonialism, immigration, and a multiplicity of transnational networks and practices. In recent years, these factors have informed both national and pan-European debates concerning the legacies of these encounters and their current reformulation with regard to transhistorical phenomena that impact ethnic minorities and immigrant populations. These concern a broad set of cultural, economic, political, and social factors that include reflection on the limits and pertinence of reparation and restitution, the study and reassessment of colonialism, the role and *instrumentalization* of memory, the status of postcolonial subjects, and ultimately the parameters of a multicultural Europe.[3]

Numerous new museums have appeared on the European landscape, altering and in some cases dramatically reconfiguring its topography. From the

Guggenheim Museum Bilbao (Spain) to the Kiasma Museum of Contemporary Art in Helsinki (Finland), and from the Tate Modern in London (UK) to the Kunsthaus in Graz (Austria), new display practices have been experimented with and in some instances even been eclipsed by the spectacular architectural projects that contain them.[4] The role of European nations in the slave trade and in colonialism has been acknowledged, although the assessment of the respective roles played by these nation-states remains contested; nevertheless, this history has been explored in a multiplicity of ways throughout Europe in such diverse spaces as the British Empire and Commonwealth Museum (UK), the Royal Museum for Central Africa (Belgium), and the Tropenmuseum (Netherlands), all of which have undergone elaborate and of course expensive refurbishment in recent years. Alongside these, the Quai Branly Museum (MQB, Musée du Quai Branly) and the National Center for the History of Immigration (CNHI, Cité nationale de l'histoire de l'immigration) in France have made significant additions; the International Slavery Museum (Liverpool, UK), the Hackney Museum (London, UK) and the National Maritime Museum (Amsterdam, Netherlands) held special exhibits.

As Carol Duncan has argued, "As much as ever, having a bigger and better art museum is a sign of political virtue and national identity—of being recognizably a member of the civilized community of modern, liberal nations."[5] Naturally, these early twenty-first-century transformations happened together with a transition in European demography, the emergence of new political constituencies, and geopolitical alignments, but there are antecedents that make such investigations all the more interesting, particularly when one considers that these mutations have occurred in some instances within the very structures (such as the Palais de la Porte Dorée in eastern Paris) initially built for ideological and propagandist ventures. Panivong Norindr has underscored this point:

> Spatial reterritorialization of indigenous buildings and monuments produced a particular understanding of the French colonial empire. Native architectural space was altered to make way for a transfigured vision of indigenous buildings that conformed better to French aesthetic and political ideals. In the 1930s, architecture was elevated to the rank of "leader" among all artistic expressions because as *art total* it was said to embrace, and even subsume, all arts. During the 1931 Exposition Coloniale, architects were invested with the authority and power to promote *l'idée coloniale*. The *palais d'exposition* was conceived as an architectonic colonial manifesto, a public and official display of French colonial policies, which determined its discourse, circumscribed its space, and revealed its ideology. Significantly, all

> of the buildings constructed for the exposition were temporary pavilions not designed to last beyond the duration of the fair, with one notable exception, the Musée Permanent des Colonies, which still stands today.[6]

Such observations naturally require additional historical contextualization given the role these institutions played as propagandist mechanisms for furthering imperial expansionist objectives, for according them legitimacy as a humanitarian undertaking, and in fostering public support for the enterprise; (this was certainly the goal of the International Colonial Exhibition of 1931 held in Paris).

There is of course a world of difference between the project of colonialism (and recourse to bodies such as the Royal Museum of Central Africa built by King Leopold II to stage Belgium's empire) and the concern with eliminating obstacles to the integration of postcolonial communities into European society (by rewriting the *national narrative,* as for example the CNHI in France has endeavored to do). However, historical precursors in both nineteenth- and twentieth-century Europe *also* reveal compelling transcolonial trajectories involving "concerted strategies by both parliamentary parties to promote the concept of a homogenous national identity and unity within Britain. Imperialism was one of the dominant ideologies mobilized to this end. The Empire was to provide the panacea for all ills, the answer to unemployment with better living conditions for the working classes and an expanded overseas market for surplus goods."[7]

The development and expansion of overseas marketing opportunities and the incorporation of these international spaces into a European economic sphere of influence are indissociable from museum history. From the monarchical sponsorship of explorers to the inventory of European conquests that resulted from massive subventions provided by government ministries, the *spoils* acquired as a result of these initiatives and subsequently placed on display in European museums as glorious symbols of geopolitical power have necessarily become a component of social processes commemorating and questioning these complicated histories. As Roger G. Kennedy has shown, the history of "triumph" is a problematic one, that is, "Hauling after you possessions taken from others—indeed, hauling *them,* too, in chains, cages, or in effigy—is a practice of many imperial peoples. Museums that present the artifacts taken at gunpoint from aborigines, or museums demonstrating the superiority of the collector to the collected, are vestiges of the triumphant school of museum-building."[8] For example, more is often known about the proprietorship of collections than the history of acquisition and the source of materials, and questions of conservation and preservation continue to be exacerbated by economic disparities between the economically prosperous zones of the world and the global south that is "preserved and displayed."[9]

As Jean-Loup Amselle has argued, this dimension is of particular concern, since

> At the Quai Branly Museum, no information is provided concerning the modes of acquisition of the objects, modes of acquisition that are of course integral to their very existence. It is not merely a question of the singular conditions under which exotic objects were acquired . . . namely through colonial pillage. Rather, the issue concerns the fact that most of the objects on display are not, strictly speaking works of art given that they were not produced by recognized individual artists who went on to add their signature to the various pieces. . . . Furthermore, within the museum itself, these anonymous objects are mixed in with the works of contemporary artists from the global south . . . , which has the effect of "primitivizing" these works by returning them to a kind of prehistory.[10]

The politics of circulation—as it relates to objects *and* subjects—also of course concerns collective histories of conquest commemoration and memorialization while complicating European debates on the singularity of genealogy.

It will therefore come as no surprise that new museological practices have overlapped with these modifications and that museums have addressed the shift in concerns and priorities that accompanied new audiences. Indeed, if, as Susan Crane has argued, museums "had begun as an elite undertaking to save, record, and produce the cultural heritage of the past and the present,"[11] then "where collections are made up of remnants of living cultures expressed by actual people, they who are 'collected' are now demanding a voice in their own representation."[12] As Anne-Christine Taylor (director of the Department of Education and Research at the MQB) has explained, the Quai Branly Museum centralized collections from the Musée de l'Homme (itself having absorbed materials from the Musée d'ethnographie du Trocadéro, the Muséum national d'histoire naturelle, the Bibliothèque nationale, Bibliothèque Sainte-Geneviève, and the Musée national de la Marine et d'Ethnographie) and the Musée des arts africains et océaniens (MAAO). The MQB thereby "has inherited two very different museologic traditions: that of the MAAO, inspired by the concern with universalizing art; and the other, closer to the interests of the Musée de l'Homme, defined by the aim of considering cultural diversity from a research perspective."[13]

The intersection between museological concerns and sociopolitical ones is quite apparent from a cursory overview of the collections and holdings of major European museums. Thus, the matter of the "representation (or absence) of non-Western traditions in Western museums"[14] and the ways in which museums "might be refashioned so as to transform them into 'differencing machines' committed to the promotion of cross-cultural understanding, especially across divisions that have been racialized"[15] remains of crucial importance. Such measures have been fraught with controversies and divisive debates in which the accuracy of historical accounts has been questioned and revisionist approaches denounced by critics for whom the very principles that informed colonial expansionism and the accumulation of objects on display require urgent recontextualization as a prerequisite for advancing community-building in postcolonial Europe. These are daunting questions for which answers often remain elusive. When one considers the extent of the French *colonial fracture*,[16] critics such as Robert Aldrich have even asked "whether these museums should be, can be, 'decolonized'?"[17] However, societies cannot circumvent these twenty-first-century issues and realities merely because they are complex; rather, they call for assiduous engagement of the kind Corinne A. Kratz and Ciraj Rassool point to, precisely because "the many ways of belonging are layered onto the museum along with other meanings and narratives, . . . redefining museum, exhibition, and public cultures in the process. It is essential to keep in mind that these recastings, remappings, and reorganizations always require negotiating the political economies of resources and power and that help define the very terms of engagement. But these are challenges that must be undertaken boldly, with no fear of friction" ("Remapping the Museum," 356).

This seems the logical point at which to turn our attention to some of the concrete ways in which museums have adapted to these imperatives and responded to new museological taxonomies.[18] To begin with, one should highlight the fact that the International Council of Museums (ICOM), which has overseen museum practices since 1946, has itself undergone some changes: "Following a thorough review of the ICOM's Code in the light of contemporary museum practice, a revised version, structured on the earlier edition, was issued in 2001."[19] These revisions have primarily concerned Article 6, given the degree to which museum collections reflect the cultural and natural heritage of the communities from which they have been derived. As such they have a character beyond that of ordinary property, which may include strong affinities with national, regional, local, ethnic, religious or political identity. It is important therefore that museum policy is responsive to this possibility. Two particular measures are of relevance to this discussion, namely 6.2 *Return of Cultural Property* and 6.3 *Restitution of Cultural Property*. In thinking about the multidimensionality of the postcolonial era, several strategies have emerged with which to confront colonial history:

(1) the willingness to rethink the ownership of museum holdings within the context of reckoning with acquisition procedures,

(2) responding to the repositioning of museological agendas from aesthetic to political ones,[20]

(3) privileging the experiential (in exhibits such as Hackney Museum's exhibition "Abolition '07"), and

(4) narrowing the representational gap between the "us" and the "them" in order to recognize that audiences are also "postcolonial" and that the parameters of the nation-state are no longer the same.

As Susan Crane has demonstrated:

> The museum is not the only site where subjectivities and objectivities collide, but it is a particularly evocative one for the study of historical consciousness. A museum is a cultural institution where individual expectations and institutional, academic intentions interact, and the result is far from a one-way street. A range of personal memories is produced, not limited to the subject matter of exhibits, as well as a range of collective memories shared among museum visitors. . . . Personal feelings and memories, whether accurate or appropriate or not, indeed are always a factor in the contexts in which historical consciousness is made, because they shape how an experience is remembered. ("Memory, Distortion, and History in the Museum," 319–321)

However, this process of constructing postcolonial memory and of foregrounding the components of a shared and constitutive history has, as we shall see, proved highly problematic.

Former French president Jacques Chirac attempted to build a twenty-first-century globalized museum (the Quai Branly Museum, centralizing holdings from Oceania, Asia, Africa and the Americas)[21] that would illustrate France's commitment to global cultural diversity, updating earlier examples of French *rayonnement* (radiance) in the world.[22] In his inaugural address (June 20, 2006), Chirac underscored the importance and urgency of combating "uniformity" and respecting "alterity," a lesson France had learned following a "tumultuous history," and which somewhat paradoxically according to him globalization threatened to erase: "Diversity is a treasure that we must preserve now more than ever."[23] Critics were quick to draw attention to the contradictions inherent to his characterization of history,[24] while of course simultaneously showing how his rhetoric—claiming for example that there are no "hierarchies between peoples" (Chirac, "Speech")—was at odds with his policies on immigration and ethnic minorities.

Today, most European countries have devoted space to museums that focus on colonial history, postcoloniality, or immigration history. In fact, commenting on the absence of such a space in Germany, Karen Margolis wrote, "It's not a solution to the problems of immigrants or their fellow citizens, but it would boost the confidence of foreigners living in Germany—it would affirm they have a place of their own in the national cultural landscape, and are here to stay."[25] Thus, in addition to the Quai Branly Museum, "one of the world's largest collections of African arts, with almost 70,000 items from the Maghreb, sub-Saharan Africa, and Madagascar" (www.quaibranly.fr), the National Center for the History of Immigration opened in 2007 in the Palais de la Porte Dorée, a space designed as the Musée Permanent des Colonies in the 1930s and later occupied by the MAAO, whose collection was incorporated to the holdings of the Quai Branly Museum.[26] Jacques Toubon, the former government minister responsible for the CNHI project, explained the importance of providing "recognition of the place of immigrant populations in the destiny of the Republic [so that] every French person arrive at a more accurate idea of French identity as it stands today, while also reconciling the multiple components that make up the French nation with those values that represent its strengths."[27]

As with the Quai Branly Museum, this initiative has also been surrounded by controversy, given that the museum's intentions have been seemingly partially undermined by the fact that the opening in 2007 coincided with newly elected French president Nicolas Sarkozy's creation of the Ministry of Immigration, Integration, National Identity and Co-Development and disquieting statements made in his speech delivered in Dakar, Senegal (July 26, 2007) in which racist constructs revealed the lingering nature of such discourses in *postcolonial* France. In the next chapter, closer scrutiny of the CNHI project will provide helpful insights into the current political landscape, the symbiotic relationship between government ministries and cultural practices, and the tenuous connections between national politics and globalization, while also suggesting the kinds of measures that will have to be taken for decolonization to finally occur. Comparative analysis on the relative effectiveness of museological projects in addressing the complexity of racial formations and historical processes can, at the very least, provide indicators on the postcolonial condition in the context under investigation.

Britain has, like other European nation-states with historical ties to slavery and imperialism, struggled to reconcile this heritage with the demands and exigencies of a contemporary multicultural and postcolonial society. Certainly, recourse to legal devices such as the Race Relations Act as early as the 1970s served to advance tangible reform and to partially recalibrate perceptions and mindsets concerning formerly colonized subjects. For example, "in 1994, National Museums Liverpool opened the Transatlantic Slavery Gallery, the first of its kind in the world. This gallery has achieved huge visitor numbers and impact, but there is now a pressing need to tell a bigger story because of its relevance to contemporary issues that face us all."[28] The success of this focused exhibit (with similar outcomes measured at numerous others held in 2007 to commemorate the bicentenary of abolition) drew attention to the interest, receptiveness, and willingness of new museum-going audiences to learn about past actions and to connect these to the present in a transhistorical framework. Likewise, the decision in 2007 to relocate the British Empire and Commonwealth Museum from Bristol (where it opened in 2002) to Britain's capital city and center of tourism reveals a commitment to focusing on the legacy of the British empire over a long history, one that includes slavery and the slave trade as well as the colonial era. As the director of the Museum Gareth Griffiths explained: "Relocation to London presents a major opportunity for the Museum to widen its reach and engage new audiences with this important and formative part of our shared past. . . . It is anticipated that the move will enable the Museum to expand upon the range of topics covered in connection with Britain's colonial past and continue to address the contemporary legacies of this history today."[29] The reformulation of the role of the museum in twenty-first-century Europe is therefore twofold: on the one hand, to rethink this role in postcolonial Europe and, on the other, to reposition postcolonial European populations in the museums themselves.

Two other major European museums have adopted analogous methodologies. In Tervuren, Belgium, the Royal Museum for Central Africa (RMCA) justified the renovation project that began in 2007 in the following terms: "The Royal Museum for Central Africa (RMCA) dates from 1910 and despite its unique charm, the presentation of the permanent exhibits is outmoded and its infrastructure is obsolete."[30] Acknowledging that "as it's displayed now, the permanent exhibition still reflects the way Europe regarded Africa in the nineteen-sixties," there is nevertheless recognition that this is "despite a radically altered social context not only in Africa but here as well" (www.africamuseum.be). In Amsterdam, the Tropenmuseum, which is part of the Royal Tropical Institute, provides an account of the multiple ways in which its *mission* has changed over time in response to the socio-cultural and socio-political climate:

> A museum has many stories to tell, and the Tropenmuseum in Amsterdam tells stories about non-western cultures. The museum promotes learning about other cultures and encourages interaction through its thousands of objects displayed in temporary and permanent exhibitions. . . . The development of the museum since it was founded at the end of the nineteenth century and the way the presentation of non-western cultures changed over the past century is a fascinating story in itself. . . . Integration into the community has been and continues to be an important focus: the aim is an even stronger emphasis on cultural exchange as a drive for ongoing change, starting here and now. Visitors can expect substantial changes to the interior, in which the collection will better express non-material values. The building will follow this trend: a remodeling of the entrance area is planned, in which the openness and transparency serve as a physical reflection of a socially relevant design. (www.kit.nl)

Elsewhere in Europe, the topography is punctuated by *traces* and *remnants* of empire and expansionist ambitions, monuments to fallen soldiers in colonial wars and to transoceanic exploits—Lisbon's Padrao dos Descobrimentos (The monument to the discoveries)[31] and the National Monument Slavernijverleden (National monument to the legacy of slavery) in Oosterpark, Amsterdam. Needless to say, heated debates are ignited each time new *memory sites* are proposed.[32]

The aim of reaching broader audiences and improving the accessibility and pertinence of museums—of *democratizing* museums—is certainly understood as an important aspect of museology today, and all the more so within a postcolonial context.[33] "The development of new narratives in art museums," as Eilean Hooper-Greenhill has maintained, "demands new ways of thinking about collections and audiences, and new ways of integrating the two. . . . The function of the museum as a communicator cannot be separated from cultural issues of knowledge, power, identity, and language."[34] During the first years of the twenty-first century, museum directors have reported increases in attendance revealing both an interest and identification with collections and history.[35] These have triggered all kinds of responses from observers who have been critical of what they perceive of as a popularization of museum exhibits and appeal to tourism,[36] while others have argued that "this is an important approach but tells museums very little about the impact they are having on those individuals and groups, and so must be seen as a way of achieving something rather than being an end in itself."[37]

One thing remains perfectly clear, though, and that is the importance migration will continue to play in twenty-first-century society *and* the challenges of interpretation and reinterpretation that will emerge from situating these experiences in national narratives. These concerns have been in evidence outside of Europe as well of course, in such places as the Museo de la Inmigración in Buenos Aires (Argentina), in Canada's Immigration Museum (Halifax, Nova Scotia), or in Australia's immigration museum (Melbourne). However, when one considers the variations of associations ascribed to the term "immigration" in American history, recent discourse serves to emphasize the degree to which histories of contact remain problematic.[38] In 2009, for example, the New Americans Museum opened in San Diego, California. Its stated objective is to serve as "a catalyst for celebration of America's past and promise, the Museum provides inspiring educational and cultural programs to honor our diverse immigrant experiences";[39] yet, as a recent newspaper article revealed, "the museum had dropped the word 'immigration' from its name to quiet objections from the community."[40] Consensus on the European colonial experience has not been reached, and measures taken to address the circumstances of postcoloniality have proved inadequate. In an ever-expanding European Union in which there have been alarming instances of cultural and socio-political intolerance, the cohabitation and coexistence of populations with diverse backgrounds will require vigilant monitoring.

One expects debate and controversy in the process of electing a new president. But there are few places in the world where political and social transition generates the degree of international attention and scrutiny that France does. A cursory glance at the early years of the twenty-first century will confirm this. In the 2002 general elections, the unpopular incumbent president Jacques Chirac gathered sufficient votes to make it through to the run-off only to discover that his opponent would be Jean-Marie Le Pen, who was at the time leader of the extreme right-wing Front National party. Le Pen had benefited and even capitalized on a complex series of strategic miscalculations on the part of a disgruntled electorate. Chirac was subsequently returned to office for another five years by a record-winning margin that underscored the widespread public embarrassment that had accompanied such a pragmatic vote.

Chirac's final years in office remain indissociable from these symbols of growing social bifurcation, and the legacy of his presidency generated much debate.

The focus here is primarily on the *Sarkozy years* (2007–2012), which has allowed us to assess the aforementioned legacy. Of course, now that Sarkozy has himself been ousted from political office (following the results of the second round run-off voting on May 6, 2012) by the Socialist candidate François Hollande, the task of revisiting that presidency is necessary. As we shall see, divisions in French society were exacerbated during Sarkozy's term in office, providing strong indication as to the prevalence of anti-immigrant sentiment in France today. But there is perhaps no better place to start than to focus on the French *grands projets* or *grands travaux,* namely those state-sponsored architectural sites that have been deployed on the Parisian landscape to immortalize successive presidents. François Mitterrand was the most pro-active in this regard, with contributions such as the Grande Arche of La Défense, the Bastille Opéra, and the Institut du Monde Arabe. With reference to these projects, Panivong Norindr has argued that these "new urban markers delimit, inscribe, and reconfigure in space an image of France as a dominant cultural center."[41] Indeed, much as Chirac's own discourse contains multiple layers of contradictions to which we shall return shortly, Mitterrand's undertakings already heralded a "shift away from ethnocultural accommodation and *la société multiculturelle* toward *La France pour les Français,*" as confirmed by "the architectural modernist design of [his] Parisian *travaux présidentiels* " ("La Plus Grande France," 249). In fact, the transcolonial and nationalistic dimensions of these ventures inscribe in powerful ways the linearity between colonial and republican ideals. Norindr, assessing the cultural climate, wrote:

> Mitterrand's public works elaborate an aesthetic and cultural shift that aims at reestablishing Paris as the cultural capital of the world through the construction and circulation of 'strong' images, which the French language captures metaphorically very well: these images are said to be *porteuses,* imparting the idea of grandeur and importance. . . . *Grands travaux* present an image of a modern, progressive, culturally and technologically dynamic "nation," one that claims to be sensitive to cultural differences. But behind the benevolent and democratic façade hides a disturbing cultural logic, one that contains and oppresses. ("La Plus Grande France," 249–250)

The vestiges of this outdated conceptualization of France's *global* status remained in evidence in Chirac's rhetoric, and as Susan Vogel rightly claims, "Things are slightly more complicated in the case of the Quai Branly because of the fact that this project was ordered by the office of the President of the French Republic and that the client was therefore the French State" ("Des ombres sur la Seine," 192). More recently, in a powerful deconstruction of the Quai Branly Museum project, James Clifford updated this perception of France, demonstrating how "Paris itself is a changing contact zone—no longer the center of Civilization (high culture and advanced science), but a node in global networks of culture and power" ("Quai Branly in Process," 9). Indeed, as I argued in *Black France: Colonialism, Immigration, and Transnationalism,* evidence of what we might describe as a "global Hexagon" can, quite paradoxically, in fact be located in the *banlieues* housing projects, marginal sites in which contact between peoples is truly transnational and globalized.[42] Additional contextualization is therefore necessary to fully understand the broader cultural, political, and social implications of these recent changes.

There have been heated debates in France concerning colonial history and postcoloniality itself. In turn, these exchanges have informed the contested terrain of postcolonial studies as a disciplinary paradigm. The tenuous relationship between revisionist historians and advocates for a more nuanced conceptualization of colonialism is exemplified in diametrically opposed scholarship, with works such as Daniel Lefeuvre's *Pour en finir avec la repentance coloniale* and Pascal Bruckner's *La tyrannie de la pénitence, Essai sur le masochisme occidental* standing in contrast with Pascal Blanchard, Nicolas Bancel, and Sandrine Lemaire's *La fracture coloniale: La société française au prisme de l'héritage colonial.*[43] Analogous manifestations of these issues have also been in evidence in the political domain. For example, on February 23, 2005, the National Assembly voted on the Debré 2005–58 Law; one requirement included in this bill was that "school programs highlight the positive aspects of the French overseas presence, notably in North Africa." Even though the clause was subsequently repealed in January 2006, the very fact that an attempt had been made to introduce the law in the first place served to underscore the degree to which colonial memory remains a mobilizing force. At a similar time, the definitive reference dictionary in the French language, *Le Petit Robert,* was to publish an updated edition in which a definition of "colonialism" described a process of "valuing, enhancing, exploiting the natural resources."[44] Indeed, as Alice Conklin has shown, when William Ponty became governor general of French West Africa in 1907, he "took several steps designed to clarify the content and pedagogical methods of education and to increase the number of schools available to Africans. Under his administration, French became the official language of the federation, the first comprehensive course plan applicable to the entire federation was drawn up, and the first manuals began to be published."[45] Given the role school textbooks played during the colonial era, this *return* to the colonial model as an extension of republican ideals in the postcolonial era, and recourse to this model of the past to shape the new citizens of the postcolonial era, is of course particularly troubling. How then, we might very well wonder, can such seemingly opposed contextualizations and interpretations of history operate alongside the potentialities of such innovative projects as the Quai Branly Museum and the National Center for the History of Immigration that opened in Paris in 2006 and 2007, respectively?

A point to accentuate is that these debates have taken place across political divides. For example, when the socialist Lionel Jospin was prime minister in 1998, concerted efforts were made toward the recognition of immigrants—the Taubira Law, changes to school textbooks concerning revolts in Sétif, the *tirailleurs sénégalais,* models of African resistance, or the justification for the mutiny of 1917. Following Jospin, the new right-wing government, with particularly militant parliamentarians in favor of the *pieds noirs* (European settlers in North Africa), altered the discourse as it concerned official mechanisms pertaining to memory and immigration, and how these would be deployed. Echoes to a colonial rhetoric reverberated in France, imbued with racist characterizations and stereotypes, and specifically targeting an electoral base in the south and southwest of France growing disenchanted with the French Right and shifting its allegiance to the Front National. Similarly, as we shall see in the next chapter, the CNHI was initially a project of the French Left, albeit one that was completed by a right-wing administration, but its conceptual origin must not be forgotten. This background helps us better understand how these questions intersect with colonial legacy, immigration, national identity, and the shifting parameters of Frenchness.

Whereas the CNHI addresses the history of immigration in France, the MQB is dedicated to the arts and civilizations of Africa, Asia, Oceania, and the Americas, and has effectively centralized the holdings of the Musée de l'Homme and the Musée des Arts d'Afrique et d'Océanie. The museum was designed by the well-known French architect Jean Nouvel (previous projects include the Institut du Monde Arabe). A staggering 300,000 objects have been moved to this new site, although only a small percentage is on actual display. As Herman Lebovics revealed in his insightful analysis of recent museum projects in France: "When President Chirac first proposed the museum, the term 'primitive art' was used in official statements to describe its contents. People who knew something of the subject immediately protested. This unacceptable label was soon dropped, to be replaced successively by the equally objectionable euphemism Museum of the First Arts [arts premiers], Museum of Societies and Civilizations, and then Museum of Man, Arts and Civilizations. The planners have ended the distasteful naming game, at least temporarily, by simply calling the museum by its street address: Musée du Quai Branly."[46] To this end, the MQB aligns itself with a longstanding French tradition of granting names to museums based on their street address; (another example is the Musée d'Orsay).[47]

The reductive associations linked to ascriptions such as "primitive art" or "tribal/first arts" were immediately highlighted and of course triggered much controversy. It is worth underlining that the project might have been very different. The anthropologist Maurice Godelier, who was initially appointed to play a leading role in the conceptualization of the museum, "wanted to make a *better* Musée de l'Homme. He wanted a modernized ethnology museum with lots of immediately accessible information available to visitors about the societies which produced the artifacts being exhibited. [Godelier] wanted to build a 'post-colonial' museum. By this he meant a museum with a cultural pluralist relationship to the peoples whose arts would be on display" (Lebovics, "The Dance of the Museums," 154–174).[48] However, Godelier was not to see the project through to completion, and his vision was restricted to the margins. On the occasion of the official inauguration on June 20, 2006, President Chirac delivered the official address. I propose to place this text under critical pressure in order to suggest how its structuring rationale is informed by an implicit ideological logic that ultimately has much to teach us about the conflicted landscape of contemporary French politics.

In the presence of Kofi Annan (then secretary-general of the United Nations) and Adbou Diouf (former president of Senegal and now secretary-general of the Organisation Internationale de la Francophonie, OIF), Chirac began by denouncing ethnocentrism: "Central to our idea is the rejection of ethnocentrism and of the indefensible and unacceptable pretension of the West that it alone bears the destiny of humanity, and the rejection of false evolutionism, which purports that some peoples remain immutably at an earlier stage of human evolution, and that their cultures, termed 'primitive,' only have value as objects of study for anthropologists or, at best, as sources of inspiration for Western artists" (Chirac, "Address," 2). Arguably, the most striking component of his speech would concern his allusion to, "Those are absurd and shocking prejudices, which must be combated. *There is no hierarchy of the arts any more than there is a hierarchy of peoples.* First and foremost, the Musée du Quai Branly is founded on the belief in the equal dignity of the world's cultures" (Chirac, "Address," 2, emphasis added).

Essentially, the structure was provided by four key components as they inform and relate to a broader francocentrist project. These include *reparation, globalization, cultural diversity,* and the *aesthetic experience*:

> Reparation
>
> France wished to pay homage to peoples to whom, throughout the ages, history has all too often done violence. Peoples injured and exterminated by the greed and brutality of conquerors. Peoples humiliated and scorned, denied even their own history. Peoples still now often marginalized, weakened, endangered by the inexorable advance of modernity. Peoples who want their dignity restored. (Chirac, "Address," 1)
>
> Globalization
>
> By showing that there are other ways of acting and thinking, other connections between beings, other ways of relating to the world, the Musée du Quai Branly celebrates the luxuriant, fascinating and magnificent variety of human creativity. It proclaims that no one people, no one nation, no one civilization represents or sums up human genius. Each culture enriches humanity with its share of beauty and truth, and it is only through their continuously renewed expression that we can perceive the universal that brings us together.
>
> *That diversity is a treasure that we must preserve now more than ever.* In globalization, humanity is glimpsing the possibility of unity, that age-old dream of the Utopians, which has become the promise of our destiny. At the same time, however, standardization is gaining ground, with the worldwide expansion of the law of the market. But who can fail to understand that when globalization brings uniformization it can only exacerbate tensions between different identities, at the risk of igniting murderous violence? (Chirac, "Address," 4, emphasis added)
>
> Cultural Diversity
>
> That is also the idea behind this museum. To hold up the infinite diversity of peoples and arts against the bland, looming grip of uniformity. To offer imagination, inspiration and dreaming against the temptation of disenchantment. To show the interactions and collaboration between cultures. . . . To gather all people who, throughout the world, strive to promote dialogue between cultures and civilizations.
>
> France has made that ambition its own. France expresses it tirelessly in international forums and takes it to the heart of the world's major debates. *France bears it with passion and conviction, because it accords with our calling as a nation that has long prized the universal but that, over the course of a tumultuous history, has learned the value of otherness.* (Chirac, "Address," 5, emphasis added)

> Aesthetic Experience
>
> A visit to this new institution dedicated to other cultures will be at once a breathtaking aesthetic experience and a vital lesson in humanity for our times. (Chirac, "Address," 1)

Now, of course, Chirac's fondness, his passion for *Arts premiers,* and even his knowledge and expertise in this area, are not in question. Rather, it is the pronounced, even radical nature of his relativism that is so troubling and that has even lead him to support France's unqualified role in "françafrique" (a term used to describe neocolonial practices, and to which we shall return in chapter 4).

Chirac's inaugural address is, effectively, that of the prestidigitator, structured on the interplay between an absence and a presence. A history of violence and of exploitative brutality is invoked: ("Peoples injured and exterminated by the greed and brutality of conquerors. Peoples humiliated and scorned, denied even their own history"), but one in which France's role remains unclear. Similarly, the role of the colonial project itself is unarticulated, as is the impact of the *civilizing mission* whose foundational, expansionist and justificatory principles are imparted in the address, most notably as far as the process of hierarchization is concerned. These linguistic formulations serve to accentuate the aesthetic project of the MQB; as such, we begin to sense a rearticulation of what could very well be construed as a kind of postcolonial *civilizing mission* that simultaneously refuses to engage in any discussion or polemic on the question of the historical origin(s) of the collection (especially the African one), thereby relegating to the margins a socio-political understanding without which any contextualization and historical framework cannot be undertaken.

As Robert Goldwater has argued, this follows a trend that has witnessed, certainly since the late nineteenth century and early twentieth century, a move "in the direction of the enhancement of the aesthetic values of the productions of the primitive peoples."[49] This privileging of *exhibiting* over *collecting* is a recent one, and "not only are typical objects less crowded in their cases, so that they may be better seen, but aesthetic standards are invoked by isolating certain works for separate exhibition on the basis of their individual excellence" ("The Development of Ethnological Museums," 136). However, as Vogel has shown, the organizing principles and rationale that inform the display of the MQB collection are on the one hand indebted to an established history of projections and stereotypes yielding "old clichés on an Africa that had only ever existed in the fevered Western imagination," and on the other structured in a critical and theoretical vacuum by "non-specialists and people who were not in the slightest informed about current debates" ("Des ombres sur la Seine," 186 and 192).[50] But the history of *collecting* must be foregrounded in the MQB project in order to gauge the transhistorical dynamic as it has mutated into/onto postcolonial French society. Failure to do precisely this would contribute to both obscuring and muffling those internal colonialisms (hierarchies?) in favor of aesthetics.

Indeed, this gesture of erasure is further instantiated by the domestic circulation of the objects themselves that have migrated from the former collections of the MAAO held at the Porte Dorée in eastern Paris (itself the site of the 1931 International Colonial Exhibition and formerly the Musée Permanent des Colonies!) to the new MQB site. Surely, this must be interpreted as a further (conscious or unconscious) gesture of amnesia, erasure, or even *oblivion*[51] that culminates in an additional degree of separation between the history of object acquisition and its new *home* at MQB, or what Bogumil Jewsiewicki has termed "decontextualization" and "dehistorization."[52] Robert Aldrich has insisted upon this aspect:

"For if the collections of exotic objects that belong to European museums, particularly in France, reflect a history of overseas expansion, they also shed light on the museological, political and moral questions that surround the exhibition of non-European works of art and artifacts. . . . Even the most occasional visitor will soon become aware of the extent of the collection of objects originally from former colonies in the holdings of Parisian museums and that colonial traces are omnipresent everywhere in French society." ("Le musée colonial impossible," 84–85)

Naturally, as I have mentioned, the complex *layering* that is at work here is only further complicated by the fact that the location selected for the CNHI is the very site vacated at the Porte Dorée.[53] But, as Clifford has illustrated, "If ethnography is present but marginalized in the permanent exhibition space, history has almost entirely vanished. . . . It's worth quickly recalling some of what is absent: histories of the cultures in question, from deep archeological time through colonial changes to their present social and artistic life; histories of the objects themselves, collecting practices, markets, prior sites of display and changing meanings; local, national, metropolitan, and transnational contexts for currently changing patterns of signification" ("Quai Branly in Process," 15).[54] As we shall see, these procedures connect in powerful ways with the politics of memory in France today, and of course with the various ways in which these are affixed and transposed onto immigrant populations and ethnic minorities.

One cannot sufficiently underscore the symbiotic nature of colonial and postcolonial discourse and their respective ties to the foundational principles of the French republican machinery. As Pascal Blanchard and Nicolas Bancel have convincingly demonstrated:

> The genealogy of the colonial State's discourse—in which the colonial is cleverly introduced as an extension of the national and as a condition of its power—will remain, all the way up to political independence, a component of the discourse concerning the necessity of diffusing the "enlightened" values of the Republic to people seen as biologically and culturally inferior. . . . From this perspective, colonialism "overseas" does not represent a rupture with the past: on the contrary, it inscribes itself as an integral element in the construction of the French nation, and through its legacy, of the Republic itself.[55]

Both the MQB and the CNHI follow this trajectory. Evidently, we all share in the responsibility of declining a monolithic version of history, "either an individual or a collective attempt to reconstruct the past that is not founded on scientific methodologies but privileges instead the formation of myths and legends in assessing the emotional relationship which individuals or groups entertain with the past" (Bancel and Blanchard, "Mémoire coloniale," 23). Acting otherwise can only, ultimately, be counterproductive. This is all the more urgent when we consider the positionality adopted by those groups that self-ascribe as the "indigènes [natives] de la République" (the recuperation and recirculation of the category *indigène* that was employed to label colonial subjects emphasizes the transcoloniality of the nature of power relations).

As Clifford indicated in his elaboration of the notion of "contact histories," "In many cities, moreover, contact zones result from a different kind of 'travel': the arrival of new immigrant populations."[56] Unfortunately, memory and immigration continue to inform and confuse the official discursive realm in France and therefore of course state-sponsored expressions of these as they are adapted to the MQB and CNHI. Additionally, these remain associated with a colonial and racist discourse.[57] To this end, the positions adopted by Sarkozy's government on the question of citizenship and nationality substantiate this point since throughout his term in office from 2007–2012 he repeatedly put into question the loyalty of ethnic minorities to the French nation, thereby invoking those very *hierarchies* whose existence Chirac had denounced in his inaugural address.

The CNHI project is a perfect example of the continued existence of these subconscious hierarchies. The overarching framework of the CNHI is structured around the following notion: "Leur histoire est notre histoire" (Their history is our history). The distance between the "we" and the "other" is reiterated (even though, as we have been informed, there are supposedly no "hierarchies" between peoples), and the paternalistic appropriation of the other—to be civilized and colonized—is now reformulated through the imperative of assimilation and integration—culminating, as Lebovics demonstrates in conjunction with the MQB, in a process whereby "all this modernizing updates the old 'we' and the 'other' of the colonial era. For when all the moving is done, the old dichotomy between the 'civilized' and the 'primitive' will literally be reconstructed" ("The Dance of the Museums," 176).[58] Ultimately, this raises at least two important matters: on the one hand (and this aspect is of paramount importance to *all* museums), the relationship between the audience *and* the exhibit, and on the other, the associations of the audience *to* the exhibit. In the case of the MQB and the CNHI, this means immigrants and ethnic minorities in France whose histories are inseparable from the objects and narratives on display (alongside other hexagonal residents of course whose own history is *also* intertwined with the objects on display).

As Sally Price has argued in the first major book-length study in English on the MQB, *Paris Primitive: Jacques Chirac's Museum on the Quai Branly*, "From an early twenty-first-century perspective, the MQB has missed precious opportunities for meaningful cultural dialogue that would have led to greater consideration of these issues" (*Paris Primitive*, 177). Invariably, these elements are representative of the more general debate erected around the concern with globalization and the supposed threat of uniformity and homogeneity, a dialogue that re-stages and reinvests France as the protector of cultural diversity in reaffirming its centrality in this process through a skillful reconfiguration of the task and responsibility as a humanistic project: "That diversity is a treasure that we must preserve now and more than ever." But given France's own colonial history and defining role in what Chirac has described as engendering "peoples injured and exterminated by the greed and brutality of conquerors. Peoples humiliated and scorned, denied even their own history. Peoples still now often marginalized, weakened, endangered by the inexorable advance of modernity. Peoples who nevertheless want their dignity restored and acknowledged"—one might expect, even demand, that the MQB, as a methodological imperative, "rethink museography and the approach to the colonial past given that so many issues remain unresolved and of pertinence to multi-ethnic France today" (Aldrich, "Le musée colonial impossible," 91). These observations call for a programmatic radical rethinking of the *hierarchization* that continues to be in evidence, and whose constructive potential is negated and undermined by the semiology. As Tomke Lask suggested with another context in mind (but one that nevertheless applies to the MQB), "The conception of who the public is should be reviewed, incorporating broader categories than the usual white urban visitor: to broadly inform on ethnic identities and their history produces better advised visitors, meaning more responsible citizens."[59]

As I pointed out earlier, attempts were made in the early planning stages of the MQB to achieve such a framework. As Lebovics indicated, "Whereas Godelier's idea was to begin the healing by remembering and displaying past injustices, the current staff has decided to turn its back on history" ("The Dance of the Museums," 163). For example, the current director of patrimony and collections at MQB, Jean-Pierre Mohen, has unequivocally insisted on the primacy of aesthetic considerations over political questions, thereby relinquishing the opportunity to situate the museum's collection in a broader historical and political context: "The visual criteria of estheticism should not impede the sacred/anthropological understanding of works. Rather, one should seek to identify each and every detail, the materials used, the techniques of fabrication, the products used for sacralization, and the functions of the object in order to appreciate its internal magical qualities that call out and move us."[60] This reductive approach is simply not functional, and the origins of the objects on display cannot be ignored in this way; the collection at MQB cannot be appropriately contextualized in a historical vacuum.[61] "Museums," Laske argues, "must find a more dignifying way to take care of the aspect of change, giving back some of their legitimization to the ethnic objects' original producers" ("Introduction," 18). The MQB accentuates what Lebovics has described as an apparatus that to all intents and purposes *envelops* "the objects it shows in yet another layer of European meaning, that of the modernist work of art. But with its high modernist aesthetic agenda, the layers will neither be seen nor evoked" ("The Dance of the Museums," 158). This process is actually a kind of "wrapping," whereby "historical stratifications of meanings [are] added to the *object*. More exactly, it is a genealogy of the imperial gaze" (Lebovics, "The Dance of the Museums," 158). Historically, as Susan Crane argues, museums "had begun as an elite undertaking to save, record, and produce the cultural heritage of the past and the present."[62] This is precisely what informed Chirac's paternalistic *mission* and idea to provide "a venue that would do justice to the infinite diversity of cultures and offer a different view of the genius of the peoples and civilizations of Africa, Asia, Oceania and the Americas" (Chirac, "Address," 1). Indeed, the MQB had—*has* —an occasion to rethink the legacy of colonial rule, the hierarchies that justified expansionist ideals, and accordingly to reascribe the positive characterizations of the objects on display to their original producers *and* to their descendants located in the *internal* colonies of France as a result of current racist and exclusionary practices in evidence in the Hexagon today—"Peoples still now often marginalized, weakened, endangered by the inexorable advance of modernity" (Chirac, "Address," 1).

These objectives have not been achieved. Sarah Frohning Deleporte's analysis assists us in gauging this missed opportunity; the process of deconstructing and dismantling these hierarchies is, however, hindered by the Republic's structuring discourse: "Since the establishment of public museums after the Revolution, the State has been training civil servants capable of overseeing the national patrimony on behalf of the public, thereby assigning them a kind of 'mission.' This opposition between civil servants (who hold power) and the general public (the beneficiaries of this knowledge) conceals another, namely that which persists between a 'we,' those who are of *French stock,* and an 'us,' those others. In this discourse, one slides easily from a duality founded on knowledge to one that is built on ethnicity."[63] Of course, this triggers a "hierarchy" between "l'Occident et les Autres" [the West and the rest] (Deleporte, "Trois musées, une question," 110). In fact, implicit to the idea of providing a *special* space for the *first arts* suggests a *separateness* within the art community and informs the landscape of museum and collection hierarchies in Paris today.

The ahistorical dimension of the MQB project is strikingly evident, echoing, as many critics have insisted, that very absence of history that had previously defined and justified the *White Man's Burden*. Even if the aim is "to hold up the infinite diversity of peoples and arts against the bland, looming grip of uniformity" (Chirac, "Address," 5), one cannot but notice how the assimilationist imperatives of the French Republic are themselves deployed to support the strategic *uniformity* of an *indivisible* Republic. Many critics have fastened on this dimension. Gilles Labarthe, for example, in his article "Histoires brouillées" (confused and muddled histories) was unambiguous in his position: "If the Quai Branly Museum's mission was to erase the past, confuse the issues, and lose us in endless games and mirror effects, well then the mission was accomplished."[64] In this process, those very populations located in the *postcolony* and *internal hexagonal postcolonies* are denied the occasion to connect with those very *cultural* objects that defined their respective diverse cultures, cultures that were dismissed by the demands of the colonial enterprise. The rearticulated exigencies of the *color-blind* Republic (in which ethnicity is secondary to the integrational demands and requirements) that claims to have moved beyond the politics of race as implied by American or British interpretations and models will, according to Lebovics: "close the colonial era for France by means of aesthetic modernism. Showing beautiful creations of gifted artists, and showing them without history, without social context, and without evidence of the relations of power that they embody—in a word, without the layers—has been now for over a century and a half the classic exhibition strategy for eliding the human reality from which the art emerged and about which it speaks. It remains today the West's oldest, and most honored, way of occulting a terrible past" ("The Dance of the Museums," 174–175). This silencing was central to Chirac's address—"France wished to pay homage to peoples to whom, throughout the ages, history has all too often done violence"—whereby France remains unnamed as the perpetrator of this "violence" for which reparation is invoked.[65] As Benoît de L'Estoile has argued, "It is precisely because colonial relations determined every interaction between Europe and the other continents and in particular available modes of representation, that one cannot escape that reality through some kind of unilateral declaration of good will. On the contrary, only by braving the multiple aspects of the colonial legacy will it be possible, not to disengage from it, but rather to learn how to live with it."[66]

In fact, the legitimate "heirs" of many of these objects were ignored in the MQB planning.[67] "No attempt was made in Paris to take into consideration the points of view of those who consider themselves the heirs of those who produced these works"; instead, Labarthe argues, "One gets the feeling one is witnessing the staging of a kind of double cultural hold-up: of those populations who have been deprived of their statues, masks, relics and cultural objects; and that of the French national museums upon whom it was incumbent to remind us of the oppressive context, and to what expansionist propagandist ends, these works were acquired" ("Histoires brouillées"). Implicit to this is a form of *official revisionism,* recycled in a transcolonial context at the service of what Olivier Le Cour Grandmaison has described as a "powerful, conquering, and generous France."[68] This *grandeur* is, as I insisted earlier, inextricably linked to the *grands projets* legacy, reformulated here as a component of France's attempt to situate itself according to the parameters of a *globalized* world and thereby extending, as Norindr has argued, "The *rayonnement de la France,* the influence France wants to exert on the rest of the world [which] is therefore cultural and economic" ("La Plus Grande France," 247). The MQB thus aligns itself with "that old tradition of the separation between the arts of great cultures and the arts of the others. Like the other creations, it projects a major rereading of the French cultural heritage. . . . Quai Branly is a new copy for which there is not yet an original of France's chosen vocation to be—in this era when globalization threatens to flatten all cultural distinction—the principal patron of the art of the small cultures of the world"(Lebovics, "The Dance of the Museums," 153).

The very fact that the MQB has so vociferously defended what amounts to a systematic argument for a perceived *democratization* of the museum space and experience highlights the recognition of the actual failure of the museum to achieve such measures as well as the more widespread *fracture* that is in fact intrinsic to contemporary France. By May 2007, a month short of the MQB's first anniversary, some 1.55 million visitors had entered the museum, and this attendance trend has continued over the years.[69] A *Le Monde* newspaper article fastened on the *composition* of visitors: 20 percent say they are not regular museum-goers, 23 percent are between 18 and 35, and some have stated that "the establishment allows them to better understand their roots—for the most part, these are descendants of immigrants" ("Un nouveau public pour le Quai Branly"). *But* the stated mission of the museum remains aesthetic and *not* political, and one has to question this newfound concern by the museum management with the demographic profile of its visitors. The MQB director, Stéphane Martin, has also commented on this dimension: "The institution must allow a new generation of twenty to thirty year olds to entertain new questions—How does one live with the other? How can one organize a constructive cultural dialogue? How does one construct identity in a plural world?" ("Un nouveau public pour le Quai Branly"). His position rejoins in powerful ways not only the republican ideal of *invisible* ethnic affiliation in relation to citizenship but also the official government line on market forces as the solution to economic (and racial) marginalization. The MQB concerns (and is concerned *with*) the circulation of *objects and* the CNHI, one could argue, with migrant *subjects*. But how can one achieve *democracy* without *people*? In conclusion, I would like to juxtapose a number of *temporary* exhibitions that have been held at the MQB with what we have discussed thus far in relation to the *permanent* collection.

Temporary exhibits have covered a broad range of artistic practices, including sculpture, photography, and print culture. Some of these include *Maya: de l'aube au crépuscule* [From dawn to dusk] (June 21–October 10, 2011), *La fab-*

riques images [The making of images] (February 16, 2010–July 17, 2011), *Dogon* (April 5–July 24, 2011), and *Maori: leurs trésors ont une âme* [Their treasures have a soul] (October 4, 2011–January 22, 2012). The exhibit "Tarzan ou Rousseau chez les Waziri" (June 16–September 27, 2009) explored the myth of Edgar Rice Burroughs's fictional character Tarzan. Some observers saw in this venture an attempt by the MQB to partially address its own display practices and staging of the *primitive*. In other words, could an ironic treatment of representation and *otherness* assist in the complex process of demythifying ethnocentrism? However, while recognizing that the exhibit can be seen as an attempt by the MQB to play with this tenuous relationship, staging within its confines the *ambiguity* of primitivistic representational practices, others, such as Jean-Loup Amselle, have argued that in the end, this can only constitute a further step in the process of "concealing the historical conditions of production, circulation and exhibition of exotic arts" (*Rétrovolutions*, 192 and 193). It is therefore in the other temporary exhibits that I propose we search instead for an engagement with people and postcolonial realities.

Two examples come to mind from the early years of the MQB's opening. The first was "Diaspora" (October 2, 2007–January 6, 2008), curated by the critically acclaimed French filmmaker Claire Denis, that featured contemporary art installations (works by Jeff Mills, Brice Leboucq, Caroline Cartier, Jean-Pierre Bekolo, Mahamat-Saleh Haroun, Yousry Nassrallah, Mathilde Monnier, and Agnès Godard) focusing on the African Diaspora.[70] Shortly thereafter, "Planète métisse: To mix or not to mix" (March 18, 2008–July 19, 2009) curated by the historian Serge Gruzinski, opened and partially extended Denis' approach by exploring the consequences of cultural intermingling and globalization.[71] In these instances, the themes touched on a range of political and social questions. MQB's responsibilities also include educational and scholarly events, and several lectures, conferences, colloquia, and symposia have been held, and in some cases organized to coincide with temporary exhibits. Thus, an international conference, "Littératures noires," was held January 29–30, 2010, in collaboration with the Bibliothèque Nationale de France, while the exhibit curated by Sarah Grioux-Salgas on the publishing house and journal *Présence Africaine* was still on display—"Présence Africaine: un forum, un mouvement, une tribune" [A forum, a movement, a network] (November 10, 2009–January 31, 2010). This was followed by a seminar series organized by Dominic Thomas (March 5–26, 2010) that brought together a broad range of scholars and writers (Françoise Vergès, Catherine Coquery-Vidrovitch, Lydie Moudileno, Zahia Rahmani, Léonora Miano, Nicolas Bancel, Gisèle Sapiro,

Pascal Blanchard, Faïza Guène, Alain Mabanckou, Jean-François Bayart, and Nacira Guénif-Souilamas) in an interdisciplinary framework to consider the ways in which postcolonial studies have informed and shaped debates on memory, reparations, museology, racial advocacy, and pedagogy in France and elsewhere. After all, the MQB's motto is "Là où dialoguent les cultures" (Where cultures communicate or enter into dialogue). However, as a state-sponsored museum, the MQB necessarily finds itself in a delicate position when it comes to justifying its activities to government ministries that control and fund it, especially when it comes to issues such as colonial history. To this end, we have been able to witness two significant and interrelated developments in 2011 and 2012 that will surely compel critics and observers to partially rethink earlier appraisals of the MQB.

Motivated by, and in response to widespread social uprisings and protests in French Guiana, Guadeloupe, Martinique, and Reunion, President Sarkozy declared 2011 the "Année des Outre-mer" (The year of France overseas).[72] The most significant event was the inauguration of a plaque at the Panthéon on April 6 in honor of the Martinican poet Aimé Césaire, on which occasion Sarkozy delivered a public address.[73] However, this would soon be followed by a public controversy. Daniel Maximin, a novelist and poet from Guadeloupe, was appointed as the commissioner of the Année des Outre-mer. However, one particular event in the program revealed extremely poor judgment, namely, the plan to stage "Un jardin en Outre-mer" (An overseas garden) from April 9 to May 8 in the Jardin d'Acclimatation in Paris to introduce visitors to the cultures of France's overseas departments and territories. What the organizers failed to take into account was the fact the site was far from *neutral* given that *human zoos* had been held there on repeated occasions from 1877 to 1931.[74] A group of public intellectuals were quick to issue a signed declaration, "Nous n'irons pas au Jardin d'acclimatation" (We won't go to the Jardin d'Acclimatation), thereby establishing a transcolonial connection with those French surrealists who had also, back in 1931, declared in protest "Nous n'irons pas à l'Exposition coloniale" (We won't go to the Colonial Exhibition). When Nicolas Bancel published an article in *Le Monde* on March 29, "L'exposition des Outre-mer au Jardin d'Acclimatation est un scandale," Marie-Luce Penchard (the minister in charge of France overseas) was forced to intervene and take immediate action.[75] Although she attended the official opening ceremony of the exhibition on April 7, she also appointed Françoise Vergès, the president of the *Comité pour la mémoire et l'histoire de l'esclavage* (CMPHE), to prepare a report "on the question of 'human zoos' and memory in ethnographic and colonial exhibitions in France, and specifically in Paris (with regards to the Jardin d'Acclimatation and the colonial garden in the Bois de Vincennes)" with the goal of "suggesting measures conducive to improving public awareness."[76] A lengthy report was submitted on November 15, 2011, *Rapport de la mission sur la mémoire des expositions ethnographiques et coloniales*, but was ignored by the minister. This prompted Nicolas Bancel to publish a second article in *Le Monde* on January 27, 2012, "Les oubliés du Jardin d'Acclimatation." Now that the Sarkozy administration has been voted out of office, it remains to be seen whether these questions will receive more favorable attention from the Hollande government.[77] While these events were unfolding, a previously scheduled international symposium for the tenth anniversary of the "Law of 21 May" (the official date on which France recognized its role in the Atlantic slave trade and slavery as crimes against humanity) went ahead as planned, "Exposer l'esclavage: méthodologies et pratiques" (Exhibiting slavery: Methods and practices in the museum) (May 11–13, 2011).[78]

All of the above-mentioned events culminated in a significant departure from the previous museographic practices of the MQB and reluctance to deal with "bodies." One cannot sufficiently emphasize the centrality of physical specimens in the history of French museums, given that entities such as the Musée de l'Homme gathered and collected human specimens for the purposes of ethnographic and scientific research, often at the service of physiological and racial argumentation that of course fueled colonial expansionism. The link between exploration, research, and display practices is therefore incontrovertible. In fact, "Scholars began to feel that studying ethnographic objects and human remains from archaeological digs was insufficient—the examination of real individuals was indispensible to any anthropologist worthy of the name. The possibilities were limited, however, for it meant either 'going into the field' by joining a major, long-term expedition, or importing 'items of study' (which might even mean 'ordering' bodies, as French scientists did in the mid-nineteenth century, and as German scholars did in the late nineteenth century and early twentieth century from southern Africa and Australia)."[79] Thus, "Exhibitions. L'invention du sauvage" (Human zoos: The invention of the savage, November 29, 2011–June 3, 2012) proved to be a groundbreaking exhibition in its attempt to bring public attention to the colonial and universal exhibitions held from the sixteenth to the twentieth centuries in Europe at which populations from Africa, Asia, Oceania, or the Americas were exhibited. The head commissioner was Lilian Thuram, former captain of France's triumphant 1998 Soccer World Cup team (now director of the Lilian Thuram Foundation, an organization that seeks to combat racism). Thuram's involvement is particularly striking, since he is both extremely well respected in general while also being adulated by France's youth; Thuram contained the promise of attracting new audiences to the MQB by offering a form of legitimacy to the museum space.[80] Alongside co-commissioners Pascal Blanchard—a historian and director of the Association pour la Connaissance de l'Histoire de l'Afrique (ACHAC), whose books and films have dramatically improved public consciousness of the colonial and postcolonial imaginary—and anthropologist Nanette Jacomijn Snoep—MQB's decision to host such an exhibit must be understood as a strategic calculation to further extend its public appeal.[81]

President Chirac, we will remember, "decided to create this museum [the MQB] to pay homage to peoples to whom, throughout the ages, history has all too often done violence." But these "people" to whom he alludes, it is crucial to remember, were once *objects,* traded as commodities on the international market. Much like the objects on display in the MQB—objects whose *history* of production is often rather vague—these same people, the *producers* of these objects, were for far too long characterized by their ahistoricity and lack of humanity. It is important to remember, "The history of human interrelationships has often hinged on the implementation of strategies of domination, which may take complex and varied forms. . . . When exhibiting others becomes a way of adopting a distance from an entire people (or exotic 'race'), when it becomes a reflection of identity or deformity—or, indeed, a combination of the two—then the process of constructing a radical alterity has begun, often as a prelude to exclusion" (Blanchard, Boëtsch, and Snoep, "Introduction, " 20). Museographic choices can either foreground that history or obfuscate it, conceal history or instead elect to challenge the imaginary and the reductive constructs that shaped it.[82] The question of presence and visibility remains pertinent to all facets of French civil society today, where the display of African arts (at the MQB, the Louvre, and elsewhere) has become common, whereas the visibility of ethnic minorities in political office has not taken place in substantial ways. An equilibrium must be sought between the ways in which objects are displayed in the permanent exhibition outside of the political context of acquisition and those subjects that are increasingly finding a space in the temporary exhibitions, if only to avoid denying contemporary populations access to their history, a history that is also constitutive of contemporary France irrespective of official governmental attempts to rewrite the past.

This Human Zoos exhibition was both timely and significant given the current political climate in France where a lack of maturity persists when it comes to talking about cultural difference. This was confirmed by the profoundly problematic nature of public statements made on February 4, 2012, by then Minister of the Interior Claude Guéant: "In view of our republican principles, not all civilizations, practices, or cultures, are equal."[83] These kinds of hierarchies exist today in French society and continue to influence cultural, political, and social perceptions of the figure of the "other." Engaged debate on these matters is needed and will require challenging the French authorities that have remained thus far incapable of "thinking critically about the *post-colony,* in other words, when it comes down to it, the history of its presence in the world and the presence of the world inside France, before, during, and after Empire" (Mbembe, "La république désœuvrée," 159). As Bancel and Blanchard have pointed out, this inability to address colonial history is informed by a longer history linking *colonialism* with *republicanism,* and thinking about these two notions *together* would invariably, "mean rethinking the foundations of the dominant hexagonal political ideology. . . . Since after all, broaching the subject of colonization necessarily entails deconstructing those very discourses that provided its legitimacy" ("Mémoire coloniale," 36).

The undividable nature of relations between the French State and museum establishments perpetuates the transcolonial legacy that has informed complex processes of acquisition and display. This was exacerbated by such developments as the Ministry of Immigration, Integration, National Identity and Co-Development (to which we shall return in chapter 3), and the concerted efforts being made to consolidate the coordinates and parameters of Frenchness without consideration or recognition for the dynamic ways in which these categories have evolved. The confusion engendered by revisionism, negationism, and the distortion of history has not assisted in this process but instead served to further accentuate exclusionary policies. How diverse hexagonal populations perceive of themselves and how they remember and interpret heterogeneous histories is of course crucial to identity construction and communication, and to the imagination and fabrication—understood here as a constructive journey rather than an endeavor to obfuscate—of shared trajectories for the twenty-first-century.

2

Object/Subject Migration

THE NATIONAL CENTER FOR THE HISTORY OF IMMIGRATION

The visual discourse of race involves a conceptual and categorical slippage between the body as object and the body as subject. A parallel slippage occurs when the material culture of everyday life, such as artifacts collected in museums of art and anthropology or forms of commodity production and consumption, participate in the construction of race discourse by supporting processes of subjection. Objects come to stand in for subjects not merely in the form of commodity fetish, but as part of a larger system of material and image culture that circulates as a prosthesis of race discourse through practices of collection, exchange, and exhibition.

—*Jennifer A. González*[1]

Constructed for the International Colonial Exhibition of 1931, the Palais de la Porte Dorée has been the home of the National Center for the History of Immigration (CNHI, Cité nationale de l'histoire de l'immigration) since it opened in October 2007.[2] This site was initially occupied by the Musée Permanent des Colonies and later by the Musée des arts africains et océaniens (MAAO) until it relocated in 2006 to the Quai Branly Museum. The symbiotic relationship between the French State and museum establishments has been clearly established, but little attention has been paid to the various ways in which this relationship has served to perpetuate a transcolonial network of power relations. This interconnectivity has also translated into a tenuous relationship in public discourse in terms of the ways history and memory have been articulated.[3] Similar projects are to be found around the world: Centre de documentation sur les migrations humaines (Luxembourg), Museo de la inmigración (Argentina), Immigration Museum and Migration Museum (Australia), Memorial do Imigrante (Brazil), Kosmopolis, The House of Cultural Dialogue (Netherlands), Museu da Emigração e das Comunidades (Portugal), MhiC—Museo de Historia de la Inmigración de Catalaluña (Spain), DOMiD (Documentation Center and Museum of Migration in Germany);[4] many of these institutions, as members of the *International Network of Migration Institutions,* seek to adhere to the UNESCO-IOM objective of "promoting the public understanding of migration."[5]

The press dossier released at the time of the CNHI's inauguration underscored its close tie with the authorities through its formal affiliation with various ministries. The tie was clear in terms of the actualization and conceptualization of the project *and* the state-sponsorship institutional partners, whereby the CHNI "is a public establishment financed by the Ministry of Culture and Communication, the Ministry of National Education, the Ministry of Higher Education and Research, the Ministry of Immigration, Integration, National Identity and Co-Development."[6] A consideration of the CNHI's objectives and mission therefore seems warranted. Civil servant and former Minister of Culture Jacques Toubon was appointed to shepherd the project through to completion; to this end, the *Mission de préfiguration du Centre de ressources et de mémoires de l'immigration* published by the Documentation Française is a useful document in order to gauge the rationale that informed the project's organizational principles. "The recognition of the place of immigrant populations in the destiny of the Republic is important," Toubon explained, "and should help every French person arrive at a more accurate idea of French identity as it stands today, while also reconciling the multiple components that make up the French nation with those values that represent its strengths."[7] The emphasis is placed on the constitutive dimension whereby immigration is to be understood as an integral part of French history.

Framing the project around the concept of "French identity" complicated the task of evaluating the history of immigration in France. The notion itself has been contested, and it has therefore proved difficult to build a project around which a lack of consensus has existed from the outset. Let us explore the CNHI's stated objectives a little further:

> Under the aegis of its research and cultural project, the public establishment aims to: outline and manage the national museum of the history and cultures of immigration, an original cultural ensemble of a museologic and research nature, responsible for preserving and presenting to the public collections that are

> representative of the history, arts and cultures of immigration; to preserve, protect and restore for the good of the State those cultural objects included in the inventory of the national museum of the History and Cultures of immigration for which it has responsibility and thereby contributing to the enrichment of the national collections; gather in a resource center all kinds of documents and information relevant to the history and cultures of immigration as well as to the integration of people who have migrated, including aspects that relate to the economic, demographic, political and social dimension, and accordingly to disseminate this information, including through digital and electronic means, to the general public and to professionals; to develop and promote a network of partners throughout France . . . in order to reach our three fundamental goals: cultural, pedagogic, citizenship. (Press Dossier, 3)

Two particular challenges are thus outlined from the outset: "The first is to incorporate the history of immigration into the common heritage as something inseparable from the construction of France and to recognize the place of foreigners in our common history. . . . The second is to place at the heart of the project the general public and the 'inhabitants', the National Center for the History of Immigration defines itself as both a space and a network" (Press Dossier, 3). As we shall see, the broad range of objectives outlined in these early statements have continued to inform the numerous attempts that have been made to examine French immigration history, attempts that have been additionally complicated by the political instrumentalization of immigration in public discourse in recent years.

The commitment to fostering an inclusive approach to French immigration history was also reflected in the particular concern for *democratizing* access (a dimension that was also important to the Quai Branly Museum project) to the collections and relocating the migrant experience within a broader national narrative. As Robert Aldrich has argued, "The record of the past and differing interpretations in words, commemorations or exhibitions today illustrate how strongly colonialism marked the landscapes, the cultures and the psyches of the colonizing countries, and also how the colonial record has become an object of contemporary contention."[8] With these kinds of considerations in mind, the rationale for the CNHI was that an appeal to a large audience through a paradigm that endeavored to account for the multidimensionality of the historical experience, in theory at least, would encourage a reinterpretation of that history with collective attributes. In fact, a special volume of the journal *Hommes et Migrations* was even devoted to this question and featured the outreach measures adopted (schools, local associations, trade unions) with this end in mind. Ultimately, the thinking was that such a method could alter and displace "negative representations of immigration and of bringing audiences closer around the recognition of the major contributions immigrants and their families have made to the construction of the Nation."[9]

Such strategic calculations were ultimately rendered all the more complex for two main reasons. Firstly, precisely because the traditional role of museums has often been to link processes of *commemoration* with those of *glorification*—of military victories, conquests overseas, and so on. Therefore, to decouple an examination of French immigration history from a concerted analysis of a transcolonial framework that would highlight French imperial ambitions and their indissociability from subsequent migratory patterns would be to obfuscate or revise a key chapter in that collective experience. And secondly, as Michel Wieviorka was right to bring to our attention, yet another problem was posed by the question of immigration given that in the current political climate of French politics, "[i]mmigration is not perceived as a historical process, but rather as a social question."[10] Thus, whereas the CNHI project emphasized a spirit of *inclusivity*, the question of historical accuracy and memory rendered the initiative all the more complicated. It thus remains crucial to foreground the terminological bifurcation of the term "immigration" in terms of its multiple signification in the French context: for "immigration" simultaneously describes the migratory act (and associated policy mechanisms) *and* immigration policy designed to address ethnic minority issues and integration in the post-migratory context.

To a certain degree, Jacques Toubon was aware of the plurality of symbolic registers associated with immigration in the French hexagon and the planning process took into consideration the question of changing mindsets: "Because of a lack of historical perspective, most of our fellow citizens understand immigration as a recent phenomenon, one that is temporary, accidental, somehow a threat to the national community, whereas in reality our experience of immigration, with its failures and success stories, emerges as a constitutive element that is important to French reality. Thus, wanting to show the key aspects of this collective construct, is to want to change current views on immigration and in turn to work toward the ongoing project of achieving integration and social cohesion" (Press Dossier, 1). As a dynamic space that will continue to host conferences, symposia, seminars, and educational visits, and to hold both permanent and temporary collections, the CNHI is not a typical *museum* project and in its capacity as a *centre national* (national center) is less interested in conservation than in narrating, documenting, and recording a particular history, namely that of migration/immigration in France. Indeed, the CNHI exceeds the parameters of the criteria established by the International Council of Museums (ICOM) definition as to what is a museum: "Article 3—Definition of Terms, Section 1. Museum. A museum is a non-profit, permanent institution in the service of society and its development, open to the public, which acquires, conserves, researches, communicates, and exhibits the tangible and intangible heritage of humanity and its environment for the purposes of education, study and enjoyment."[11]

The challenge of altering received notions and perceptions of *étrangers* (foreigners) and *immigrés* (immigrant communities), of questioning the lines of demarcation between *indigenous* or *native* populations and *immigrants,* and of rethinking popular constructions of insiders and outsiders, necessarily entails a complex engagement with the social and political apparatus of national identity formation. As Wieviorka points out, rethinking the role of immigration in French history would "imply looking at the construction of national identity in quite different ways and finding a degree of pride in having been a country of immigration for a good century and a half" ("Inscrire l'immigration," 8).

The reconfiguration of immigration as a constitutive element of French history goes against the historical characterization of the question given that immigrants have tended to be defined in terms of their supplementary status in the national narrative. Nancy Green's comparative analysis of the American and French context confirms these key differences given, as Alexandra Poli, Jonna Louvrier, and Michel Wieviorka have argued, that in the American context the Ellis Island experience "inscribes immigration at the heart of the national story."[12] The insistence on immigration as an essentially late nineteenth- /early twentieth- century phenomenon therefore resists the notion of immigration as a foundational component of the nation and perpetuates the hierarchization between *national* and *immigrant* categories. (Somewhat paradoxically, similar tensions have resurfaced in the United States in recent years, in which the positive attributes that had come to be associated with immigration discourse have been reformulated—around the figure of the *illegal* and *undocumented*—as an undesirable component of globalization rather than as a positive historical phenomenon.) Clearly and unambiguously, the CNHI insists that the nation *came first* and that immigration was grafted upon this pre-existent body, something to be embedded in that pre-existent history.

As visitors to the CNHI embark on the journey through this history, they are immediately oriented in this direction by a large information panel:

> For two centuries, immigrants from all over the world have been shaping France. Unlike France's European neighbors who have experienced *emigration,* France became very early on a country of *immigration.* The French Revolution provided the foundations for a new way of conceiving of the nation. As early as the 19th century, the nation-state emerged along with citizenship. From that point on, foreigners and citizens were distinguished in juridical terms. . . . Initially of European descent and later from the old territories of the French colonial Empire, immigrants have come from all over the world. . . . Each successive group has its own history, its own memory. For a long time we ignored these; yet, one cannot begin to understand contemporary French history without according them the space that is justly theirs in our shared past. Our permanent exhibit is devoted to this history.

On the surface, this information panel appears to adhere to the principle of incorporation and to a constitutive interpretation of national cohesion and history. However, rather than inscribing migration in everyone's genealogy, this genealogy is problematized by the insistence on the post-nineteenth-century experience, that is, as a supplement to a pre-existing national identity. In fact, as Poli, Louvrier, and Wieviorka have signaled in their research on French education and curricular structures, "migratory movements are only rarely inscribed in history" ("Introduction," 11).

The CNHI seeks to promote the symbiotic aspect of the national-immigrant relationship, precisely in order "to explain what France owes to immigration, to provide millions of inhabitants of this country the possibility of situating their individual history in a much larger whole without it disappearing or having to be dissolved,"[13] but this configuration comes up against an opposing logic pertaining to the foundations of the French nation. Not surprisingly, this historical narrative, which cultivates monolithic interpretations of history and identity, coincides with the version that is reproduced and transferred to successive generations in the French classroom. "This then constitutes an obstacle to the process of taking into consideration the experience of alterity and of various particularities introduced by the theme of immigration," Poli, Louvrier, and Wieviorka argue, since "the nation is preexistent, and the Republic itself assumes that particularities be dissolved. Or that they remain confined to the private space, and there is no room either in the national imaginary or for that matter in the very functioning of republican institutions for heterogeneous or diverse elements inherent to immigration" ("Introduction," 12).

The French Museum landscape has evolved dramatically in recent years, and certainly from the late twentieth century onward as an outcome of former president François Mitterrand's aggressive cultural program. Panivong Norindr convincingly demonstrated how "the continuity between Mitterrand's *grands travaux* and the politics of urban design of his predecessors since the Second Empire can be located in the ways these new urban markers delimit, inscribe, and reconfigure in space an image of France as a dominant cultural center."[14] The interesting shift that has taken place more recently reveals a disquieting concern with French identity, especially as we witnessed throughout Sarkozy's term in office (2007–2012). The French authorities are evidently struggling to redefine France's position and role in a rapidly mutating and globalized environment in which antiquated conceptions and interpretations of human relations have been superseded by new forms of human interaction and community formation, preconditions, and logical outcomes of an increasingly interconnected world. As Fabrice Grognet has argued, "For a decade, France has been recomposing the various identities it plans on presenting in various museums. . . . The Cité involves the constitution of new national collections (artistic, ethnographic, oral and written archives) around immigration, in order to show how the *Other* has been present in France for a long time and contributed implicitly to the process of expanding the composition of the French Nation."[15] Already with the Quai Branly Museum the objective had been to provide a space devoted to the cultures of the *other,* thereby further perpetuating segregated arrangements in the cultural and political domain; in the case of the CNHI, the defining umbrella rubric for the project is specified by the statement "Leur histoire est notre histoire" (Their history is our history). In each instance, the relationship between the *other* and the *we* remains exceptionally vague, confused and complicated by the question of appropriation, as well as the specter of republican ideals and values.

Not surprisingly, the creation in 2007 by newly elected president Nicolas Sarkozy of the Ministry of Immigration, Integration, National Identity and Co-Development triggered controversy. The Ministry sought to control migration by privileging "immigration choisie" (chosen and selective economic migration) and dramatically reducing family reunification. We will explore the implications of these new policies in the next chapter; what concerns us here is the tenuous relationship between the objectives of the CNHI and those of the Ministry. The CNHI's intended role was to *humanize* the migratory and immigrant experience, in other words, to treat migrants as *subjects* rather than as *objects.* However, since 2007, we have observed an intensification of a discourse that dehumanizes these populations as they continue to be characterized as economic and social burdens. Recourse to such categories in official governmental rhetoric and policies ends up dissociating the harsh measures and policies adopted by the authorities from any reference to the migrants' own experience. Additionally, the commitment to a dramatic reduction in family re-unification occludes the constitutive dimension of the collective migration experience over a much longer historical timeframe while encouraging suspicion and xenophobia, obstacles to the kind of reconceptualization and re-contextualization necessary to achieve a constitutive and incorporative understanding of the migration experience alluded to earlier.

These developments only serve to further accentuate the degree of interconnectivity between the work of the *ministries* and the *museums*. The CNHI was initially a project of the French Left, since the socialist prime minister Lionel Jospin commissioned the first planning report in 2001. But the project was only given the go-ahead in 2003 by the right-wing government of Prime Minister Jean-Pierre Raffarin and President Chirac, and it was the latter who subsequently assigned the project to Jacques Toubon. Under Sarkozy's presidency, the institution found itself under the joint control of several ministries (Culture, Education, Research), as well as under the Ministry of the Interior, since the latter absorbed the Ministry for Immigration, Integration, National Identity and Co-Development in 2010. "Whilst its statutes [the CNHI's] are intended to guarantee the institution considerable editorial autonomy," Mary Stevens has pointed out, "it should from this brief overview be evident the extent to which this is a highly politicized project that cuts to the heart of long-standing debates about what it means to be French in a globalized, interdependent world."[16] Indeed, as Florence Bernault has argued, "Today, the return of the colonial, and the return of the colonized, does not spare any terrain, from the political to the cultural, the academic, and the popular, and the land of the imagined universals. Everywhere the colonial paradigm has proved, for better or for worse, highly disruptive of established routines and polite discussions. Syndrome or revulsion, the freezing of the past has broken down, and a few deceptions with it."[17]

On May 18, 2007, eight members of the CNHI's distinguished research council (Marie-Claude Blanc-Chaléard, Geneviève Dreyfus-Armand, Nancy L. Green, Gérard Noiriel, Patrick Simon, Vincent Viet, Marie-Christine Volovitch-Tavarès, and Patrick Weil) resigned in protest because of the Ministry of Immigration, Integration, National Identity and Co-Development's agenda, which for them was contrary to the objectives of the CNHI. A public statement by these researchers reiterated the CNHI's commitment to dismantling rather than reaffirming narrow interpretations of "identity":

> This space was conceived with the aim of changing the ways in which people looked at their society by reminding them how, over two centuries, foreigners, arriving in successive waves, have contributed to the development, transformation, and enrichment of France. Accounting for diverse histories and individual and collective memories, making them a part of everyone's history, with its moments of glory and its "shady zones," helping in this manner to move beyond prejudice and stereotyping, these are the things that brought us together in this project. The creation of a "ministry of immigration and national identity" puts into question these objectives. Words are symbols and weapons in politics. Defining *identity* does not come under the purview of a democratic state. Linking *immigration* with *national identity* in a ministry is without precedent in our Republic: such a creation by this presidency inscribes immigration as a "problem" for France and the French. . . . Bringing together these two terms is to associate a discourse that stigmatizes immigration with a nationalist tradition founded on suspicion and hospitality towards foreigners experienced during times of crisis. The challenge of the CNHI was to bring people together and to look to the future, gathered around a shared history that all may identity with, yet this ministry threatens on the contrary to instill the kind of division and polarization whose toll history has shown. That is why we are resigning today from our official responsibilities at the CNHI.[18]

These contradictions point in the direction of a failed decolonization and to greater problems that are today part of the fabric of French society.

Another way in which this dissent has manifested itself has been in the debates surrounding the location of the CNHI in the Palais de la Porte Dorée itself, given the history of the site. Rather than obfuscating the longer history of the building, France could have seized the opportunity to reckon with its colonial past. Instead, the burden has been shifted to former colonial subjects and their descendants *in* Africa and to postcolonial communities residing *in* France to move beyond the past. On December 17, 2008, at the École Polytechnique, Sarkozy delivered his "diversity speech," in which he argued, "We must change our behavior, we must change our habits. We have to change so that the Republic can remain alive. We have to change so that no French person ever feels like a foreigner in their country."[19] While echoing some of the objectives of the CNHI planning document, these rhetorical ploys were undermined by the semiology and stereotypes inherent in Sarkozy's broader discourse.

Numerous arguments and heated debates have taken place in France in recent years concerning multiple facets of French society, from colonial history, memory, and postcoloniality,[20] including exchanges that have informed the contested terrain of postcolonial studies as a disciplinary paradigm,[21] the memorialization of slavery,[22] the legacy of Algeria,[23] and the educational sector.[24] The fact that the Palais de la Porte Dorée could never be a neutral site may seem obvious. "The dominance of the metropole over its colonies," Maureen Murphy has argued, "is clearly expressed in the choice of architecture: the purpose was not merely to display products from the colonies but also to convey the subordination of the latter to France's power"[25] and, as the only structure that would survive the exposition, the "permanent museum of the Colonies" was conceived with the aim of giving the discourse deployed in the Bois de Vincennes an enduring presence. At that time, the hope was that the condensed historical, artistic, and economic image that was offered of the Empire would encourage visitors to invest in those products brought back from the colonies, perhaps even to settle overseas. The building, as well as the frescoes that decorate the internal space and that are still visible today, bear witness to an ideology tainted by contradictions."[26] Migration is today a central component of globalization, but the *global* reach of empire is inscribed in the architecture, whereby "the bas-reliefs, ordered according to geography, illustrate the benefit of the colonies to the metropole," and in turn the frescoes themselves found inside the building "illustrate France's influence in the world" (Murphy, *Un Palais pour une cité,* 29 and 33). These displays of colonial power and of colonial labor working tirelessly at the service of France's imperial ambitions and expansionist drive throughout the world share a complex linearity with the *subjects* on display in the CNHI that are featured as migrant laborers having made invaluable contributions to France's economic, military, and political power. The disconnect between these *positive* attributes and the increasingly harsh measures invoked by the French authorities in order to combat *negative* immigration are therefore particularly striking. Of course, as we saw in the previous chapter, the longer history of displaying and representing the *other* cannot be ignored particularly when we are reminded that the CNHI now finds itself at the site of the 1931 Colonial Exhibition.

The colonial past is inescapable and remnants are to be found everywhere in colonial and postcolonial rhetoric and scientific discourse. "For if exotic objects on display in European museums, in particular in France, reflect the history of French expansion overseas," as Robert Aldrich has shown, "they also shed light on a broad range of museological, political, and moral questions relating to the exhibition of non-European works of art and artifacts. . . . Even the occasional visitor will soon become aware of the sheer number of objects in the collections of Paris museums that have come from former colonies and that the traces of colonialism are omnipresent throughout French society."[27] *Their history* may well be *our history,* but *they* remain the *other* when they enter national territorial boundaries and are subjected to control, categorization, and objectification as subjects. In actuality, we are left with a "subordination of distinct group identities to a monolithic notion of a homogenous citizenry," Mary Stevens writes, whereby "once (im)migration was understood as the crossing into *national* territory then questions of internal migration, both within the hexagon and between the constituent parts of the French empire had to be excluded. In one simple move, immigration was uncoupled from colonization, despite the avowed inherence of the former to the latter."[28]

In reality, the CNHI's presence at the *Porte Dorée* serves to "accentuate an absence for which it can never fully compensate: namely the lack of a museum that would really take on the necessary but unenviable task of dissecting France's colonial past."[29] Indeed, activists and researchers have insisted that the vacancy of the Palais de la Porte Dorée was a missed opportunity to inscribe the experience of immigration as a chapter in a broader and more pertinent history that would have included slavery, colonialism, and the postcolonial era. There has been inadequate engagement with that history and with its legacy in public consciousness, a legacy that is perceived in transhistorical terms as confirmed by the ethnic minority advocacy group *Les Indigènes de la République* who conceive of themselves as "descendants of slaves and deported Africans, daughters and sons of the colonized and of immigrants"[30] and by the *Comité pour la mémoire de l'esclavage, Mémoires de la traite négrière, de l'esclavage et de leurs abolitions* that explicitly situates slaves in French history, whereby "Their history and culture are constitutive of our collective history."[31] The *objects* that were formerly on display at the MAAO may well have *migrated* westward across the city, but the images of human subjects on display at the CNHI remain forever connected with their ancestors. As Mary Stevens has argued, "The *Palais de la Porte Dorée* was conceived as a vehicle for colonial propaganda and remains inseparable from it," a "euphemistic appellation—named for its address rather than its content" ("Still the Family Secret?" 247) in which postcolonial realities emerge "as a radical and comprehensive break with the colonial past rather than the working through in a metropolitan context of the colonial legacy," culminating in "continued occlusion" ("Still the Family Secret?" 248–249).

The CNHI collection brings together a disparate range of objects, photographs, digital archives, and installations, organized in such a way as to stage and perform immigration.[32] The permanent collection is divided into subsections demarcated by pillars inscribed with headings that include "Ici et là-bas" (Here and there), "Au travail" (At work), "Face à l'état" (Facing the State), "Émigrer" (Emigrating) and "Diversité" (Diversity). Each explores aspects of the "migrant" experience, pointing out how "The past is not erased when one leaves ones country. All migrants bring with them their mother tongue and culture and seek out compatriots upon arrival in order to recreate micro-communities. . . . More often than not, it's the next generation that begins to distance itself from this origin . . . " (Ici et là-bas). This kind of narrative is interrupted by a combination of descriptive accounts of *socioeconomic* and *sociocultural* problems associated with assimilation and integration, including housing, given that "Upon arrival, with only limited means or a settlement plan, migrants often find themselves in precarious living conditions. . . . Access to adequate housing will later symbolize the migrant's gradual settlement in the host society. From the 1950s on, the State will actively develop public housing" (Ici et là-bas), spaces that will become emblematic of contemporary urban diversity. In the section on work: "Emigrating is a phenomenon often determined by factors that are outside of the individual's control but that is lived at a human level" (Émigrer). In turn, the section on "diversity" reflects the sociocultural reality of a vibrant multicultural France with migrations from multiple locations and in multiple forms—"a space for multiple cultural encounters . . . that continue to enrich the French national heritage" (Diversité). In reality, though, efforts at defining a common or shared French (and for that matter European) identity remain far more complicated.

Photographs, audio-visual resources, posters, family objects, and legal documents, among others, endeavor to document the manifold facets of the migrant experience to/with France, components augmented with a number of installations. Certainly one of the most striking is Barthélémy Toguo's *Climbing Down* (2004), a twenty-foot construction in which single beds have been stacked one upon the other and draped with cheap multi-colored shopping bags from the discount department store Tati, bags often used by poor migrants as luggage, thereby addressing notions of social displacement and mobility. The descriptive label informs us: "*Climbing Down* refers to immigration shelters. The artist is tackling serious problems relating to separation and precarious housing. The work reveals the tensions that can arise in the public space and in the shelters, in the shared space and in the private space where individuals recreate a micro-universe, marked out by bags and suitcases that contain traces of the homes they have left. The relationship between the individual and the collective and the interior and exterior becomes a tenuous one" [CNHI information panel, Bathélémy Toguo, *Climbing Down,* 2004]. Isabelle Renard has fastened on the "oxymoronic"[33] quality of the title contained in the juxtaposition of "climbing" with "down"; the artist addresses the psychological challenges that come from separation, an often overlooked component of the migratory struggle given the imperative of attaining a successful economic outcome, notions implied by the link one is compelled to make because of the allusion to *social climbing* and to upward mobility.

Several video installations also focus on the question of loss. Zineb Sedira's *Mother Tongue* (2002) traces the violence of cultural alienation and displacement, as communication is interrupted and limited across generations between a grandmother, her daughter, and granddaughter.[34] The information panel explains:

> The artist examines notions linked to preservation and loss of cultural identity. Through a matrilineal chain, the artist, her mother and daughter dialogue, two at a time and on three screens, each in their respective mother tongue and in three languages: French in the case of Zineb Sedira, Arabic for the mother, and English for the granddaughter. However, dialogue appears to have been broken between the granddaughter and the grandmother who do not seem to understand one another; if the artist's triple language skills bear witness to her diverse identity, then the cultural differences engendered by the diasporic experience are revealed at between her mother and daughter. (CNHI information panel, Zineb Sedira, *Mother Tongue,* 2002)

The looping video installation takes place over three sequences: (1) Mother and I [Arabic-French]; (2) Daughter and I [French-English]; (3) Grandmother and Granddaughter [Arabic-English]. Naturally, the notion of a mother tongue is further complicated here, since the point of the installation is that they *do not/no longer* share language. The installation is simultaneously about words and silence, revealing what is lost and disrupted in translation and migration. One is forced to reflect on how such outcomes might well differ in other transnational diasporic settings.

In another montage, *Mother, Father and I* (2003), Zineb Sedira projects concurrently on separate screens interviews she conducted with her parents on the subject of the 1954–1962 French-Algerian war. This results in a polyvocal account of her family's ties to Algeria and to how the war is remembered. The disparate and gendered accounts that result from this act of memorializing a troubled history serve to question the mechanisms that have been deployed for recording official historical memory while also articulating perspectives and observations that might not otherwise have been known. How, for example, might the father have access to the mother's private position, and how might gender deliver certain variables? The originality comes from the fact that the daughter (Sedira herself) remains symbolically silent in her capacity as observer, filmed on a different screen that is set up facing her parents' testimonial narratives. The communication that takes place between her father and mother is not structured around direct exchange but rather emerges from the space *between* them as a reciprocal engagement with history. The intimacy of the disclosure is maintained while Sedira is able to confirm that ultimately, no single, monolithic narrative of immigration can exist: "Zineb Sedira's private history, along with her family's, who left Algeria for France, constitutes the privileged subject in the artist's piece."

Mother, Father and I deals with themes relating to multiple identities, the war, departure, travel, and her life in France. Zineb Sedira's work follows a historiographic mode, but the documentary style she adopts is also influenced by traditional story-telling techniques. The use of her own image also allows her to question her history and identity. Her parents in fact speak at the same time but *not* to each other. They have shared their lives and histories living side by side, but ultimately their respective *experiences* of that history warrants autonomous validation, offering through the intimacy of disclosure what is arguably a more accurate contextualization of that collective journey, introducing new forms of communication and dialogue. In this regard, this installation provides a compelling alternative to the corpus of works known as *beur* literature produced by the children of North African immigrants living in France from the 1980s on.[35]

One of the most original concepts developed at the CNHI is that of the allocation of a space to a "galerie des dons." Through a symbolic acknowledgment of Marcel Maus's influential work on the "gift" and the fluid nature of "value" as it is accorded to objects across cultures, the CNHI has endeavored to encourage individuals and families to share with the general public personal symbols of their respective migratory experience, thereby further foregrounding the human and personal dimension. As Fabrice Grognet has remarked, "Objects that had previously only been family heirlooms, identity papers, expired job contracts, personal or institutional archives swell the ranks of objects that serve as 'witnesses' to immigration in France. . . . Added to the inventory, this artificial grouping of objects of different nature and origins find unity as components of a *national collection*" ("Quand 'l'étranger' devient patrimoine français," 30).[36] Naturally, these concerns are not specific to the French context, and other European Union members have been implementing measures aimed at heightening public awareness of the precariousness of migrant workers and immigrant families.

In Spain, for example, the office of the Secretary of State for Immigration and Emigration has launched (with other partners) a sensitization initiative that has included a mobile exhibit, "Los deseos cerca de Tí en La Ruta Prometida: une exposicíon donde podrás compartir tu deseo" (Desires Near You on the Promised Route: An Exhibition Where You Could Share Your Desire), that addresses the dangers of ocean crossings and immigrant conditions. These kinds of initiatives now define the work being done by the office of the United Nations High Commissioner for Refugees (UNHCR): "Climbing over razor wire fences, taking to sea in leaking boats or stowing away in airless containers, refugees and migrants around the world risk their lives every day in desperate attempts to find safety or a better life. Behind the dramatic headlines and the striking images of people on the move, there are personal stories of courage, tragedy and compassion. Although refugees and migrants often use the same routes and modes of transport they have different protection needs."[37]

However, in order to meet the stated goals of the CNHI—in other words, to reach an improved understanding of the role immigration has played in French history—a concerted effort will have to be made to denounce those paradigms and stereotypes that were initially disseminated by the Ministry of Immigration, Integration, National Identity and Co-Development, and individuals and institutions encouraged to abandon and relinquish a one-dimensional genealogical apparatus at the service of nationalistic tendencies. Given the current political climate in France and the E.U. in a more general way, this is unlikely to happen in the near future. On the contrary, the 2012 French elections brought to light evidence of regression.

In 2007, Sarkozy appointed Hervé Lemoine (the director of the Museum of French Monuments, subsequently promoted to head the French National Archives, under the aegis of the Ministry of Culture and Communication) to prepare a report, "La Maison de l'Histoire de France,"[38] that was to "provide a concrete proposal for the establishment of a research center and for a space that could house a permanent collection dedicated to France's civil and military history" (Lemoine report, 2). Submitted on April 16, 2008, this initiative provides further indication as to the nature of collaborative measures between various government ministries. However, the Lemoine report also reiterates the importance of France's "long historiographic tradition" and insists that "*historical culture* be accorded a central place in national identity and in French national sentiment" (Lemoine report, 16). Sarkozy validated this project in a speech in Nîmes on January 13, 2009, "Vœux aux acteurs de la Culture": "We have decided to create a French History Museum. This museum will be located on a site that is emblematic of our history, a site that we have yet to decide upon but that will be identified."[39] The fact that the project to create this "French History Museum" was co-sponsored by the Ministry of Culture and Communication *and* the Ministry of Defense, might, for obvious reasons, be a source of concern. Closer scrutiny of the Lemoine report reveals a restricted and monolithic conceptualization of French identity. As Tzvetan Todorov has argued, "There is no such thing as a country with a totally homogeneous culture . . . ; A country's culture is always multiple and in constant evolution."[40]

The most conspicuous aspect of the Lemoine report concerns the emphasis on historical figures rather than events. As Olivier Le Cour Grandmaison has demonstrated, the practice of "invoking a monumental past makes it possible to believe in a return to grandeur and power while also restoring the belief and confidence in a glorious future, since what has been can surely be achieved again."[41] Indeed, recourse to Louis XIV, Napoleon, and de Gaulle conveniently avoids more "awkward" historical chapters. "Given how the report and the key questions it poses are framed," Nicolas Bancel and Herman Lebovics have convincingly argued, "it is not improbable that the grand narrative of France which the museum will present will have little or nothing to say about the social conflicts of the Great Revolution or any others in subsequent history: the story of women and of gender, French imperialism and colonialism, slavery and the slave trade, the year's of Vichy government . . . or France's history as the greatest immigrant nation in Europe."[42] The real issue here concerned of course Sarkozy's desire to distance himself from that *other* French history museum, namely the competing project that is the CNHI, and which to Sarkozy symbolized "another example of national fragmentation: a history museum dedicated to special interests, in this instance, one that celebrated differences, and, most unappealingly, the coming of various new communities. . . . This was not the President's idea of how to tell the story of his nation" (Bancel and Lebovics, "Building the History Museum to Stop History," 272). Thus, whether or not Sarkozy was committed to inscribing himself in that French tradition of *Presidential museum projects* through the creation of a French history museum—of course, Sarkozy only completed one term in office and did not, as some of his predecessors did, leave behind a landmark cultural project that would be associated with his legacy—was in actuality secondary to his concern with instrumentalizing history through a "reconquest of 'national identity'" precisely via "the denunciation of the enemies within," and by fostering patriotic fervor through examples of "uplifting and edifying" role models that will "supply moral and civic instruction" (Bancel and Lebovics, "Building the History Museum to Stop History," 272 and 273). In the next chapter, the implications of these measures are explored through a focus on Sarkozy's immigration policies, the actions of the Ministry of Immigration, Integration, National Identity and Co-Development, and the significance of the *National Identity Debate* launched by Éric Besson, the minister of the aforementioned ministry, in November 2009.

3

Sarkozy's Law

NATIONAL IDENTITY AND THE INSTITUTIONALIZATION OF XENOPHOBIA

He spoke in public several times a day, and on each occasion puffed out his breast like a pigeon and engaged in peculiar contortions in order to liven up his pronouncements, the substance of which was of less importance than the form itself, which in any case varied depending on his audience. . . . In spite of his limited attractiveness, he was able to negotiate and build alliances like no other. This Hungarian aspired to unify the French and the Visigoths in Gaul against a declining Roman Empire, and to recreate it to his advantage.

—*Patrick Rambaud*[1]

The temptation to build walls is certainly not a new one. Whenever a culture or civilization has failed in thinking the other, in thinking self and other together, and thinking the other in the self, stiff and impenetrable preservations of stone, iron, barbed-wire, electric fences, or closed-minded ideologies have been erected, collapsed, only to return with newfound stridency.

—*Edouard Glissant and Patrick Chamoiseau*[2]

Behind bars and handcuffed, he still loved France. He was a patriot.

—*Delphine Coulin*[3]

We asked for manpower, and we got human beings.

—*Max Frisch*[4]

As I embark upon this chapter, I am reminded of the importance of taking into consideration a broad range of comparative examples. Whether or not one agrees with the effectiveness of such mechanisms as *Affirmative Action* in the United States or the *Race Relations Act* in the United Kingdom, these devices represent at the very least recognition that *race* constitutes a category for discrimination. Ethnic or diversity monitoring has been extensively debated in France in recent years, a country in which all citizens are considered equal and indistinguishable before the law.[5] Yet, official racial *invisibility* has complicated discussions on difference, especially given that a general consensus has emerged with regards to the ineffectiveness of assimilation, insertion, and integration policies. This tenuous situation is perhaps best exemplified in the diametrically opposed interpretations of contemporary politics provided by two French philosophers, namely Alain Badiou and Alain Finkielkraut. For the former, "A definition of the population based on identity must reckon with the fact that populations in our contemporary world are composite, heterogeneous and multifaceted. . . . The aim of identifying what 'French civilization' may be, an entity I am at odds to describe, can only be futile and ultimately serve to point out those who don't belong under that category," whereas for the latter, "A form of loathing is to be found among a significant element of the new French populations . . . militant *francophobia*."[6] Certainly, the relationship between national identity and immigration policy is neither new to France, nor for that matter unique to its sociocultural history. Yet, in recent years, these questions have found themselves at the forefront of the policy-making agenda.

The French authorities have instrumentalized the theme of migration—and particularly migration from Africa—arguing that "uncontrolled migration" threatens France (and therefore also the European Union), and thereby justifying the control systems and responses that have been implemented. As Éric Fassin has shown, "The Minister [of Immigration, Integration, National Identity and Co-Development] is there in order to give life to a problem that in turn allows him to exist."[7] In his book *Non-Persons: The Exclusion of Migrants in a Global Society,* Italian sociologist Alessandro Dal Lago provides a lucid analysis of the ways in which government discourse and media representations operate, shape public opinion, while informing and structuring what he has described as a "Tautology of Fear":

> Foreigners are a threat to citizens because the *clandestine* [illegals or irregulars] are usually criminals → Subjective definition of legitimate actors: "We're afraid.

> Foreigners make us feel threatened" → Objective definition in the media: "Foreigners are a threat" → Transformation of symbolic resource into dominant frame: it has been proven that the *clandestine* threaten our society and therefore "the authorities must act" → Subjective confirmation of legitimate social actors: "We can't stand any more. What are our mayors, police, and government doing?" → Intervention by "legitimate social representatives": "If the government won't intervene, we will defend our own citizens" → Legislative political and administrative measures that confirm the dominant frame.[8]

As we shall see, this framework has proved to be highly-effective in building electoral constituencies and mobilizing support for policies, because insisting on the *perpetual* nature of the danger or threat to the national or E.U. community presented by clandestine/illegal/irregular migrants has in turn enabled governments (in France, Italy, Spain, and so forth) to demonstrate the effectiveness of their reactive policies by establishing "arrest quotas/goals,"[9] and then publicizing the number of repatriated/expelled migrants, thereby "politicizing the repression of illegal immigration, and transforming a bureaucratic practice into a political objective."[10] The authorities have argued that recourse to the rule of law merely constitutes the application of fundamental democratic and republican principles, thereby invalidating the criticism formulated by opponents to what they see as a "legitimate power."[11] Indeed, public statements made in 2010 by French president Nicolas Sarkozy pertaining to the "failure of multiculturalism" and German chancellor Angela Merkel, who evoked the "utter failure" of German *Multikulti* policies, alongside British prime minister David Cameron's assessment in 2011 that "it's time to turn the page on the failed policies of the past," have only further accentuated the centrality of these issues to twenty-first-century existence. In order to further elucidate the various ways in which the French authorities have exploited the above-mentioned "tautology of fear," I propose to juxtapose official assessments and declarations with the findings of agencies and organizations that monitor migration and integration.

For example, the Expert Council of German Foundations on Integration and Migration (Sachverständigenrat Deutscher Stiftungen für Integration und Migration) has observed consensus among the German political parties around the sentiment and perception that "integration has failed": for the Left, "Integration has failed, because natives and members of the majority populations have obstructed the integration efforts of immigrants," whereas on the Right, "Integration has failed, because large parts of the immigrant population in

Germany are neither willing nor able to integrate."[12] Yet, such statements are at odds with the conclusions of the French Haut Conseil à l'Intégration (HCI, High Council on Integration) that uses indicators such as political representation (local, regional, and national), educational achievement, employment, professional advancement, and mobility in order to evaluate integration. In fact, their findings offer signs of progress in many of these areas, predominantly when it comes to comparing integration outcomes between migrant parents and their children.[13] However, a considerable discrepancy exists between the findings of research groups (whether governmental or independent) and the *impact* of government discourse in shaping public perceptions of migrants and immigrant communities.

During the 2006 and 2007 French presidential campaign, candidate Sarkozy made immigration and national identity central questions.[14] To this end, he sought to capitalize on the tough positions he had taken as Minister of the Interior during the 2005 urban uprisings in France and the harsh declarations he directed at minority ethnic groups at that time.[15] Not surprisingly, statistics relating to the 2007 presidential elections revealed that 77 percent of practicing Catholics had voted for Nicolas Sarkozy, while 80 percent of Muslims had supported the Socialist candidate Segolène Royal, and 64 percent of Sarkozy supporters believed there were "too many immigrants in France." In debates on *immigration* during the 1980s and 1990s—a term which refers simultaneously in French to the physical act of migrating *and* to race relations[16]—the focus had been almost exclusively on what Etienne Balibar has described as "the insurmountability of cultural differences, a racism which, at first sight, does not postulate the superiority of certain groups or peoples in relation to others but 'only' the harmfulness of abolishing frontiers, the incompatibility of lifestyles and traditions."[17] Yet, the social uprisings that occurred during the fall of 2005 in several French *banlieues* housing projects located in urban peripheries served to highlight exclusionary realities based on class *and* racial structures.[18]

Often referred to as the French "Katrina"—an attempt to establish parallels between the socioeconomic circumstances of disadvantaged populations that were exposed as a consequence of the devastating impact of Hurricane Katrina in Louisiana and the profound inequities in French society which the 2005 uprising brought to public attention—the existence of a *global south* within metropolitan France served to accord a key place once again to issues relating to immigration. On June 20, 2005, then Minister of the Interior Sarkozy had visited the Cité des 4000 housing project outside of Paris (in La Courneuve) claiming that he would "clean it out with high-pressure hose" (nettoyer au Kärcher). Later, during a visit to the Argenteuil *banlieue* on October 25, 2005, he promised one resident he would rid the project of its "scum/rabble" (racaille). These irresponsible comments served to further exacerbate tensions between *banlieue* residents and the authorities, such that—when on October 27, 2005, a fifteen-year-old boy named Bouna and seventeen-year-old Zyed (both ethnic minorities) were electrocuted at Clichy-sous-Bois in an EDF power plant as they ran from police officers—riots ensued. The authorities were quick to deflect responsibility, attributing blame instead to cultural and religious practices (such as Islam and polygamy) at odds with republican ideals and values, even declaring on November 8 a state of emergency justified by a preexisting law (the decree of April 3, 1955) previously adopted to prevent French citizens from organizing against the war in Algeria. These measures served to further underscore the nature of transcolonial alignments, introducing disturbing echoes of a colonial past, updated in this case in the guise of repressive mechanisms and racial profiling. Many argued that these events signaled the failure of economic integration; instead, one could also argue that social protest of this nature—albeit one that lacked organizational cohesiveness and failed to articulate specific claims for social and economic reparation—inscribes itself in a long French tradition of fighting against injustice, pointing instead to an appropriation of republican ideals in order to highlight inconsistent applications of justice to an identifiable spectrum of the French community.

As Pierre Tevanian and Sylvie Tissot have shown, the prevailing official rhetoric had for some time privileged a juridical and security-based vocabulary that included terms such as "délinquance," "insécurité," "incivilité," "préoccupation majeure des Français," "responsabilisation," "tolérance zero," and expressions such as "préférence nationale" and "problème de l'immigration," namely what Gérard Noiriel has called a "vocabulaire de menace" (vocabulary of threats).[19] As we shall see, these linguistic signifiers highlight "illegality," "irregularity," and the "clandestine." The manipulation of public opinion has served to justify the toughening of border control mechanisms and the introduction of new legislation. A vast discrepancy can be identified between the resources allocated to the fight against illegal immigration and those aimed at integration efforts; in reality, these procedures have been accompanied by a decline in the rights of foreigners and migrants.[20] Furthermore, populist sentiments have been driven by media coverage of a declining global economy and repeated public statements made by political leaders in which examples (*laïcité,* headscarves, veils, and burqas) function as evidence of the assault on republican ideals and values and therefore rationalize protectionist acts.[21] In turn, this has given rise to widespread xenophobia, what Jérome Valluy has described as "the range of declarations and actions aimed at designating foreigners as a problem, risk or threat to the host society, whether these foreigners find themselves elsewhere, or whether they are already present or settled in the society."[22]

Government discourse has already had a tangible and real impact.[23] A report published in 2010 by the German Marshall Fund, "Transatlantic Trends—Immigration," reveals a deterioration in recent years in French perceptions of immigration: "In 2010, however, only 38% of the French said that immigration is an opportunity for France, and their perceptions of immigrants' impacts on culture, labor markets, and crime has become more negative. . . . On the issue of crime, for instance, only 31% of French respondents thought that illegal immigrants increased crime in 2009. By 2010, that number had increased to a majority of the French (55%) linking illegal immigration and crime rates. . . . When asked about culture, 58% of the French in 2010 thought that immigration enriches French culture, down from 68% in 2009."[24] Likewise, one finds increased concern for "illegal immigration" and similarly elevated negative perceptions of Muslims: "26% of European are 'concerned' about immigration, 67% are 'preoccupied' by illegal immigration."[25] Since 2005, when the social uprisings brought unparalleled attention to the degree of social exclusion and racial segregation in French society, racial affirmation and debate has returned to the political agenda, in an attempt to raise public consciousness and therefore to counter the views mentioned above.[26] Included in these discussions has been the question of political underrepresentation in elected office (in 2011, only one *visible minority* deputy out of 577 was elected to the Assemblée Nationale, fewer, one should note than during the 1950s), a priority for activist organizations endeavoring to displace the status quo. Having said this, the multidimensionality of the ethnic minority question in France makes analysis at once compelling and intriguing, and inquiries into this specific domain inevitably entail a consideration of a broad set of political and social factors with roots in the slavery, colonialism, immigration, as well as in postcolonial history.

Attention has been drawn to these historical connections and layers of immigration that go back centuries in French history as a way of offsetting official state discourse that obfuscates the constitutive nature of demographic realities as well as the multiple contributions immigrants have made to building contemporary France culturally, economically, and socially. Collaborations between artists, intellectuals, public personalities, and political activists have yielded published declarations such as "Identité nationale et histoire coloniale" (National identity and colonial history) by the collective *Pour un véritable débat,* and the *Appel pour une République multiculturelle et postraciale.*[27] These have been augmented by a substantial corpus of publications focused on these questions: Pascal Blanchard, Nicolas Bancel, and Sandrine Lemaire (*La fracture coloniale: La société française au prisme de l'héritage colonial,* 2005); Nicolas Bancel, Pascal Blanchard, Achille Mbembe, Françoise Vergès, and Florence Bernault (*Ruptures post-coloniales: Les nouveaux visages de la société-francaise,* 2010); Rama Yade-Zimet (*Noirs de France,* 2007); Gaston Kelman (*Je suis noir et je n'aime pas le manioc,* 2003, *Au-delà du Noir et du Blanc,* 2005, and *Parlons enfants de la patrie,* 2007); Jean-Baptiste Onana (*Sois-nègre et tais-toi,* 2007); Patrick Lozès (*Nous les noirs de France,* 2007); Claude Ribbe (*Les Nègres de la République,* 2007); Pap Ndiaye (*La condition noire: Essai sur une minorité ethnique française,* 2008); Christiane Taubira (*Egalité pour les exclus: La politique face à l'histoire et à la mémoire coloniale,* 2009); Rokhaya Diallo (*Racisme: Mode d'emploi,* 2011); Pascal Blanchard, Sylvie Chalaye, Éric Deroo, Dominic Thomas, and Mahamet Timera (*La France noire. Trois siècles de présences des Afriques, des Caraïbes, de l'océan Indien, et d'Océanie,* 2011); and Alain Mabanckou (*Le Sanglot de l'Homme Noir,* 2012).[28] Likewise, racial advocacy groups, building on shared experiences of discrimination, have been infused with new energy or emerged on the political landscape and are passionately combating policies that draw upon racist principles as a way of enlisting support, notably the *Conseil représentatif des associations noires* (CRAN) and the *Indigènes de la République, S.O.S. Racisme, Collectif Égalité,* or the *Alliance noire citoyenne,* and organizations such as the *Association pour la Connaissance de l'Histoire de l'Afrique* (ACHAC), which have been actively engaged for almost twenty years in bringing to public attention (through books, films, and visual archives) the various ways in which the colonial and postcolonial imagination has been shaped.[29]

Efforts at applying qualitative and quantitative sociological data to the immigrant experience—insisting, for example, on France's long history of immigration, providing statistics on job and school performance and information on access to healthcare and housing—have often proved futile precisely because politicians have successfully capitalized on the populist appeal and capital that negative characterizations of immigrant populations offer.[30] In the previous chapter we explored the museographic challenges confronting the CNHI when it came to structuring and representing the French *architecture* of immigration. Let us now turn our attention to a competing interpretation of this discourse and history.

The Ministry of Immigration, Integration, National Identity and Co-Development

The creation in 2007 of the Ministry of Immigration, Integration, National Identity and Co-Development essentially completed a project Nicolas Sarkozy started as Minister of the Interior (2005–2007).[31] In that capacity, Sarkozy had already made the fight against illegal immigration a priority, resulting in dramatic increases in expulsions: 35,921 in 2005, 34,127 in 2006, and 20,411 during the first six months of 2007, representing a 19 percent increase over the similar period in the previous year.[32] (Prior to the 2012 general election, the Minister of the Interior indicated that the goal for the upcoming year had been raised to 35,000). The ministry was established by "Décret n°2007–999 du 18 mai 2007 relatif aux attributions du ministre de l'immigration, de l'intégration, de l'identité nationale et du codéveloppement," and Article 1 outlined its responsibilities: "[To] prepare and implement the government's immigration, asylum, and integration policy, and promote national identity and co-development." In April 2008 the last part of the name was changed to "Développement solidaire" (thereby expanding the "co-development" component to suggest the "solidary," "bilateral," and "inter-governmental" nature of these agreements, measures, and policies). Furthermore, during the November 2010 cabinet reshuffle, the ministry was absorbed into the Ministère de l'intérieur, de l'outre-mer et des collectivités territoriales (Ministry of the Interior, Overseas Departments and Territories, and Local Government) and a new organizational chart published.[33] Given that many of these responsibilities had previously been those of the Ministry of Foreign Affairs and that the Office français de protection des réfugiés et apatrides (OFPRA) had already been transferred from the Ministry of Foreign Affairs to the Ministry of Immigration, Integration, National Identity and Co-Development in 2007, a significant blurring of domestic/national and foreign policy has taken place, providing us with interesting insights into Sarkozy's conceptualization of these matters.

There are of course antecedents to these transformations, and these must be inscribed in a longer history of immigration reform in France. The "Law of August 10, 1932" had given French hexagonal workers priority, and French

West African (Afrique occidentale française, AOF) "indigènes" (natives) were required to read and write French and to demonstrate "proximity" to French civilization. Since African independence around the 1960s, the French government has attempted to structure and control immigration policy, including movement from its French Overseas Departments into metropolitan France after 1963 with the creation of the Bureau pour le développement des migrations dans les départements d'outre-mer (the Bumidom). Later, the 1977 "Circulaire Bonnet" provided sub-Saharan immigrants subventions to encourage repatriation ("aide au retour"), and the "Barre-Bonnet Law" (1980) specifically targeted "clandestine" immigration. President Valéry Giscard-d'Estaing (1974–1981) called for "zero immigration" during the mid-1970s, and the attention shifted to internal populations with a focus on integration contracts and increased scrutiny of immigrant lifestyles. The most repressive period followed during the 1980s and 1990s in the guise of what are known today as the "Pasqua-Debré Laws" (86–1025 [1986], 93–1027 [1993], and 97–396 [1997]), laws that delineated new restrictions on the right of entry and residency and implemented visa requirements for high-risk migrants ("risque migratoire," a cryptonym of course for "Africans"), thereby breathing new life into colonial categories that had established distinctions between "desirable" and "undesirable" groups.[34] A succession of disquieting statements are linked to this new chapter in French immigration history, beginning with Jacques Chirac's declaration in 1984 (as mayor of Paris), that "[t]he rise in insecurity [threats to public order] is due to the uncontrolled influx for the past three years of poor quality clandestine migrants," and followed shortly thereafter by other politicians: President François Mitterrand claiming that the "seuil de tolérance est dépassé" (the threshold of tolerance has been reached, 1989), Prime Minister Michel Rocard that "France cannot welcome the weight of the world ("la misère du monde," 1990),[35] Giscard-d'Estaing evoking an "invasion" (1991), and finally Chirac again, this time alluding to an "overdose d'immigrés" (1991). Today, new technocratic language and "management" of migration and security have replaced this type of language.[36] New distinctions have also appeared between an "immigration choisie" (controlled, chosen, and selective) and "immigration subie" (endured or uncontrolled).

These issues were foregrounded by Sarkozy during the 2006–2007 presidential campaign. Thus, by establishing the Ministry of Immigration, Integration, National Identity and Co-Development, he was effectively following up on campaign promises. However, his ability to implement policy was facilitated by the methodical and systematic discourse applied to immigrants and ethnic minorities. This was particularly evident in speeches such as the "Discours sur le nation" he gave in Caen on March 9, 2007:

> France has a long history. Its identity and personality have been molded over centuries; this must be respected, and cannot be erased or ignored. . . . In the end, we have every reason to be proud of our country, of its history, and of what this has and continues to embody in the eyes of the world. Because France has never succumbed to totalitarianism. France has never exterminated a people. She has never invented a final solution or committed a crime against humanity, or committed genocide.

And:

> Those who want to live in France are asked to recognize that France existed long before them, that it expects to be loved and its values respected, its history shared, and that they be actively involved in its destiny. For those who want to live in France, we offer the pride of being French. Those who despise France, those who have contempt for her are not obliged to stay. . . . If one loves France, one has to assume its history and that of all those French people who have contributed to its greatness.[37]

The parallels with Alain Finkielkraut's "francophobia" are of course striking.

Under the leadership of his close friend and political ally, Brice Hortefeux, for whom "a substantial component of what held the French nation together has become dislocated," the new ministry endeavored to capitalize on the widespread belief that *national identity* had been eroded.[38] For example, UMP deputy Thierry Mariani sponsored a bill that would allow DNA testing as a "scientific" way for "foreign families" to prove their ties to France.[39] Defining newcomers to France differently from their French counterparts has instead served to support prevalent assumptions that visible minorities and immigrants belong to a distinct social configuration, outside the dominant order of things, while also relegating all other individual and human attributes in order to "arrive at a supposedly irrefutable truth located somewhere in the genes or bones."[40] Likewise, reforms to immigration policy have overlapped with both the consolidation of extreme right-wing positions in Europe or with policies being mainstreamed by a range of political parties; calls for increased border control, heightened security, and the expansion of police powers have become routine in many European countries. As Achille Mbembe has argued, "This surge of legislative and repressive arrangements prevent entry into the country, of course, but each new law also renders ever more precarious the lives of foreigners who are already established in France."[41] The new preoccupation with border security, while reviving discussions on the singularity of European identity and integration, has encouraged monolithic interpretations of history that fail to account for the fact that European populations are more intimately related to non-European ones than some European people wish to believe.

The structure of the ministry was organized around four main priorities:

1. *Controlling migration flows.* Fighting illegal migration remains a top priority, with an annual objective of 25,000 people brought back to the border. Migrants destined for staying for a long period on the national territory will be selected according to France's welcoming capacities and economic needs. At the same time, asylum policy, which consists in protecting persecuted foreigners, will remain a moral imperative for us.

2. *Encouraging development partnership.* The stake of co-development is to provide southern states and their citizens the means to trust themselves and to build a future on their own territory. It will primarily consist in mobilizing the tools allowing migrants to act in the interest of their country of origin. We will also need to ensure that the cooperation and development policies of the countries of origin pay greater attention to immigration control.

3. *Favoring integration.* A foreigner allowed to stay and willing to establish himself in France must master the language and respect republican principles in order to benefit from a 10-year residence permit. In the same way that a foreigner has duties, so does the State. Access to housing, education and training will be favored in order to make integration easier. At the same time, the work of associations contributing to fight discrimination on the ground will be facilitated.

4. *Promoting our identity.* French identity consists of both our historical heritage and the future of our national community. Article 1 of the Constitution of the Fifth Republic states that "France is a Republic, indivisible, laïc [secular], democratic and social. She ensures the equality of all citizens before the law, without distinction of origin, race or religion." The promotion of our identity constitutes a response to communitarianism and aims at preserving our Nation's equilibrium. Immigration, integration and national identity are complementary and very closely linked. Because of her own identity, which she can be proud of, France has had

> the means to integrate those immigrants who respect our values, and can therefore organize immigration in a confident way.[42]

Foremost among these measures one can therefore register the implementation of chosen/selective immigration based on certain skill sets, development partnerships, a renewed emphasis on what are presented as core republican values, and an objective of dramatically reducing family-related immigration (i.e., reunification) in favor of economic migration. To this end, *domestic* policy and *foreign* policy can no longer be decoupled, since they unambiguously concern both facets of immigration: namely, the dynamics of internal race relations and policies aimed at controlling the entry of migrants into France. Naturally, these mechanisms reinforce existing paradigms concerning the criminalization of poverty in the *banlieue,* and these have been transferred to economic models that essentialize the criminality of immigrants.[43] These labels emerge as inseparable components of the illegal/irregular migrant's *clandestine* status in the E.U., a presence that is therefore assumed a priori as a *risk* factor, while also being structured around comfortable and shared negative representations.

Meanwhile, the politics of "co-development" essentially reproduce age-old patterns of labor acquisition in the *global south;* all that has changed is that the coordinates of human capital exploitation have shifted from the healthiest and the strongest (slaves) to the best and the brightest (employees). In this context "immigration choisie" serves to designate the new "desirables," not a "brain drain" according Hortefeux, but rather a "circulation of competence."[44] This position calls for further consideration since neither the nature of neo-colonial relations and the circumstances that trigger migration, usually in the guise of perilous Mediterranean crossings whose recalibration echoes an earlier *middle passage,* nor the broader unidirectionality of the process of labor circulation are accounted for in Hortefeux's conjecture. In fact, France has been actively establishing quotas with African-sending countries, agreeing for example on February 25, 2008, with Senegal to issue "competence and skills cards" to young Senegalese workers in return for assistance in fighting illegal immigration, improving border control, and streamlining the process of repatriating illegals (similar deals have being pursued with Benin, Congo, DRC, Gabon, Morocco, and Togo). As Nathalie Kotlok has argued, "the term 'co-development' implies a notion of partnership, but if one looks at statistics, all we find are adjustment policies that serve to implement a security-based rhetoric."[45]

France and the European Union

Sarkozy assumed the rotating presidency of the E.U. on July 1, 2008, under acrimonious conditions triggered by the June 13, 2008, Irish "no" vote on the Lisbon Treaty. Nevertheless, France's new president, a man who took pride in having been France's *top cop* and who had developed a reputation for the action-packed behavior usually attributed to comic-book heroes (in addition to having a terrible temper and a proclivity for swearing and hurling insults in public), was able to obtain virtually immediate consensus on two significant and connected initiatives: the *European Union Pact on Migration and Asylum* and the *Union for the Mediterranean project* (both of these measures receive extended attention in chapters 7 and 8). Closer scrutiny of these French priorities provides interesting insights into broader debates on the contested parameters of a European identity.

Recent developments in Europe shed new and disquieting light on the original organizing principle of the E.U., according to which the E.U. was to become a "family" of democratic European countries. E.U. membership has continued to grow (adding new members in 2004 and 2007), and this growth has been accompanied by the liberalization of internal frontiers. These measures have also coincided, however, with heightened concerns over border control and the vulnerability of *Fortress Europe*. France has, historically, played an extremely important role in defining E.U. identity, and policies and measures concerning migration and security preceded the Sarkozy administration. In the *Third Annual Report on Migration and Integration* (2007), the E.U. emphasized the point that the "integration of third-country nationals is a process of mutual accommodation by both the host societies and the immigrants and an essential factor in realizing the full benefits of immigration."[46] However, French determination to impose and extend a key domestic policy agenda item throughout the E.U. zone has resulted in a shift away from policies concerned with the integration of migrants toward an emphasis on protecting its *own* citizens from migrants through more restrictive laws, regulations and restrictions.

Before we look at the ways in which the French government has sought to extend these policies to the E.U., we should briefly consider earlier E.U. initiatives. In October 1999 E.U. leaders at a European Council meeting in Tampere, Finland, "called for a common immigration policy which would include more dynamic policies to ensure the integration of third-country nationals residing in the European Union. They agreed that the aim of this integration policy should be to grant third-country nationals rights and obligations comparable to those of citizens of the E.U. The European Union is keen to promote economic and social cohesion throughout its territory. As such, integrating third-country nationals has become a focal point of the European Union's immigration policy."[47] For many years, E.U. leaders have underscored the importance of fostering prosperity, solidarity, and security alongside immigration. This has resulted in the intensification of control over third-country nationals or migrants, that is, "any person who is not a citizen of the Union within the meaning of Article 17 (1) of the Treaty and who is not a person enjoying the Community right of free movement, as defined in Article 2(5) of the Schengen Borders Code,"[48] wanting to cross the E.U.'s "frontières extérieures" (external borders).[49] Thus, this latter measure, extended on June 19, 1990, effectively introduced a new border separating non-Europeans (Wihtol de Wenden, *L'Immigration en Europe,* 29) and has made it possible "to differentiate between two types of borders in the union: the so-called interior borders and the so-called exterior borders,"[50] and "these texts have also outlined measures aimed at increasing the surveillance of Europe's external borders."[51] Operating according to the key principle that common borders would necessitate coordinated policy, the E.U. has worked toward reaching these objectives over the years. Among the most significant of these was the *European Union Pact on Migration and Asylum,* initially presented to the European Council of Ministers of Home Affairs/Interior and Justice on July 7 and 8, 2008, in Cannes, by Brice Hortefeux, and subsequently adopted by the European Council of October 15–16, 2008. At the meeting in Cannes, Hortefeux underlined the imperative of achieving uniformity among the disparate national mechanisms currently in place and the need to regulate legal immigration and asylum policy concerning third-country migrants (i.e., any person who is not a national of an E.U. member state). Proposed measures were targeted at developing a common and coordinated policy, one that would endeavor to harmonize approaches to legal and illegal immigration: introduction of a European Blue Card Scheme designed to address internal labor shortages, and a newly integrated series of security measures (consisting of deportation, detention, expulsion, regularization, repatriation, and return directives). Approved measures included:

- to organize legal immigration, to take account of the priorities, needs and reception capacities determined by each Member State, and to encourage integration;

- to control illegal immigration by ensuring that illegal immigrants return to their countries of origin or to a country of transit;
- to make border controls more effective;
- to construct a Europe of asylum;
- to create a comprehensive partnership with the countries of origin and of transit in order to encourage the synergy between migration and development.[52]

As Claire Rodier has pointed out, "two out of the five measures—the second and the third—have the objective of repelling and keeping migrants at a distance rather than welcoming them."[53] More recently, via the *Union for the Mediterranean project* (UfM, Euro-Mediterranean Partnership, EUROMED), formerly known as the *Barcelona Process: Union for the Mediterranean,* the E.U. has been seeking partnerships with several countries that border the Mediterranean and that will extend these policy objectives.[54] As Évelyne Ritaine has shown, "Confronted with migrations originating (or in transit) on the African continent, the European Union has taken upon itself to seal off the Mediterranean. Surveillance is now the responsibility of maritime and aerial intervention units operated by Frontex."[55] This will seem all the more paradoxical that at a moment in history when economic disparities are greatest and when recent political upheaval (such as the "Arab Spring") has increased migratory pressure, the E.U. is "reinforcing its borders so that only those migrants it needs can enter."[56]

The idea of *Fortress Europe,* as the E.U. has come to be known in official *Eurospeak* with reference to the multi-country juridical border control mechanisms deployed under its aegis, and *Fortress Europe* as it is constructed and perceived in the minds of global migrants attempting to enter the geographic zone it now contains—provides a compelling framework for sociocultural and sociopolitical inquiry into the multidimensionality of practices associated with this space. These points of referentiality may be symbolic, but they nevertheless serve to circumscribe both what they keep out but also what they contain, and simultaneously refer to concrete mechanisms that relate to identity formation and community-building in the E.U. In recent years, E.U. member states have privileged the selectivity and choice of migrants, implementing three components, "procédures d'obstacle," "triage," and "rétention" (Ritaine, "Des migrants face aux murs," 157–158), while emphasizing legal paths to E.U. residency and integration, as well as engagement with *sending* countries. But this new philosophy of immigration has often not paid sufficient attention to the humanitarian dimension while also revealing deep-seated prejudice toward populations from the *global south.* Ultimately, as observers have argued, "they have in common the desire to make such policies a reality, in other words to 'lock out' the undesirables" (Ritaine, "Des migrants face aux murs," 157). These instruments therefore discriminate between those who can circulate freely and those who cannot, determining the conditions and terms according to which participation in the global economy can occur. "This wall thus reveals," Ritaine argues, "the intrinsic asymmetry of contemporary territorial and statutory limits. It is indifferent to that which exits as it focuses on controlling access, allowing capital to circulate freely while restricting the movement of people, protecting the community while repressing *outsiders*" ("Des migrants face aux murs," 163).

Analysis of these policy developments reveals a shift in the approach to immigration, whereby the implementation of "immigration choisie" now "emerges as a reaffirmation of sovereignty,"[57] and in which one can identify the "generalization of discourse in which immigration is presented as a threat to Western countries, particularly as far as national identity is concerned."[58] In fact, between 2007 and 2012, we witnessed a shift from the focus on the causes and problems of *immigration* (undocumented and illegals) to a commitment to reduce the proportion of foreigners to the French population while dramatically limiting entry and circulation into France (debates on the residency status of foreign students, on extending voting rights to foreigners, etc.). Likewise, rather than addressing multiculturalism, integration, and diversity, the authorities focused instead on outlining *expectations* of outsiders, tangible indication of adherence *to—and* respect *of*—republican ideals and values. This thinking is reflected in the distinction between chosen/controlled/selective and endured/uncontrolled immigration, given that "recourse to these terms serves to present migration policy as the privileged expression of national sovereignty: after all, a sovereign nation should be able to select its guests and not have to resign itself to being subjected to their presence."[59] Naturally, the question of citizenship and belonging—and therefore the extent to which individuals are protected by the State—becomes crucial, and the E.U. has struggled with this. This has been reflected in complex debates on national identity and sovereignty[60] precisely because of the intergovernmentality and supranationality of the E.U. itself, not only when it comes to monetary and juridical matters, but also to the very idea of building a *European family.* When Brice Hortefeux was promoted to Minister of the Interior, his successor at the helm of the Ministry of Immigration, Integration, National Identity and Co-Development,

Éric Besson, turned the question of *family* and *belonging* into a central issue in the *National Identity Debate* he launched in November 2009.

The National Identity Debate

Éric Besson claimed that a *National Identity Debate* would help rekindle patriotic fervor and adherence to French republican ideals and values in response to the feeling of a dissolved or disappearing French identity.[61] After all, one of the stated goals of his ministry was to "Promouvoir notre identité" (Promote our identity). In reality, though, the debate served to confirm the disconnect between the French authorities and the sociocultural realities of French society today. Perhaps not surprisingly, the *National Identity Debate* culminated in the release of a new legislative document, a "Projet de loi relatif à l'immigration, à l'intégration et à la nationalité, April 1, 2010 (Immigration, Integration and Nationality Bill), in which French national policies are outlined in terms of their relevance to the E.U. zone:

- Make Europe and France more attractive destinations for work-related immigration;
- Accelerate access procedure for acquiring French citizenship for foreign nationals who have more rapidly integrated into French society;
- Ensure that obtaining French nationality through naturalization would be conditional upon the signature of a chart of the rights and duties of the citizen;
- Improve the fight against illegal immigration;
- Transpose into French law the European Union directives on "return" and make sure these are implemented in the E.U. zone.[62]

What we can retain from these priorities is the objective of achieving "rapid integration." As Gérard Noiriel has stressed, the French government has set itself "the task of selecting today's immigrants according to criteria relating to 'republican values,' while affirming at the same time that one is protecting French identity in the future" (*A quoi sert "l'identité nationale,"* 99).

Didier Fassin has addressed the growing evidence of such stratifications (*borders* and *boundaries*) and disquieting hierarchies, arguing that "By External borders, I have in mind the limits of the national territory or, increasingly, of a supranational European territory. . . . Whereas by internal boundaries, I am thinking of the limits between the racialized social categories inherited from the double history of colonialism and immigration."[63] The ultimate expression of this can be located in the "confusion between borders" (Fassin, "Frontières extérieures, frontières intérieures," 14) evidenced in the name of the Ministry of Immigration, Integration, National Identity and Co-Development that associates "the threat posed by immigration" with the task of "protecting French identity," processes that contradict in important ways the diversity and plurality that is so crucial to E.U. principles. This raises the issue of European identity itself,[64] its foundations, organizing principles, and the distinction between a member State (that provides its citizens with *nationality*) and a European citizenship that does not exist.

The relationship between the *us* and the *them*—that informs a negative model of identity construction informed by exclusionary rather than inclusionary criteria—updates previous sociological paradigms used to describe hierarchies between the "established" and "outsiders,"[65] structuring in this instance categories of "desirables" and "undesirables" (powerful reminders of colonial era debates in which such terminology informed immigration policy).[66] "When it comes to immigration control," as Alexis Spire demonstrates, "the opposition between the 'us' and the 'them' is strengthened by the sentiment that it embodies the State and its authority before those suspected of threatening its integrity" (*Accueillir ou reconduire,* 47). As mentioned earlier, this is even more likely to be the case in a context in which "immigration is equated with national identity"[67] and where an "ennemi intérieur" (enemy within)[68] has been identified. In these circumstances, even the signifier "immigrant" introduces "terminology that makes it possible to define both the Other that has already settled and the one who is arriving," and "has more often than not also been ethnicized and racialized through recourse to the notion of a non-E.U. community third-party national, an expression that always summons images of poor people located for the most part in the southern hemisphere.... That 'particular immigrant,' lacking the necessary resources to be a good consumer, has in turn become accountable for society's ills" (Bigo, "Contrôle migratoire," 170).[69] Indeed, this "State-sanctioned xenophobia" in order to "protect the cohesion of our national community"[70] systematizes the politics of fear we discussed earlier: "The objective is always to achieve a definition of national identity by denouncing its opposite, through a classical logic that juxtaposes the 'them' with the us.... One must also point out that unlike the National Front, Nicolas Sarkozy does not name the group he has in mind ... but rather, through allusions, leaving it up to his commentators and electoral supporters to fill in the gaps" (Noiriel, *A quoi sert "l'identité nationale,"* 95–96). The *National Iden-*

tity Debate was therefore inextricably linked to broader questions pertaining to the very definition and understanding of French history, as confirmed by the special section on the ministry's website devoted to a "bibliothèque"—essentially a recommended reading list with accompanying abstracts.[71] These texts therefore enable us to identify the kinds of works that have structured official thinking on a broad spectrum of twenty-first-century issues while also providing insights as to how the Panthéon mausoleum—whose façade is inscribed with the phrase "Aux Grands Hommes La Patrie Reconnaissante" (To the great men, the grateful homeland)—has also been used (notably by Sarkozy) to strengthen the indissociability of "greatness" with the "homeland."

The response to Besson's initiative was quite surprising. On the one hand, Besson interpreted the thousands of *hits* on the official website as confirmation of the public interest in this question (although he did have to admit to deleting multiple blog entries and posts—"dérapages" (blunders, as they were called—because of their explicitly offensive racist and xenophobic tone); but he was also forced to reckon with widespread opposition that drew further attention to just how out of touch the government was with public sentiment on the question among large segments of the French population. The online journal *Mediapart* announced, "Nous ne débattrons pas!" (We will not debate!) and launched a petition;[72] SOS Racisme joined ranks with opponents, urging "Mr. President, put an end to this debate!";[73] and gay rights organizations Panthères roses/Act Up released a badge stating, "My identity is not national." Besson's official "Lettre de mission" outlined the rationale for this undertaking: "The promotion of our national identity should find itself at the heart of your action. . . . Our pride in being French will facilitate the integration of those foreigners we welcome to our country. How can one expect them to love France if we don't love her ourselves? In the eyes of new migrants, we should not only assume our pride in being French, but also celebrate it."[74] With these guidelines in mind, Besson's *digital* and *cyber* debate confirmed his commitment to this mission: "Welcome to the website we have created for the debate on national identity. This initiative keeps a promise made by Nicolas Sarkozy when he was a [presidential] candidate. At that time he had said: 'I want to promote our national identity, promote our pride in being French, and encourage the French people to identify with these fundamental values, with these republican ideals.' And so we are going to do this together and we have asked you a few simple questions on the web-site. 'What does it mean to be French today?'"[75] During the 2006–2007 electoral campaign, then candidate Sarkozy relied heavily on the importance of expressing undivided and unqualified pride in French history, beliefs encapsulated in his oft-repeated offer: "Ceux qui n'aiment pas ce pays, qu'ils ne se gênent pas pour le quitter" (Those who do not love France should feel free to leave), echoing Philippe de Villiers' (the leader of the Mouvement pour la France, MPF, a conservative political group) comment that "La France, tu l'aimes ou tu la quittes" (France, either love her or leave her). Not surprisingly, such notions have infiltrated statements made subsequently by Besson, whereby "being French means loving France, which means knowing its history."[76]

Let us consider how Besson interpreted this history: "Our nation has been built over the centuries by welcoming and integrating people of foreign origin. This great debate must recognize the contribution of immigration to national identity, while offering us measures that will improve the appreciation of the values of national identity at each stage of the integration process. How can we improve the way in which we share the values of national identity with those of foreign origin entering or spending time on our national territory?"[77] These efforts have also entailed a recuperation of some of the central tenets associated with the extreme-right-wing policies of the Front National since the 1970s, including the national anthem: "All young French people should sing the national anthem at least once a year, if need be after a class session devoted to this theme."[78] These campaign strategies and post-election discourse have come under heavy criticism, not least from scholars: "This instrumentalization is purely strategic. . . . One is witnessing a compulsive recourse to history and to the emergence of a mechanism aimed at the consecration of the past."[79]

Olivier Le Cour Grandmaison has deconstructed this language in an incisive analysis, arguing that "Evoking a monumental past in this way creates the illusion that one can recapture grandeur and power and therefore rekindle belief and confidence in a radiant future, since of course what has been must be achievable again."[80] In light of such analysis, the aforementioned "bibliothèque"[81] on the ministry's website thus became all the more significant. Of course, those works included tell us as much as those which were excluded; selected texts, for the most part, do not challenge or question republican ideals and values, but rather adhere to or espouse nationalist and patriotic tendencies, and are not of course indicative of the diverse range of scholarship and thinking on questions of national identity, minority/ethnic politics, debates on reparations, or for that matter of inroads that have been made in recent years in France in the field of postcolonial studies. Authors and works range from Max Gallo's *Fier d'être Français* (2006) and *L'âme de la France: une histoire de la nation des origines à nos jours* (2007) and Daniel Lefeuvre's and Michel Renard's *Faut-il avoir honte de l'identité nationale?* (2008) to non-threatening *apologist* narratives such as Gaston Kelman's *Je suis noir et je n'aime pas le manioc* (2005, at one point an advisor at the Ministry of Immigration, Integration, National Identity and Co-Development) and Léopold Sédar Senghor's "Prière de paix" (1948), not ignoring of course well-known and celebratory speeches such as those made by Charles de Gaulle—the "Discours de Bayeux" (1946) and Discours de Rennes (1947)— and André Malraux's "Discours du 4 septembre 1958" (in defense of the Fifth Republic) and the "Discours sur Jean Moulin" (on the occasion of the transfer to the Panthéon of the remains of the French resistance hero in 1964).[82]

Late in 2009, Sarkozy anticipated the terms of the debate in a speech he gave to farmers in Poligny in the Jura on October 27, 2009, "Un nouvel avenir pour notre agriculture" (A new future for agriculture):

> France has an almost carnal relationship to its agriculture, and I dare use the word, its land. The word land (terre) has a special significance in France and I was elected to defend French national identity. I'm not afraid of these words; in fact, I proclaim them. France has a distinctive identity that, while not being above others, is nevertheless its own. I don't see why people should think twice about utttering the words "French national identity." These words are not aggressive toward anyone. They are quite simply an expression of the respect we owe the generations that came before us, who shed their blood and gave their lives to make France what it is today. Well, the land is a component of French national identity. And this French national identity is made up, notably, of the singular relationship French people have with this land.[83]

One cannot but be struck by these metaphorical inferences to "the land" and by the broader allusions to colonial territorial expansion, reaffirmed in the unmistakable links that can be made with the Algerian landscape in, for example, the writings of Albert Camus. Yet, paradoxically, another dimension exists that relates to the consequences of these imperial ambitions and the resulting political consciousness exemplified by such influential works as Frantz Fanon's *Les damnés de la terre* (The wretched of the earth, prefaced of course by Sartre!), whereby "For a colonized people, the most essential value, because it is the most meaningful, is first and foremost the land: the land, which must provide bread and, naturally, dignity. But this dignity has nothing to do with 'human' dignity. The colonized subject has never heard of such an ideal."[84] The transcoloniality of these mechanisms is thus confirmed here, revealing longstanding constructs pertaining to the formation of otherness.

During a session at the French National Assembly held on December 8, 2009, devoted to the *National Identity Debate,* Besson claimed, "People may well have a personal history and be proud their roots, but there nevertheless exists a melting pot: namely the French Republic and French nationality which for me, impose a hierarchy between forms of belonging."[85] Paradoxically, rather than fostering neo-universalist sentiments among populations with different historical links to France and strategically capitalizing on colonial paradigms according to which Frenchness was not at issue because of its perceived synonymous link with wider notions of humanism, the authorities instead promoted hierarchies and structures of differentiation. Writing on the *National Identity Debate,* Albin Wagener has shown that two central elements defined the parameters of the debate: "How can we improve the way in which we share the values of national identity with those of foreign origin entering or spending time on our national territory?" and "How can we improve the way in which we share the values of national identity with foreign nationals who become members of our national community?"[86] These questions were partially rhetorical given that obvious answers were to be found in policy: "immigration" and "national identity" were, as inscribed in the ministry's name, symbiotic, since the newly established Contrat d'accueil et d'intégration (CAI, Welcome and Integration Contract) includes the provision of assisting immigrants in achieving a "better understanding of life in France"(Wagener, 28), while also outlining measures that would expand the "republican pact" in order to require evidence of linguistic competency (itself a fairly standard requirement in international immigration policy making) along with an improved knowledge of republican values.[87] The purpose of the *National Identity Debate* was of course to reaffirm what the authorities defined as republican ideals and values or at the very least to point the finger at those who most threatened them—Muslims, the *sans-papiers,* illegals, irregulars, the undocumented, and so forth.

I have described these repressive immigration debates between 2007 and 2012 as *Sarkozy's Law,* an attempt to capture the broad range of incredibly repressive policies that defined his time in political office. The Front National has been equally effective under the new leadership of Marine Le Pen (Jean-Marie Le Pen's daughter) in fostering analogous debates. To this end, one can actually talk about policy convergence between the FN and UMP, and the 2012 presidential election campaign certainly confirmed this.[88] In fact, one is often hard pressed distinguishing between those statements made by Sarkozy's administration and the pronouncements of Marine Le Pen; observers in fact started to characterize this phenomenon in terms of a "droitisation" (shift to the far-right) of the UMP. During the March 2010 regional elections, for which the FN slogan had been "Pour défendre l'identité nationale, il n'y a que le Front National!" (In defense of national identity, the only choice is the National Front),[89] Marine Le Pen announced that the "great decline of French identity the FN has been warning French people about is gaining momentum," and that "at the root of this great identity question one finds, as expected, problems related to extra-European immigration and the equally important question of Islam and its place in the public sphere."[90] *Both* parties, and *both* leaders—Nicolas Sarkozy and Marine Le Pen—have attempted to build support by fostering the sentiment that France is under threat and therefore in need of a *protector.* For the philosopher Alain Badiou, "Sarkozy stands for a society that is afraid and in search of protection. . . . This fear comes from, I believe, the fact that after what was a long and glorious history, in the end, France has become a middle power, albeit one with considerable privileges and wealth, but nevertheless a middle power in a world dominated by emerging giants such as China and India or at least countries that are considerably more powerful such as the United States. France's future is therefore uncertain."[91] Following urban uprisings in the city of Grenoble, Sarkozy made an extremely strong statement on July 30, 2010, in which he connected—much as his predecessor Jacques Chirac had done in 1984—"insecurity" with "immigration," attributing the threats to public order and an array of societal ills to "fifty years of inadequately controlled immigration" and warning (much like Marine Le Pen had done) that "it is our values that are gradually disappearing."[92] The role of the *National Identity Debate* was, as we have seen, to reawaken patriotic zeal.

However, as Nicolas Bancel has argued, this "national and security-based ideology in which explicit links are made between immigration and delinquency and in which minorities are stigmatized" and these "target groups" blamed for "insecurity" and the "decline in the nation's values"[93] will achieve very little in the manner of addressing social dissymmetry. Effectively, what Sarkozy juxtaposed was an opposition between those who represent "true France" and those that belong to France's "multicultural populations" (Bancel, "La brèche," 18).[94] In this equation the question of race is pervasive—a dimension we will soon turn our attention to when we examine the racial overtones in Sarkozy's 2007 Dakar Speech—since "[w]e are not [the French]," as Alain Badiou argues, ever considered in these declarations, "in opposition to others of course—an inferior race" and a "true French person has no reason to question the legitimacy of France."[95] The figure of the "clandestin" emerges as "an individual who neither speaks nor writes the national language, who does not respect the law or republican values, and who makes no effort to integrate" and can therefore be readily substituted as the "antithesis of the French person," whereas the "communitarian" materializes as the "antithesis of republican values" (Noiriel, *A quoi sert "l'identité nationale,"* 93–94). In the end, we are left wondering whether the very *communitarianism* assigned to ethnic minorities is itself more appropriately to be attached to the *français de souche,* those members of the French population deemed of *pure French stock* or *ethnically French* who see in globalization and diversity a menace to their historical *Frenchness.*

Brice Hortefeux's successor at the Ministry of the Interior for the final fifteen months of the Sarkozy presidency (February 2011–May 2012) was Claude Guéant, Sarkozy's former chief of staff at the Elysée. He wasted no time in making provocative statements that re-emphasized national identity and immigration as priorities. The comments that received the most attention were those he made during an interview he gave on March 17, 2011, on Europe 1 radio: "Because of uncontrolled immigration, French people can at times feel as if they are no longer at home, or that practices incompatible with our social life are being forced upon us."[96] However, what has received less attention is the specific impact such rhetoric has had on the targeted populations. We have already examined the findings of such research groups as the German Marshall Fund; conclusions of a 2008–2009 study conducted by the Institut national d'études démographiques and the Institut national de la statistique et des études économiques (Ined-Insee) revealed elevated levels when it came to evaluating feelings of "exclusion" amongst French Overseas populations and the children of immigrants—as many in fact as 40 percent have stated that they "feel they are treated differently to their compatriots."[97]

Without Papers, or Rights

Economic migrants, faced with these new pressures, have recently become increasingly vocal in their demand for social and political rights. *Illegals* around the world are slowly beginning to emerge from the dubious *safety* of legal invisibility and have begun to press more directly for public representation. During April and May 2008, several French businesses (with support from the CGT and other trade unions) went on strike to support the workers known as the *sans-papiers* and called for regularization.[98] This action also served to counter popular misconceptions and stereotypes concerning illegals and irregulars, bringing attention to the *legal* work they perform and contributions they make, but also signaling the dangers of restrictive employment laws in exposing workers to exploitative employment practices that E.U. workers would find unacceptable.

E.U. laws designed to punish abusive employers exist, notably Article 5 of the Charter of Fundamental Rights that concerns the Prohibition of slavery and forced labor: (1) No one shall be held in slavery or servitude; (2) No one shall be required to perform forced or compulsory labor; (3) Trafficking in human beings is prohibited.[99] The European Court of Human Rights in Strasbourg is also committed to ensuring these rights are protected. Nevertheless, abusive practices have been widely tolerated and extensively documented. Hugo Brady has shown that "The Commission estimates that there are around 8 million illegal immigrants in the E.U., and that this number increases by 500,000 to 1 million every year. . . . These workers are drawn to Europe mainly by the knowledge that they can find work illegally in the construction, agriculture, cleaning and hospitality industries. Many end up doing under-paid or dangerous work."[100]

Fabrizio Gatti, the recipient of the 2006 award "For diversity—against discrimination" has provided a compelling account of the glaring failure of the E.U. to address exploitative labor practices. Gatti has even got so far as to equate current employment conditions with slavery: "In order to pass a week undercover amidst the slave laborers it is necessary to undertake a voyage that takes one beyond the limits of human imagination. But this is the only way to report on the horrors that the immigrants are forced to endure. . . . They're all foreigners; all employed as so-called 'black workers,' the name used to describe illegal, untaxed and underpaid work scams. . . . Down here they also ignore the Constitution: articles one, two and three, as well as the Universal Declaration of Rights."[101]

Considerable disparities persist in the E.U. concerning integration and the required degree of adherence to national codes and values. The *Union for the Mediterranean project,* as we shall see in chapter 7, extends both the economic and the social priorities of the *European Union Pact on Migration and Asylum* while simultaneously promoting the circulation of goods but not people. Efforts at defining a common or shared European identity have been informed by such categories as desirable and undesirable subjects, yet the introduction of "integration contracts" reveal the degree to which the authorities subscribe to and embrace a long-held belief that a European identity either exists or can be achieved. What is less clear is the degree to which any such identity will depend on an increasingly rigid polarization of *insiders* and *outsiders,* on the increasingly paranoid resentment that divides privileged members of the "family of democratic European countries" from their extra-European cousins. In Toulon, December 1, 2012, Sarkozy reassured his supporters that "We will defend our identity, our culture, our language, our way of life, our social model. Thus, we will not accept uncontrolled immigration, since that would drain our social welfare system, destabilize our society, perturb our way of life, and disturb our values."[102]

Repeated attempts have been made to connect the fight against illegal immigration to a discourse of human rights concerned with the protection of vulnerable subjects from fraudulent traffickers and employers. Yet, the findings of demographers demonstrate Europe's long-term need for cheap labor. Instead, obsessive concern with the apparent need to delineate a European identity in a newly uncertain global landscape has encouraged legislators to approach immigration exclusively in terms of security and economic policy, without adequate mechanisms for ensuring that basic standards of equality and justice apply to the new global migrant working class. Abundant evidence points to growing insensitivity to migrants, resulting in dehumanization and labeling as economic burdens (immediately scapegoated during downturns in the global economy), factors that have made it easier to expel them and to dissociate such harsh measures from any reference to the migrants' own experience. Additionally, the commitment to a dramatic reduction of family reunification in favor of the economic migration needed to build a more cohesive "European family" ignores and occludes the collective migration experience over a much longer historical time frame. As we will see in subsequent chapters, filmmakers and writers have endeavored to accord a voice to those populations who have been traditionally unheard or silenced by disparaging depictions.[103]

"New Europe," Old History

In the absence of such attention, questions about the nature of "Europeanness" are difficult to address. Current talk about the emergence of a new Europe remains exceptionally vague. E.U. member states have denounced evidence of ultra-nationalism and human rights abuses in countries seeking E.U. membership, but do not always adhere to those standards themselves. Proposed measures in Italy to fingerprint and register Roma populations (communities who were previously expelled by Mussolini in the late 1920s and subsequently exterminated during the Second World War), along with the similar treatment in Portugal, Spain, and elsewhere, are a case in point. E.U. Justice Commissioner Viviane Reding warned France in September 2010 to abide by and respect the E.U. Directive on freedom of movement when it targeted the Roma for expulsion.[104] Sarkozy had explicitly already talked about the "Roma problem" in his Grenoble speech in July; faced with such criticism from the E.U., the

French authorities initially denied specifically targeting the Roma.[105] However, a document (Subject: "Evaluations des campements élicites") prepared, signed, and dated August 5, 2010, by Éric Besson's Chief of Cabinet, Michel Bart, contradicted that position: "Last July 28, the French President had outlined precise objectives concerning the evacuation of illicit camps: namely 300 illicit camps or implantations must be evacuated over the next three months, with priority given to Roma ones."[106] In fact, as Éric Fassin has argued, this is indicative of a far more important question, given that "the Roma question touches upon the whole ambiguity of the European Union: is this a political or an ethnic project? Is European identity juridical or rather racial?"[107]

European immigration policy increasingly depends on multilateral and nonreciprocal Euro-Mediterranean agreements and partnerships that serve to restrict population movements and duplicate age-old historical patterns of exploitation and uneven exchange.[108] French-African relations were conceived from the beginning in terms of culturalist and racist supremacy, and they continue to define patterns of neo-colonial domination and exploitation that contribute directly to the very problems of destitution and emigration France bemoans. E.U. subsidies and biased trade policies ensure that "co-development" policies largely perpetuate African poverty. E.U. immigration policies pay concerted attention to the problems associated with poverty in the global south, yet, as Philippe Bernard has shown, for every migrant who tries to move illegally from Africa to an OECD country there are more than four people who migrate illegally from one African country to another (4 million and 17 million people respectively).[109]

As we will see in the next chapter, much of the argumentation and language in the speech Sarkozy delivered in Senegal in July 2007 was informed by notions that were first developed, in the nineteenth century, in response to those *indigènes* of Algeria or the Ivory Coast who stubbornly refused to appreciate the virtues of the French *mission civilisatrice.* Naturally, such negative representations continue to both influence and structure policy-making and to guide principles and inform strategies adopted to address the claims, issues, and problems of concern to ethnic minorities in France. What remains obfuscated in these constructs are African (among others) contributions to that *long history* and the constitutive nature of African-French relations. As Catherine Coquery-Vidrovitch has suggested, there is an urgent need to "relocate that historical object that is 'France' according to its . . . complexity, plurality."[110] For, "seeing Africans chained together like criminals prior to forceful repatriation," Mauritanian filmmaker Med Hondo has argued, "is a spectacle that does little to honor those states who claim to embrace the rights of Man and democratic ideals. Nothing is worse for a person than humiliation. This has become the daily lot of immigrants in the countries of the North."[111]

No matter what interpretation finally prevails or proves satisfactory, the fact nevertheless remains that Sarkozy's administration forever altered the configuration of ethnic minority discourse in France. Whether talking about *laïcité,* polygamy, female excision, headscarves, veils, or burqas, "all of these references to immigration serve as symbols of the decadence and crisis of values in France today" (Noiriel, *A quoi sert "l'identité nationale,"* 97) and therefore rationalize the necessity for monitoring threats to republican ideals and values. The interchangeability and mutability of referents applied to minority populations have been studied by Azouz Begag, the author, sociologist, and former Minister for Equal Opportunities (2005–2007). In his book *Ethnicity and Equality: France in the Balance,* Begag provided a list of the different appellations (second-generation, of North African descent, Muslim, etc.) defined by "territorial, ethnic, religious, and temporal criteria"[112] to describe these populations, thereby emphasizing what Etienne Balibar has shown as the figure of the "foreigner" of which the "immigrant" functions as signifier for a broad range of cultural, political, and social issues, which "the less the social problems of the 'immigrants,' or the social problems which massively affect immigrants, are specific, the more their existence is made responsible for them."[113] In other words, more attention is commonly granted to the *problems* associated with social integration rather than to the *obstacles* to that objective. How, after all, can one be born an immigrant? Antecedents are to be found in the United Kingdom where Enoch Powell spoke during the 1970s of "invading hordes" of immigrants "lacking inherent cultural qualities and the desire to integrate with indigenous society and polity"[114] in his "Rivers of Blood" speech. In France too, Jacques Chirac had, as mayor of Paris, alluded in 1991 to the "bruit et l'odeur" (the noise and the smell) of immigrants, carefully outlining how "*[t]hey* come over here with their three to four wives and twenty or so children . . . think about the poor French worker . . . and on top of that he has to deal with the noise and smell."[115] Sarkozy promised a *rupture* and new models for dealing with these questions, yet statements such as the one that follows have become only too familiar: "One needs to respect France's rules, which means that you don't practice polygamy, excision on girls, that you don't slaughter sheep in your apartment, and that you respect republican rules."[116]

Ultimately, the more central question concerns of course the matter of who belongs and who does not belong in/to France, and the creation of a new Ministry for Immigration, Integration, National Identity and Co-Development in 2007 indicated the degree to which this is a concern. Patrick Weil has convincingly shown in his book *How to Be French: Nationality in the Making since 1789* that access to French nationality has been far from a straightforward process.[117] For Sarkozy's government, the solutions to all these questions were anchored in shortsighted policies. Yet these measures, public declarations, and speeches reveal deep-seated subconscious patterns that reinforce global dissymmetries. If ethnic mobilization during the 1980s had served to underscore the deficiency of assimilation, insertion, and integration policies, then the uprisings of 2005 must surely be understood as the glaring failure of decolonization *and* the survival of transcolonial structures of inequity in the metropole. Sarkozy's appointment in 2007 of three high-profile ministers—namely Rachida Dati as Minister of Justice (now a representative at the European parliament), Fadela Amara as Junior Minister for Urban Affairs (both women of North-African origin), and the Senegalese-born Rama Yade as Secretary of State for Foreign Affairs and Human Rights (later Secretary of State for Sports)—did little to alter the French political landscape since their incorporation into politics contrasted with the racist overtones and policies that were either proposed or implemented. (All three ministers were eventually terminated in cabinet reshuffles that took place in 2009 and 2010.)

At the same time, assertions of national sovereignty have taken on an increasingly shrill and reactionary intensity, raising important questions about belonging, cohesiveness, and the sanctity of the E.U.'s original structuring aspirations and objectives. Drawing on more recent historical memories, the French government has also established target figures for the expulsion of illegal migrants that have resulted in often arbitrary "rafles" (roundups) of subjects—a term that evokes the 1942 "rafle du Vel d'Hiv," which led to the deportation of French Jews to Nazi concentration camps. As a character in Faïza Guène's 2006 novel *Du rêve pour les oufs* (Dreams from the Endz) states, "Since the decree of 2006 and its aim of expelling 25,000 people a year, it's like there's a smell of gas in the queue in front of the immigration office."[118] Europe cannot afford to ignore such antecedents when its leaders have recourse to terminology and procedures of this kind. The racial profiling of "insiders," the return of biology and race, rising Islamophobia, and the demonization of asylum-seekers—all these phenomena directly relate to the most troubling sequences in European history. Any searching genealogy of the European family yields a lesson, first and foremost, on the institutionalization of xenophobia. Responsibility for "State-sanctioned xenophobia and a politics of fear" in order to "protect the cohesion of our national community"[119] can only be attributed to a deliberate "political objective" (Bancel, "La brèche," 18). As European nation-states seek to redefine national identities in relation to new European configurations, they will surely have to remain particularly attentive and cautious as to the ways in which the past is rewritten as a way of shaping the present and therefore the future.[120]

4

Africa, France, and Eurafrica in the Twenty-First Century

The tragedy of Africa is that the African has not fully entered into history. The African peasant, who for thousands of years has lived according to the seasons and whose life ideal has been to live harmoniously with nature, has only ever known the eternal renewal of time, punctuated by the endless repetition of the same gestures and the same words. In this imaginary world where everything starts over and over again there is no place for human adventure or for the idea of progress.

—*Nicolas Sarkozy*[1]

Strange dawn! The morning of the Occident in black Africa was spangled over with smiles, with cannon shots, with shining glass beads. Those who had no history were encountering those who carried the world on their shoulders.

—*Cheikh Hamidou Kane*[2]

On February 23, 2011, a group of French diplomats, calling themselves the *Marly collective* (after the Paris café at which they had gathered), published an anonymous statement in *Le Monde* newspaper in which they lamented the loss of French geopolitical significance, underscoring the following points: "Europe is powerless, Africa is slipping out of our hands, the Mediterranean is avoiding us, China has tamed us, and Washington ignores us."[3] The question of France's cultural, economic, and political position in a newly configured twenty-first-century landscape has been the subject of much debate. Indeed, the concept of a "sphere of influence," first elaborated at the Berlin Congress held between November 15, 1884, and February 26, 1885, as a way of capitalizing on the "rising nationalist tendencies and technical progress in Europe," is of course inextricably associated with a very different era of power alignments.[4] However, as we saw in the previous chapter, the rise of new global economic leaders has compelled several European nation-states, most notably France, Germany, Italy, Spain, and the United Kingdom to rethink and recalibrate their *identity*. During the 2007 French presidential elections, then-candidate Nicolas Sarkozy addressed this issue in a much-commented speech delivered in Toulon on February 7, 2007: "The United States and China are already busy conquering Africa. How long is Europe going to wait before it starts building the Africa of tomorrow? While Europe wavers, others are forging ahead."[5]

This chapter explores France's complex historical relationship with its former African colonies in order to assess the manner in which the French authorities have, in the context of demands and exigencies linked to a *new world order*, revisited the multiple components (defense, immigration, security) of their *Africa* policy.[6] Naturally, such an approach must necessarily include a consideration of European Union policy, since it has become increasingly difficult to disentangle strictly *national* policies from those resulting from E.U. inter-governmental and supranational governance.

A number of late twentieth-century political transformations, including the dismantling of the Soviet Union, the official end of South African apartheid, E.U. expansion, the emergence of new economic powers, and so forth were of course key factors in motivating shifts in French foreign policy.[7] One such example, as Catherine Coquery-Vidrovitch has shown, concerns the "Asian stake in commercial exchanges [that] has tripled" between 1990 and 2008.[8] Likewise, as Jean-Pierre Dozon has argued, after 1994, greater involvement by the E.U., the World Bank and the International Monetary Fund "in the macroeconomic regulation of African countries" decreased the magnitude of Franco-African relations.[9] Yet, the longer history of Franco-African colonial and postcolonial ties has provided for a mutually constitutive dynamic, whereby "Africa continues to sustain France as a national State as well as its capacity, within new global and European configurations, to maintain its status as a world power. [In turn] France appears to remain for francophone African countries a friendly power in the North, most likely to speak up for them, to plead their case" (Dozon, *Frères et sujets*, 346).

A cursory overview of Franco-African interaction provides substantial evidence that corroborates these observations: the numerous visits made to Africa since 2006 by Nicolas Sarkozy, first as Minister of the Interior (2005–2007) and subsequently as President (2007–2012); the steady flow of African heads of state welcomed at the Elysée Presidential Palace in Paris (such as

Ellen Johnson-Sirleaf [Liberia], Denis Sassou-Nguesso [Republic of Congo], Omar Bongo [Gabon], Idriss Déby [Tchad], Paul Biya [Cameroon]); France's active role in recent political events in Ivory Coast;[10] and its influence over political transition in Gabon, as well as its close involvement in international responses to the political and social upheaval commonly referred to as the "Arab Spring" (especially in Egypt, Libya, Morocco, and Tunisia). One could also mention the highly controversial guest-of-honor status accorded to those African leaders (including representation from Cameroon, Burkina Faso, Chad, Congo, Senegal, Mali, Togo, Central African Republic, Benin, Mauritania, Gabon, Niger, Ivory Coast, and Madagascar) invited to attend the July 14, 2010, French Independence Day celebrations and to commemorate the fiftieth anniversary of independence from colonial rule. Critics have drawn attention to the questionable nature of these associations, pointing to the unresolved question of French colonialism (exemplified in the lingering presence of revisionist discourse pertaining to colonial history) and the under-appreciation for the contributions and sacrifices made by African soldiers during both the First and Second World Wars. Of course, the fact that many of the political leaders present at the July 14th festivities had a record of governance that is considered absolutist, authoritarian, and dictatorial, in other words contrary to the very ideals and principles initially invoked on Bastille Day in 1789, did not help matters.[11] Given that most of the presidents of francophone sub-Saharan African states are recipients of the Légion d'Honneur, France's highest civil recognition given to foreigners for "services rendered to France by persons of great merit" (Article R.128 of the Code de la légion d'honneur), the Franco-African interface thus serves to highlight the privileged attention the French authorities assign to this region of the world and the competitive and strategic advantage they hope to maintain while simultaneously bolstering notions of French *grandeur.*

As we saw in the earlier consideration of the Quai Branly Museum, Universal Exhibitions (the first such exhibition in France dates back to 1885) have played a key role in fostering France's "rayonnement civilisateur" (civilizing radiance). In 1889, France established a protectorate over Ivory Coast and the Union coloniale française was founded shortly thereafter in 1890 to promote French overseas expansionism. The creation of the Ministère des Colonies (Ministry for the Colonies) in 1894 formalized the process, and the Afrique occidentale française (AOF, French West Africa) was inaugurated in 1895 (incorporating under its aegis Dahomey, French Sudan, Ivory Coast, Guinea, Mauritania, Niger, and Senegal Upper Volta), and the Afrique équatoriale française in 1910

(AEF, French Equatorial Africa, grouping Gabon, Middle Congo, Chad and Oubangui-Chari). Later, at the Brazzaville Conference (held between January 30 and February 8, 1944), the governors of African territories met to discuss the question of political autonomy and transition within the framework of the Union française. The 1958 referendum was a defining moment when colonial territories in the Union française voted almost unanimously to join the Communauté franco-africaine, with the exception of Guinea which had voted "no" on this project in a referendum held on September 28, 1958. De Gaulle's objective to establish a new Franco-African community was therefore derailed, and the French authorities were forced to rethink how their economic and political interests would best be served within the parameters of a newly configured map of Africa.[12]

France was nevertheless successful in capitalizing on this apparent defeat, effectively manipulating the outcome of the referendum by "claiming to be a 'decolonizing' power while simultaneously maintaining increasingly privileged ties with the bulk of its former colonies" (Dozon, *Frères et sujets*, 241). François-Xavier Verschave has studied these developments and demonstrated how de Gaulle "decided to officially grant independence to France's sub-Saharan colonies. . . . At the same time, de Gaulle entrusted his right hand man, Jacques Foccart, who was already responsible for the Gaullist Party, its covert financing, and the secret service, etc., to serve as his behind-the-scenes operator in doing precisely the opposite of what he claimed publicly, namely to maintain a structure of dependence."[13] "At the same time, France's old African possessions were abandoned to their tyrants, who received, through corruption and military aid, generous political and ideological support from the French ruling class."[14] A recent documentary on the question, *Françafrique, 50 années sous le sceau du secret*, by Patrick Benquet, has brought further attention to *Françafrique* and been screened on French television.[15]

Independence was, for all intents and purposes, formulated and conceptualized within those borders and boundaries determined and delineated in Berlin in the late nineteenth century, yet, as Achille Mbembe has shown, "Far from being simple products of colonialism, current boundaries thus reflect commercial, religious, and military realities, the rivalries, power relationships, and alliances that prevailed among the various imperial powers and between them and Africans through the centuries preceding colonization proper. . . . At the time of conquest, their main function was to mark the spacial limits that separated colonial possessions from one another, taking into account not ambitions but the actual occupation of the land."[16] By 1961, entities such as the

Ministère de la France d'outre-mer (Ministry of France Overseas) had been folded into the Ministère de la Coopération (Ministry of Cooperation) and were ultimately integrated by 1999 into the Ministère des Affaires étrangères (Ministry of Foreign Affairs).[17] At one level mere lexical changes, yet the political and social events that have transpired over the past fifty years compel us to examine the *degree* and *extent* of "independence" since the transition from colony to postcolony occurred.

The asymmetrical nature of exchanges between Africa and France has been encapsulated in the notion of *Françafrique.* As François-Xavier Verschave has pointed out, "The French thought that they were in the process of decolonizing when in fact de Gaulle was doing all he could, with Jacques Foccart's help, to extend colonialism into a neocolonial period. This is what I have called la Françafrique."[18] The objective of this alignment was of course to "maintain these colonies in the Western orbit" (Verschave and Hauser, *Au mépris des peuples,* 9). "With colonization and fifty years of influence in Africa," Sylvain Touati writes, "a network has been created between French and African elites: 'la Françafrique.' French policy-making is developed within this special network consisting of politicians, state officials, military officers, heads of oil and weapons firms and members of the African elite. It is a grey zone of diplomacy."[19] The term *Françafrique* itself designates the narrow imbrication of French-African neocolonial economic and political relations, the "binary complex," as Christopher L. Miller has shown, linked with "forms of extraction and dissemination that took place during the centuries of the Atlantic triangular trade, on the one hand, and the postmodern, postcolonial forms of globalization of our own times."[20] In French, it may be worth noting, the word "frique" is a colloquial way of saying "money." This component is far from coincidental since the French colonial authorities established a specific currency for their AEF and AOF territories known as the CFA franc. Initially an abbreviation for Colonies françaises d'Afrique, the CFA itself evolved along with political changes, becoming the Communauté française d'Afrique and eventually the Communauté financière africaine. As Jean-Pierre Dozon has explained, "The invention of such a monetary system was without parallel, not even to be found in the British Commonwealth, and was vital to the capitalist machinery of the French-African State" (*Frères et sujets,* 263).

To this end, President de Gaulle established the Secrétariat aux Affaires africaines et malgaches (Secretariat for African and Malagasy Affairs) in 1960 and appointed Jacques Foccart to head it with the specific objective of maintaining "French interests in their former colonies"[21] and, as François-Xavier

Verschave has shown, *Françafrique* "was in reality a spin-off of the Foccartian system deployed in 1958 by General de Gaulle's closest collaborator. Francophone sub-Saharan African countries thus found themselves, at independence, entangled in a web of political, military, and financial 'cooperation' agreements that effectively placed them in trusteeship."[22] Jacques Foccart (1913–1997) was, without a shadow of a doubt, the most influential French figure in twentieth-century Franco-African relations.[23] He was a close adviser to several French presidents, and he headed the Africa cell between 1958 and 1981, then from 1995 to 1997, and even though French presidents—Georges Pompidou, Valéry Giscard d'Estaing, François Mitterrand, and Jacques Chirac—all set up their own "Africa" networks, they nevertheless continued to draw on the insights of the "Foccartian system" until his death in 1997.[24] As Samuël Foutoyet has shown, this was purely geostrategic: "This strategy made it possible to maintain a form of colonial domination and exploitation while giving the impression of decolonizing. . . . It also allowed France, a middle-sized power, to maintain a dominant position in international institutions such as the United Nations to the extent that francophone African states, even though officially independent, usually vote along with the former metropolitan power" (21).

Naturally these arrangements have been criticized and scrutinized. Mongo Béti, for example, the Cameroonian activist and novelist, denounced the exploitative nature and practices associated with Franco-African relations, anchoring his critique in such works as *Main basse sur le Cameroun, Autopsie d'une décolonisation* (1972), and *La France contre l'Afrique, Retour au Cameroon* (1993). These works presented a transcolonial historical framework in which a seamless transition from the colonial to the neocolonial operated.[25] In this context, both the French authorities and African leaders (in this instance the Cameroonian government) are the target of his critique, in the case of the latter for establishing a situation "which the Élysée perpetuates" (Béti, *La France contre l'Afrique,* 146) and in the former, because the ruling elite "are completely cut-off from reality due to their passion for luxury and sole preoccupation with protecting the exorbitant privileges they have accumulated for over thirty years" (Béti, *La France contre l'Afrique,* 146). In his capacity as Minister of the Interior (2005–2007), during the 2006–2007 electoral campaign, and then as President (2007–2012), Nicolas Sarkozy endeavored to (re)define Franco-African relations, evoking a "rupture" with previous arrangements. In many ways, these changes have coincided with those global realignments evoked earlier in this chapter that have resulted in a diminution of national influence in favor of non-State actors in the guise of multi/transnational corporations. For Odile

Tobner (Mongo Béti's widow), a harsh critic of Franco-African relations, "what can be considered new is the competition today between predators."[26]

Sarkozy folded the "cellule africaine" (Africa cell) into a diplomatic cell in which a Conseiller diplomatique adjoint chargé de l'Afrique (Deputy Diplomatic Advisor for Africa) reported directly to the president's own Conseiller diplomatique (Diplomatic Advisor Jean-David Lévitte, former French ambassador to the United States). However, the new structure maintained an analogous pattern when it came to oversight: "The 'Africa cell' may well have disappeared, but Nicolas Sarkozy has maintained control over Africa policy, outside of all parliamentary oversight" (Foutoyet, 89). Sarkozy was of course mayor of Neuilly from 1983 to 2002, a French department that is "the wealthiest in France, a kind of emirate" (Verschave, *Noir silence,* 436), where many of France's major corporations such as Elf, Bouygues, Total, Bolloré-Rivaud, and so on have their headquarters.[27] The symbiotic link between major corporations and the French State is well known; however, the transcolonial nature of this dynamic[28] is disquieting given that for businesses such as the Groupe Bolloré, "In this region [Africa], the Bolloré Group's interests are closely tied with those of the French State; . . . the Bolloré Group owes much of its fortune to its colonial history" (Foutoyet, 79).[29] Claude Guéant is widely considered "a specialist of Franco-African questions" (Foutoyet, 42–43), and his proximity to Sarkozy—going back to the prefecture of the Hauts-de-Seine (1986–1991) where he was deputy Cabinet director under Charles Pasqua—and later in the Elysée Palace helped strengthen the African network. Thus, as Verschave has written, "In conclusion, it is no longer the Republic or for that matter the Élysée that determines or carries out French policy in Africa, but instead a dubious group of economic, political and military players" (*La Françafrique,* 296).

In order to better evaluate the kinds of adjustments that have been made to France's Africa policy, past statements by French leaders, including Charles de Gaulle (1958–1969), Georges Pompidou (1969–1974), Valéry Giscard d'Estaing (1974–1981), François Mitterrand (1981–1995), and Jacques Chirac (1995–2007) need to be briefly considered.[30] François Mitterrand's "Discours de La Baule" (June 20, 1990), delivered on the occasion of the Sixteenth Africa-France Meeting of Heads of State, provides helpful contextualization to this discussion: "It is not our intention to meddle with internal affairs. This subtle form of colonialism that consists in endless preaching to African states and their leaders is as perverse as any other form of colonialism. It implies that certain people, who alone know the truth, are superior and more capable than others, but I know the great efforts being made by so many leaders who love their people and are intent on serving their interests."[31] Mitterrand's words can be inscribed in a much longer history, one that goes back at least to General de Gaulle's much-cited "Discours de Brazzaville" at the Conférence africaine française, January 30, 1944:

> We believe that the African Continent should be treated as a whole so far as the development of resources and communications are concerned, but in French Africa, as in all the other countries where men live under our flag, no progress will be possible if the men and women on their native soil do not benefit materially and spiritually and if they are not able to raise themselves to the point where they are capable of taking a hand in the running of their countries. It is France's duty to see that this comes about. This is our aim. We know that it is a long-term program. . . . When the moment comes it is for the French nation and for her alone, to proceed with the major structural reforms on which she will decide. But in the meantime we must start planning for the future today. You will study the spiritual, social, political, economic and other problems in each territory with a view to advising the Government on how they can be solved and so that the development and the progress of the populations concerned enables them to integrate with the French community without losing their personality, their interests, their aspirations or their future.[32]

The concerns evoked in these speeches serve to highlight the mutually constitutive nature of Franco-African relations, and the degree of historical interpenetration between the two spaces. In fact, the existence of Franco-African summits, dating back to the inaugural meeting in 1973 organized by President Pompidou, reflect this symbiotic relationship, and each successive meeting has stressed the important concerns and issues of the day: "Reforms to models of cooperation" (1973), "International economic questions and Franco-African cooperation" (1977), "Good governance and development" (1996), "Security in Africa" (1998), "African youth" (2005), and in 2010, "Major political issues in the 21st century." Ultimately, then, the task at hand is to assess what Sarkozy outlined as "rupture" with the past and determine whether or not this characterization is in fact pertinent.

Sarkozy's most well-known speech pertaining to Africa was the one he gave in Dakar, Senegal, on July 26, 2007, shortly after his election. Prior to engaging in a detailed analysis of that speech, earlier speeches provide useful indicators as to the kinds of arguments he would develop on that occasion. In 2006 in Cotonou (Benin), Sarkozy talked about how

> [a]bove all, this relationship must be transparent. The time has come to do away with the networks of the past and with the unofficial emissaries [émissaires officieux] who act with no legitimacy. The normal operations of political and diplomatic institutions must prevail over those unofficial networks responsible for so much harm in the past. The time has come to turn a new leaf, once and for all, on complacency, secrecy, and ambiguities. . . . The relationship between Africa and France is old and profound; we have a common history, one that has known instances of violence and even at times tragic episodes. I am aware of this and respect the necessary duty of memory [devoir de mémoire] we share with regards to this common history, including its darkest moments.[33]

In this instance, the historical longevity of the privileged partnership was evoked, the unofficial networks attributed to another era, and the need to "turn a new leaf" in the name of a new era of relations invoked. Subsequently, however, Sarkozy was cautious to avoid questioning the historical dissymmetry of the relationship, partially acknowledging the complex and complicated history, yet also introducing ambiguity when it came to attributing blame and culpability: "The truth is that few colonial powers have striven so hard for civilization and development and so little for exploitation. One can condemn the principle of colonialism while being honest enough to recognize that fact."[34] Each speech was carefully tailored to the specificities of the country visited, both within the francophone sphere (Congo, DRC, Gabon, and so on) and beyond in those regions France is endeavoring to build new ties (Angola, South Africa). As we saw earlier in the consideration of immigration policy in the E.U. context, analogous conclusions can be drawn when it comes to examining the link between French interests in Africa and the need to develop a common policy for Africa. We shall return to this aspect later.

The actions of politicians often leave people incredulous. Occasionally it will be argued that decision making is informed by considerations that cannot always be explained (because of their complexity) or shared (for security reasons). However, when it comes to considering Sarkozy's speeches pertaining to Africa, the one he delivered in Dakar on July 26, 2007, at the prestigious Cheikh Anta Diop University, has received the most attention. Commentators have been at a loss when it comes to interpreting the import of such a strikingly paternalistic and reductive view of Africa. Naturally, Sarkozy had multiple audiences in mind for this speech: on the one hand, addressing the question of repentance and colonial history provided the opportunity to appeal directly to certain electoral constituencies and lobby groups that helped get him elected, while on the other hand, targeting "African youth" (referred to interchangeably as "jeunesse africaine," "jeunes," "jeunes d'Afrique" and mentioned no fewer than fifty-six times in the speech), at whom a broad new range of immigration reforms, regulations, and co-development policies deployed by the newly established Ministry of Immigration, Integration, National Identity and Co-Development were explicitly aimed:

> I have not come to erase the past because the past cannot be erased. I have not come to deny mistakes or crimes—mistakes were made and crimes committed. There was the black slave trade, there was slavery, men, women and children bought and sold as so much merchandise. And this crime was not only a crime against the Africans, it was a crime against man, it was a crime against all of humanity. . . . But no one can ask of the generations of today to expiate this crime perpetrated by past generations. No one can ask of the sons to repent for the mistakes of their fathers. . . . The colonizer came, he took, he helped himself, he exploited. He pillaged resources and wealth that did not belong to him. He stripped the colonized of his personality, of his liberty, of his land, of the fruit of his labor. The colonizer took, but I want to say with respect, that he also gave. He built bridges, roads, hospitals, dispensaries and schools. He turned virgin soil fertile. He gave of his effort, his work, his know-how. I want to say it here, not all the colonialists were thieves or exploiters. There were among them evil men but there were also men of goodwill. People who believed they were fulfilling a civilizing mission, people who believed they were doing good. They were wrong, but some were sincere.

Thus, while acknowledging that "they were wrong" (ils ont eu tort) and that "colonization was a huge mistake" (la colonisation fut une grande faute)—*accusing* while simultaneously *excusing* French actions overseas—Sarkozy then argued in favor of reconciliation so that *both* Africans *and* the French could now "face the future together." "I have come to propose to you to look together, as Africans and as French, beyond this pain and this suffering. I have come to propose to you, youth of Africa not to forget this pain and this suffering that cannot be forgotten, but to move beyond it. I have come to propose to you, youth of Africa, not to dwell on the past, but for us to draw together lessons from it in order to face the future together. I have come, youth of Africa, to face with you our common history." Indeed, as Achille Mbembe has demonstrated, "In all relations in which one of the parties is not free nor equal enough, the act of violation often begins with language—a language which, on the pretext of simply expressing the speaker's deepest convictions, excuses all, refuses to expose its reasons and declares itself immune whilst at the same time forcing the weakest to bear the full force of its violence."[35] By the same token, the implied separation between *them* and *us* can only, invariably, lead to a "politics of *difference*."[36] The place of Africa in the political and social imaginary thus remains of crucial importance here, especially as one assesses the role such constructs and perceptions continue to play in policy making and in shaping perceptions of Africa (as continent), Africans (as people), and ethnic minorities and diasporic populations (in France and the E.U.). As Éric Fassin has argued, this "inconscient politique" (political unconscious) yields new forms of "racism" and "state xenophobia" that are located in the "effects produced by immigration policy" and that can in turn be extrapolated from "the repeated *dérapages* [blunders] made by politicians."[37] One is compelled to wonder how such a "paternalistic and hackneyed vision" continues to be in evidence on the contemporary French political landscape (Mbembe, "Sarkozy's Africa"). Yet, of course, the origins of this discourse has been extensively documented in a range of influential works, notably by Christopher L. Miller in *Blank Darkness: Africanist Discourse in French,* Valentin Y. Mudimbe in *The Idea of Africa,* and Achille Mbembe in *On the Postcolony.*[38] It should be noted that this ignorance can also be partially explained by exploring the institutional roots of the discipline of African history in France where the restructuring of the field of "colonial history," itself a branch of the colonial enterprise itself, toward the study of contemporary history has been particularly problematic.[39]

Africa, according to Sarkozy, "is an ahistoric, undeveloped world, entirely prisoner of its natural spirit and whose place remains on the threshold of universal history." In fact, "The tragedy of Africa is that the African has not fully entered into history." This "dialectic of lack and incompletion" (Mbembe, "Sarkozy's Africa") had been powerfully countered by Aimé Césaire over seventy years ago in 1939 in his *Notebook of a Return to a Native Land:*

> Those who invented neither powder nor compass
> those who could harness neither steam nor electricity
> those who explored neither the seas nor the sky but who know
> in its most minute corners the land of suffering
> those who have known voyages only through uprootings
> those who have been lulled to sleep by so much kneeling
> those whom they domesticated and Christianized
> those whom they inoculated with degeneracy.[40]

Why then, one may ask, are we confronted by this imperative to engage in revisionist interpretations of history, to reframe colonialism as a humanitarian project, to persist in adhering to "the refusal to 'repent' . . . inspired by the speculations of the likes of Pascal Bruckner, Alain Finkielkraut, and Daniel Lefeuvre. . . . Who's going to swallow that to create a humane world, you must throw morals and ethics to the wind because in this world, there's no justice for complaints or justice for causes?" (Mbembe, "Sarkozy's Africa"). It is well known that Sarkozy's adviser Henri Guaino is instrumental in writing many of the president's official speeches.[41] Of particular interest here is the indirect dialogue that has taken place between Guaino and some of his harshest critics. Achille Mbembe has, for example, stated that "Henri Guaino contented himself to lifting, almost word for word, passages from the chapter Hegel devotes to Africa in his work *Reason in History*" ("Sarkozy's Africa"), and Guaino himself wrote in *Le Monde:* "On the other hand, this speech owes nothing to Hegel. Too bad for those who thought they'd spotted an instance of plagiarism."[42] Closer comparative analysis of Sarkozy's speech and Hegel's writing will allow us to settle this dispute.

I have already quoted extensively from Sarkozy's speech, so the following citations from Hegel's *Philosophy of History* (1822) should help us further elucidate what is at stake here.[43]

> What we properly understand by Africa, is the Unhistorical, Underdeveloped Spirit, still involved in the conditions of mere nature, and which had to be presented here as only on the threshold of the World's History. (Hegel, 157)
>
> Africa proper, as far as History goes back, has remained—for purposes of connection with the rest of the World—shut-up; it is the Gold-land compressed within itself—the land of childhood, which lying beyond the day of self-consciousness, is enveloped in the dark mantle of Night. (Hegel, 148)
>
> The peculiarly African character is difficult to comprehend, for the very reason that, in reference to it, we must quite give up the principle which naturally accompanies all *our* ideas—the category of Universality. . . . The Negro, as already observed, exhibits the natural man in his completely wild and untamed state. We must lay aside all thought of reverence and morality—all that we call feeling—if we would rightly comprehend him; there is nothing harmonious with humanity to be found in this type of character. (Hegel, 150)

Certainly, the survival of these "remarkable amalgamations of ideas about Africa" (Miller, "The Slave Trade," 242) provided the justification for a French civilizing mission, and therefore questioning these would be tantamount to questioning the very foundations of French *grandeur.* "To recognize in public that colonial abuses took place (something which no one denies)," as Catherine Coquery-Vidrovitch has argued, "would run the risk of besmirching the Republic's honor. To explain away such abuses would be tantamount to engaging in 'repentance,' to handing minorities arguments that could undermine the one and indivisible nation" (*Enjeux politiques,* 133).[44] There is simply too much at stake in revising the official narrative, even though few would argue that this age-old view of Africa, developed in Hegel's thought, provided the ideological (and moral) premise for the European colonial *adventure.* But as Jean-Pierre Chrétien has argued, "The colonial regime did not simply consist in exporting 'progress.' . . . Rather, it was a very particular invention that brought together two parallel societies that were supposed to cohabit around the model proposed by the dominant power."[45]

Intellectuals, scholars, and writers immediately denounced Sarkozy's Dakar speech. Shortly thereafter (August 10, 2007), *Libération* newspaper published a "Lettre ouverte à Nicolas Sarkozy," signed by Jean-Luc Raharimanana and other writers, including Boubabar Boris Diop, Kangni Alem, Patrice Nganang, Makhily Gassama (a noted Senegalese professor and former Minister of Culture, also the editor of a collective response, *L'Afrique répond à Sarkozy: Contre le discours de Dakar,* 2008), and Adame Ba Konaré (Malian historian, married to former president Alpha Oumar Konaré), the editor of *Petit précis de remise à niveau sur l'histoire africaine à l'usage du président Sarkozy* (2008).[46] Above all, the most disturbing pattern in evidence in the speech concerned the manner in which nineteenth-century discourse found itself "réactualiser" (reactivated)[47] in the guise of a paternalistic mode that allowed Sarkozy, according to Mwatha Musanji Ngalasso, "[t]o position himself, *de facto,* in a hierarchical position" before his audience and thereby legitimize his role as all-powerful "master."[48] In this instance, colonial- era references to barbarism and savagery were updated with examples of poor governance, genocide, the prevalence of disease, famine, and poverty, yielding, as Laurence de Cock has shown, an Africa "stripped of all historicity so as to better justify domination by the European powers as the only bearers/carriers of progress."[49] The architecture of the speech connects in interesting ways with the earlier discussion of the museology at the Quai Branly Museum. As noted historian and art critic Bogumil Jewsiewicki has argued, "Let us consider the permanent exhibition at the Quai Branly Museum where Africa ends up being dissolved in the authoritative aesthetic presentation offered by the curator. Is this not precisely the problem with Sarkozy's speech? No doubt genuinely taken by surprise, the author of the speech failed to understand the clamor of indignation since in his estimation he was doing Africans a real favor."[50] What then, one may well ask, are the links between this discourse and the actual reality of policy making, particularly when it comes to extending these concerns and interests to the E.U.?

Sarkozy was a strong supporter of E.U.-Africa relations, and the French authorities have been proactive in encouraging the E.U. to "develop a common policy toward Africa."[51] Initiatives have included collaboration with the African Union, schemes such as the European Neighborhood Policy (ENP), and partnership treaties (with countries such as Burkina Faso, Congo, the DRC, Mali, and Senegal), and in 2000, 2007, and 2010, E.U.-Africa summits were held. The Joint Africa-E.U. Strategy (JAES) is composed of four main priorities: (1) improving the Africa-EU political partnership; (2) promoting peace, security, democratic governance and human rights, basic freedoms, gender equality, sustainable economic development, including industrialization, regional and continental integration, ensuring that all the Millennium Development Goals are met in all African countries by 2015; (3) effective multilateralism, and (4) a people-centered partnership.[52] Clearly, as we saw in chapter 3, (im)migration policy and the *management* of migration remain a central concern and issue for France.[53] Sarkozy stated in Cotonou as early as 2006: "Immigration has become a central issue in relations between France and Africa"; it is thus worth repeating that domestic *and* foreign policy cannot be decoupled when it comes to considering this question. French support has been concentrated on the idea of *Eurafrica,* conceptualized by privileging the geostrategic importance of the Mediterranean (defined by a body of water which of course connects France to the African continent) around the *Union for the Mediterranean Project.*[54] "To those in Africa," Sarkozy explained in Dakar, "who regard with suspicion the great *Union for the Mediterranean Project* that France has proposed to all countries bordering the Mediterranean, I want to say that in France's spirit it is not at all about side-lining sub-Saharan Africa. On the contrary it is about making this Union the pivotal point of Eurafrica, the first stage of the great dream of peace and prosperity that Europeans and Africans are capable of conceiving together" ("Dakar Speech," translation slightly altered). Later, in South Africa (2008), Sarkozy underscored the "indissociability" of France/Europe and Africa and alluded to the geographic proximity of the two continents, separated by a mere "14 kilometers at the Straits of Gibraltar," points he later emphasized in 2010 in his opening speech at the twenty-fifth Africa-France summit, whereby "France and Europe need Africa as much as Africa needs us."[55] Critics have been quick to deconstruct what is at stake in this particular vision of *Eurafrica,* one in which "two Africas" emerge: "one that would be 'useful' to Europe," offering a "kind of shield that would protect it from the assault of clandestine migrants," and the "other, with a vocation to become its periphery, 'useless' because 'problematic', and sheltering, according to the President, 'too much famine and too much misery.'"[56] Here again, the specter of Hegel is in our midst:

> Africa must be divided into three parts: one is that which lies south of the desert of Sahara—Africa proper—the Upland almost entirely unknown to us, with narrow coast-tracts along the sea; the second is that to the north of the desert—the European Africa (if we may so call it)—a coastland; the third is the river region of the Nile, the only valley-land of Africa, and which is in connection with Asia. . . . The northern part of Africa, which may be specially called that of the *coast-territory* (for Egypt has been frequently driven back on itself by the Mediterranean), lies on the Mediterranean and the Atlantic; a magnificent territory, on which Carthage once lay—the site of the modern Morocco, Algiers, Tunis, and Tripoli. This part was to be—*must* be attached to Europe: the French have lately made a successful effort in this direction. (Hegel, 148–150)

In his "Discours à Toulon" in 2007, Sarkozy had outlined the contours of the shared European and Mediterranean "dream" in the following terms:

> The European dream needs a Mediterranean dream. It shrunk when the dream that had propelled in days of yore the knights from all corners of Europe on their expeditions to the Orient [the Crusades] was broken, a dream that had drawn so many emperors of the Holy Roman Empire and so many French kings to the south, a dream that had been Bonaparte's in Egypt, Napoleon III's in Algeria, and de Lyautey's in Morocco. This dream that was not so much a dream of conquest as it was a dream of civilization. Let's not tarnish our past.[57]

In his book *Rétrovolutions. Essais sur les primitivismes contemporains,* Jean-Loup Amselle has contrasted French colonial policy in sub-Saharan Africa and the Maghreb, showing how proponents of the *civilizing mission* in sub-Saharan Africa partially justified it in opposition with the context of Morocco, where the figure of Maréchal de Lyautey (1854–1934) continues to "valorize" the patrimony and therefore *grandeur* of Maghrebi civilization itself.[58] Sarkozy embraced this trans-Mediterranean geopolitical configuration because, according to him, "the Maghreb . . . *has* genuinely entered history" and "the real difference therefore is to be found in the opposition between France (and therefore Europe) and sub-Saharan Black Africa, since the latter, albeit the cradle of humanity and therefore the bearer of the world's wisdom, is nevertheless hindered, because of its attachment to tradition, from fully committing itself to modernity and globalization" (Amselle, *Rétrovolutions,* 46 and 47, emphasis added). Such formulations would have been unacceptable in relation to Morocco where Sarkozy in 2007 in his "Discours de Tanger sur le projet de l'Union de la Méditérranée" developed "age-old divisions between the Maghreb and 'Black Africa,' juxtaposing (in an orientalist reading) the Maghreb of Carthage, Rome, and the Great Arabo-Musim or 'Arabo-Hispanic' (Andalusian) legacy with a [Conradian] *heart of darkness"* (Amselle, *Rétrovolutions,* 47).[59] These constructs ultimately contributed, "beyond the implicit cultural references at play in this text, to re-establishing a racial hierarchy between Europe, the Maghreb and sub-Saharan Africa" (Amselle, *Rétrovolutions,* 46, emphasis added), while simultaneously outlining a distinction between "great nations" and "small nations" based on historical "precedence."[60] As with Sarkozy's project to open a French history museum and as highlighted by the *National Identity Debate,* the "attachment to tradition" evoked by Amselle and so heavily criticized in Sarkozy's characterization of Africa and Africans, may very well explain France's own struggle with "modernity and globalization" and failure to recalibrate its foreign policy according to new geopolitical coordinates.

In 2008, the NGO Transparence International along with Sherpa, Survie, and the Fédération des Congolais de la diaspora brought a case seeking investigation into the assets located in France of three African leaders: Omar Bongo (Gabon), Denis Sassou-Nguesso (Congo), and Teodoro Obiang Nguema (Equatorial Guinea). This has become known as the "Affaire des biens mal acquis [BMA]" (The Ill-Gotten Assets Affair), and, as Xavier Harel and Thomas Hofnung have argued in their recent book *Le scandale des biens mal acquis. Enquête sur les milliards volés de la françafrique,* this marked a "genuine turning-point," since the case brought by the NGOs challenged the heretofore "near-total impunity enjoyed by leaders" and "resulted [in] a major diplomatic crisis between Paris and several African capitals, notably Libreville and Brazzaville."[61] Even though President Sarkozy had repeatedly promised a "rupture" with the "incestuous relations" that shaped *Françafrique*—what Angelique Chrisafis has characterized as the arrangement that permitted the "kickbacks, petrodollars and privileged relations that defined Paris's foreign policy towards its former colonies"[62]—and even though a "rupture of sorts" effectively took place during Sarkozy's mandate, Paris "remains reluctant and even unwilling to act against rulers still in power" (Harel and Hoffnung, 213–215) and "African leaders are [now] seeking out alternative havens that will enable them to conduct their lucrative business unobstructed" (Harel and Hoffnung, 212).

The symbolic fiftieth anniversary of African independence *celebrated* in 2010 provided the occasion to reflect on political and social developments during this timeframe. For the most part, criticism has focused on *Françafrique,* the duplicitous nature of French foreign policy, or the misguided IMF, World Bank, and structural adjustment policies as mechanisms for prescribing, assessing, and evaluating economic performance.[63] Ultimately, we are left with a paradoxical situation in which postcolonial politics—debates on repentance, immigration, cultural difference, accountability, and transparency—have complicated the relationship of former European colonial powers with their ex-colonies and rendered their attempts at forging comparative advantage increasingly complex, whereas, at the same time, new global powers have emerged and new alignments been forged independently of Western powers and without the ethical pressures confronting the aforementioned decolonizing powers.[64] One will have to remain attentive and vigilant in monitoring rapidly mutating economic, migratory, political, and social networks and trends, in order to ensure that a new generation of leaders is held accountable and prevented from replicating *Françafrique.*

5

From mirage *to* image

CONTEST(ED)ING SPACE IN DIASPORIC FILMS (1955–2011)

And then there was no more Empire all of a sudden
Its victories were air, its dominions dirt . . .
The map that had seeped its stain on a schoolboy's shirt
Like red ink on a blotter, battles, long sieges.

—*Derek Walcott*[1]

The symbiotic ties linking Africa and France are incontrovertible facts of history. The French presence in Africa has received extensive scrutiny, yet more recently attention has shifted toward those populations of African descent (usually former colonial subjects), immigrants or ethnic minorities (either naturalized subjects or citizens), residing in the French hexagon.[2] Findings have underscored the complexity and multidimensionality of this phenomenon and pointed to a broad range of discourses organized around such diverse cultural, political, and social questions as assimilation, incorporation, Islam, globalization, and secularism. On the one hand, European metropolitan centers have continued to exercise a magnetic effect in attracting labor from the *global south,* yet on the other we have witnessed a disquieting increase in anti-immigrant sentiment and intolerance toward migrant subjects. This has generated revisions to government policy and in some cases blurred the gap between domestic and foreign policy.

Research has privileged late twentieth- /early twenty-first-century experiences and in some cases obfuscated the longer history of bilateral relations between the two continents. Yet, much can also be learned from displacing our focus and according attention to the late-colonial/early-postcolonial period, and from relocating developments during both a pre-independence and post-migratory period. Several films with Afro/Francocentrist concerns made in France by African filmmakers during the 1950s and 1970s offer improved contextualization.[3] Examination of the gravitational forces at work in *pulling/pushing* Africans to Paris provides insights to the complex process of demystification and the various ways in which *mirages* of the metropolis, disseminated through colonial schooling and accompanying propagandist mechanisms, have been dismantled. In turn, these films have also emerged as precursors to recent debates on the politics of hospitality and treatment of clandestine, illegal, irregular, or undocumented subjects. Patterns of immigration and government responses to these have become inseparable from the actual subjects addressed by African and/or minority filmmakers. Films have provided an effective mechanism with which to explore territorial displacement and spatial reconfiguration and to more accurately contextualize the shifting global landscape of African/French postcolonial relations. Additionally, films have also included production at extra-hexagonal sites within the European Union itself as a consequence of new intra-European funding structures and modifications to regulations concerning population mobility within that geographic zone. These adjustments are historically relatively recent and have not always been sufficiently anticipated or accounted for by film critics. For example, while acknowledging the vibrancy and "the diversity of movements in African cinema" at the end of the 1980s, Manthia Diawara's prognostic for African cinema remained for the most part very much Africa (as continent) centric.[4] In contrast to Diawara's ideas, not only Africa but also *both* Africa *and* Europe are now relevant for African cinema.

A cursory overview of box office figures provides us with interesting information on the broad range of themes that have provided the subject matter of films made about African, Antillean, and ethnic minority populations in France (See Table 5.1). Whether made by established French filmmakers or newer directors whose backgrounds (Algeria, Martinique, Tunisia, and so forth) reflect the long history of African-French contact, these films allow us to better gauge the treatment and presentation of the history of race relations in France while also indicating a correlation between political debates and audience interest in a range of thematics and sociocultural issues. The breakthrough occurred in 1986 with the release of Thomas Gilou's film *Black Mic Mac,* which provided a humorous treatment of the African community in Paris. Rachid Bouchareb's *Indigènes,* on the subject of North African soldiers who fought for France in the Second World War, was a major domestic and international

Table 5.1. Films made in France on Black communities/presence, the *banlieues*, memory, and slavery

Director	Film	Theme	Box Office	Year
Rachid Bouchareb	*Indigènes/Days of Glory*	Memory/North Africa	3,227,502	2006
Mathieu Kassovitz	*La haine/Hate*	Banlieues	2,042,070	1995
Lionel Steketee	*Case départ/Back to square one*	Slavery	1,768,971	2011
Laurent Cantet	*Entre les murs/The Class*	Banlieues	1,612,356	2008
Lucien Jean-Baptiste	*La première étoile/Meet the Elizabethz*	Black communities and presence	1,647,603	2009
Euzhan Palcy	*Rue cases-nègres/Sugar Cane Alley*	Slavery	1,410,511	1983
Thomas Gilou	*Black Mic Mac*	Black communities and presence	1,228,154	1986
Luc Besson	*Banlieue 13/District B13*	Banlieues	961,850	2004
Abdellatif Kechiche	*L'Esquive/Games of Love and Chance*	Banlieues	373,618	2003
Jean-François Rivet	*Ma 6-T va crack-er/My Project is Going to Crack*	Banlieues	69,534	1997

Source: http://jpbox-office.com/ [September 7, 2011]

Note: Mathieu Kassovitz, *La haine* (Canal +, 1995), Euzhan Palcy, *Rue cases-nègres* (NEF Diffusion/Orca Productions, 1983), Thomas Gilou, *Black Mic Mac* (DVD Studiocanal, 1986), Rachid Bouchareb, *Indigènes* (Tessalit Productions, Kiss Films, France Cinéma, 2006), Lionel Steketee, *Case départ* (Légende Films, 2011), Abdellatif Kechiche, *L'Esquive* (Lola Films and CinéCinémas, 2003), Lucien Jean-Baptiste, *La première étoile* (Vendredi Film, France 2 Cinéma, 2009), Jean-François Rivet, *Ma 6-T va crack-er* (Actes prolétériens, 1997), Luc Besson, *Banlieue 13* (Europa Corp, TF1 Films Production, Canal +, 2004).

success, released just a year after heated debates on colonial memory (the 2005 Debré Law, for example). The French *banlieues* have provided a significant source of inspiration to filmmakers since Mathieu Kassovitz's 1995 hit *La haine.*[5] Three films preceded the 2005 urban uprisings: Jean-François Rivet's *Ma 6-T va crack-er* (1997), Abdellatif Kechiche's *L'Esquive* (2003), and Luc Besson's, *Banlieue 13* (2004) were distributed internationally and have continued to introduce new audiences to the complex fabric and challenges of French society, and one major success came later, *Entre les murs* (winning the Palme d'Or in Cannes, 2008). Since Euzhan Palcy's *Rue cases-nègres* (1983), the history of slavery and the slave trade has provided the subject of many films and documentaries. The official recognition by the French Parliament in 2001 of French involvement in the Atlantic slave trade and slavery as a crime against humanity paved the way from commemorative initiatives and discussions of this history, and in many ways have yielded an improved understanding of this past in French society (something that is certainly not true when it comes to exploring colonial history).[6] In many ways, one could argue, this may help to explain the box office success of Lionel Steketee's film *Case départ,* which was seen in France by almost two million spectators during summer 2011. The film features the actors Fabrice Eboué and Thomas N'Gijol (both have at least one Cameroonian parent), playing brothers who travel back in time to the era of slavery. Recourse to comedy has perhaps helped alleviate tensions while providing a forum for discussion and debate on key social issues. In a similar vein, Lucien Jean-Baptiste's *La première étoile,* a comedy about a black family that decides to go on a ski holiday, was also very popular when it came out in 2009. Visible minorities are today enjoying not only an increased presence on French television and in films but also an improvement in the quality of the roles they are playing.[7]

Colonialism and Diaspora

What is important to keep in mind at this juncture is the fact that the production and distribution of African and diasporic films remain inextricably linked to a longer cultural, economic, political, and social history of interaction between Africa and France. An analysis of the long-standing connections between Africa and the French metropolis of Paris introduces questions pertaining to French policy in Africa, historical transition, and the incorporation of the African continent into significant post-industrial changes in Europe while also naturally triggering a broad range of cultural, economic, political, and social bilateral and transversal networks associated with globalization. Lines of demarcation between those films made in Africa and/or in France have been blurred as a result of this complex network of influences, and ultimately contested in these concrete and imaginative spaces. Indeed, as Manthia Diawara has shown: "For a film historian, it is a complex task to explain the emergence of Francophone African filmmaking. One would have to determine the role played by the French government and individuals in furthering film production in their former colonies. . . . One would have to clarify the extent to which the French involvement is political, and merely reproducing in the domain of cinema, too, the structures of neocolonialism as it has been the case in other areas of the transfer of technology between North and South" (*African Cinema,* 21–22).

Diawara appropriately links the colonial and postcolonial framework, highlighting control patterns governed by legal and financial factors. Not surprisingly, given the degree to which the French authorities endeavored to foster a *civilizing mission* with the specific objective of forming French cultural prototypes and as a foundational component of a colonial policy of direct rule, interference in the domain of visual culture was also in evidence.[8] Such a program would have recourse to the multidimensional qualities offered by film as a propagandist mechanism, and the *Comité de Propagande Coloniale par le Film* was inaugurated as early as 1928. The *Décret Laval*—named after the French minister of the colonies—and signed into law in 1934, announced the concern of the colonial authorities for the potential of film as an insurrectionary tool. Paulin S. Vieyra had "argued that the development of movie soundtracks in 1928 was what prompted the French government to take measures to control film activities in the colonies, lest the involvement of Africa in these activities become subversive or anticolonialist" (Diawara, *African Cinema,* 22). The French authorities knew only too well how film could be used for consciousness raising and wasted no time imposing restrictions on autonomous modes of film production while extensively exploiting this medium for the purposes of information dissemination. In fact, "From 11 March 1934 on, the administration alone decided which films were made in Africa."[9] The *Comité de Propagande Coloniale par le Film* confirmed this, since "[t]he promotion of colonial educational cinema was auxiliary to a vision of colonial humanism . . . that linked economic development to moral, political, intellectual, educational, and social values."[10] David Murphy and Patrick Williams corroborate this argument: "The colonial period brought film to Africa, and in some instances its introduction was a deliberate part of colonial policy."[11] Thus, "the purpose of the Laval decree was to control the content of films that were shot in Africa and to minimize the creative roles played by Africans in the making of films" (Diawara, *African Cinema,* 22). Though "rarely invoked," as Murphy and Williams claim, "it was nevertheless used to prevent Paulin Vieyra . . . from filming in his own country of Senegal . . . ; however, the law did not prevent him from filming in France" (12). As we shall see, in a somewhat paradoxical manner, these restrictive measures were to play an unexpected role in African film history. Vieyra was able to exploit what essentially constituted a *loophole* in the Laval decree and bypass these early rules and regulations governing film production, obtaining both training and competence in filmmaking in the Parisian metropolis, and then turning this newly acquired skill toward the production in 1955 of *Afrique-sur-Seine,* a film "cited in history as the first directed by a black African" (Diawara, *African Cinema,* 3). Such developments and complex reformulations of national and territorial affiliation epitomize the broader sphere of francophone African film production and the resulting negotiation that has taken place between African and diasporic films.

The interesting aspect of French colonial film policy concerns its pluridimensional objectives; on the one hand, to structure constructs of Africa at the service of colonial expansionist objectives, and on the other, to disseminate perceptions of the French capital itself: "At the same time as cinema was representing Africa to the West and beyond, it was being used in different ways to represent the West to Africa" (Murphy and Williams, 2007, 11). But the fundamental point remains that "interest in Africa grew, as did the number of films set there, or purporting to be about the continent and its people. . . . All of these, when not straightforwardly racist, at least confirmed colonialist stereotypes about Africans and African culture among the cinema-going populations of the West, and as such contributed toward the ideological justification of the colonial enterprise in a period when its legitimacy was increasingly being questioned" (Murphy and Williams, 2007, 11). African filmmakers would join forces with key literary works by such important writers as Mongo Béti, Aimé Césaire, Cheikh Hamidou Kane, Ferdinand Oyono, and Léopold Sédar Senghor, who had engaged in the dual project of challenging widespread stereotypes about Africa and questioning those myths in circulation concerning the metropolis. As Peter J. Bloom has convincingly illustrated in his book *French Colonial Documentary: Mythologies of Humanitarianism,* "Making France known to the colonies, and the colonies known to France was the guiding policy for colonial film education . . . , an instrumental part of the broader architecture of colonial documentary educational filmmaking" (127). Furthermore, as a broader constitutive component of a simultaneously deployed internal and external agenda, "Educational cinema, as a cinema of reform for the education of children in metropolitan France, was exported to the colonies as a means of rhetorically transforming colonial subjects into citizens. . . . The language of conquest as a form of instruction was part of a broader strategy attempting to position France at the apex of a hierarchy of mind, knowledge, and civilization" (Bloom, *French Colonial Documentary,* 127–140). In this case, film history is intimately linked to the project of citizenship-formation, built around carefully coded practices and promises. "An entirely different approach to representing the West to Africa was that adopted in the French Empire, which was simply to show French films to Africans, since the French colonial ideology, embodied in the notion of 'la mission civilisatrice,' worked on the premise that their colonized subjects could, or would soon be able to, appreciate the products of French culture" (Murphy and Williams, 12). This propagandist element, at the service of a system perpetuating Occidentalist superiority, was to be deconstructed in film and literature, and in particular through travel to the metropole. Two dimensions are important here: the first concerns the actual content of those films that were being made, and, second, how these Occidentalist constructs would be countered. As Vieyra observed, "As a result, in the hands of the colonizer, Africa was used primarily as a location and Africans as the backdrop for stories with European audiences in mind. Later, under the influence of colonialist thought, films merely served to support this Western view of the world" (*Le cinéma africain,* 37). And "one could say that Black Africans only appeared on screen, in the best of cases, as objects of scientific curiosity, and only when they were not either consciously or unconsciously being used to justify some form of questionable exoticism" (Vieyra, *Le cinéma africain,* 55). The circulation of reductive films *about* Africans stands of course at the very origin of the African response to such paradigms, thereby confirming the indissociability of African and French filmography.[12]

The process of adopting a conscious response to colonial filmmaking practices cannot be decoupled from the more important activism inaugurated during the 1950s by a burgeoning global black consciousness. The actual historical moment coincided with a cultural and political environment that included a multiplicity of factors, ranging from the creation of the influential journal *Présence Africaine* (1947) and publishing house of the same name (1949), processes that inscribed the Parisian metropolis as the hub of the black intellectual community.[13] Additional formative events included the Afro-Asiatic

Conference held in Bandung in 1955, conflict in Algeria, and developments in the cultural realm that brought together interlocutors at such gatherings as the First International Congress of Black Writers and Artists (Paris, 1956), the Second International Congress of Black Writers and Artists (Rome, 1959), and the First World Festival of Black Arts (Dakar, 1966) where, as Bennetta Jules-Rosette has indicated, cinema became an important issue: "In Dakar, with the emphasis on art and performance, cinema emerged as an important strategy for shaping national consciousness and discourses in the arts" (*Black Paris,* 69). Whereas Vieyra's film *Afrique-sur-Seine* was released in 1955, his writings *on* cinema remain to this day important archival documents on the history of francophone sub-Saharan Africa cinema. Clément Tapsoba, in his essay on Vieyra, "Portrait de Paulin S. Vieyra (1925–1987)" foregrounds these contributions: "The film critic, whose numerous essays and publications on African cinema allowed it to be better known and to find a place in the history of world cinema, is more familiar than the filmmaker."[14]

Vieyra's numerous essays, such as "Quand le cinéma français parle au nom de l'Afrique noire" (When French cinema speaks for Black Africa), "Propos sur le cinéma africain" (Throughts on African cinema), and "Responsabilités du cinéma dans la formation d'une conscience nationale" (The role of African cinema in building national consciousness), were published in *Présence Africaine* from 1956 on, and most were subsequently gathered in a single volume published in 1969 entitled *Le cinéma africain.*[15] These provided an interesting background to his dual role as filmmaker and advocate for an autonomous African cinema. From his essays, Vieyra surfaces as a committed activist, indicating various obstacles and restrictions on African filmmakers, and campaigning for policy changes. His initiatives can be read as an early manifesto for African cinema, one that indeed provides us with insights on the various challenges confronting African cinematographers. The problems and limitations are associated with a nationalist and anti-colonialist struggle, from which the promise of emancipation would deliver the prerequisite conditions for African films: "In those days, wanting an African cinema and working toward its advent was their way of fighting for Independence; they were convinced that the conditions necessary for films to express an authentically African reality would only be possible with national sovereignty" (Vieyra, *Le cinéma africain,* 1969, 8). The need to redress this imbalance and issues of representation was deemed essential in order to allow "young African filmmakers . . . to express themselves" (Vieyra, *Le cinéma africain,* 1969, 145). Vieyra's call for a "federally-funded film department" (*Le cinéma africain,* 46) committed to "the promotion of an authentically African cinema" (47) constituted basic preconditions for growth and development through the implementation of circumstances that would contribute to the "emergence of a cinematographic art specific to the African people" and to the elimination of "stereotypical images of Africans as obedient children and noble savages, in order to reveal instead the true face of Africa" (55). The model he elaborated included concrete suggestions and ideas for financing, the provision of studio space, and the establishment of a technical training program, while also insisting on the retrieval of films about Africa and the creation of archival resources and distribution networks, all of which would assist in the process of bringing Africa up to date with technological developments pertaining to cultural production and dissemination. In many ways, Vieyra was to anticipate the objectives of the 1969 Fédération Panafricaine des Cinéastes (FEPACI), whose role Diawara has described as "crucial to an understanding of the development of African film production. . . . The efforts of FEPACI in Francophone Africa contributed to the creation of national film centers in different countries, to the setting up of an inter-African film distribution center (CIDIC), to production (CIPROFILM), and to the creation of the Ouagadougou festival as a way of promoting African films" (*African Cinema,* 35). These policies would later resonate with concerns shared at the 1974 Ouagadougou conference in their desire to address the following question: "How the cinema can present the human, social and cultural realities of Africa and make Africans think about their destiny."[16]

Evidently, meaningful transition would be achieved only gradually, primarily for financial reasons, and the ongoing struggles confronting African filmmakers have been extensively documented. As Nwachukwu Frank Ukadike has indicated, colonial-era control was to be transferred into the postcolonial period: "French aid for the production of African films is problematic. Though useful, it is regarded as paternalistic at best and imperialistic at worst" (1994, 70). The Ecrans du Sud, for example, a funding mechanism implemented following the 1991 Sommet de la Francophonie had the objective of placing "filmmakers from the South in contact with professionals from the North to promote the emergence of an African cinema which would meet the demands of the hour. . . . The aim was to give southern-hemisphere filmmakers an instrument that was more independent, less bound up with the state and hence not so dependent on the political developments which might possibly constrain the various government departments."[17] However, one of the problems with the funding structure of the Ecrans du Sud was its insistence, irrespective of the director's residency, that

> a film must be made in Africa. For filmmakers who have, in many cases, lived in Paris for a long time, this condition is very restrictive; it attests to an inability to consider a foreigner with his or her own culture as a full member of French society. . . . The African director is irremediably Other, who, as a consequence of his cultural difference cannot be integrated; on the other hand, he is already part of French society and is helping cross-fertilize it at a deep level. The effect of this is the almost total absence of films relating to the experience of the black community in Europe. (Barlet, *Africans Cinemas,* 269–270)

Effectively, colonial structures of control were reversed in this instance, as the French authorities have continued to attempt to exercise control over both the production and content of African films, albeit displacing the initial concern with anti-colonial oppositionality toward an updated version revealing an apprehension toward denunciations of the contemporary treatment and social status of postcolonial African minorities in France itself. Throughout the 1990s, the French Ministry of Co-Operation continued to play a key role, "wishing to preserve its direct aid, which enabled it to intervene independently; [it] has acquired a key role, through its direct aid and its historic significance, in choosing which proposals receive backing" (Barlet, *African Cinemas,* 269). For Med Hondo, though, as Madeleine Cottenet-Hage has explained, the "[d]ifficulties in finding backing for his films are in no way unique, but they illustrate a state of affairs that the Mauritanian filmmaker has been denouncing repeatedly—the colonization of Black Africa by Western cinema."[18]

Any treatment of ethnicity and race in France is inevitably infused with broader questions pertaining to republican notions of citizenship, and comparative analysis with other European countries reveals the particularity of these circumstances. As Carrie Tarr has indicated: "The system inevitably encourages self-censorships, and there is no structural support for minority filmmakers within the French film industry and TV industry comparable to the BFI and Channel Four in Britain. As a consequence, filmmakers from France's former colonies, many of whom have studied and/or worked in France, or live in France on a more or less permanent basis . . . find themselves making films that primarily address a French/European art-house audience."[19] Official French policy in the cultural domain reflects adherence to those principles of republican citizenship that concern undifferentiated subjects, and as Melissa Thackway has argued, "French critics and audiences, conditioned by a tradition of 'assimilationist' policies and an official anathema to the existence of communities, still have difficulty in accepting a critical African gaze in their own country."[20] There remains much confusion around the attempt to categorize these films, "whether such works are better seen as part of a 'Black French', rather than an 'African cinema'" (Thackway, *Africa Shoots Back,* 145), questions that were answered decades ago across the Channel where the coordinates of a multicultural infrastructure had been carefully delineated. Nevertheless, "how the European films made by Francophone African directors are received in France and what this says about the position they occupy in the French cinematographic landscape" (Thackway, *Africa Shoots Back,* 145) can contribute to a more nuanced understanding of the general context but also to the manner in which obstacles and prohibitions have not succeeded in preventing the emergence of committed films that replicate the "cultural nomadism of African filmmakers."[21] The *nomadism* or *mobility* of African filmmakers relates both to the funding structure elaborated earlier that necessitates adaptability and flexibility but also to displacement patterns that are intrinsic to global historical experiences that in turn have provided the material for films made in Africa or in diasporic contexts: "Access to funding, technical expertise, distribution and exhibition is of primary importance in determining what films get made and whether they get seen" (Tarr, "French Cinema," 60).[22] Archival and commercial resources have been limited, restricted to specialist organizations such as California Newsreel or the Médiathèque des Trois Mondes, and at one point the Cinémathèque Afrique funded by the Cultures France project, or established film festivals such as the Panafrican Film and TV Festival of Ouagadougou (an annual festival since 1969) and venues such as the Edinburgh Film Festival. Only in recent years have critics been addressing these issues and seeking new ways of enhancing the availability of African films.

However, prior to these developments, and because of the Laval decree, "Permission to film in Africa was denied Paulin S. Vieyra, the first African graduate of l'Institut des Hautes Etudes Cinématographiques (IDEHC). In the face of this impossibility to film in their own countries, Vieyra and his friends, Le Groupe Africain du Cinéma, resigned themselves to making *Afrique-sur-Seine* (1955, 21 minutes), a film about Africans in Paris" (Diawara, *African Cinema,* 23). It is to this paradox of history that I propose to turn our attention, including two other short films (court-métrage), namely Inoussa Ousseini's *Paris c'est joli* (1974) and Ben D. Beye's *Les princes noirs de Saint-Germain-des-Prés* (1975).[23]

Filming Africa, in *France*

It would be unreasonable—perhaps even anachronistic—to expect Vieyra's film to offer an all-encompassing view of the political and social climate at the time. Nevertheless, his exploration of an African presence in Paris during the 1950s, the focus on the intellectual dynamism and inclusion of images of African workers in the Parisian metropolis, serves as a kind of vignette of the times. Indeed, the politically charged context is reflected in the important discussions that took place whereby "[u]nresolved debates issued from the definition of antithetical Africa, in which black consciousness was an intermediary step rather than a solution to Africa's problems. Delegates at the 1956 congress were unable to achieve an equilibrium between cultural and political action or to define the terms of their artistic expression in a unified manner" (Jules-Rosette, *Black Paris,* 73). The bifurcated agendas of an engaged intelligentsia and an active colonial state provided the conditions for the contestation of the future of colonial control and the privileging of decolonizing imperatives. Vieyra's film was thus the first film made by an African filmmaker outside of the African continent, and the *Comité du Film Ethnographique* provided financial support. Shot in black and white, the framework is supplied by the world of students and intellectuals in Paris as they come into contact with the topographic objects of their colonial education gathered on both banks of the Seine River that traverses the French city.[24]

The film opens with a sequence providing somewhat idyllic images of young African children enjoying recreational activities in the ocean off the west coast of Africa. A voice-over inserts the ominous threat of departure, a hint of the pending territorial separation that will accompany displacement to the Parisian metropolis: "We had to grow up, leave home for Paris, the capital of the world, capital of Black Africa. Here, the fog has replaced the sun. The cries of machines those of nature." The camera then crosses the waters and adjusts its focus away from the shores of Africa to the iconic landmarks of Paris, those identifiable *realms of memory,*[25] observed from the elevated heights of Montmartre. Melissa Thackway, in her comprehensive analysis of "immigrant narratives" in film, underscores the import of this landscape:

> The film also focuses on Paris and its monuments to such an extent that they too become a subject rather than just a setting, avoiding simply reversing the ethnographic gaze that characterized so many Western representations of Africa at the time. This allusion to an "ethnographic gaze" is not fortuitous, for the film, whose opening credits present "under the patronage of the Museum of Mankind's ethnographic film committee," widely adopts contemporary ethnographic filmmaking style. This is conveyed through the characteristic exteriority of the filmic gaze, the physical distance from the characters (most of the film is shot in long and mid-shot), and the silence of the characters whose voices are replaced by the film's omniscient voice-over commentary and music.[26]

The francocentrism of the various protagonists is characterized by a fascination with those symbols of modernity in the metropolis, of mobility and motion exemplified in accelerated modes of circulation that include repeated scenes of cars, buses, scooters, or the metro, all captured and recorded on camera. The realm of childhood dreams has become, the narrator informs us, "the Boulevard St. Germain, the rue de l'Odéon, the secondhand bookstalls along the Seine, Molière's house, the Place de la Colonie." The *mirage,* inculcated in/onto the colonial imaginary, has been actualized and transferred into an *image,* as monuments such as the Panthéon and the Eiffel Tower unfold on screen alongside neighborhoods, streets, and squares such as the Latin Quarter, Sorbonne, Champs-Elysées, Place de la Concorde, Tuileries gardens, Trocadero, and Place de la Bastille. As Lieve Spaas has shown, the film "pictures Paris through the African eyes and deals with the illusions the Africans have about the much-idealized city, the center of hope and promises. . . . This is a film about the estrangement experienced by Africans who arrive in a city they feel they already know through years of colonization. This kind of false 'mother'-land betrays the fascination Paris exercises on the French-African imagination, between the imagined Paris of promise and its bitter reality."[27] African students in the film are forced to confront the myth with the reality itself: "In our quest for Paris, the future Seine river, we had the hope of meeting up and joining together, of finding civilization. Let us pay tribute to the genius of mankind, the freedom that comes from equality, to those moving victories of tired men, the monuments in Paris, witnesses to past and present glory."

Various Africans appear on screen and are engaged in a broad range of activities; the camera follows and monitors quotidian routines: a young man wearing a suit walking along the streets of Paris, a mixed-race couple taking pleasure in each other's company, a black couple greeting customers at a restaurant during the lunchtime shift, and so forth. At no point during the film does the spectator witness the actual content of dialogue or exchanges between subjects on the screen (although we are informed: "In the Latin Quarter, people come together, assimilate . . . so as to come closer, to better understand one another"). The soundtrack is exclusively restricted to a voice-over narrator and to music, the former operating as a guide, conducting the viewer through different events that punctuate the daily life of the city (weddings, social gatherings): "Paris, unique in its variety," "Paris, where fraternity was born," later juxtaposed with statements such as "Paris, endless days, days without hope" and "Paris, the merry-go-round of hope for a brighter future." The ambiguity confronting a whole generation of protagonists in the main texts of francophone sub-Saharan African fiction published prior to this film by such authors as Ousmane Socé (*Mirages de Paris*) and Camara Laye (*L'Enfant noir*), and subsequently in works by Cheikh Hamidou Kane (*L'aventure ambiguë*) is to be found in this film.[28]

Writers such as Daniel Biyaoula, Gaston-Paul Effa, Alain Mabanckou, and Simon Njami will update these questions in postcolonial-era narratives. While the solitude of the African migrant is evoked, what is in fact put into question is the more complex mechanism of colonial assimilation, through travel to the metropole—triggering a realization of the limits/limitations of the promises made. As Vieyra pointed out, in those films screened in Africa, "Africa is presented with an inaccurate view of Europe" (*Le cinéma africain,* 41). The process of representing Africa was not a unidirectional phenomenon, but rather one that was also mediated through a construction of France as a cultural and civic prototype to be emulated.

Afrique-sur-Seine does not formulate an explicit critique of the historical relationship between Africa and France. Nevertheless, the importance of this film (document?) comes precisely from the fact, as Thackway has shown, that "[m]ade at a time when African characters were either entirely absent or visually marginalized in French film productions, *Afrique-sur-Seine* was the first work to provide a panoramic overview of the African community in France" (*Africa Shoots Back,* 121). Statements by the narrator concerning signs of racial solidarity across different communities in Paris (Africans, Asians, Europeans) should by no means be understood as a conscious attempt to either disguise or ignore the political turbulence of the 1950s. Rather, the simultaneous rethinking of the centrality of the *mythic* metropolis deployed in the imperial imaginary that goes along with physical relocation materializes in conjunction with a global solidarity—made somewhat paradoxically available in the metropolis through French colonialism's centrifugal apparatus that brought students together at institutions of higher education in Paris. Beyond what may be perceived as "the relatively convivial climate of the student milieu in the Fifties" (Thackway, *Africa Shoots Back,* 123), this crucial moment in the articulation of colonial subjectivity and in the formulation of a global black consciousness (what Thackway has described as an "interracial fraternity," *Africa Shoots Back,* 141), partially driven by a vibrant Black American presence, was of course extensively theorized in the work generated by *négritude* philosophers.[29] Thus, rather than disguising a defining political moment, images of fraternity and entente propose a model of solidarity and a consciousness of belonging implicit to nationalist liberationist struggles and to the mission of revising and dismantling the coordinates of colonial ideology; in turn, the celebration, conquest, and glorification associated with France's *grandeur* overseas is put into question.

Afrique-sur-Seine must also be understood as a precursor to a whole new corpus of films made about Africans in France, featuring immigrants, refugees, or ethnic minorities. Perhaps most significantly, a counterpoint is introduced that highlights the constitutive nature of African-French history as a trans-colonial—that is, a colonial and post-migratory phenomenon: "By bringing characters to the screen who reflect Europe's cosmopolitan make-up, they also reflect a resolutely African point of view that challenges the absences, stereotypes and misrepresentations of immigrant characters in the vast majority of European films" (Thackway, *Africa Shoots Back,* 120). Françoise Pfaff has emphasized the contribution Vieyra's film made to a broader context: "Although the work depicts the aspirations and occupations of Paris's Black population, it was also the first time the French capital and its inhabitants were seen through non-Western eyes, by African students . . . returning the anthropological gaze, first looking at their colonial metropolis and subsequently to their continent and the world. African cinema was to become a unique instrument of cultural self-examination and self-assertiveness (while rejecting the stereotypical images of Africa found in Western tarzanistic jungle melodramas) within a shifting context of modernization and urbanization."[30] In films that came after *Afrique-sur-Seine,* African filmmakers shifted their attention to the complexity and diversity of the African presence in the metropolis.

In *Les princes noirs de Saint-Germain-des-Prés* (1975, color, 16 minutes), Ben Diogaye Beye enacts an intertextual gesture to the Parisian metropolis featured in Vieyra's earlier film, selecting Paris's well-known Left Bank Latin Quarter as the topographic site in which to explore the particular interaction between young African men and white French women. This allows the director to comment on the legacy of various colonial processes that inform this relationship. In this film, as Madeleine Cottenet-Hage has argued, Beye "portrays penniless but foppishly dressed young Africans who would seduce young European women by claiming princely ancestry in faraway African kingdoms."[31] The importance of projecting the appearance of success involves, in this instance, a dual process of deception: an external component through which the men have recourse to ostentatious vestimentary codes in order to simulate an image of success, and an internal dynamic through which the women knowingly assist and sustain the illusion by allowing these "penniless" men (African princes no less!) to serve as a repository of dreams. As Pierre Bourdieu has commented, fashion serves as "the motor of cultural life as a perpetual movement of overtaking and outflanking."[32] Indeed, an analogous system can be found in the practice of *La sape,* a phenomenon that designates the Société des Ambianceurs et des Personnes Elégantes (Society for Ambiencers and Persons of Elegance). In both instances, the Parisian metropolis is crucial to the accomplishment of these coded conventions, since passage there is required in order for the title of *sapeur* and accompanying cultural capital to be conferred on the individual. Furthermore, the *sapeurs* require opportunities to wear, display, and exhibit their clothes, and "[t]he *sape,*" as Didier Gondola observes, "is there to conceal his social failure and to transform it into apparent victory."[33] Ultimately, Beye's film investigates this gendered arrangement between former colonial subjects and French women in postcolonial France, while also providing insights as to how each respective group assembles this social pact.

The opening sequence follows an unidentified man walking along a Parisian boulevard, window shopping, carrying a yellow and dark-striped umbrella, wearing sandals and clothed predominantly in traditional African garments. At this stage, the spectator does not get to see his face. Several seemingly independent scenes unfold, and only gradually are we able to arrive at some kind of logic from these fragmented sections. In one scene, two African men are stationed at a metro exit and cruising for women. As a young black woman approaches the exit, the first man comments, "She's not bad, eh? But can't you tell she's an African (a *négresse*). Who cares about African women?" The process of mis-identification is revealing, and all the more so as the scene unfolds. Refusing to abide by his friend's assessment of the young woman's African origins (signified in the label *négresse*), "You're crazy. She's obviously American," he runs after her to ascertain her identity. Her response effectively silences him, since rather than potentially claiming insufficient knowledge of the French language as a barrier to communication, she mirrors back to him the African component of his identity, claiming that it is instead her lack of familiarity with Luba that hinders dialogue (a language of the Bantu peoples of Central Africa), "I don't speak Balouba. Um, I mean, I'm American, sorry, sorry." Whereas this sequence reveals the failure to connect with a female subject, the following scenes are on the contrary quite opposite.

Two French women are engaged in conversation in a café, during which one of the women informs her friend about her new African boyfriend. As her friend gains familiarity with developments in her private life, the viewer also begins to gauge information on various protagonists:

My boyfriend is called Guy.

Where's he from?

Senegal. He's from the Serer ethnic group, just like the president, a big deal there.

Really! So he's of noble birth?

Yes. If I'm not mistaken, the president is his first cousin or perhaps even his uncle. In fact, he's a crown prince. But you know, with all their revolutions and independence in Africa, well, it's a real shame.

Make sure you look at his right hand. He wears a strange bracelet. His grandfather gave it to him. It's a *unique* bracelet. The symbol of his rank, . . . he's majestic, beautiful, beautiful, so beautiful.

Beyond the accumulation of adjectives, the new boyfriend is invested with regal status and is not therefore an *ordinary* African, although as we learn, his uniqueness is built on ignorance given that his ethnic affiliation with the *serer* merely places him in Senegal's second largest ethnic group, one to which Senghor's father belonged. At this stage, the young man the camera had been following in the opening sequence reappears and he has now undergone a mutation. Sporting a blazer, vest, neck scarf, and handkerchief in his breast pocket, he parades confidently down the street, whistling, embracing the mode of the *flaneur* and *dandy.* As he joins them at the café, making a dramatic entry, his girlfriend gazes at him, clearly infatuated, mesmerized by the calculated exhibition of his apparel and rehearsed gestures. The bracelet he is wearing resembles the same generic bracelet present in repeated shots of African men, thereby providing the visual evidence that the narrative recounted about him contains inconsistencies. After complimenting her on her appearance, kissing her on both cheeks, his hand slowly moves toward her purse from which she discreetly hands him cash, complicit in sustaining the deception. We now discover that the unidentified figure we have been following since the film began—and whose *biography* has been narrated by his girlfriend—is in actuality diametrically contrary to the image delivered. Beye thus employs a clever device for unfolding and exposing the identity of the subject and the complex layers of disillusionment in operation.

Meanwhile, in another café, an African man is busy seducing his female companion. He also borrows money from her in order to place a call from a public phone. The conversation he has with his interlocutor, from whom he wants to borrow an apartment, confirms his objective of seducing the woman, commenting on the manner in which the "le coup du masque" (the mask trick) is working wonders on his latest victim. The "mask trick" turns out to be a variation, an adaptation of a master narrative circulating in the African diasporic community. Returning to the table, he asks the woman: "Do you know what this mask symbolizes? It's really, really important. Important because of its uniqueness. It belonged to my grandfather who was the divine protector of the village's secret." At this stage his hand moves gently across the area between her breasts in order to delineate the imagined geography he is evoking. His home village, that is simultaneously "fantastique" (fantastic), "un printemps perpétuel" (a perpetual Spring), and "beau" (beautiful) is supposedly to be found somewhere in close proximity between Mauritania and Gabon. The fact that the former is a northwest African country on the Atlantic ocean and sharing borders with Senegal, Mali, Algeria, and the Saharan desert, whereas Gabon is located in west central Africa with just over two thousand miles separating their respective capital cities of Nouakchott and Libreville, is secondary to the actual account he offers since these names and locations are only of import for their capacity to enhance the exoticizing qualities of his story whose familiar discursive realm has its roots in colonial rhetorical constructs. The tenuousness comes from the respective ways in which these dual narratives work; how Africa has been understood, and also how Paris itself lures African subjects who have been equally influenced by misconceptions of the metropolis. The film leaves us with an on-screen phrase: "Fifteen years since Independence, and still the same fantasies," insisting on the degree to which the decolonization of the unconscious remains incomplete.

In *Paris c'est joli* (1974, 23 minutes) by Inoussa Ousseini, one enters into a new phase of African-French relations. The earlier colonial nature of exchanges and interactions are now displaced, and these concerns have shifted toward a postcolonial framework defined by the irruption into the political domain in France of immigration as a central problem, organized around questions associated with nationalist imperatives and in which the limits of integration are put under pressure. Indeed, during Valéry Giscard d'Estaing's presidency (1974–1981), the question of the "suspension" of immigration had been much discussed in response to shifting global economic alarm linked to rapidly rising oil prices. After all, this was the era of the "Circulaire Bonnet" issued by the Ministry of the Interior according to which sub-Saharan immigrants were to be provided with "aide au retour" (repatriation) subventions. Shortly thereafter, the "Loi Barre-Bonnet" of January 10, 1980, targeting clandestine immigration was in effect, and "France, like other labor-importing countries decided to close her borders to fresh inflows of immigrant workers because of fears of rising unemployment."[34] *Paris c'est joli* must then be located in this context. The film begins with the televised broadcast of a news report: "The police have just intercepted a convoy of trucks at the border with Spain transporting people from sub-Saharan and North Africa. Hidden away in animal cages, they were of course trying to enter France illegally. Overtaken by panic, the traffickers and their clients fled and are now scattered in the open countryside. This is the not the first time we have related such a story. Think back to last winter. Ladies and gentlemen, if you happen upon strangers in your area, kindly inform the authorities or accompany them to the nearest police station."[35] The official shift in the responsibility for security away from the exclusive domain of the authorities toward the collective exercise of a vigilant form of citizenship heightens xenophobic tendencies in the process of solidifying the parameters of the national family through exclusionary measures targeted at a threatening clandestine outsider readily identifiable because of ethnic markers and somatic features. In a discussion of the codes of hospitality in the context of 1990s French politics, Mireille Rosello has written: "In the case of illegal foreigners, it is even more problematic to be forced to make no distinction between hospitality and identity. . . . The host must now see himself as an immigration officer and must visualize the threshold of the house as the equivalent of a national frontier. . . . It was clear that hospitality (and not only immigration) was constructed as a question directly related to the law rather than to apparently private notions of generosity and goodwill."[36]

More recently, these kinds of mechanisms aimed at solidifying categories of exclusion have been in evidence in a number of ways. Firstly, with the creation of the Ministry of Immigration, Integration, National Identity and Co-Development in 2007, that effectively institutionalized xenophobia, and secondly, in debates on DNA testing as a way of establishing genealogy in immigration cases. This had the effect of reinforcing the distinction between the *français de souche* (a term that literally means "indigenous French people," or people of French "stock," in other words white French people with a multigenerational presence on French soil) and second-class French citizens, while establishing different standards for the French family than the immigrant one, for whom the only legal basis of family becomes biological. These actions potentially fix the notion that visible ethnic minorities originate from immigration, thereby relegating them to an alternative status beyond Frenchness whose homogeneity is in turn inextricably linked back to whiteness. The history of colonial cinema revealed the various ways in which the French propagandist project was concerned with shaping simultaneously images of Africans *and* of France itself, and the ways in which these constructs and categories have survived and informed the Sarkozy presidency have been striking.

Following the news report, the camera fastens on an African man walking in the French countryside, carrying two bags. His visibility has been heightened by news coverage, and we find ourselves, as spectators and viewers, inserted into the dynamic of racial profiling and therefore complicit in the process of identifying the outsider. In this instance, we initially have no reason to suspect that this individual is *clandestine;* he appears disorientated, which has the effect of raising our attention, but it is above all through our amplified sensitivity to a racialized *blackness* that Ousseini succeeds in making us attentive to the potential threat this man represents. The man meets the criteria evoked by the television news report, his blackness inscribed as a kind of *wanted* symbol in our now hyper-vigilant minds that allow us to readily distinguish between insiders and outsiders. He is eventually picked up as a hitchhiker, sexual advances are made by a white Frenchman who articulates a whole range of stereotypes, thereby transposing the colonial projections and phantasms evoked in Beye's film to a homosexual context. The next person that offers him a ride responds to his inquiry on the presence of other Africans in the area: "Yes, that's for sure. More and more. But I have nothing against them." These sentiments concerning the *growing* African presence suggest that the French "seuil de tolérance" (threshold of tolerance) is being tested, and naturally the fact that he feels the need to supplement his statement by insisting on his own openness is questionable, while at the very least pointing to the fact that this *is* a problem for others. Subsequently, Ousseini's *wanted* subject is swindled by a prostitute and another African man, who relies on his presumed sense of solidarity to violate that trust and exploit the precariousness of his status. The conclusion of the film returns to those very myths disseminated during the colonial era pertaining to the representation of the Parisian metropolis, enforced by the migrant subject's realization of the disconnect between the representation of the metropolis and the reality; yet, he cannot accept the consequences of a failed migration to the north and the additional pressures of success that those in the south have invested financially and psychologically in him. Cottenet-Hage has explained this process, showing how "[c]ultural mimicry brings us back to notions of geographical and social space because adhering to exogenous models implies seeking legitimacy for one's own values and practices beyond one's own territory. Such 'looking beyond' takes on an additional significance for Africans, since that space beyond the Mediterranean is invested with hopes for material success" ("Images of France," 118).

We thus observe him writing home on a postcard that features the Eiffel Tower, that most iconic of symbols: "My darling sweetheart. I had an uneventful journey. All is well. People are very nice. Paris is beautiful. Make sure you tell the children." He makes a decision to sustain and perpetuate the myth. In Alain Mabanckou's novel *Bleu, Blanc, Rouge*,[37] an official "form letter" circulated in the migrant community, a prototypical narrative that reproduced the accepted coordinates of a metropolis and north, what Lydie Moudileno has characterized as a "foundational text in the imaginary of migration."[38] The mailbox into which he ultimately places the postcard offers two choices of destination, "Paris seulement/Autres destinations" (Paris only/Other destinations), metaphorically inscribing the bifurcation between those who belong in the metropolis and those who do not.

Not surprisingly, these films anticipated a significant thematic evolution. Dreams of the north are naturally linked to broader migratory processes and to developments in the global economy. Much in the same way that the colonial era incorporated Africa and African labor into a post-industrial world economy, so too have more recent factors associated with a globalized economy also become important.[39] Historically, as Michael T. Martin has argued, "The racial and ethnic formations that have evolved were forged largely by Third World immigrants who have historically served as a source of cheap labor in the post-war period."[40] Links between the north and the *global south* have become central to discussions on the subject of globalization. Elisabeth Lequeret has argued with reference to Vieyra's film how it belongs to the rubric of north-south relations.[41]

These films were innovative and have contributed to the expansion of the parameters of *both* African *and* French filmography. Thematically, they augment a long list of films that have addressed the living conditions of ethnic minorities and immigrants, "their asymmetrical relationships with French individuals, their negative interactions with French authorities, and the poverty, racism, and unemployment that plague the young people."[42] "The emergence of a cinema that has begun to portray the real rooting of the African community in France" (Thackway, *Africa Shoots Back*, 145) has been important to the process of diversifying the ways in which this population is represented. Analogous developments also occurred in the United Kingdom, and there has been progress from 1987 when Paul Gilroy claimed in *There Ain't No Black in the Union Jack: The Cultural Politics of Race and Nation* that "the categories of blackness and Britishness were mutually exclusive" and twenty years later when he sounded more optimistic in his discussion of the contributions made by Black British populations who contain the "promise of making Britain into a different place: somewhere more at ease with the irreversible fact of black settlement and more able to reconcile itself with the ongoing consequences of its long colonial past."[43]

In the French case, "Mainstream comedies of the 1990s indicate significant shifts in the representation of ethnic minorities and mixed-race relationships. . . . However, films from the cinemas of the periphery tell a different story" (Tarr, "French Cinema," 72–73).[44] Whereas French films have endeavored to address the presence of immigrant populations, the primary concern has been either with the integrational obstacles confronting these groups or with the alleged problems they present to France's assimilationist ideals.[45] Filmmakers such as Ousmane Sembene with *La noire de . . .* (1966) explored the myth and disillusionment that accompanied earlier historical migration. Med Hondo's films have focused extensively on the evidentiary mode of African immigrant circumstances, and in *Soleil O* (1970), as Cottenet-Hage has shown, "[t]he feeling of alienation, the experience of racism that he encountered during these years, the exploitation of cheap, imported manual labor, and the living conditions of immigrant communities all became material" (Decolonizing Images," 174). Similarly, a later film such as *Les bicots nègres, vos voisins* (1973) stands as "a lucid, sincere and intricate political film, it demonstrates how French neocolonialism exploits migrant labor and exerts a cultural imperialism over their minds."[46]

These themes have been adopted by filmmakers such as Idrissa Ouedraogo, Jean-Marie Teno, and José Zeka Laplaine and in later films by Med Hondo in order to reflect and account for the sociopolitical circumstances of late twentieth-century migrations. A number of films have addressed the question of the deportation of the *sans-papiers* residing in France but also of course in Fortress Europe: Hondo's *Lumière noire* (1992) turns to the deportation of Malians from France, and *Watani: Un monde sans mal* (1998) examines racism, xenophobia, and the *sans-papiers,* a subject Laplaine had also worked on in *Clandestin* (1996). The legacy of colonialism informs current production, and filmmakers such as Hondo have felt compelled to tackle these questions: "Confronted with racist representations of Africa in the media, I could only try and respond in my own way and with the means at my disposal in order to offer another version that was closer to reality. . . . Westerners continue to have a caricatural view as to who we are."[47] The precarious status of immigrants/ethnic minorities is evident. As Carrie Tarr has shown, "Ethnic minority filmmakers bring a 'double consciousness' to bear on their experiences, a biculturalism that, in itself, challenges the hegemony of dominant French republican culture."[48] These trends can also be found in works of nonfiction such as *Ahmed de Bourgogne* by Azouz Begag and Ahmed Beneddif, and in the personal testimonies of the *sans-papiers,* such as Madjiguène Cissé's *Parole de sans-papiers* and Abacar Diop's *Dans la peau d'un sans-papiers.*[49]

All of these films and texts confirm the centrality of the metropolis. As Cottenet-Hage contends, "The existence of the French 'space' remains, at least for the time being, intricately bound to African cinema, if not always as 'real' space, at least as 'phantasmic space'—the location of hopes, dreams, references, disappointments, uncertainties, divided loyalties. . . . Perhaps resentment and recognition are subtly intertwined in the representation of a country that, like an unwanted parental presence, continues to be felt" ("Images of France," 121). President Sarkozy's attention to the labor market and implementation of new measures aimed at "selective/chosen" immigration cannot be separated from his negative conception of Africa. Consideration of the earliest African films thus offers the kind of contextualization necessary in order to unpack those discourses that continue to circulate in contemporary France, and that will surely continue to influence the subject of African filmmaking, whether focused on Africa, immigrant communities, or on the transversal movements and circuits that are a reality in the increasingly globalized networks and patterns of the twenty-first century.

Since at least the 1970s, Africa-centered films have successfully evaded simple categorization, and the degree of interpenetration has been reflected in films featuring African populations in Africa, in the diasporic communities of France and Europe, and among ethnic minorities and immigrant populations. In turn, the multiplicity of topographic spaces in which these films have been located announce a significant expansion and decentralization of the parameters of French-language film production, a phenomenon that has also been accompanied by a thematic evolution. Analysis of recent developments in diasporic films necessarily engages with the dual components of this equation, namely those elements pertaining to the new spaces in which film production operates *and* the actual evidentiary mode represented by an African presence in these spaces.

Post-Migratory Experiences

An exhaustive account of these circumstances would call for a much longer and sustained analysis; nevertheless, consideration of a selection of films by Med Hondo (Mauritania), Zeka Laplaine (Democratic Republic of the Congo), Idrissa Ouedraogo (Burkina Faso), and Jean-Marie Teno (Cameroon) can serve to highlight the multiple ways in which films in and about the diasporic context and in dialogue with the African continent have been constant elements of Franco-African film collaborations. The degree to which these new films have challenged the cultural and political landscape of the hexagon and accordingly generated contestation over space and discourse are exemplified in Olivier Barlet's suggestive question, "Are the new films from Africa really African?"[50] Barlet delineates a chronology that runs from early debates around the question of multiculturalism during the 1980s through to the issues of the 1990s that included both urban riots and discussions over the appropriate treatment of undocumented/illegal migrant subjects, collectively ascribed the label *sans-papiers.* These questions have served to further highlight the degree to which race and social exclusion remain important problems while simultaneously questioning France's ability to ensure the application of equality.[51]

The social and political context cannot be decoupled from the analysis of these films. Not surprisingly, these issues have disproportionately impacted minority populations and played a central role in the amplification of francophone film production away from a uniquely hexagon-centric model. Certain films, set in multiple locations, accentuate this pluridimensionality, and such is the case for Med Hondo's *Lumière noire* (1992) set in Paris, Idrissa Ouedraogo's *Le cri du cœur* (1994) in Lyon, José Zeka Laplaine's *Clandestin* (1996) in Portugal, and Jean-Marie Teno's *Clando* (1996) in Germany. As Mathilde Blottière has pointed out, a new figure has emerged, whereby the "new pariah of a globalized world where everything and everyone circulates freely except him, the outlaw immigrant has become, in a few years, a hero on the big screen."[52] Films by both French and other European directors such as Gilles de Maistre, *La Citadelle Europe* (Lost in Transit, 2003), Eliane De Latour, *Les Oiseaux du ciel* (Birds of Heaven, 2006), Sylvestre Amoussou, *Africa paradis* (2007), and Olivier Masset-Depasse, *Illégal* (2010) turn their attention to twenty-first-century migration patterns, as protagonists struggle to enter the E.U.[53] Thus, to talk about film today means ultimately going beyond the reductive parameters of a nation-centric paradigm in order to acknowledge that any discussion about France necessarily also includes the E.U. In *We, the People of Europe: Reflections on Transnational Citizenship,* French philosopher Etienne Balibar was one of the first to expose the broader implications of such an articulation of shared identity:

> There is another aspect that has been forced on our attention by the problems relative to the treatment of asylum seekers and the modalities of control of so-called clandestine immigrants in Western Europe, which pose serious problems of the protection and institution of human rights: the system of identity verifications (generally occurring within the territory) allowing a triage of travelers admitted to and rejected from a given national territory. For the mass of humans today, these

> are the most decisive borders, but they are no longer "lines": instead they are *detention zones* and *filtering systems* such as those located in the center or on the periphery of major international airports.[54]

Mireille Rosello, in her analysis of the 1996 film *La promesse* by Belgian film directors Jean-Pierre and Luc Dardenne, a film that focuses on the symbiotic relationship (both personal and legal) between an illegal immigrant and an illegal employer, indicated: "It may take a while before directors choose to reflect on the most recent evolution of migration patterns and to portray undocumented immigrants" (*Postcolonial Hospitality,* 137). Rosello is of course correct to assume that films would gradually reflect an evidentiary mode linked to changing debates on immigration. Films such as Med Hondo's 1998 *Watani: Un monde sans mal* explored the racism, xenophobia, and right-wing politics in France that informed the political climate when on August 23, 1996, over one thousand armed CRS (Compagnies Républicaines de Sécurité) mobile police units stormed the Saint-Bernard de la Chapelle church in Paris's eighteenth arrondissement and forcibly removed the *sans-papiers* who had sought refuge there while awaiting a decision on their request for *régularisation* (amnesty and legalization). Yet, as we have seen, precursors to these films, such as Ousseini's *Paris c'est joli* have existed since at least 1974, highlighting the changing political climate in France toward immigrants.

The compelling dimension of the *sans-papiers* question concerns the mutation and transfer into public discourse *and* onto film from invisibility to visibility. As Rosello points out, developments operated against the logic of legal invisibility, "because the 'sans-papiers de Saint-Bernard' were deliberately fighting the myth of their clandestinity, because they opted for full visibility, they also gave up on the illusory freedom conferred upon individuals by the anonymity of huge cities" ("Representing Illegal Immigrants," 149–150).[55] This has coincided with other developments; for example, the question of visibility was also important during the riots that took place in French cities and *banlieues* in October and November 2005 (often referred to as the "revolt of the invisibles"), although in this case the predominantly disadvantaged and disenfranchised urban populations who collectively abandoned and relinquished their economic and social invisibility in order to render observable those feelings of disaffection were predominantly French citizens. Shortly after Senegalese Independence, Ousmane Sembene's 1966 film adaptation of his 1962 short story *La Noire de . . .* had treated the question of racism, powerfully connecting modern forms of racism with transhistorical slavery inscribed in the allusion to the Island of Gorée (a former slave-trading center), as the central protagonist Diouana travels to France to work, "Leaning out of the wide window overlooking the sea, transported, Diouana watched the birds flying high above in the immense expanse of blue. In the distance she could barely make out the Island of Gorée."[56]

In *Soleil O* (1969), Hondo criticized the racism confronting Africans in France and also established correlations between the slave trade and labor practices in the economically prosperous zones of Western Europe. Cottenet-Hage, describing this situation, stated that "[t]he feeling of alienation, the experience of racism that he [Hondo] encountered during these years, the exploitation of cheap, imported manual labor, and the living conditions of immigrant communities all became material for this film and the following one" ("Decolonizing Images," 174)—themes to which Hondo returned in *Les bicots nègres vos voisins* (1973). With reference to *Les bicots-nègres vos voisins,* Hondo explained how he had "wanted to show that these workers aren't eating anyone else's food, and that they hardly get what is theirs by right. And to show how they live, and what their problems are, their difficulties, their contradictions, all of them things that European workers know but poorly."[57] But for Hondo, this corresponds to a very particular and profound political commitment, "This is the main reason why I make films. Confronted with racist representations of Africa in the media, I could only try and respond in my own way and with the means at my disposal in order to offer another version that was closer to reality."[58] According to David Murphy and Patrick Williams, "Med Hondo is acknowledged as one of the great postcolonial chroniclers of the lives of the unrecognized and unrepresented masses in the various waves of the African diaspora" (*Postcolonial African Cinema,* 70).

The kinds of reformulations of the parameters of French cinema addressed earlier are exemplified by Hondo's claim that *Lumière noire* is to be considered "my first French film" (quoted in Signaté, *Med Hondo,* 111), a statement that is further complicated by the fact that we are left to fathom what he really means. After all, the film deals with previously tackled subjects such as racial discrimination and is anchored in *both* an African space (in this case Mali) *and* France. What this film does confirm, however, as Cottenet-Hage has argued, is the fact that "the existence of the French 'space' remains, at least for the time being, intricately bound to African cinema" ("Images of France," 121). Faithfully adapted from Didier Daeninckx's 1987 novel by the same name, the action is organized around a severe blunder by the police (a "bavure policière") during which Gérard Blanc, a technician employed at Air France, is shot and killed.[59]

Yves Guyot decides to investigate the suspicious death of his best friend, an undertaking complicated by conflicting "official" reports and depositions that claim to be concerned with establishing the truth: "My objective," insists Judge Berthier, "is to verify all the information I am given and to synthesize the different points of view I am given" (Daeninckx, 16).

Two additional inquiries are also being conducted, one by the police and the other by an administrative review team; these serve to further confuse the complex process of arriving at an accurate account of events. A climate of fear and escalating xenophobia triggered by the imminent threat of a terrorist attack provides the background that partially explains the agitation and anxiety of the authorities. "Faced with a concerned population, they find themselves forced to justify their mission" now that "France has been under threat of terrorist attacks for two months. The fact that specific terrorist targets have not been identified has increased levels of anxiety and as each day passes the population further discredits those responsible for their safety." When they killed an innocent Gérard Blanc, they realized the negative effect this would have on public opinion: "Our task is to terrorize the terrorists, not the people we are supposed to protect!" (Daeninckx, 181). This leads them to hastily elaborate a scheme that would implicate Gérard Blanc in criminal activities, "thereby justifying, after the fact, his assassination" (Daeninckx, 182), and in doing so to deploy a complex web of lies to support their version of reality.

The original incident took place in proximity to Paris's Charles de Gaulle International Airport, and Guyot soon learns that there was a witness to the "crime," a Malian *sans-papiers* who was being held in detention and awaiting deportation at a nearby hotel. It turns out that the entire seventh floor of the hotel had been requisitioned for the police authorities by the Ministry of the Interior: "It's not exactly a secret, but they're afraid that it will harm the reputation of the Artel chain if the information gets out. The Bobigny police department, or the Ministry of the Interior, well, they're the same thing I suppose, detain illegal immigrants in the rooms until they can find an aircraft to send them off. . . . They're mostly from sub-Saharan or North Africa, . . . illegals who got caught without papers" (Daeninckx, 54). In the established tradition of thrillers and detective stories, it turns out that the Malian witness Boudjougou (Babemba in the novel) enjoyed *a room with a view* and that his perspective from *the rear window* would be a crucial component in the process of reconstituting the events of the night in question and in solving the enigma of the crime. All the ingredients of a classic police investigation are set in motion, and Guyot's parallel investigation leads him to visit several Paris neighborhoods, where he finds assistance from an expansive diasporic network. Having obtained information as to Boudjougou's whereabouts, he sets off on a voyage to Mali to follow in his trail. This component of the story had served as the motivating point for Hondo, since as he has claimed, "The spectacle in French airports of Africans chained together awaiting deportation is nauseating" (quoted in Signaté, *Med Hondo,* 113).[60] The gradual and systematic reconstruction of events, including images of handcuffed Malians being transported to the hotel, fabricated testimony and newspaper reports, the extra-judicial elimination of witnesses, and inconsistent police reports, all serve to juxtapose a documented reality with the fabricated version of events proposed by the police authorities.

The on-screen postscript offers suggestive associations between the struggle to arrive at a truthful account of the events of the fateful night in question and racial tensions and dynamics: "This is the battle between day and night. I see black light." Drawn from Victor Hugo's well-known utterance, and partially reproducing the epigraph to Daeninckx's novel, the combat between darkness and light juxtaposes the natural element with the struggle for justice addressed in the film, reconfigured around the post-revolutionary Déclaration des droits de l'homme et du citoyen (as the symbolic culmination of the Enlightenment). In this case, the application of the key principles of that document are interrogated, and articulated by Hondo when he claims that "Seeing Africans chained together like criminals prior to forceful repatriation is a spectacle that does little to honor those States which claim to embrace the rights of Man and democratic ideals" (quoted in Signaté, *Med Hondo,* 72). Thus, Hondo's film ends up rejoining the newly politicized discourse for visibility of the *sans-papiers* that would be enunciated a few years later, as the expression of their awareness of those fundamental rights and their unambiguous assertion that those rights be extended to them.

In José Zeka Laplaine's short black and white silent film *Clandestin* (15 minutes), we witness the arrival of a cargo ship loaded with multiple containers busy docking in Lisbon's harbor.[61] A crate opens to reveal the lone figure of a young clandestine African man, abandoned on the perilous crossing by a now-deceased fellow traveler: "I traveled with an injured Angolan man. He was going to ask for political asylum." As he attempts to find his way out of the docks, he is chased by a black security guard equipped with a truncheon (the irony of this individual's responsibility for patrol and surveillance is of course striking). The rapid action and movement on screen adapts some of the devices associated with animated films: a chase ensues through the streets of the Alfama,

Lisbon's oldest quarter; the sound of a clock ticking away heightens the tension and suspense; the young man stops and starts, visibly petrified, tracked down like a wild animal; he gets away once, is then caught by the guard who keeps resurfacing, and then escapes again from his clutches. The act of temporarily outrunning the guard allows the camera to provide images of the lives of other Africans living on these shores, some in conditions of squalor, others driven by the precarious economic status to exploiting new arrivals. The turning point comes when he is run over by a car. Lying unconscious and one assumes dead in the street, the guard takes umbrage when the driver mumbles some inaudible comment, reproduced on screen in text as the term "Negro" and followed by an exclamation point. Miraculously, the fallen *adventurer* gets up again, unharmed, and the chase ensues.

An element of humor characterizes this game of cat and mouse, and one gradually senses a growing solidarity between the actors, a shared sentiment of vulnerability that comes from being perpetually scrutinized, inspected, kept under observance and surveillance. Having already seen him emerge from a container, we now learn from an on-screen inscription of the motivation for the adventure the central protagonist has begun: "My dear cousin, you must be wondering what I am up to. Well, as planned, I hid in a container and tried to join up with you in Europe. What an adventure that turned out to be." Yet, the claustrophobia of the container in which he traveled across the ocean serves to designate another metaphor of containment, namely the plight of the clandestine undocumented subject newly arrived on the inhospitable shores of Europe. Blinded by daylight upon exiting the container, Laplaine's *Clandestin* operates a kind of intertextual gesture with Hondo's film *Lumière noire* through the invocation of the shortcomings of Enlightenment ideals as symbols of hope and emancipation, promises that have not been actualized for these displaced subjects. The choice of Portugal's capital city as the topographic space for the unfolding of the narrative is far from coincidental. Lisbon's numerous monuments conjure up a comprehensive historical subtext that has much to reveal concerning the film's broader message: the history of the Alfama and the well-known symbol of the Torre de Belém. Perhaps more importantly the city's most famous monument, namely the Padrao dos Descobrimentos (the Monument to the Discoveries). Lisbon was, of course, the point of departure for so many navigators and explorers. These earlier *adventurers* are commemorated here for their voyages of conquest and of discovery to other shores, thereby conjuring associations between the expansionist policies of the European colonial powers and contemporary neo-colonial factors that hat have engendered the economic unevenness between the *global south* and economically prosperous north and provoked the emigration of subjects across the Mediterranean.

Laplaine's film, however, warns of the dangers of such a voyage and reveals the futility of these crossings, recording instead the harsh realities of the north. "Cousin," the young man writes, "I ended up being turned away. I don't regret anything though, except for my poor Angolan companion. For the time being, I have decided to stay in Africa and to try and make things work. Take good care of yourself, your cousin." Thus, rather than falsely glorifying the economic possibilities in Europe, Laplaine adopts the kind of standpoint that serves to demystify migration to the north, warning young people against leaving Africa.[62] Analogous conclusions are to be found in Jean-Marie Teno's film *Clando* (1996) set partially in Germany where, as Sheila Petty shows: "Teno interrogates migration as a solution to Cameroon's problems by suggesting that it is ultimately self-defeating for the nation."[63]

In *Le cri du cœur,* Idrissa Ouedraogo turns his attention to a different facet of the African presence in France, namely the question of family reunification, a much-contested issue today as new policies have prioritized selective economic immigration. The opening sequence features Ibrahim, the father of the central protagonist Moctar, depositing a letter in a French mailbox. Only later when the letter is delivered to his wife (Saffi) in Africa, do we learn through the declarative "We are leaving for France" that after years of hard work he has now achieved a level of economic security that enables him to have his wife and son come and join him in Lyon. The originality of the screenplay in this case originates in the fact that Moctar was actually born in France. Interestingly enough, this shift has stimulated critiques pertaining to "Ouedraogo's decision to move away from his West African homeland to make a film about an African family in France" (Murphy and Williams, *Postcolonial African Cinema,* 154). Also noteworthy is the fact that the film was produced as a co-production of the Centre européen cinématographique, the Centre national de la cinématographie de la Communauté Européenne économique, and the Ministère français de la coopération and the Agence de coopération culturelle et technique (ACCT), a funding structure that has set into motion partnerships that ultimately translate into a decentering of the sites and locations at which *African* films are made.

The *return* that takes place here is to the metropole rather than the more common reverse journey. This has the effect of forcing the viewer to rethink a number of stereotypical representations of immigrant communities, the most obvious of which concerns the perceived unwillingness of immigrants to seek integration into French society. Ibrahim's determination to reunite his family provides the motivation for enduring separation and for overcoming the obstacles he encounters to his incorporation into the French economic sphere. Paradoxically though, in this occurrence, his son experiences difficulties relinquishing his connection to the continent of Africa. This manifests itself in the recurrent and persistent haunting visions and sightings he has of a hyena, events that prompt those around him to question his mental health. Cottenet-Hage sees in these episodes "the nightmarish translation of his anguish at separation from both his grandfather (whose totem is the hyena) and his native village" ("Images of France," 108). Moctar's difficulty with acculturation and transplantation emerges as paradigmatic of broader assimilationist issues concerning immigrant populations, since Moctar's difficulties at school render him visible to his teachers and the authorities (social workers, doctors, psycho-therapists). Ibrahim states, "He's acting out to draw attention to himself" and reminds his mother, "We're foreigners here" and "You need to understand that we must be discreet. Unwanted attention could make things difficult for us." The central objective, as he sees it, is to abide by codes of republican indistinguishability.

Ibrahim's perspective must be framed in the context of his larger struggle with employment, and his "five years of sacrifice" that allowed the family to be together again. Evoking the hardships related to work, he expresses how "[t]imes are tough," a statement that activates an intertextual reference to the wider discourse on migration when a news story is interjected into the narrative featuring the deaths of migrants on a recent attempted crossing of the Mediterranean. Paradoxically, while the family has now been brought together after years of separation marked by an ocean, the realities of their long working days in France, during which they hardly see each other as a family, introduces new forms of separation and distance whereby each family member occupies an autonomous space in two different worlds, within the physical topography of France but also in the imaginative configuration in which Moctar finds refuge. When Moctar goes away for a few days to the countryside to clear his mind, the visit with his uncle Mamadou allows him to interact with one of his cousins who has not been to Africa. "What's it like over there?" his cousin asks. Moctar's response provides us with an indication as to some of the contributing factors to his condition, namely his feelings of isolation as a result of the long hours he spends alone while his parents strive to make ends meet, exemplified by the fact that he remembers Africa as a space in which one is never cold or alone. Responding to the imperative of achieving integration in France, Moctar's father (unlike the protagonist Paulo who befriends and listens to Moctar) is not able to equip his son with the tools he requires for transition, perhaps because he embodies the ambiguity and confusion that exists around the notion of *fatherland,* but also because he figures as a symbol of absence for the child who has erased him from the sentiment of *togetherness* he connects to Africa.

Not surprisingly, as Thackway has shown, "The emergence of the latter themes in film is an interesting contemporary development that reflects the real fragility of immigrant status as Europe has begun to tighten its borders" (*Africa Shoots Back,* 135). Filmmakers have become increasingly determined to address this precariousness and have rekindled their efforts at warning fellow Africans as to the realities that await them in Europe. Images of unsuccessful Mediterranean crossings painfully stir up memories of earlier generations whose forceful displacement cannot be occluded. Connecting and insisting on the longer history of African/French/European relations effectively brings to the surface the shortcomings inherent in monolithic interpretations of history that fail to adequately account for the constitutive aspects of the African/French experience, one that extends to cross-cultural influences in film and literature. These influences will receive additional attention in several chapters as the focus shifts to the pluridimensionality of the migrant experience: the Mediterranean (chapter 7), detention centers in northeast France and the English Channel (chapter 8), and finally in documentary films in France's *banlieues* (chapter 9).

The symbiotic nature of African-French relations alluded to in the opening section of this chapter continues to inform a broad range of film production. In fact, questions of belonging—and therefore of identity—are intrinsic to African and diasporic filmmaking. Moussa Sene Absa's *Ainsi meurent les anges* (And So Angels Die, 2001) follows the protagonist Mory as he struggles to reconcile the life he has built up as a resident in Paris with family influences in Africa; in Cheik Doukouré's *Paris selon Moussa* (Paris According to Moussa, 2002), a Guinean man arrives in Paris in order to fulfill an assignment for his village and finds himself shortly thereafter navigating his way through the networks of the diasporic community.[64] Alain Gomis's *L'Afrance* (2001), a loose adaptation of Cheikh Hamidou Kane's 1961 novel *L'aventure ambiguë* (Ambiguous Adventure), perhaps best encapsulates the *ambiguity* of the transnational ocean crossing and experience, producing what Sathya Rao has described as a "new space" (via the recombination of the two components of his identity, "Africa" and "France" in order to achieve "L'Afrance") and through a "montage that, by introducing a series of flashbacks and ruptures, breaks with the traditional linearity of narrative in order to embrace El Hadj's meandering subjectivity."[65] This is a theme we also find in S. Pierre Yaméogo's *Moi et mon blanc* (Me and My White Man, 2003), which follows an African student confronting problems with his residency papers.[66] As all these films confirm, and as recent trends in film production and thematic orientation have emphasized, not everyone is satisfied with the government's positions on these issues, and people in France are interested in obtaining an improved contextualization and understanding of African-French relations—historically *and* in terms of addressing the specific realities of multiculturalism today. The excavation, through archival research, performed in films such as *Paris couleurs* by Éric Deroo and Pascal Blanchard (2005) are a step toward demystifying official governmental rhetoric and attempts at instrumentalizing the past.[67] Whether or not consensus is achieved around the various interpretations of this historical relationship or in terms of delineating the topography of a roadmap for a diverse twenty-first-century French society may very well, in the long-term, prove secondary to the efforts made by individuals, groups, and funding sources in this direction. Documentaries such as *Diaspora. La communauté noire en France* (Dir. Medhi Kabara and Régis Chaoupa, 2006), *Jambé Dlo, une histoire antillaise* (Dir. Emmanuelle Bisou and Fabienne Kanor, 2008), *Des Noirs et des hommes* (Dir. Amélie Brumet and Philippe Goma, 2009), and *Noirs de France de 1889 à nos jours: une histoire de France* (Juan Gélas and Pascal Blanchard, 2011) signal this interest.[68]

6

The "Marie NDiaye Affair," or the Coming of a Postcolonial évoluée

Conrad portrays a void; Hamidou Kane celebrates a human presence and a heroic if doomed struggle. The difference between the two stories is very clear. You might say that difference was the very reason the African writer came into being. His story had been told for him, and he had found the telling quite unsatisfactory.

—*Chinua Achebe*[1]

The awarding of the Prix Goncourt to Marie NDiaye on November 2, 2009, for her novel *Trois femmes puissantes* (Three Strong Women) may at first sight appear to have brought further confirmation of the "Copernican revolution," which, according to signatories of the manifesto "Pour une 'littérature-monde' en français," has been sweeping through the world of literatures of French expression, casting aside hierarchical distinctions inherited from the colonial era.[2] Yet scarcely had the announcement of NDiaye's triumph been made when it unleashed a public controversy that showed her to be trapped in a web of identity politics which, in the optic of the manifesto, had supposedly been consigned to the trash can of history. Though the word was not publicly used, NDiaye was, I will argue, treated as a latter-day *évoluée.*

While deferring unconditional membership to that privileged club that was Frenchness, the French colonial authorities coined the category of *évolués* in order to designate certain colonized subjects which, through exposure to colonial educational and assimilationist mechanisms, had internalized French cultural and social norms. The racial advocacy organization founded in 2005 and known as *Les Indigènes de la République* has emphasized the transcolonial and transhistorical connections inherent in such mechanisms of hierarchization in terms of their representation of "descendants of slaves and deported Africans, daughters and sons of the colonized and of immigrants."[3]

The treatment meted out to the distinguished and critically acclaimed writer Marie NDiaye highlights the complex positions the writer has negotiated in the process of *belonging* in France as a person of African descent (her mother is a white French woman and her father a black Senegalese man) in a nation-state whose republican ideals and values are supposed to render ethnicity indistinguishable. In practice, NDiaye's racial differentiation explains the disquieting statements formulated by an elected member of the French National Assembly (Eric Raoult) in response to comments she had made concerning the impact on ethnic minorities and immigrants of President Nicolas Sarkozy's policies. In Raoult's view, these statements put into question her allegiance to France. Raoult's claims betrayed deep-seated expectations concerning the standards to which immigrants—treated in effect as postcolonial incarnations of *évolués*—should adhere. Wider social tensions on these issues have been heightened since November 2009 when the French government launched the *National Identity Debate* seeking to define what it means to be French, a debate implicitly structured around outdated notions of a pristine, white Europe-bound French history.[4] At the same time, NDiaye herself has been outspoken concerning the limits of her *Africaness* and her conceptualizations and paradigms of Africa in her own writings also raise important questions. The complex web of issues makes it particularly challenging to situate NDiaye clearly in relation to existing theorizations of a *littérature-monde* in French and also highlights the potential pitfalls inherent in seeking to situate writers according to a single identity.

The connection between *littérature-monde* and major literary prizes in France has been foundational to the process of thinking about the parameters of such a literary model. In response to the award of three important prizes in one season to *non-natives,* Jonathan Littell (Goncourt), Alain Mabanckou (Renaudot), and Nancy Huston (Femina), the initial manifesto "Pour une 'littérature-monde' en français" (Toward a World Literature in French) published March 16, 2007, in *Le Monde* proclaimed: "The center, from which supposedly radiated a franco-French literature, is no longer the center. Until now, the *center,* although less and less frequently, had its absorptive capacity that forced authors who came from elsewhere to rid themselves of their foreign trappings before melting in the crucible of the French language and its *national history:* the center, these fall prizes tell us, is henceforth everywhere, at the four corners of the world" ("Toward a World Literature in French," 54). *Francophone* prize-winning precursors had of course included Tahar Ben Jelloun, Patrick Chamoiseau, Andreï Makine, Amin Maalouf, and Ahmadou Kourouma, and new authors have added their names to an ever-expanding list of twenty-first-century prize recipients—Atiq Rahimi (Goncourt, 2008) and Tierno Monénembo (Renaudot, 2008), a list further augmented by the award of the Prix Goncourt to Marie NDiaye and the Prix Médicis to Dany Laferrière in 2009. Naturally, not all of these writers were signatories of the original manifesto.[5] Certainly, since the award of the Goncourt prize in 1921 to René Maran (a Black French Guyanese author) for his novel *Batouala: véritable roman nègre*, the question of diversity—both gendered and racial—has been inseparable from the para-discourse that has accompanied prize giving.[6] Competition between publishing houses is fierce, and it might be worth reminding ourselves that since the Goncourt was established in 1903 and the Renaudot in 1926, the overwhelming majority of awards have gone to male authors (less than twenty women in total or one out of every ten awardee) published for the most part by the three most prestigious publishing houses (Gallimard, Grasset, and Seuil) or by commercial branches of these (L'Olivier, Denöel, Mercure de France, etc.). In this context, the Editions du Seuil's commitment to francophone African and Caribbean authors has translated into a much stronger track record with the Renaudot at least, with laureates including Edouard Glissant (1958), Yambo Ouologuem (1968), René Depestre (1988), Daniel Picouly (1999, born in Paris of Martinican parents), Ahmadou Kourouma (2000), Alain Mabanckou (2006), and Tierno Monénembo (2008).[7]

Given the considerable media and scholarly attention devoted in recent years to these questions and to the national and international impact of the debates on *littérature-monde*, the award of the Prix Goncourt in 2009 to a mixed-race woman published by the Editions Gallimard thus becomes all the more interesting particularly when one considers the range of responses this announcement has triggered. After all, as one of the Goncourt jury members Tahar Ben Jelloun claimed after the announcement was made at the Drouant restaurant, "It is good to remind people that France has writers that are not lily white. In the end, Marie NDiaye is a mixed-race French woman with a Senegalese father and mother from Burgundy." However, such statements warrant further analysis. Why, one may well ask, is this "good"? How does Marie NDiaye's own understanding of her racial identity connect with such a statement? And, how do such statements correlate with republican imperatives concerning racial invisibility or for that matter with broader questions pertaining to racial constructs in France today? And finally, to what extent can NDiaye's work—to rejoin Maran's title—be considered a "véritable roman nègre" (authentic negro novel)? Lydie Moudileno provides a compelling analysis of these complex factors, revealing how NDiaye: "has controlled the conditions of her visibility and entry into the institution through a systematic strategy involving multiple positions. The first has entailed playing down, or at least distancing herself from her 'African' origins. When she first published, though her family name gave away a connection to Senegal, her physical body, and therefore her 'race,' remained invisible. Furthermore, books published by the Editions de Minuit [her previous publisher] are recognizable for their blank white covers and the fact that they do not include photographs of the authors."[8] Of course, NDiaye's case is all the more interesting precisely because of her background and the comments she has made pertaining to francophone literature in a more general manner.

Marie NDiaye is not the first Black woman on the French literary scene. In 2006, with reference to Calixthe Beyala (a Cameroonian writer who resides in France), Nicki Hitchcott had written that "Only Marie NDiaye has experienced anything close to comparable commercial success with her novels published by the prestigious Editions de Minuit. . . . However, born in France of a French mother and a Senegalese father, NDiaye has never been represented (nor represented herself) as a black African writer; indeed, she is keen to reject any suggestion that she is 'francophone' rather than 'French.'"[9] In response to a questionnaire prepared by Beverley Ormerod and Jean-Marie Volet in their book *Romancières africaines d'expression française: le sud du Sahara,*[10] NDiaye emphasizes how "Never having lived in Africa, and having scarcely known my father (I am of mixed race), I cannot be considered to a be a francophone novelist, that is a French-speaking foreigner."[11] However, as Hitchcott rightly suggests, "NDiaye poses an important question about what constitutes an African woman writer, especially as her fiction is not recognizable as that of an African author since it has neither an African context nor African characters" (*Women Writers in Francophone Africa,* 24). As African literature has become increasingly globalized, diasporic and transnational, many of these questions have gained in complexity. African authors and/or writers of African descent are now located on every continent, thereby complicating the question of defining that which constitutes an *African* work of literature: Does the author, for example, have to be the bearer of a passport from an African country, reside on the African continent, write in *African* languages, or for that matter situate the narrative in Africa? As I have argued elsewhere:

> What is particularly striking . . . in texts produced by francophone sub-Saharan African authors who have chosen to situate their narratives in both Africa and France . . . is the variety of ways in which transnational communities are organized

> outside the homeland, how cultural practices are maintained, challenged and transformed as they are subjected to multiple influences. . . . At what point, then, does Beyala stop being a Cameroonian novelist and become an Afro-Parisian one? Is she, for example, Afro-Parisian when she writes about immigration in France . . . and Cameroonian when the focus is Africa.[12]

Likewise, other African and/or Franco-African authors such as Fatou Diome have authored works that address the challenges that come with having to negotiate multiple identities as both they *and* their protagonists circulate between Africa and France *and* Africa in France.[13] Beyala's perception of the French literary establishment becomes all the more interesting when one considers recent developments. As Hitchcott has shown, "Throughout these various tactical shifts, the one constant has been Beyala's emphasis on her 'otherness.' . . . Her adopted position of victim extends to her disingenuous explanation of her failure to win the Prix Goncourt: 'I'm not going to kid myself: to give the prize to a Black African woman, even me, that would be a bit much for the Goncourt.'"[14] To a certain extent, Beyala's condemnation has now become redundant, because a "Black African woman"—whether NDiaye accepts this categorization or not may well be secondary since the range of responses to her recognition have only further confirmed her *Africaness*—has now won the Goncourt. But for NDiaye, the question has always posed itself differently than for Beyala and Diome: At what point, one may ask, does NDiaye stop being a French novelist and *become* an African one? Such a reversal to the conditions of analysis accrues currency given that the Goncourt has been awarded to what is unambiguously her most *African* book—in terms of geography, choice of protagonists, engagement with global migration patterns, human rights issues, and so on. Perhaps then, what the *World Republic of Letters* has deemed the most authentic, the most "véritable" (authentic) of African works, produced by a writer who exceeds the norms of Frenchness and who as such, though the self-proclaimed "least" African of "Black" writers in France, is nevertheless simultaneously equipped with the unquestioned authority of a *native* informer when she writes *about* Africa, and in particular when she writes in the way she does about the continent.[15] Such an argument would find support in the conclusion Nelly Kaprièlian reaches, "There is no one better positioned to deal with this monstrous era in which 'outsiders' are treated so poorly."[16] As such, NDiaye is invested with an ethnographic authority which, as we shall see, rather than destabilizing and displacing prevalent constructs, paradoxically reproduces and performs the kind of comfortable and reductive representations of Africa that fulfill the expectations of readers whose projections cannot then be decoupled from popular views of Africans and African migrants that influence insensitive policy-making initiatives. These observations require further analysis, and we will return to them later. But the important point to retain at this juncture is that while NDiaye is *indigenous* to France—she was born *on* French soil—the manner in which she is treated by certain elements in French society is analogous to the treatment of *indigènes* (natives) in French colonies, namely those individuals who were considered *évolués* and therefore deemed unworthy of rights.

In the past, NDiaye has invoked her lack of familiarity with the African continent as a way of pointing to the inappropriateness of the label and category "francophone" to describe her. In *Trois femmes puissantes,* Africa becomes an imagined topographic space, mediated through a broad range of constructs, territorial associations, and references. According to Kaprièlian, the novel emerges "as an antidote to the traditional linear novel that embodies bourgeois norms, a one hundred percent French literature."[17] Somehow, the framework adopted by NDiaye can no longer be accommodated by traditional categories ascribed to the French novel; it is now marked by its otherness, its difference, its non-Frenchness. Kaprièlian stops just short of adding it to the library of *littérature-monde* in French, of calling it *francophone.* Alain Mabanckou has explored this tenuous relationship between the French and the francophone, preferring to think of the contributions of the latter in terms of an expansion of the horizon of writings in French:

> For a long time, somewhat naïvely, I dreamed of the day when Francophone literature would be integrated into French literature. However, over time, I gradually came to realize that there was another way of looking at the question. Francophone literature is a vast ensemble whose tentacles reach out across several continents whereas French literature is a national literature. Rather, it is French literature that should see a place within the vast Francophone ensemble. . . . If French literature is going to stay alive, France is going to have to conceive of itself as an element of the broader Francophone space.[18]

In one of the first mainstream appraisals and assessments of NDiaye's new novel, Kaprièlian asked the author: "Your characters are African. Your father is Senegalese. Do you proclaim an African identity?" ("Marie Ndiaye: aux prises avec le monde," 31). NDiaye replied: "I would claim such an identity and feel proximity to it if I actually had a dual culture. . . . The *only thing* that is different when one's origins are African is that one is Black, this difference is visible. . . . But I was raised in an environment that was one hundred percent French.

And so in my life, African origins don't mean very much—except for the fact that I can't hide it because of my surname and the color of my skin" ("Marie Ndiaye: aux prises avec le monde," 30–31, emphasis added). This "only thing," though, cannot be downplayed since this racialized identity informs the status of citizens in the postcolonial French Republic (even those who have participated in every aspect of French life), and serves as a constant reminder of a marginal status in a context in which there exists little ambiguity concerning the parameters of Frenchness.[19] Kaprièlian takes NDiaye's responses at face value and does not go on to challenge her further on this, pointing to the fact that she refuses to "justify her literary work through this biographical element. Much in the same way that her novel is not to be interpreted as an allegory for relations between France and Africa" ("Marie Ndiaye: aux prises avec le monde," 29); yet she goes on to argue how "Marie NDiaye recounts stories of lives torn between Africa and France. There is an interrogation on the human condition today: migrations and questions of belonging. . . . It is them, these human beings rendered vulnerable by racial mixing, migration, emigration, class structures, the monstrosity of families as microlaboratories of collective barbarism, beings that are out of place, that exceed categorizations, and that are *so rarely represented in French literature,* and that Marie NDiaye offers a place to thanks to writing" ("Marie Ndiaye: aux prises avec le monde," 29–30, emphasis added). But the fact nevertheless remains that these subjects—which she claims are "so rarely represented in French literature"—do pertain to contemporary relations between France and Africa, providing the structure and theme of the third section of the novel (pages 247–317) which, while fictionalizing perilous Mediterranean crossings, remain *fictions* anchored in decipherable evidentiary modes that have captured the author's attention: "I was very interested and shaken by accounts of refugees arriving on the shoreline in Malta or in Sicily or elsewhere" (Kaprièlian, "Marie Ndiaye: aux prises avec le monde," 30). In fact, "For this section of the book, I decided to rely less on fiction, with no magic, or very little at least, preferring instead to account for these circumstances, while still producing a literary object rather than a *documentary*" (Kaprièlian, "Marie Ndiaye: aux prises avec le monde," 29, emphasis added). Could NDiaye's consciousness of racial hierarchies in France have allowed for identification with and greater sensitivity to circumstances in Africa?

Possible answers are perhaps to be found in an interview with Lucie Clair, "La discrète empathie," published in October 2009.[20] The notion of "empathy" emerges as a key indicator here as to NDiaye's relationality to the plight of Africa and Africans, and a review of *Trois femmes puissantes* written by Clair confirms this connection. Clair writes, "This is also the site . . . where the problem of contemporary slavery and forced marriages is to be found."[21] But this "empathy" Clair alludes to as a "site" happens to be a *real* geographic zone, namely sub-Saharan Africa; the context is precise, identifiable, it becomes a "documentary" in nature. We know that such violence exists, has been recognized as such, and that these are sites (among numerous others) of patriarchal oppression. They are thus not products of the imagination but rather concrete realities, albeit realities that also inform the collective European imagination when it comes to Africa and that have often been recuperated at the service of a paternalistic France, the kind of France that invests in debates on a twenty-first-century *national identity.* As Gérard Noiriel has demonstrated, "The objective is always to achieve a definition of national identity by denouncing its opposite, through a classical logic that juxtaposes the 'them' with the us. . . . One must also point out that unlike the National Front, Nicolas Sarkozy does not name the group he has in mind, . . . but rather, through allusions, this leaves it up to his commentators and electoral supporters to fill in the gaps."[22]

In a discussion of works produced by second-generation Maghrebi women authors, Alec G. Hargreaves had identified a disturbing pattern, whereby "There is also a danger that narratives denouncing the subjection of minority women to sexual and other forms of abuse may play into the hands of those who argue that today's postcolonial minorities are as inherently barbarous as were yesterday's colonized 'natives'. . . . Their personal testimony is all too easily ensnared in the public circulation of stereotypes inherited from the colonial period which to a large extent rob them of the ownership."[23] With reference to texts about African immigration in France, I have also argued that these "have often resorted to a documentary-testimonial format in which a sensationalist rhetoric associated with widespread oppression is evidenced. Accordingly, these texts essentially narrate and record the immigrant experience, and are fictional only in that the names of various protagonists are changed, but otherwise recounting actual events."[24] An assessment therefore remains to be made as to the extent to which NDiaye's novel inscribes itself or not within this tradition.

The evidence is certainly there when it comes to ascribing the work with a sense of political commitment, a dimension NDiaye has not ignored: "There is a reason why these characters flee hardship; it is the result of policies, of inadequate governance" (Kaprièlian, "Marie Ndiaye: aux prises avec le monde," 29).

These comments pertain to the third section of the novel where the focus is provided by the sociological circumstances of migration from the African continent into the European Union. In this instance, the reader observes these conditions through the eyes of the central protagonist Khady, as she contemplates the spectacle of human suffering: "Just like her, others were waiting, seated on oversize Tartan plastic carrier bags or cardboard boxes roped together tightly" (*Trois femmes puissantes,* 269). *Regarding the pain of others*[25] (a pain that is now also hers), "She glanced at an undifferentiated mass of packages and beings" (*Trois femmes puissantes,* 276), gathered here with shared hopes and expectations for what lies beyond, in anticipation "that there might one day come a day in Europe" (*Trois femmes puissantes,* 286). As in so many migration narratives, the protagonists share in their concern with fulfilling the hopes and expectations of those they have left behind: "You must not come back, she whispered into Khady's ear. You must send us money as soon as you get there. If you don't make it, don't come back . . . as was the case with most of the men who came to see her, who had been drifting in the area for years now, losing count of the exact number of years, hailing from countries where their families assumed they were dead since they didn't dare, ashamed as they were of their situation, keep in touch" (*Trois femmes puissantes,* 261–309). It has become common knowledge that globalization has exacerbated economic dissymmetries, and NDiaye's characterization of the political climate in France since President Sarkozy was elected in 2007 is apt: "I find this France monstrous. . . . Besson, Hortefeux, all these people, I find them monstrous," promoting "the atmosphere of a police state" ("Marie Ndiaye: aux prises avec le monde," 32). But NDiaye also shares in the responsibility of exercising caution when it comes to representing sociocultural dynamics in Africa itself, because the overwhelming image one gets from her novel is one of violence and despair.

In the epigraph, Chinua Achebe distinguishes between the works of Joseph Conrad and Cheikh Hamidou Kane, pointing to the former's presentation of Africa as a void. This re-emerges in NDiaye's novel, for while she acknowledges the complexity of gender relations, she nevertheless reintroduces a Conradian take on Africa, filled with an overwhelming range of negative representations and stereotypes. Thus, as argued earlier, the risk is that her novel serves to reassure a French audience with received notions as to what constitutes Africa *and* Africans—thereby perpetuating the kinds of negative constructs that have become all too common in France today and that operated at the service of those repressive measures implemented by the Ministry of Immigration, Integration, National Identity and Co-Development and which NDiaye has denounced. Ultimately, her novel can be potentially "reconstructed as a sensational rhetoric that appeals to an official French audience whose prejudices [therefore] can only be further confirmed by the authenticity of a narrative delivered by an African 'native' informer?" (Thomas, *Black France,* 140). Furthermore, when NDiaye claims that her work provides a space for beings "so rarely represented in French literature," she reveals the degree to which she is blinded by her own ignorance of the vast corpus of works that has already addressed these postcolonial concerns in recent years, including works by Abdourahman A. Waberi (*Aux États-Unis d'Afrique*), Laurent Gaudé (*Eldorado*), J. R. Essomba (*Le paradis du Nord*), Antoine Matha (*Épitaphe*), Fatou Diome (*Le ventre de l'Atlantique*), Alain Mabanckou (*Bleu-Blanc-Rouge*), and Mahi Binebine (*Cannibales: Traversée dans l'enfer de Gibraltar*); writers that have been warning people for years that a "monstrous France" awaits them beyond the ocean.[26]

These entangled transcolonial and transnational histories are intrinsic to NDiaye's novel, and she has not herself been immune from racist critiques. Her comments concerning Sarkozy's France first appeared in print in the August 2009 interview she granted the magazine *Les inrockuptibles* with Nelly Kaprièlian—therefore several months before receiving the Goncourt prize and not therefore in an attempt to exploit the platform and visibility accorded to recipients of such prestigious awards. However, upon being awarded the prize—an award which coincidently was given on the very same day that Minister Éric Besson launched the *National Identity Debate*—Éric Raoult (UMP [Union for a Popular Movement] mayor of Raincy and elected deputy for the Department of Seine-Saint-Denis) got wind of NDiaye's remarks and immediately wrote a letter to Frédéric Mitterrand, the minister of Culture and Communication. This letter is worth quoting at length:

> Mr. Éric Raoult would like to draw the attention of the Minister of Culture and Communication to the *principle of moderation* (devoir de réserve) expected of Goncourt Prize winners. The fact is that this prize, both in France and elsewhere in the world, is considered France's most prestigious and closely observed literary prize by numerous authors and amateurs of French literature. Winners of this prize must uphold national cohesion and the image of our country. Marie NDiaye's statements . . . are unacceptable. Her words exhibit a rare degree of violence, are disrespectful if not even insulting to the ministers of the Republic and even more so to the Head of State. It would seem to me that freedom of expression cannot be transformed into a right to insult or used to settle scores. A personality who carries the French literary flag must show a certain respect toward our

institutions, their role and what they represent. This is why I believe it would seem useful to remind the winners of this prize of the need to observe the principle of moderation, in other words to act responsibly and be of an exemplary nature.[27]

One could perhaps have ignored the disturbing implications of patriotic fervor (references to "the French literary flag") and the "principle of moderation" if it weren't for the fact that additional statements by Raoult also accompanied these comments: "*We* awarded her the Goncourt Prize because she has talent. . . . Now that she has received this prize, she can think as she likes, but as it happens she now has to be a kind of ambassador for our culture. . . . France has given her the Goncourt Prize" (emphasis added).

Yun Sun Limet has provided an insightful deconstruction of Raoult's statement which leaves us with no reason to think that NDiaye has a place in his conceptualization of the national "nous":

> *We:* who is this "we"? Is this speaker a member of the Goncourt jury? No, but this "we" stands for France, where the Goncourt jury operates as the symbolic representative of France, in which it includes itself, so as to better exclude and establish a distance from this other "her." "Us" against "her." . . . *For our culture:* "our," that echoes back to the "us/her" at the beginning of his statement; this "our" is clearly possessive and refers back to the speaker who can thus exclude from this culture the person identified with this "her."[28]

The context of the *National identity Debate* is of course all-important, since it (willfully?) stirred up racial tensions, and as Kaprièlian has argued:

> It is no coincidence that an elected UMP official should have attacked the author—moreover one of Senegalese origin—of such a book at the height of the debate on national identity. It would be a mistake to see in Éric Raoult little else than a kind of rogue moron, as the UMP would have us believe: the reality is that these statements are symptomatic of the insidiously racist climate and of the onslaught on freedom that have come to characterize Nicolas Sarkozy's France; Raoult says out loud what others are think. His utterances are serious: they express a willingness to censor criticism, opposition, freedom of expression, and they reveal a contempt for writers, and by extension for their freedom. ("Écris et tais-toi," 10)

Effectively, Raoult sets in motion a mechanism in which outdated expectations and hierarchies associated with an assimilated colonial *évolué* category are here reorganized and rationalized only to then be subsequently mapped onto the postcolonial subject. We are reminded here of NDiaye's inability to escape her perpetual status at the periphery, dependent on admission according to the imperatives of the dominant racial class, and sanctioned here for not having properly learned the *assimilation* lesson. Exemplars of assimilation and integration exist and have been rewarded, such as Gaston Kelman whose book, *Je suis noir et je n'aime pas le manioc* [I'm Black and I don't care for manioc], represents a kind of *defense and illustration* of the possibility of successful insertion into a color-blind Republic that can be called upon to invalidate the assertions and claims of visible minorities.[29] Kelman's public statements on race afforded him the appointment as adviser for a while to Éric Besson at the Ministry of Immigration, Integration, National Identity and Co-Development.

In the public debate that ensued, both NDiaye and Raoult called upon the Minister of Culture and Communication to weigh in. "I expect him to finally answer the question Éric Raoult put to him, to take a clear stance on this matter, and put an end to this unseemly saga,"[30] NDiaye explained. When Mitterrand finally intervened on November 12, 2009, in *Le Monde* newspaper, he was non-committal and merely defended the principle of free speech: "The Goncourt Prize is a private entity, and a remarkable one at that. And so, writers who are awarded this prize, and Marie NDiaye is a great writer, have every right to say whatever they like"; extending these principles and rights can also, therefore, protect Raoult the elected official, "a friend and worthy man who, as a citizen, as a parliamentarian, also has the right to say what he thinks."[31] The background to the question of belonging in French society can only be fully understood by returning to some of the objectives of the *National Identity Debate* as well as other recent incidents that have underscored the lingering presence of racial constructs in French society.

In his appointment letter of March 31, 2009, Besson is reminded that: "The promotion of our national identity should find itself at the heart of your action. . . . Our pride in being French will facilitate the integration of those foreigners we welcome in our country. How can one expect them to love France if we don't love her ourselves? In the eyes of new migrants, we should not only assume our pride in being French, but also celebrate it."[32] This question of belonging has emerged as a central tenet in contemporary French politics. During a session devoted to the debate at the French National Assembly on December 8, 2009, Besson presented the main issues and then responded to questions from other deputies. Among his most controversial claims was the suggestion that there exist a "hiérarchie entre les appartenances" (a hierarchy between forms of belonging) that could be employed to distinguish between different forms of societal belonging: "We belong to several things. As for me—and this remains up for debate—I believe there exists a hierarchy when it comes to belonging. People may well have a personal history and be proud their roots, but there nevertheless exists a melting pot: namely the French Republic and French nationality which for me, impose a hierarchy between forms of belonging."[33] Naturally, the subtext here has everything to do with what it means *to be* French—not in and of itself—but rather in contradistinction to what it means *to not be* French, namely a goal that can ultimately only be achieved by measuring the "integration of those of foreign origin" and by proposing "measures that will improve the appreciation of the values of national identity at each stage of the integration process," that is by implementing an apparatus that would enhance the dissemination of "the values of national identity with those of foreign origin entering or spending time on our national territory."[34] Thus, when Raoult (cited earlier) calls upon NDiaye to "uphold national cohesion" and to "carry the French literary flag," he is merely echoing Besson's call for patriotism, as exemplified by such requests: "all young French people should sing the national anthem at least once a year, if need be after a class session devoted to this theme."[35]

There is a fascinating precedent to this polemic. Senegalese-born Rama Yade, who held different ministerial appointments (Secretary of State for Human Rights and Secretary of State for Sports), developed a reputation in the French media as an outspoken member of Sarkozy's administration in which she served until 2010. She has been described as "insoumise" (rebellious, insubordinate) and criticized for not being a "team player" and for refusing to tow the Party line.[36] In *Comment je suis devenu français* (How I Became French), a book edited by Jacqueline Rémy, Rama Yade evoked her surprise at being informed of the need to respect republican values in the official letter of notification she received informing her that her petition for French citizenship had been successful.[37] When Yade added that she had received the news at a time in her life when she had not yet come to terms with her biculturalism and "national allegiance" (she was only twenty-one), "In those days, I often said to myself that if war broke out between Senegal and France, I'd be on the side of my country of origin," two UMP deputies (Jacques Myard and Christian Vanneste) denounced this "double allégéance" (divided allegiance).[38] To observers in Britain and the United States, to cite just two examples, such a reaction to the perceived incompatibility of national origin with citizenship may seem striking, yet in France the very individuals concerned by these responses have often been the first to reject the positive qualities of such diverse backgrounds. "Why," Yade is asked by the journalist François Soudan, "why don't you acknowledge your dual belonging, your two identities? Just declare that you are in the position you are in because you are competent and because you are black?" And for Yade to respond: "You'll never hear me say that. My trajectory is a classic one, that of the republican meritocracy. Nicolas Sarkozy [the President] and François Fillon [the Prime Minister] trusted me because of my capabilities. If you just needed a black face, well there were other choices in the UMP Party. I don't want to be judged based on my appearance, but rather for what I do. One should never allow oneself to be contained by skin color."[39] The parallels between Marie NDiaye's and Rama Yade's exposure to the French authorities are compelling, sharpening the need to further disentangle the knotted intersection of government, press, and cultural discourses in evaluating the question of race in French society today.

In the case of NDiaye, there was already an interesting way of approaching this, given that she had written the preface to her brother Pap Ndiaye's (they have elected to spell their surnames differently, in his case with a lower case "d" following the capitalized "N") 2008 book *La condition noire: Essai sur une minorité ethnique française.*[40] The intersection therefore of their respective intellectual trajectories—the one as a writer of fiction and the other as a social scientist—around the question of *race* and *Africa* is interesting. The short story, "Trois sœurs" (Three Sisters),[41] which is positioned as a preface to her brother's essay on ethnic minorities in France, addresses the complexity of multiracial identities, divided allegiances, and the self-definition of identity balanced against the perceptions and expectations of others. Indeed, as Catherine Coquery-Vidrovitch has argued, "Marie NDiaye's short-story, written to introduce her brother's book, conveys the situation admirably: whether a black person pretends to ignore it or suffer from it, the first contact with a fellow citizen (a white person from the hexagon) is, whether we like it or not, a reaction based on color (or facial features), experienced as a need to prove that, even though one is black (or *beur*), that one is French."[42] In fact, NDiaye has stated that her growing awareness of being black came as a result of discussions with her brother and from reading his work: "'I never asked myself the question until I read his work, and he talked to me about it" (Kaprèlian, "Marie Ndiaye: aux prises avec le monde," 32). In other words, a *discovery* that must have been relatively recent given that Pap Ndiaye's own research had focused almost exclusively on the United States and the Black American experience[43] until after the 2005 uprisings in France and the creation of the Conseil représentatif des associations noires (CRAN, Representative Council for Black Associations), in which he has been active. This new way of conceptualizing and interpreting a complicated African-French history as a colonial and postcolonial experience—affording a mixed-race novelist a newfound "empathy" with African women and a social scientist a shift in fieldwork orientation from ethnic minorities in the United States to those in contemporary France—has surely infused the narrative of *Trois femmes puissantes.* To this end, the arguments formulated by Pap Ndiaye in his *La condition noire* become relevant because of the insights they can offer us. A symbiotic link can therefore be established between the preface to a work of social science and the findings of social science in turn refracted into a work of fiction.

For Pap Ndiaye, new forms of identification and solidarity originate in the shared experience of discrimination. His inquiry is structured around "phenomena through which specific groups, 'minorities,' experience discrimination, find themselves the object of differential treatment because of illegitimate criteria" (*La condition noire,* 21–24). When one relocates visibility within French republican structures as the primary factor in the experience of discrimination—that is, of social exclusion—then one can only conclude that "the difference between black French people and other French people whose parents came from elsewhere is that the French identity of the former will always be treated suspiciously" (Ndiaye, *La condition noire,* 42). With this realization in mind, with the acknowledgement and recognition that *race* continues to operate as the symbolic marker of difference, "It thus becomes a priority to identify those discriminations founded on ethno-racial criteria, and to name them if one wants to fight against them, rather than covering them up by adopting a pseudo-republican approach" (*La condition noire,* 285). As we saw in chapter 3, the *National Identity Debate* fostered perceptions that some French people are *more* French than others and gave credence to the idea that social hierarchies exist. These constructs have roots that can be traced back to the colonial era because "The idea of race—understood as the hierarchical difference between groups—concerns republican citizenship. Some are more citizens than others: the creation of a *colonial citizenship* in 1946 that was different to the citizenship applied in the metropole, was the most striking example of this."[44] Yet, Pap Ndiaye's conclusions are that "For the most part, France's blacks hold on to their French identity and their eventual association with this category has its roots in a minoritarian logic rather than a factionalist one" (*La condition noire,* 368). However, repeated public statements by the authorities have contributed to dissatisfaction, disidentification, and disengagement.

For the writer Faïza Guène, who grew up in a French *banlieue* (housing project), this has given rise to a form of oppositional politics: "I realized something important, which is that not many people from my background, with my social and cultural origins, are represented in the media or have a voice.

I got this opportunity, and now I realize I don't have the right to pass it up. It's rare for someone to speak out, especially in a field that's not normally reserved for us. 'French literature'—I've got no right to touch it!"[45] When interviewing NDiaye, Kaprèlian raised an important question: "In England and in the United States, there are many writers from different ethnic backgrounds, such as Zadie Smith, Monica Ali, Hari Kunzru, and so forth. In France, we don't have the same kind of writers. How do you account for this?" ("Marie Ndiaye: aux prises avec le monde," 33). In response, NDiaye remarked: "For the most part, writers are people who have pursued advanced studies, who know how to handle language, and that might not be the case yet for our minorities who feel left out of a certain kind of knowledge . . . *Most French writers seem to come out of an enlightened bourgeoisie,* they are educated, and this is a fairly restricted milieu" ("Marie Ndiaye: aux prises avec le monde," 33, emphasis added). Raoult's comments reveal deep-seated assumptions and prejudice against certain categories of French people; they are reprehensible and to be denounced as such. Yet, as much as NDiaye's work has endeavored to feature those "victims" of African social relations, those "so rarely represented in French literature," one has to wonder whether her experiences before and after the Goncourt have altered her way of conceiving internal (domestic) cultural and political dynamics and to recognize that "French writers DO NOT ALL come out of an enlightened bourgeoisie" (my capitalized alterations) but rather from diverse ethnic backgrounds and *banlieues* neighborhoods, often those very spaces in French society in which the experience of "monstrous France" has been most tangible.[46] As Moudileno has argued:

> When NDiaye issues an almost legal disclaimer of any affiliation with the category "romancière africaine" (African woman novelist), she is not only resisting the identity attached to this socio-literary label but also defending her position according to which she believes that such an identification would ultimately exclude her from the French hexagonal corpus she has worked so hard to conquer. Having resisted that label earlier in her career, she has, in a way, refused the temptation of celebrity. Thus, having elected to distance herself from such categorizations—a repression which may very well have provided the circumstances for absolute, unequivocal fame in French *belles lettres*—she now finds herself years later in a position to allow the postcolonial origin to find its way back into her private and professional identity. (Moudileno, 72)

In fact, for a long time, NDiaye claims, she was "shelved in the Francophone section in the FNAC, because of her name."[47] Having now vacated a space on the "francophone" shelves and joined the *literary we,* it remains crucial for the author to remain attentive to and aware of the existence of those *others*—writers who have often been left behind *in* and *by* France. Their names are Faïza Guène, Mehdi Charef, Abdourahman Waberi, Ferrudja Kessas, Farida Belghoul, Fatou Diome, Azouz Begag, Soraya Nini, Thomté Ryam, Gaston-Paul Effa, Léonora Miano, Alain Mabanckou, Mohamed Razane, and Rachid Djaïdani. A similar critique can be made of the *littérature-monde* movement which, in its own concern with having "the center placed on an equal plane with other centers" ("Toward a World Literature in French," 56), also neglected to include any *Beur* or *banlieue* authors in their original manifesto.

The fact that Marie NDiaye currently resides in Berlin may seem all the more paradoxical given that the twentieth anniversary of the dismantling of the Berlin Wall has only just been celebrated. Coinciding with this historic moment, a petition circulated calling for the dismantling of another symbolic wall—the Ministry of Immigration, Integration, National Identity and Co-Development—one that was being erected brick by brick with fear-mongering and ignorance in Germany's neighbor to the west, where "[r]efugees and migrants, in particular those who originate from the Mediterranean region and Africa, and their descendants, are separated by a national 'we' that is not only imaginary since its boundaries are evident at material, administrative and ideological levels."[48] As one reflects on the cultural, economic, political and social challenges that have come to define existing forms of global communication, contact and exchange, one can only hope that it will be possible—now that the Sarkozy presidency has ended—to move beyond the kind of divisive discourse epitomized by political figures such as Besson, Raoult, and Sarkozy (among a long list of others, of course, and especially in the guise of Marine Le Pen and the Front National) when the homeostasis is displaced and those mechanisms deployed at the service of the imposition of hierarchies of belonging rendered obsolete by newly configured models of empathy.

7

The Euro-Mediterranean

LITERATURE AND MIGRATION

Africa is not fiction. Africa is people, real people.

—*Chinua Achebe*[1]

One has to understand that the most basic comfort level
necessary to survive here during the Winter
is something people dream of over there

—*Dany Lafferière*[2]

Economic, political, and social asymmetries account for transitions in migratory patterns within countries and continents and beyond strict national/continental borders. This has been convincingly demonstrated by migratory movements triggered by the "Arab Spring," whereby new geopolitical realignments revealed the extent of the interpenetration of global politics and globalized societies and new arrivals at the European Union's external borders in Corsica, Cyprus, Greece, Malta, Italy, and Spain. These prompted the E.U. to publish a "Communication on Migration," stating that "recent events of historic proportion in the Southern Mediterranean have confirmed the need for a strong and common EU policy in the field of migration and asylum."[3] We have seen how politicians have instrumentalized the precariousness of displaced populations (France's leader of the extreme right-wing Front National, Marine Le Pen, for example, made a much-publicized visit to the Italian island of Lampedusa on March 14, 2011). Recourse to the *global south* as a category has made it possible to circumscribe those disadvantaged regions from which emigration is most significant, while also highlighting the unidirectionality of human mobility toward those economically prosperous geographic zones in the E.U.[4] Naturally, these migratory routes and patterns inscribe themselves alongside a multiplicity of other twenty-first-century transnational networks.[5] Indeed, if migration has emerged as a key geometric coordinate of globalization today, then so too has the concern with *controlling* the planetary circulation of human beings (labor forces, asylum seekers, refugees), particularly when it comes to the African continent. As Paul Gilroy has argued, "The war against asylum seekers, refugees, and economic migrants offers a chance to consider not just changing patterns of governmentality, commerce, and labor but to examine the cultural and ethical contours of Europe where the notion of public good and the practice of politics seem to be in irreversible decline—undone by a combination of consumer culture, privatization, and the neoliberal ideology."[6]

Political leaders recognized the benefits to national interests of harmonizing European imperial ambitions in Africa, and this awareness provided the rationale for the 1884–1885 Berlin Congress. Such historical antecedents to trans-colonial developments in E.U. policy-making are hard to ignore particularly when one considers changes in immigration rules and regulations. "Africans were citizens of the French Union according to the 1946 Constitution and in theory at least free to circulate on French territory," Pap Ndiaye has reminded us, and: "Independence did nothing to alter this relationship given the bilateral agreements that were signed between African countries and France. French industry needed labor, . . . and in those days it was easy to enter France, even illegally, find work and later put one's papers in order. But a decisive change occurred in 1974 when the borders were closed off to work-related immigration from non-European countries."[7] In relative terms, though, policies implemented during the later years of the twentieth century could very well be considered moderate when one compares them to more recent incarnations. As Saskia Sassen has shown, "Strengthening control is what the European Union is gearing up to do when it comes to immigration from outside its borders . . . moving toward the construction of a sort of Berlin wall across the Mediterranean and into the Atlantic."[8]

These observations can be illustrated with a number of concrete examples. As we have seen repeatedly throughout this book, the creation of the Ministry for Immigration, Integration, National Identity and Co-Development underscored the urgency for Sarkozy's government of controlling migratory flows and collaborating with *sending* countries. France was successful in extending these policy objectives to other E.U. member-states, and achieving a *common* and *coordinated* policy has also been made possible as a result of modifications to economic and political alignments—and treaties via the E.U. Neighborhood Policy with its southern neighbors—between different regions of the world, most significantly in relation to the Mediterranean where "part of North Africa is drawn toward the Mediterranean. Without necessarily espousing Europe's cultural values, it is trying to bind its economic future to that of Western Europe."[9]

The first matter to address concerns the very conceptualization and definition of the Mediterranean for the purposes of policy-making and international agreements. As we shall see, this approach bears no resemblance to the kind of Euro-Mediterranean alignment proposed by Etienne Balibar in his book—*We, The People of Europe? Reflections on Transnational Citizenship*—in which a longer history of imperial and postcolonial interconnectedness correlates with the realities of twenty-first-century existence.[10] Sarkozy—who was been a long-term opponent of Turkey's accession to E.U. member status, repeatedly explained and sought to justify his position by arguing that Turkey was a "Central Asian" country. Given that French Overseas Departments (Guadeloupe, Martinique, French Guiana, Reunion, and Mayotte) are connected with Africa, Latin America, the Caribbean, and so forth, the E.U.'s external borders have thus *never* been strictly those of the continental boundaries of Europe. The way in which Sarkozy thinks about identity is therefore disconcerting, crucial in fact in order to better understand France's particular interest in promoting the *Union for the Mediterranean Project* (UfM, Euro-Mediterranean Partnership, EUROMED), formerly known as the Barcelona Process.[11] The UfM has thus far established cooperation agreements with twenty-seven E.U. member countries and sixteen Southern Mediterranean, African, and Middle Eastern countries. As Virginie Lydie has argued, "European initiatives such as the 'Euro-Maghreb' process, 'Lisbon process,' and 'Barcelona process' take us toward greater interdependence" and have contributed toward actualizing the reality of such a union.[12] In turn, the objectives of the UfM can only be understood by examining the context of E.U. policy objectives.[13]

The UfM has established certain priorities that include cooperation on questions such as environmental and civil protection initiatives, education, transportation networks, and business. However, the question of migration has been foregrounded and inscribes itself as an extension of existing E.U. priorities. In 2007, the E.U. published its *Third Annual Report on Migration and Integration,* seeking to "analyze changes and describe actions taken on the admission and integration of third-country nationals at the EU and national level. They provide an overview of policy developments and contribute to strengthening integration measures and the promotion of policy initiatives for the more effective management of immigration in Europe."[14] The first priority for the French authorities (who were certainly not alone of course in seeking consensus on this question) was to find agreement that would allow for greater articulation, coordination, and harmonization of immigration policy.[15] The foundation for such an agreement had been carefully delineated in MEMO/08/402 on June 17, 2008 ("A Common immigration policy for Europe: principles, actions and tools"), in which E.U. members confirmed and reasserted that "further developing a common immigration policy complementing Member States' policies remains a fundamental priority in order to respond to the challenges and opportunities of globalization."[16] This would shortly be followed by a major new agreement, namely the *European Pact on Migration and Asylum.*

Adopted by the European Council of October 15–16, 2008, the Pact outlined five key areas:

- To organize legal immigration to take account of the priorities, needs and reception capabilities determined by each Member State, and to encourage integration;
- To control illegal immigration by ensuring that illegal immigrants return to their country of origin or a country of transit;
- To make border controls more effective;
- To construct a Europe of asylum;
- To create a comprehensive partnership with countries of origin and of transit in order to encourage synergy between migration and development.[17]

Subsequently, a "Final Statement" was issued November 3–4, 2008, concerning the "Barcelona Process: Union for the Mediterranean," providing a comprehensive outline of the structure of such a "Union":

> The Heads of State and Government agreed to build on and reinforce the successful elements of the Barcelona Process by upgrading their relations, incorporating more co-ownership in their multilateral cooperation framework and delivering concrete benefits for the citizens of the region. This first Summit marked an important step forward for the Euro-Mediterranean Partnership while also highlighting the EU and Mediterranean partners' unwavering commitment and common political will to make the goals of the Barcelona Declaration—the creation of an area of peace, stability, security and shared prosperity, as well as full respect of democratic principles, human rights and fundamental freedoms and promotion of understanding between cultures and civilizations in the Euro-Mediterranean region—a reality.[18]

Of central concern here is of course the issue of "irregular immigration," on which the E.U. has made a formal declaration: "Migrants entering the EU clandestinely via land and sea routes, or those who have acquired false travel documents, often put themselves at the hands of criminal organizations. In some cases, migrants continue to depend on these criminals after they have arrived in the EU. Several thousand people are trafficked into the EU or within the EU every year. With a view to tackling human trafficking networks and smugglers, the EU has established tougher rules for action against criminals involved in trafficking in human beings, combined with better assistance for victims."[19]

Inadequate models and principles of governance—resulting from internal corruption and external exploitation—have resulted in deterioration in the standard of living in many parts of Africa. As South African author Breyten Breytenbach has argued:

> Europe is not serious about Africa; it even neglects to service the consequences of its own earlier bargains, then made in the name of the colonial pact and ill-considered structural adjustments. Now the European Union recommends a neo-liberal economy, which in practice means the perpetuation of authoritarian regimes, condemning Africa to further military turmoil and civil wars. . . . The logical outcome will be further decay of the social and political fabric, the continuing decline of conditions of life, the desperate attempts of people to get into Europe at all costs—and Fortress Europe's only response will be police repression.[20]

Breytenbach's assessment of the situation has of course proved accurate, and Navianetham Pillay, the United Nations High Commissioner for Human Rights publicly criticized on May 30, 2011, certain E.U. countries for discussing migrants as "burdens." Prior to this, February, 25, 2010, Éric Besson (as the French Minister of Immigration, Integration, National Identity and Co-Development), had argued at the E.U. on the occasion of a meeting devoted to the fight against irregular immigration in the Mediterranean, that the E.U. should focus on proposed measures designed to strengthen the protection of external borders and fight against clandestine (illegal) immigration: training border patrol officers, dismantling human trafficking networks, implementing new surveillance technologies, integrated border management strategy, expansion of EUROSUR (European Border Surveillance System) and FRONTEX (European Agency for the Management of Operational Cooperation at the External Borders), common standards on return and readmission (known as the "return directive"), and collaborative efforts between countries bordering the Mediterranean of coastguard and naval services.

Many writers have turned their attention to these realities by focusing on a broad range of thematic issues associated with the phenomena of child soldiers, genocidal practices, and disintegrating state structures, thereby introducing new forms of political commitment and narrating the latest biographical chapter in the history of African-European relations, while also pointing to new directions for African literature.[21] Hakim Abderrezak has even coined the term "illiterature" as "a deliberate compression of 'illegal' and ''literature' to re-appropriate illegality" in an attempt at describing this new category of writing.[22] Some fifty years since the majority of colonized African countries achieved political independence, one is left with the task of evaluating the role of literature in documenting and recording the evidentiary mode. How effective has literature been in humanizing individual and collective experience and in raising political consciousness with regard to contemporary governance and the impact of twenty-first-century globalization?

As recently as 2001, in her insightful analysis of the question of hospitality in the context of European immigration, Mireille Rosello suggested that "It may take a while before [film] directors choose to reflect on the most recent evolution of migration patterns and to portray undocumented immigrants."[23] Today, there does exist a wide range of works by authors from both north and south of the Sahara (and from numerous other geographic locations), addressing postcolonial circumstances, exhibiting a particular concern with the plight of migrants, asylum seekers, and refugees.[24] Ursula Biemann has explored the prevalence of news stories featuring the new points of contact between Europe and the African continent, describing "Capsized boats and clandestine immigrants washing up on European shores: these are the dramatic images that put Europe's southern border in the news again and again. The media seem to say that these images communicate the essence of the border in its most compressed and climactic form. But there is no defining, dramatic image that can narrate the endless story of inclusion and exclusion. There can be no violent icon to which the event of crossing is reducible, only the plurality of passages, their diverse embodiments, their motivations and articulations."[25]

When perusing the expansive shelves of the African literary canon, one will invariably be faced with the incontrovertible fact of the importance of circulation and movement in both colonial era texts (Ferdinand Oyono, Camara Laye, Ousmane Socé, Cheikh Hamidou Kane, and Bernard Dadié) and postcolonial and/or post-migratory narratives (Gaston-Paul Effa, Alain Mabanckou, Calixthe Beyala, Simon Njami, Fatou Diome, and Léonora Miano). Whether the engagement is with *migritude, Parisianism,* or *Afropeans/Afrodescendants,*[26] cross-cultural and transnational encounters remain inextricably connected with the symbolic value of Europe. Whereas disillusionment had often accompanied the adventures of (post)colonial protagonists, the historical relationship with the *global south* has today been updated and reformulated according to new coordinates associated with an economic *Eldorado*—access to and demand for which have become more difficult with the dramatic increase in border-control mechanisms. The result has been an exponential rise in the death toll of vulnerable economic migrants attempting to reach the southern landmarks of *Europe* that are Lampedusa, Gibraltar, Sicily, the Canary islands, Ceuta, and Melilla (the last two being Spanish enclaves on the *African* continent).[27] Naturally, these questions have also been examined in several works of non-fiction, such as those by Omar Ba, Serge Daniel, Fabrizio Gatti, Emmanuel Bribosia, and Andrea Rea, and in films by Costa-Gavras (*A l'ouest l'eden,* 2009) and Merzak Allouache (*Harragas,* 2010).[28] The focus here will be provided by the sociocultural and geopolitical *new world order* as it is treated in a selection of works published between 1996 and 2009 by authors (from Europe, the Maghreb, the United States, and sub-Saharan Africa) as diverse as J. R. Essomba, Mahi Binebine, Alain Mabanckou, Salim Jay, Abdourahman Waberi, Tahar Ben Jelloun, and Abasse Ndione, committed to the process of drawing attention to urgent humanitarian challenges.

The symbolic value of France (and its capital city Paris, in particular), has informed the francocentrist quests of young African protagonists for generations.[29] Tanhoé Bertin's opening words in Bernard Dadié's 1959 novel *Un nègre à Paris*—"Good news, my friend, good news! I have a ticket to Paris . . . yes, Paris! The very same Paris we've so often talked and dreamed about!"—confirm this.[30] Yet, both the jubilant tone and physical possession of legal documentation for entry into France emerge as distant echoes to earlier arrangements between Europe and Africa. For today, "Europe," what was once "an idea, a belief, a conviction," has changed: "What is a human endeavor worth if it is not founded on an idea, a common idea, a shared idea (or to be shared), a commitment to look to the future with a little more humanity."[31] The lure of former colonial centers cannot be underestimated: transcolonial connectivity remains a powerful vector in determining the migratory objectives, although this is no longer the exclusive factor and African-European relations have been reconfigured. The Mediterranean has emerged as a privileged site for exploring global dynamics, containing both proximity and distance, constituting a link but also an obstacle and a barrier, "a magnet that attracts us. . . . A magnet fourteen kilometers in size right there in the Mediterranean."[32]

Discrepancies are to be found in the way in which these Mediterranean crossings are presented. Some critics, ignoring the E.U.'s demographic and labor needs, often characterize migrants as opportunistic and burdensome to national economies, whereas other analysts have tended to reframe the issue by attributing responsibility to capitalistic market forces. As Juan Goytisolo has argued, "Immigrants who have reached our shores, having overcome all kinds of obstacles and risked their lives, deserve humane treatment and respect. Immigration will remain inevitable as long as its causes subsist—the monstrous inequality between the North and South."[33] Demand for cheap labor partially explains certain *pull* factors. As the Belgian comic book author and illustrator Jean-Philippe Stassen observed in his project "Les visiteurs de Gibraltar," "The Strait of Gibraltar, through which the Atlantic Ocean enters the Mediterranean (or through which the Mediterranean opens into the Atlantic), is the closest point between Africa and Europe."[34] The symbiotic levels of interpenetration between Africa *in* Europe and Europe *in* Africa are exemplified by the tangible presence of Spanish enclaves in Morocco (Ceuta and Melilla): "I'm speaking of Africa because people over there have walked for days to get this far, to Tangiers, and they are told that Tangiers is already Europe, you can smell it, you can see Europe and its lights, you can touch it, it smells good, it's waiting for you, all that is left is for you to cross fourteen little kilometers, or better even, just go as far as Ceuta and you'll already be in Europe, yes, Ceuta and Melilla are European towns, you just need to scale the barbed-wire fence."[35] Yet, in Laila Lalami's novel *Hope and Other Dangerous Pursuits,* Murad wonders "how fourteen kilometers could separate not just two countries but two universes."[36] Not only is history blurred and ambiguous, but so is geography, revealing complex colonial and postcolonial relations. The journey from different locations on the African continent to the Mediterranean coastline is itself hazardous—Fabrizio Gatti's findings published in *Bilal sur la route des clandestins* corroborate such statements—yet, "when you reach the Mediterranean the worst will still be to come."[37]

What then might be the potentialities of literature in humanizing these experiences? According to Alain Mabanckou, "History brought us face to face," and "The report has been written (or is yet to be written) in the books that will be read by the generations to come" (*L'Europe depuis l'Afrique,* 31). Postmigrant narratives have provided disquieting accounts of the social conditions in Europe. But what motivates individuals to emigrate; what are the *push* factors? In J. R. Essomba's *Le Paradis du nord,* the central protagonist Jojo is ready to risk everything to live in France: "Others would throw themselves at their bible or their rosary to pray, but every morning when he woke up or before going to sleep at night, he would be engrossed in a map of France. . . . Yes, just like the freeways in France, his dreams converged on Paris. . . . For him, Paris was synonymous with paradise."[38] The myth of a French "paradise" to which he subscribes is juxtaposed with the local "hell" (Essomba, *Le Paradis du nord,* 35), a chaotic postcolony where "The country's future was like an ellipsis" and in which extraterritorial influences have merely updated colonial ones, reflecting rapidly mutating global alignments whereby "Today it's the Cowboy embassy and tomorrow it'll be the red, white and blue consulate; . . . everyone just wants to get out of this shit-hole of a country."[39]

A long list of factors has contributed to this exodus, including weak economies, limited employment prospects, sub-standard governance, dysfunctional nation-states, poor environmental conditions, and industrialized offshore fishing practices, driving young people to seek "a better future in Europe."[40] A conversation between Azal and his neighbor Malika in Tahar Ben Jelloun's novel *Partir* summarizes this desperation:

> What do you want to do later?
> Leave.
> Leave? But that's not a job!
> Once I get out of here I'll have a job.
> But where do you want to go?
> Anywhere, across there, for example.
> To Spain?
> Yes, Spain, França, whatever, I'm already living there in my dreams. (*Partir,* 120)[41]

For this generation, "forced to leave" (Ndione, *Mbëkë mi,* 24), even "hope" has become a "dangerous pursuit" (Lalami). Poverty, this "epidemic" (Ben Jelloun, *Partir,* 186), exacerbated by new economic disparities, compels the young to flee "their countries classified Heavily Indebted Poor Countries [PPTE], inhabited by people who were worn-out, sickened and weighed-down by waste, cholera, insecurity, water, fuel and gas shortages, the unpredictable power cuts, high-cost of basic commodities, massive financial scandals, the factories and companies that were closing down, arbitrary arrests, the repeated assaults on journalists and opponents that went unpunished, recurrent floods, barefaced corruption reaching the highest levels of government, the administration and legal system, chronic unemployment among young people"(Ndione, *Mbëkë mi,* 11). These inequities become all the more apparent when one considers the rules and regulations that govern the circulation of people. Tourism thus emerges as a paradoxical issue given that many of the sites along the Mediterranean are popular destinations for European travelers. Salim Jay concentrates on this aspect of global circulation in *Tu ne traverseras pas le détroit,* and Mahi Binebine, in *Cannibales: Traversée dans l'enfer de Gibraltar,* describes the manner in which locals covet European passports:

> What a waste, don't you think, all those red, blue, green and maroon passports moldering in the pockets of all those ripped jeans. Ah, now if I had one, I'd have taken care of it, I'd have cosseted it, pressed it to my heart, I'd have hidden it somewhere the thieving and envious wouldn't have been able to find it, sewn it into my own skin, right in the middle of my chest, so I'd only have to unbutton my shirt to show it when I was crossing borders. What were they after, these foreigners, poking around in our poverty? What did they want from us, these people who taunted us with their freedom to come and go as they pleased?[42]

Having elected to leave, the physical journey exposes migrants to a whole range of dangers precisely because the illegality of the Mediterranean crossing they are poised to attempt heightens their vulnerability. Smugglers and human traffickers negotiate the transportation of stowaways and human cargo, navigating makeshift, overcrowded, precarious boats and unseaworthy crafts. African migrants are now joined at the gates of *Fortress Europe* by a global underclass hailing from other parts of the world. It will seem all the more paradoxical that "just when the economic, environmental and social gap between the two sides of the Mediterranean is widening, forcing more and more people away from their homes into exile, Europe is reinforcing border protection in order to allow access only to those migrants which it needs."[43] However, and as mentioned earlier, as demand for entry has grown so too have preventive measures: "Europeans are fighting a war right now against clandestine immigration" (Essomba, *Le Paradis du nord,* 47). No matter the degree to which border control mechanisms are strengthened, these will do little to curb migratory flows and "immigrants will carry on clamoring at the gates of Europe, ever poorer and even hungrier. The batons will only get harder but the damned will always come faster" (Gaudé, *Eldorado,* 246). As Alessandro Dal Lago has convincingly argued, "Equating the migrants with the enemy might seem misleading in so far as it is associated with a political definition of foreigners. It goes without saying that no war has ever been declared against migrants; and they don't display, obviously, their relative status as enemies. But migrants are in fact treated as enemies because they have the temerity to invade our national space. It is in fact typical of legislation to intern, expel, or deprive 'enemies of the state' of their rights" (*Non-Persons,* 57). Confronted with media images and statistics on death tolls attributed to Mediterranean crossings, one has to reflect additionally on the limits of empathy and tolerance and how literature can articulate such frameworks, particularly as a way of countering the debasing official discourse and accompanying claims that Europe is being invaded and its social fabric eroded.

Literature provides a space in which new social configurations can be mapped out and in which one can reflect on ties between the *local* and the *global,* the individual and the collective. These are questions that have taken on new meaning as globalization has increased the possibilities of interconnectedness and interculturality. Thus, when confronted with the "undesirables" (Jay, *Tu ne traverseras pas le détroit,* 49) of the contemporary era, one has to wonder along with Salim Jay what it will take for "people to put themselves in our shoes" (*Tu ne traverseras pas le* détroit, 55). This is, of course, a matter of perspective. Dany Laferrière has contemplated what might be at stake in achieving awareness of this dynamic and reversing the perspective:

> Everything is on the move on this planet.
> From above one can see the south
> In constant movement.
> Entire populations heading
> North in search of better lives.
> And once everyone has gathered there
> We will fall overboard. (*L'Enigme du retour,* 47)

A shift in focus can allow for an apprehension of the other. In *Aux Etats-Unis d'Afrique* (In the United States of Africa), Franco-Djiboutian author Abdourahman Waberi reverses the parameters of north/south economic relations as a way of thinking the relational.[44] Thus, "The cream of international diplomacy also meets in Banjul; they are supposedly settling the fate of millions of Caucasian refugees of various ethnic groups . . . not to mention the skeletal boat people from the northern Mediterranean, at the end of their rope from dodging all the mortar shells and missiles that darken the unfortunate lands of Euramerica" (Waberi, *In the United States of Africa,* 4). The resulting critique of Europe shares points of commonality with the works of a number of eighteenth-century French authors (Montesquieu, Voltaire, and others) who had also experimented with such constructs as a way of formulating political and social critiques by inverting accepted norms and standards so as to mirror back discourse. The "federation of the United States of Africa" (Waberi, *In the United States of Africa,* 5) is now the site of vibrant globalization, made possible because of an extensive system of highways connecting different regions of the continent. This new paradigm extends to a longer history—anchored in slavery and colonialism as a way of highlighting the contributions these systems made to wealth and prosperity, and the *French Atlantic Triangle* described by Christopher Miller now finds itself with new coordinates, "Twenty-three. That is the number of slave ports in Eritrea, Nubia, Somalia, and all of blessed northeast Africa . . . Ports once watered with the sweat and blood of bold workers from the West" (Waberi, *In the United States of Africa,* 32).[45] The juxtaposition of these two worlds allows for a humanization of oppression, pointing to the capacity for exploitation and xenophobia on *both* sides, whereby "the least scrupulous of our newspapers have abandoned all restraint for decades and fan the flames of fear" (Waberi, *In the United States of Africa,* 8), thereby unifying the community against a common alien: "The Southern cattlemen, the Maghreb mounted police, the Tibesti rattlesnakes, internal security agents, the border patrol, the coast guards, the Sherpas of Kilimanjaro—everybody eagerly jumped into the hunt for immigrants" (Waberi, *In the United States of Africa,* 20).

Rather than Africans seeking entry into *Fortress Europe,* we have to contend with the fact that "[t]oday even more than yesterday, our African lands attract all kinds of people crushed by poverty: trollops with their feet powdered by the dust of exodus; opponents of their regimes with a ruined conscience; mangy kids with pulmonary diseases; bony, shriveled old people. People thrown into the ordeal of wandering the stony paths of exile" (Waberi, *In the United States of Africa,* 15). Thus, whether in Waberi's fictional world or in the context of contemporary Italian politics, as examined in Laurent Gaudé's novel *Eldorado,* law enforcement officers and border patrol agents accept their mission to "protect" their territory. In training, the advice is, "They said we were there to guard the gates of the citadel. 'You are the city walls of Europe.' That's what they told us. 'This is a war, gentlemen. Make no mistake. There's no shooting or bombing but it's a war and you're the front line. You mustn't let them overrun you. You have to hold out. There are more and more of them and Fortress Europe needs you'" (Gaudé, *Eldorado,* 65–66). However, gradually achieving greater awareness of this spectacle of human suffering that defines his job patrolling the coastline, Salvatore Piracci (the main character in *Eldorado*) identifies the mutually constitutive nature of his activities, of his symbiotic connection to global migrants, whereby his success is possible "only because others failed" (Gaudé, *Eldorado,* 244). The realization of the futility of the mission is also mediated by the recognition and identification—the encounter with the other—where empathy materializes as a bidirectional process in which the other is no longer *othered.* "Deep down," Salvatore realizes, "the whole business of immigrants and frontiers was meaningless. . . . There was one boat looking for another. Men setting out to save other men, in a sort of tacit fraternity. Because they could not let the sea swallow up boats, or let the waves close over other people's lives without making some effort to find them" (Gaudé, *Eldorado,* 72–73).

The practice of humanizing complex economic, political, and social issues remains one of the greatest challenges of twenty-first-century globalization. Indeed, each generation has invariably been confronted with new forms of societal dissymmetry; today, complex diasporic networks serve to emphasize that "European identity cannot be shaped by excluding those who contributed to its grandeur. Those of us with African origins are watching Europe and hoping, for its own salvation, that it will also look at us" (Mabanckou, *L'Europe depuis l'Afrique,* 45). The dynamism of contemporary writing (whether Francophone African or other), as clearly evidenced by both the qualitative and quantitative nature of literary output since 2000, remains incontestable. In fact, it is literature that is best-equipped to imagine and define the kinds of human interrelationships that will enable translation and mediation—for exchange that is cultural and political—introducing a process of identification and therefore humanization in which one is left asking: And what if "we" were this "other"? Maybe, after all, that is what the character Adama Traoré secretly hopes for:

> If narratives can bloom again, if languages, words, and stories can circulate again, if people can learn to identify with characters from beyond their borders, it will assuredly be a first step toward peace. A movement of identification, projection, and compassion. That's the solution. And it is exactly the opposite of the worried—and worrying—identity so widely cultivated. Instead of the "we" so proudly trumpeted, the "we" flexing its muscles, puffing up its pectorals, it is another "we," diffracted, interactive, translated, a waiting, listening "we"—in short a dialoguing "we" will be born. (Waberi, *In the United States of Africa,* 106)

8

Into the European "Jungle"

MIGRATION AND GRAMMAR IN THE NEW EUROPE

Neither you nor I speak English, but there are some things
that can be said only in English.

—*Aravind Adiga*[1]

The official vocabulary of African affairs is, as we might suspect,
purely axiomatic. Which is to say that it has no value as communication,
but only as intimidation. . . . In a general way, it is a language which
functions essentially as a code, i.e., the words have no relation to
their content, or else a contrary one.

—*Roland Barthes*[2]

In the first caption to her 2008 volume *Aya de Yopougon,* Ivorian comic book author Marguerite Abouet offers an ironic statement on the trials and tribulations awaiting new arrivals in France: "We are about to land in Paris' Roissy-Charles-de-Gaulle airport. It is 6:30 AM and the temperature is 12 degrees. Thanks for choosing Air Afrique."[3] Asylum seekers, migrants, and refugees enter the increasingly patrolled and protected borders of the European Union by air and land, though in recent years the dramatic and hazardous ocean crossings to which they have had recourse have received more attention. Indeed, the gray sky and heavy rainfall in Abouet's opening sequence also serve as indicators of the challenges associated with the post-migratory experience, whereby "in addition to the dangers associated with travel to Europe (extortion, theft, the perilous crossing of the desert or ocean), one must also add the dangers encountered in Europe itself."[4] As we have seen, these components of twenty-first-century migration have been explored in a significant corpus of documentaries, films, novels, and plays, recording distressing sociopolitical evidentiary modalities, while also contributing to the demystification of constructs and perceptions relating to economic opportunities in the E.U. Accounts intersect around the analysis and treatment of disintegrating national experiments, inadequate governance, limited accountability, and both regional and national conflict, factors that have contributed to economic hardship, social disruption, displaced populations, and translated into growing disparities and dissymmetries between regions.

What remains indisputable is the globalized nature of these dynamics and the power relations that exist *between* Africa and that structure the increasingly coordinated nature of the E.U.'s relationship *with* Africa. Research has confirmed that "Migrants are therefore pushed to leave their country and pulled toward countries that need them. Because of the combination of both push and pull factors, migration is likely to continue, despite the growing restrictions put on human mobility."[5] In fact, the acceleration of exchanges and circulation have become defining characteristics of society today, and as such, difficulties associated with these new forms of human mobility are now intrinsic to the very nature of population movement.[6] For example, the International Convention on the Protection of the Rights of All Migrant Workers and Members of Their Families (ratified on July 1, 2003) states: "The human problems involved in migration are even more serious in the case of irregular migration and . . . appropriate action should be encouraged in order to prevent and eliminate clandestine movements and trafficking in migrant workers, while at the same time assuring the protection of their fundamental human rights."[7] The difficulty resides in the tension that exists between those engaged in the *fight* to control immigration and those ensuring that rights do not recede.

In this context, the issue of multilingualism and plurilingualism is of course crucial, and the E.U. has repeatedly expressed its commitment to linguistic diversity. The provision of documents in the twenty-two official languages of the E.U. is perhaps the most concrete example of this assurance. Furthermore, 2001 was officially declared the European Year of Languages and E.U. objectives were outlined in 2005 in *A New Framework Strategy for Multilingualism,* geared toward "ensuring that citizens have access to E.U. legislation, procedures and information in their own language; underlining the major role that languages and multilingualism play in the European economy; and finding ways to develop this further by encouraging all citizens to learn and speak more languages, in order to improve mutual understanding and communication."[8] However, as we shall see, wider questions arise concerning *language* when analysis focuses not exclusively on *communication* but also on its usages as a *linguistic tool*. Multilingualism, in this chapter, is not defined exclusively as the presence of several official, minority or migrant languages. Migrations *into* and *within* the E.U. redefine what it means to communicate successfully and indicate that learning one *European* language, or several, is not going to be the solution. How, for example, might one begin to address the challenges confronting practitioners of languages spoken *within* the E.U. that are not officially recognized by the E.U. itself? Such questions naturally redefine multilingualism and plurilingualism especially given that language policy in the E.U. "family" has been very deliberate in using (even in conserving/preserving usage of certain lesser-spoken languages) all member languages.[9]

Instead, I want to explore the *new language of migration* that is emerging, that does not coincide with any of the current languages of the E.U., but that nevertheless is being learnt by Europeans and non-Europeans alike, because it helps organize our perception of migration within and into Europe. The issue of sharing referentiality is as crucial as the mastery of already identified languages and a shift is clearly occurring as a new lexicon is installed according to exclusionary concepts and principles. As Claire Kramsch has argued, "If grammar is not, as many language textbooks present it, merely a system of linguistic structures, if it has conceptual meanings that are grounded in our experience, foreign language learners are faced with the challenge of catching native speakers' conceptual world in the vocabularies of their own experience."[10] In other words, a new grammar of migration that infuses the linguistic practices of a community is as significant as other forms of language-based transfers in terms of influence and in determining affective responses, particularly given the prevalence of such terminology and the powerful referential categories and constructs to which they are connected.[11]

The objective then is to raise questions about the semantic framings of these relationships, to explore sociopolitical connections, and to analyze some of the ways in which cultural productions can be helpful in achieving a better understanding of these complex phenomena. As we consider policies adopted by the E.U. and the pressures toward cultural, economic, juridical, linguistic, and political standardization, questions pertaining to plurilingualism and pluriculturalism find themselves inextricably linked to immigration policy given that it has become virtually impossible to disassociate or disentangle these facets of twenty-first-century existence. According to its founding principles, the E.U. was to be "a family of democratic European countries, committed to working together for peace and prosperity"; inclusivity and tolerance were thus non-negotiable defining characteristics. Yet, when one investigates the vocabulary employed by officials, the language of conventions, treaties and pacts, a new grammar of migration comes into evidence whose referentiality, signifying power and linguistic coding highlight forms of intolerance—of what has been described as a "phobic democracy"[12]—and which are increasingly providing the organizing principles for forms of belonging and solidarity. In fact, as Michel Agier has shown in his book *Le couloir des exilés. Être étranger dans un monde commun,* "the aim of achieving a techno-policy aimed at 'controlling flows' within a logistical framework that ends up associating security-based policies with a care-based language" ultimately yields a "langue onusien" (essentially, a form of "UN-speak").[13]

The genealogy of these developments can be traced, in many ways, and as we saw in the previous chapter, to E.U. negotiations that began in the 1980s and then to the subsequent application of the Schengen agreements that resulted in the abolition of checks at the common borders between E.U. member countries, allowing for greater circulation of E.U. nationals; (as we shall see, the implications of the United Kingdom not signing on for the elimination of border control will prove important). Article 17 of "The Schengen *acquis*" outlined these changes, whereby "With regard to the movement of persons, the Parties shall endeavor to abolish checks at common borders and transfer them to their external borders. To that end they shall endeavor first to harmonize, where necessary, the laws, regulations and administrative provisions concerning the prohibitions and restrictions on which the checks are based and to take complementary measures to safeguard internal security and prevent illegal immigration by nationals of States that are not members of the European Communities."[14] These policy measures raise analogous challenges to those addressed earlier relating to the pertinence of E.U. language policy, particularly in terms of their universal applicability. As it turns out, belonging to the E.U. family is determined according to specific criteria that ultimately serve to include as much as they exclude. One either speaks an "official" E.U. language, or one does not. Likewise, what happens to individuals and groups when legal rights are limited or restricted?[15] As Henri Courau has argued, the *family principle* does not apply in the same way to *non*-E.U. members: "Foreigners are denied the *right to have rights,* held captive, arbitrarily detained and often expelled without having had the time to begin legal procedures and in spite of protection from deportation. . . . The impossibility of communicating or of obtaining an interpreter therefore condemns some individuals to isolation" (Courau, *Ethnologie,* 83–84). These linguistic shortfalls—"the impossibility of communicating or of obtaining an interpreter"—serve to highlight the symbiotic connections between language and rights—and are of course grounds for concern given that E.U. protectionist measures geared toward border control and security serve to generate *illegals* and *irregulars.*[16] Migration can effectively produce multilingual encounters that the monolingualism of border spaces has yet to address.

As we have seen, rather than dealing in a concerted manner with the multiple *push* factors that inform twenty-first-century global migration patterns, migration policy has primarily focused on criminality and transborder crime, and the fight against human smugglers and traffickers. As a repressive mechanism, migration policy reframes its motives as a commitment against oppression, a will to protect vulnerable subjects from fraudulent traffickers and employers. But in reality, things are quite different, and adequate mechanisms for ensuring that basic standards of equality and justice are applied to the new global migrant working class are often sorely lacking. As Henri Courau has shown, language is crucial here in supporting and upholding such constructs, since the terminology itself is ambiguous—"Zone d'Atttente" (holding areas, found at airports, ports, train stations) and "Centre de rétention administrative" (administration detention center or facility), immigration removal centers, holding centers for foreigners awaiting expulsion/deportation, holding areas for foreign nationals refused entry onto French soil and asylum seekers awaiting decisions—"describe these sites of enclosure through euphemistic terms that soften their presence in the public space" (Courau, *Ethnologie,* 82).

Decades ago, Roland Barthes had drawn similar conclusions in his essay "African Grammar," in which he demonstrated how "[t]he official vocabulary of African affairs is, as we might suspect, purely axiomatic. Which is to say that it has no value as communication, but only as intimidation. . . . In a general way, it is a language which functions essentially as a code, i.e., the words have no relation to their content, or else a contrary one" (103). Today, the terminology includes detention zones, detainees, refugee camps, expulsions, roundups, arrest quotas, detentions, forced repatriation, filtering systems, the clandestine, the undocumented, illegals, overstayers, return directives, deportees, maximum periods of custody, bans on re-entry into the E.U., illegal stay, overstayers, return decisions, removal, entry ban, risk of absconding, voluntary departure, asylum seeker, illegal, refugee, hospitality, and vulnerable persons (Rodier, "Europe et migrations," 259–282). This *list* represents a new alphabet, a grammar that travels conceptually *across* and *into* languages. This is evident in the efforts that have been made by humanitarian agencies to both standardize and increase the effectiveness of response services. As Henri Courau's research concludes, "Humanitarian agencies need to be able to speak the same language, to be on the same wavelength so to speak, in order to be able to coordinate their activities on the ground. . . . The working language these days is English, an indispensable tool in order to be understood" (*Ethnologie,* 57). This linguistic pragmatism—"The working language these days is English"—rejoins the implications of my first epigraph, pointing to forms of monolingualism *in the field.* Examples of such *campspeak* include "proposal," "draft," "assessment," "guideline," "implementing partner," "network," "monitoring," "sustainable," and "briefing" (Courau, *Ethnologie,* 57–58). But other phenomena are to be noted, "In terms of various practices, the world of humanitarian agencies is a creative arena in which codes and guidelines are in constant circulation" (Courau, *Ethnologie,* 59), and recourse is made to abbreviations for the sake of expediency—"Camp de réfu." (refugee camp), "Distrib." (distribution), and "Eval." (evaluation) (Courau, *Ethnologie,* 58)—or for that matter to synonyms in order to "avoid using certain terms in potentially sensitive situations"—so, for example, one finds the backslang term "Beser" instead of "Serbe" or usage of the word "Bravo (commonly used in the international alphabet)" (Courau, *Ethnologie,* 59). *Common denominators* have been deployed to allow for a *symbolic relationality* between member countries: "Centre fermé pour étrangers" (Belgium), "Centre d'internement pour étrangers" (Spain), "Centre de résidence temporaire" (Italy), "Zone d'Attente pour Personne en Instance" (France), "Removal Centres" or "Reception Camp" (U.K.), and "Centre de départ volontaire" (Germany) (Courau, *Ethnologie,* 82–83). In fact, the E.U. itself, in its commitment to translating documents into the languages of the member states has addressed the technical challenge this presents, as it confronts numerous acronyms, abbreviations, decrees, treaties, constitutions, directives, declarations, objectives, policies, strategies, regulations, and decisions. To this end, the E.U. set up *EuroVoc,* a multilingual thesaurus for the E.U. that includes regular updates outlining new "approved terms for release." Thus, *EuroVoc* "is a multilingual, multidisciplinary thesaurus covering the activities of the E.U., the European Parliament in particular. It contains terms in 22 E.U. languages."[17] In many ways, this provides an example of building a common culture, though one that is structured according to "a common *vocabulary,* an ensemble of *beliefs* and especially of common *habits* that determine a particular way of thinking and of seeing things."[18] Similar conclusions can also be made when it comes to considering other "systems"—Sophie Dulucq, Jean-François Klein, and Benjamin Stora have shown how the era of colonialism was fashioned by "terms that wove the fabric of colonialism," and

Pierre Tevanian how the widespread usage by the authorities and in the media of terms such as "délinquance," "insécurité," "incivilité," "préoccupation majeure des Français," "responsabilisation," "tolérance zéro," and so on shaped "Sarkozysm."[19]

Ultimately, though, this terminology (detention zones, filtering systems) makes it possible to establish a conjunction between language and the evidentiary mode it seeks to *communicate,* while also allowing for an analysis as to the ways in which these terms subsequently enter the popular imagination via media dissemination. As Barthes showed us, "Try as the official rhetoric will to reinforce the coverings of reality, there is a moment when the words resist it and oblige it to reveal beneath the myth the alternative of lie or truth: independence is or is not, and all the adjectival designs which strive to give nothingness the qualities of being are the very signature of culpability" (109). As we have already noted, Henri Courau's ethnological research has revealed the prevalence of such dehumanizing practices and the manner in which such negative associations/representations have been mainstreamed: "Newspapers use terms such as 'migrants,' 'refugees,' 'clandestines,' 'asylum seekers,' and 'undocumented' interchangeably. . . . In addition to these appellations, numerous other words have been used: *passing shadows, dark shadows, ghosts, les bougnoules* [disparaging term designating North Africans], *foreigners, them, those from Sangatte, the immigrants, the Kosovans* and more frequently: *the refugees.* This wide ranging vocabulary indicates that no one really knows who these people are and in the end what it is that they want" (*Ethnologie,* 17). The vocabulary thus operates simultaneously as a descriptive category *and* as a communicative tool, whose vagueness and interchangeability produces a metaphorical meaningfulness that emphasizes the particular threat posed to the officially diverse yet *also* necessarily homogeneous European family (a prerequisite for existence and sustainability of the *official* entity that is the E.U.). The E.U. authorities recognize that camps and detention zones *within* the E.U. constitute sites of resistance to reductive paradigms of belonging and association (while also serving as a disquieting reminder of earlier chapters in European history), thus the imperative of inscribing spaces like Sangatte as "exceptional sites in which the rights and collective existence of individuals are organized according to special regimes" (Courau, *Ethnologie,* 68).

When subjects do not speak the same languages, the consequences are often misunderstanding, which may lead to conflict. And while such situations are viewed as undesirable, at least the area of *dissensus* is identified. In this case, a euphemized referentiality is imposed as a new and invisible language and the consequences are more insidious. Institutions have more latitude and the possibility to contradict or contest is diminished: legal mechanisms remain exceptionally vague as does the application and implementation of the law: "In the field of immigration, the imprecise nature of juridical criteria has invariably afforded those in charge of implementing them considerable room for maneuver."[20] The exaggeration of the threat posed by *non-Europeans* as a device for defining and consolidating the collective *we* through recourse to oppositional configurations and negative identity composition explains the expansion of coordinated efforts and systems such as Frontex and Rabit (Rapid border intervention teams). Éric Fassin has shown how "European identity is defined today, above all, in negative terms, and in opposition to 'migratory pressures'" and how Sarkozy was able to "impose this logic on Europe."[21] As we know only too well, "The choice of words can also serve to conceal the reality" whereby "to retain is to detain," and "to deport is to expel."[22] The dichotomy that emerges, that separates and disassociates the "us" from the "we" has been convincingly explored in recent years in several documentaries, films and novels, that have exhibited varying degrees of political commitment in treating the limits of human empathy.[23]

Besson in the Jungle

These mental and imaginative arrangements are rendered additionally complex by the physical nature of the borders and boundaries in question, located at the perimeters of the E.U. (such as the coastlines of France, Italy, Spain, Malta, and Greece), the exit points of the *global south* (such as Manilla, the Spanish enclave in Morocco[24]), or sites such as Sangatte along the northeast coastal perimeter of France, the sea border with Britain, and the Schengen free circulation area. In the case of Sangatte, the situation is all the more complex because France was effectively merely a transit country for third-country nationals seeking entry to the United Kingdom, which lies *outside* of the Schengen Agreement. As Violaine Carrère has shown,

> In the case of Sangatte, the problem arises on the way out of the Schengen space where the border is blocked. However, this is in fact only an illusion since those who are prevented from passing are only faced with this obstacle because they were not welcomed earlier onto the Union's territory even though they were permitted to cross the country. The creation of "pockets" in which migrants find themselves blocked thus highlights both a closure and an opening: the camp certainly points to a border yet it is filled with people that have been allowed in, all the while pretending not to notice them.[25]

As a consequence of a broad range of economic, social, and political factors that triggered large-scale migration initially in the late 1990s, individuals and groups of Afghans, Iranians, Iraqis, Kurds, and Kosovans (among other nationality groups) found themselves unable to cross the Channel and (therefore legally) enter the U.K.[26] An emergency humanitarian center (Centre d'hébergement et d'accueil d'urgence humanitaire, CHAUH)[27] was opened in December 1998 and administered by the Red Cross,[28] but then officially closed down in November 2002 by then–British Home Secretary David Blunkett and French Minister of the Interior Nicolas Sarkozy. Seeking an expedient solution to what became a visible political problem, procedures were followed in order to render the broader humanitarian problem invisible. However, these efforts proved futile, and although Sarkozy encouraged a "toughening of immigration policy"[29] ("Après Sangatte" 2009, 199) all the way through to 2007, evidence showed that some 28 percent (roughly 17,377) of all undocumented foreigners taken in for police questioning in France were in the Pas-de-Calais area ("Après Sangatte," 198). New migrants kept arriving, and a group of Afghan Pashtuns eventually sought refuge in a wooded area that became known as the "jungle." "In Pashto and Persian," Jérôme Equer has explained, "the word for forest is *djangal,*"[30] and was soon transformed into "jungle," thereby adopting a metonymic quality that revealed pejorative concepts and disparaging associations to savagery and animalistic qualities (the poor living conditions also served to reinforce these perceptions), while also of course encouraging public disidentification with the plight of the migrants.

Migration patterns and changes in E.U. law have yielded new challenges and responses. Migrants have literally found themselves *welcomed* (we shall return to this term) in camps, a term with a longer history whose usage and pertinence to the contemporary context of migration has been contested.[31] However, the transhistorical connection to the earlier examples of camps actually turns out to be all the more compelling today as a direct consequence of the toughening of immigration policy. Not only have border-control mechanisms been enhanced as a way of managing the external perimeter of *Fortress Europe* and locking third-country nationals out, but these measures have been accompanied by a dramatic increase in *camps* throughout the E.U. in the guise of detention zones, deportation centers, and refugee holding areas used to detain and hold third-country nationals.[32] Points of commonality in terms of the genealogy of the term are to be found in the work and activities of such migrant-rights organizations as Cimade that had previously worked with refugees under German occupation. In the discipline of geography, knowing *where* places are has often been of less importance than knowing *why* they are there.

More recently though, the relationship between marked and unmarked spots and areas on maps, between visibility and invisibility, has been additionally complicated, and we have witnessed the expansion of covert military installations,[33] the re-classification of outsiders as threats to sovereignty,[34] extraordinary rendition measures,[35] the construction of "espace-camp,"[36] as well as the creation of camps and detention centers[37] throughout the E.U., as monitored by the organization Migreurop.[38] Sangatte therefore offers a new and challenging way of apprehending the situation and therefore of thinking about contemporary migration where borders (*Fortress Europe,* the US-Mexico border, etc.) are designed to restrict entry, keeping people in rather than out. In this instance, tougher regulations have proven counterproductive.[39] Furthermore, these instruments discriminate between those who can circulate freely and those who cannot. "Walls reveal," Évelyne Ritaine has argued, "the intrinsic asymmetry of contemporary territorial and statutory limits."[40]

Éric Besson finally oversaw the dismantling of the "jungle" in September 2010. Though the closing of the "jungle" took place amid controversy, this was also the culmination of a lengthy process that received considerable attention from human rights activists, filmmakers, and writers. French author Olivier Adam's novel *A l'abri de rien* (Sheltered from Nothing, 2007) is clearly and unambiguously situated in the Nord-Pas-de-Calais region of France. Although Adam does not actually name the camp in Sangatte, the social and political context of migration and asylum provides the framework for the novel. Adam was one of the screenwriters for the film *Maman est folle* (Mother Has Gone Mad, 2007), which follows very closely the story of *A l'abri de rien,* and he also worked on the original screenplay (with Philippe Lioret and Emmanuel Courco) for Philippe Lioret's film *Welcome* (2009) which treats analogous issues. The very notion of a "welcome" therefore proves to be somewhat oxymoronic given the questions under investigation and the connection between the word "abri" used by Adam—namely a "shelter," something that is linked with a broad range of synonyms that include asylum, a safe haven, or even a sanctuary. In theory at least, such spaces provide protection, even if temporary, or at the very least a refuge. These works feature protagonists trying to get to Britain, yet who for the most part are unable to get beyond the final geographic point in their migratory ordeal. The Channel and its physical crossing corresponds to a barrier, but the situation for the migrants is all the more problematic since they now find themselves located outside of the law—they neither seek legal representation in France nor do they aspire to obtaining legal residency or asylum in that space. Their visibility—as groups that are gathered at the extreme perimeter of the Schengen zone heightens their vulnerability and in turn triggers increasingly tougher responses from the authorities eager to demonstrate the effectiveness of their stated policies aimed at countering *illegal* migration. In an interview, Philippe Lioret, described Calais as "our own version of the Mexican border,"[41] thereby making important connections with broader twenty-first-century global migration issues and patterns.

The release of the film *Welcome* triggered considerable public debate and brought attention to the complexity of contemporary migration. On March 2, 2009, a "Débat sur les migrations" (Debate on migration) was held on France 3 television between Éric Besson and the film's lead actor Vincent Lindon. Besson rejected the usage of the word "rafle" (roundup) to describe the treatment of migrants at the hands of the police, but was countered by Lindon who brought evidence of the existence of such practices: "They sleep in a place called the jungle, under cardboard boxes, and run away like wild beasts."[42] We have already seen how various signifiers operate, but recourse to animalistic allusions and metaphors have been common in this context. As Marc Bernardot has argued, "A hunting lexicon is omnipresent in the language and imaginary of the police. These images are predominantly linked to animals and game."[43] In Adam's novel, we also hear that "[t]he roundups were more and more frequent, the cops were organizing beatings for game in the forest" (*A l'abri de rien*, 217). Besson then visited the "jungle"—however, rather than softening his relentless assault on migrants, he continued to advocate for stricter regulations and even proposed an expansion of Frontex and of E.U. coordination measures.[44] Naturally, Besson has sought to demonstrate the efficacy of his policies through repeated recourse to statistics: "The measures we have taken over the past few months have already yielded good results: we arrested 200 smugglers in 2008 and 250 since the start of the year. The number of clandestines now in Calais has dropped from 1,500 in April to less than 500 today,"[45] while reaffirming that "[d]ismantling the jungle is not the end of the fight against clandestine networks in Calais."[46] The rationale informing his policy making expresses awareness of a fundamental dilemma, whereby "it would be absurd to provide a shelter for these people in anticipation of their crossing to England while simultaneously deploying significant resources aimed at preventing such crossings."[47] However, addressing these matters exclusively through the prism of deterrence serves to conceal a broader agenda that concerns the differentiation between desirable and undesirable partners in the European space—and of course the need for perpetual vigilance in monitoring the presence of the latter.

On April 1, 2010, Besson published his "Présentation du projet de loi relatif à l'immigration" and prioritized two areas: (1) Strengthen the welcome and integration for legal immigration and (2) Improve the fight against illegal immigration.[48] Later, on September 28, 2010, Besson provided an update on the situation, "Demantèlement de la 'jungle' à Calais: Point de situation," in which he stated that the "operation to dismantle the 'jungle'" had been a "success," thereby demonstrating a deliverable outcome, "restoring a state of law,"[49] and reaffirming objective number 2. Comparing Besson's assessment with a report published by the Coordination française pour le droit d'asile (CFDA, an umbrella organization monitoring asylum rights, *La loi des "jungles." La situation des exilés sur le littoral de la Manche et de la Mer du Nord* [The Law of the "Jungle": The Situation of Exiles on the shore of the Channel and the North Sea]) is revealing.[50] What emerges is a direct indictment of French action and policy: "The proposals are organized around five topics: the respect of the right of asylum, the obligation to provide for reception conditions to migrants (including asylum seekers) respecting their dignity, the protection of vulnerable persons, a stop to police harassment, and the rights of persons kept in detention."[51] Among the set of recommendations, France is called upon to adhere to and respect "those rights protected by international conventions and ratified by France. There exists, in particular a mandatory rule according to which no person can be sent back 'to the frontiers of territories where his life or freedom would be threatened', or if he/she could be 'subjected to torture or inhuman or degrading treatments or punishment'. This principle of non-refoulement is binding on all States for all the people present on their territory, regardless of their administrative status. In order to respect this principle, States must refrain from such expulsions" (*The Law of the "Jungle,"* 1).

As such, Adam's novel and the films of Améris and Lioret provide a perspective on an oft-neglected facet of the E.U. and the broader implications and impact of policy on local communities and regions. In this instance, these works reveal the responses of people actually residing in those areas where the E.U. experiment is playing out. As with much of Adam's work, the demographics concern lower-middle-class families; in *A l'abri de rien,* for example, the father is a bus driver and the mother, who has a history of clinical depression, has recently been fired from her position as a cashier at a local supermarket. The coastal landscape of the region is juxtaposed with new urban development zones that now include large outlets and stores such as Go Sport, Conforama, Darty, Etam, and André, themselves symbols of new market conglomerations and global distribution networks. There is nothing glamorous about quotidian existence: "And yet there was nothing I really had to do. Nothing important. Nothing to really think about. What did I do all day? Pretty much just pace up and down, biting my nails, trying to get rid of my anxiety that was gnawing at my insides, not really knowing why I was feeling that way, and trying to hold back the tears" (Adam, *A l'abri de rien,* 20). Shopping takes place at discount or bulk purchase stores such as Ed and Carrefour: "That's what life is like for most of us, and usually not much more than that. . . . And then there's the debt, the rent that's much too expensive, the lack of funds, and the struggle to make it through the month" (Adam, *A l'abri de rien,* 15–19). In fact, while the Eurostar may enter and exit the tunnel in this region of France on its way to and from Britain, most members of the local community in question do not engage in such circulation and find themselves in many ways situated at the margins of this new and mobile Europe. Yet, these are often the spaces in which contacts and confrontation with the other take place. The novels and films—and therefore the characters themselves—provide a counter-discourse, an alternative language with which to confront the sociopolitical realities in their coastal landscape.

Marie, the main character, is aware that the refugees have names that do not correspond to their national identity: "There were all these guys standing around; they looked dirty and worn-out, and looked so skinny in their torn clothes. Everyone referred to them as *Kosovans,* but they were mostly Iraqis, Iranians, Afghans, Pakistanis, Sudanese, or Kurds" (Adam, *A l'abri de rien,* 23). An encounter takes place between these global migrants—what might be considered a global migrant working class—and local working communities who, in turn, discover the willingness to question the euphemisms of the system and to propose new forms of referentiality. Marie's comments also point to the fact that the closures of the various camps and centers have not eliminated the flow of migrants, but instead worsened the migrants' situation. As Andrea Rea has shown, "The reality is that [suppression] of internal border control in the European Union has led to an increase in external border control."[52] Likewise, the harsh discourse of the authorities and heightened border-control mechanisms have produced "gray areas [such as Sangatte]"[53] and are actually indicative of shortcomings in the E.U. policy of "harmonization."

"Contrary to what Nicolas Sarkozy announced when he was Minister of the Interior," CFDA's report argues, "the closing and subsequent destruction of the Sangatte camp in December 2002 is far from having solved the problem of migrants trying to get to the U.K. Every day, refugees having transitioned through other European countries are still piling into the city of Calais on their way further north" (*The Laws of the "Jungle,"* 1, text slightly altered). In fact, Marie's language proposes that the real change is not from "camp" to the "end of camps," but instead from "camps" to "camp out on the streets": "A great big tent had been erected in front of the Mayor's office when they had closed the camp. I never understood why they had closed it, that camp. Things had only gotten worse. There were just as many of them as before and they were still looking for ways to cross over to England. The only difference was that they were really on the streets now" (Adam, *A l'abri de rien,* 23). Throughout Adam's novel such observations corroborate the findings of sociological fieldwork and research.

Didier Bigo has shown how "The haste with which expulsions take place renders them arbitrary and the deportation of clandestines does not reduce the number of illegal entries."[54] Such conclusions have resulted in a growing awareness and consciousness among local residents of the precarious situation migrants find themselves in: "I don't see why they don't just send all these people back to their country" (Adam, *A l'abri de rien,* 107). A breakdown in communication occurs between institutions and locals who no longer speak the same language because their own referentiality is competing with their government's discourse. What then happens when the micro-national community begins to reject adherence to centralized rules and regulations that don't adequately take into consideration factors on the ground? What are the possibilities when the contours of human empathy are redrawn and identification with the *other* occurs without previously attributed limitations and dictates? When individuals relinquish the status of disinterested subject and passive observer, and discover the *other*? "I had never thought about these things before" (Adam, 2007, 91), Marie acknowledges. In her case, it is the confrontation with the spectacle of violence and suffering that allows for identification and empathy: "I took a few steps and saw them, guys wearing uniforms with their dogs off the leash, carrying shiny, polished holstered guns. . . . And the heavy pounding on their bodies, their bones scraping on the flooring, the thud made by the impact of their skulls on the steps, I can still hear all these sounds, all I have to do is close my eyes and I can see it all again, I stood there petrified, terrified, wide-eyed and with my mouth open" (Adam, *A l'abri de rien,* 28–29). From the previously undifferentiated mass, "They all wore the same kind of clothing, beige corduroy trousers full of holes, two or three layers of sweaters under a worn out leather jacket, or else sweat suits, bonnets and anoraks that were too short" (Adam, *A l'abri de rien,* 60), individuals begin to emerge with actual names (Jallal, Drago), life stories (families left behind and families waiting for them across the Channel), necessary stages in the process of humanization. Recourse to depersonalized linguistic signifiers such as "populations," "overvalues or depreciates at will certain intentions: *populations* installs a euphoric sentiment of pacifically subjugated multitudes; but when we speak of *elementary nationalisms,* the plural aims at degrading further, if it is possible, the notion of (enemy) nationalism, by reducing it to a collection of mediocre units" (Barthes, 108). For some, such identification allows for a new political consciousness from which there is no return and from which henceforth only engagement will be possible.

The various dangers associated with such choices can only confirm their validity. The act of "lending a hand" (Adam, *A l'abri de rien,* 63) and of sharing in a collective act of complicity which has already landed some in the legal system proves affirming: "Isabelle [who works at a distribution center] let us read her copy of *Libé* [abbreviation of *Libération,* the French daily newspaper] and suddenly I was brought back to reality. There was a story about the guy who had been sheltering refugees. It spoke of his trial, of the various associations, the petition that was circulating, the opposition and the whole bloody mess. There was also an interview with the Minister of the Interior, and a photo of him smiling like a reptile" (Adam, *A l'abri de rien,* 89). The reference to the authorities is not fortuitous since it confirms the symbolism of this oppositionality and also the rejection of the xenophobia proposed as a way of unifying E.U. nationals in the name of some as yet unspecified and homogeneous family. Naturally, this resistance community is not representative of the whole, and through the voices and actions of local schoolchildren we gain a perspective and insight as to how others conceive of these questions, since "There were kids at the school who wouldn't sit next to them, who insulted them, calling their mother a whore and saying that she slept with refugees. . . . Some of those kids were yelling on the bus and Lucas was there, do you understand, they were yelling your wife blows Kosovans" (Adam, *A l'abri de rien,* 144). Here, the word Kosovan "had become a generic term locally to designate immigrants of all origins since the time a few years back when Kosovan refugees had started flooding into Calais" (Rolin, *Terminal Frigo,* 150). Furthermore, the fact that it is illegal to provide shelter for these "illegals" serves as the ultimate indication and expression of the incapacity of the authorities to achieve empathy, voiding therefore the very precondition for communal existence and respect for the other that informs, in theory at least, the foundations of the social contract that is the E.U. family.

The "welcome" presented in the title of Lioret's film places the concept of "Délit de solidarité" (offence of solidarity) under pressure, asking us to think about what a crime of hospitality may correspond to, and how the authorities can *criminalize* citizens who decide to reach out to refugees.[55] Thus, the new grammar of migration evoked earlier finds itself deployed here as "avis d'expulsion" (deportation order), "convocation" (summons), "centre de retention" (detention facility), "titre de séjour" (residency permit), and "passeur" (smuggler) (Adam, *A l'abri de rien,* 70, 140, 141, 160, 161). These developments raise important questions concerning the monocultural and nationalistic tendencies of certain E.U. member states, belief-systems that contradict the diversity, plurality and principles of coexistence that informed the conceptualization of the E.U.[56] The regulation of circulation practices remains problematic, challenging prevailing discourse on globalization, as does the very idea of a "shelter" given its broader concrete and metaphorical uses—economic (tax shelters), legal (protection, citizenship), political (governance and representation), cultural (diversity and pluralism), and social (housing, healthcare). As Ryszard Kapuscinski has argued, "There are many other difficulties, question marks and even mysteries on the road to our encounter with Others. Yet this encounter and coexistence on our globalizing planet is inevitable, because we live in a multicultural world. . . . What is new today is that awareness has grown of the presence and importance of these cultures: awareness of their multiplicity, of their right to exist and to own a separate identity. And this has coincided with the great revolution in communications, which has enabled these cultures to have multiple encounters, a polyphonic, many-sided dialogue."[57]

What then does it really mean to be European? Some have suggested that only greater integration will accord coexistence any genuine validity;[58] others have underscored how such evolving structures must not be accompanied by inclusionary/exclusionary mechanisms, resulting in a "lock down of the Schengen space" or an even more questionable and alarming "illusory quest for common roots."[59] How can we better define "identity"? "The refugees continue to file past the window," the novelist Caryl Phillips writes, "I want to tell this man that whether economic or political migrants, these people's lives are broken and they are simply looking for a chance to begin anew. A chance to work, to contribute, to make something of themselves. To begin again at the bottom of the pile."[60] Ultimately though, the question remains to be answered and defined. Being an undesirable and unwanted *guest* is one thing, but being asked by a *host* to *fit in* is quite another, particularly when the demands and exigencies associated with such a request are especially vague. Pierre Tevanian has succinctly summarized this condition, demonstrating how the emphasis has been placed on immigrants to integrate rather than on the social issues they face; but, to be *integrated*, "to be *included* and to have a *place* is surely better than being excluded, but this tells us nothing about what place we mean. A servant has a place, sh/e may well be included and integrated while still being subjugated, despised and exploited."[61]

These are the kinds of questions tackled by the theatre director Ariane Mnouchkine in *Le Dernier Caravansérail* (Odyssées): Part I: Le Fleuve cruel; Part II: Origines et Destins [The Last Caravanserai (Odysseys): Part I: The Cruel River; Part II: Origins and Destinies].[62] Initially performed in France at the Cartoucherie de Vincennes in 2003, a film adaptation was also released in 2006.[63] The focus is provided by the context of global migration; the political oppression that has driven people away from their countries of origin, and later the circumstances they face as asylum seekers and refugees in Australia and Europe. *Le dernier caravansérail* juxtaposes several forms of violence (in the country of origin, in juridical immigration procedures, and as exemplified by the interaction between migrants and the smugglers and traffickers seeking to capitalize on their vulnerability) with forms of intimacy (personal sacrifice, generosity, family, lovers, and so on), resisting simple binaries. But rather than privileging one, or a handful of voices, Mnouchkine's play is structured instead around sixty-two scenes (fifty in the film version) a polyphonic arrangement, a "collage,"[64] an "assemblage" of "vignettes" that "were created from improvisations based on documented stories."[65] The diverse characters have names, names that are absent in the discourse of the authorities where refugees are often reduced to their case number. Thus, through Bulgarian, Dari, English, Farsi, French, Kurdish, and Russian (among others), "The premise is thus," Judith Miller writes, "from the first, to preserve memories, to allow the exiled to tell their own stories through the conduit of the actors of the Théâtre du Soleil," and "In addition to improvising around the stories told by the refugees, the actors studied films, documentaries, and images depicting exile and refugee life" (Miller, "New Forms for New Conflicts," 216 and 214). The plight of migrants thus receives much-needed personalization—thereby simultaneously humanizing them—but this process also broadens the problem invoked by underlining the global scale of things as confirmed by the plural linguistic geography in evidence in the camps and detention centers. "The choice to perform in the languages of the refugees interviewed acknowledges that language is about all that refugees have left in life. Mnouchkine insists on foregrounding their voices" (Miller, "New Forms for New Conflicts," 215). Likewise, recourse to supertitles during the staged performance and subtitles in the film serves to defamiliarize the audience, heightening their receptivity.

A powerful example is to be found in Sequence 7, Origins and Destinies: "Refugee review tribunal, October 2001" in the film. Salahaddin Al Bassiri (File number, 0031569) is a political refugee who has been detained for over eighteen months. His appeal takes place in Farsi, via a video-conference monitor and an interpreter. There are repeated instances of miscommunication (in one instance, driven to extreme frustration, the interpreter protects his interests by simply communicating that he is confused rather than actually conveying what he said) that are perceived as indication of his unwillingness to fully cooperate. But most importantly, Mr. Al Bassiri is positioned as a *criminal defendant,* bound by his initial deposition, and cross-examined by a hostile immigration arbitrator seeking to identify inconsistencies in his narrative that in turn would confirm the illegitimacy of his claim for refugee status. All these devices are reinforced by the physical surroundings, since Mr. Al Bassiri speaks from a detention center, flanked by a federal guard. But these life stories—*odysseys*—as the subtitle reminds us, are now recounted at the new "caravanserai" (traditionally a roadside shelter, safe haven, or refuge at which caravans and traders alight) where the "weight of the world" have gathered, "as Ulysses answers to the Cyclops Polyphemus, 'Nobody': stateless, kinless, and nameless."[66] Metaphors of mobility frame the performance, and from this fragmented choreography that "speaks to dislocation and dismantlement, rather than to a continuous, linear, potentially sense-making trip" (Miller, "New Forms for New Conflicts," 217) we are implicated, along with the actors, in a deliberate "discipline of decentering" (Lauwaert, "Comme une écaille sur le mur," 168), one that leaves us with no alternative but to navigate our way to the other.

What remains incontrovertible is the manner in which the E.U. authorities have attempted to impose a specific form of monolingualism that functions across linguistic referentiality in order to address questions pertaining to migration. As we have seen, these mechanisms have also come to inform the work of humanitarian agencies, and at times this monolingualism has even been contested from within the same framework by minority characters capable of reading and reappropriating official discourse. Ultimately, both official discourse and counter-discourse end up coexisting in a complex network of tenuous relations which, rather than culminating in *consensus,* instead generate a kind of *state of dissensus.* Certainly, novels such as *A l'abri de rien,* films like *Welcome,* and pioneering theatrical projects (*Le Dernier Caravan-sérail*) confront this new grammar of migration. The introduction of oppositional figures who are unwilling to abide by the obligations and requirements made by the authorities end up challenging attempts at securing monocultural and monolithic interpretations of nationality and belonging, and interrogating belief-systems that contradict the diversity, plurality and principles of coexistence that informed the conceptualization of the E.U. The *new* Europe needs to be particularly attentive to the ways in which it engages in community building, to the bidirectionality of policy, and to those most vulnerable global citizens that find themselves *sheltered from nothing.*

9

Documenting the Periphery

THE FRENCH *BANLIEUES* IN WORDS AND FILM

We're not given the same chance, we don't have the same France.

—*H-Magnum*[1]

Because this country, our country, has all it needs to become exemplary again, as long as it accepts itself as it is rather than as it was; We, artists, have decided to join forces and to work together against inequality and injustice; We, the children of a plural France, want to promote this diversity which is an asset and an opportunity for tomorrow.

—*quifaitlafrance*[2]

Thus far, the focus has been provided by various incarnations of official discourse pertaining to *outsiders,* including asylum seekers, illegals, irregulars, and refugees. In this chapter, we turn our attention to another facet of the immigration question, namely to the writings and films made by French ethnic minorities located at the social periphery in the *banlieues.* This will allow us to assess *internal* responses to complex debates on immigration and national identity and to obtain important insights on the *other* France. Most observers of French politics will agree that the early years of the twenty-first-century have been turbulent ones: from the 2002 presidential elections in which the extreme right-wing Front National obtained sufficient votes to advance to the final round to the "no" vote on the new E.U. constitution in 2005, and from the October–November 2005 urban riots to the CPE (Contrat première embauche) student demonstrations in 2006. If examples of ethnic mobilization during the 1980s

(S.O.S. Racisme, the Marche pour l'égalité et contre le racisme [Marche des Beurs], and Convergence 84) served to underscore the deficiency of *assimilation, insertion,* and *integration* policies, then the riots of 2005 can surely be understood as indicative of the glaring failure of decolonization *and* the survival of transcolonial structures of inequity in the French métropole.

In his study of *beur* writing—works by the children of North-African immigrants in France—Alec Hargreaves emphasized the process of cross-cultural negotiation, and identified "the key problematic which has preoccupied Beur writers [as] the articulation of a sense of personal identity, forged in the particular circumstances which are those of an ethnic minority in France. . . . While such conflicts may be experienced commonly in everyday personal relations, they are rooted in the juxtaposition of radically different cultural systems consequent upon large-scale international population movements."[3] Postcolonial writing in France has been studied through a broad range of interrelated categories, including immigrant literatures, Afro-Parisianism, Black Paris, and *banlieue* writing, all of which share points of commonality naturally with *beur* writing.[4] Rather than demarcating the specific attributes of each of these groupings, I prefer to insist on the transversal qualities and mediation that exists between these texts. As I argued in *Black France: Colonialism, Immigration, and Transnationalism,* further-broadening the framework to include colonial era texts allows us to simultaneously question the inclination of the French authorities to treat immigration as an undifferentiated postcolonial paradigm, one that contributes to obfuscating European and French debates on history and identity.[5] More recently, *banlieue* writing has emerged from this historical experience and made it possible to examine the pluridimensionality of the ethnic question in France today. Whereas *beur* literature was essentially constituted by a Maghrebicentric corpus, *banlieue* writers cannot be contained by a single ethnic group.[6] Furthermore, whereas *beur* authors focused primarily on issues that closely-related to the challenges of "first generation" immigrants or their descendants, the *banlieue* generation are, for the most part, one generation further removed from those concerns. Their corpus has instead yielded a *new writing for new times,* confronting both analogous matters but also reflecting a thematic historical evolution.

Azouz Begag, arguably the most well-known and prolific *beur* author, recently adopted the term "jeunes ethniques" (young ethnics) to designate ethnic minorities: "I called them *young ethnics* because they are the children or grandchildren of immigrants from former French colonies who have been stigmatized by members of the majority population, many of whom feel that people of non-European origin do not deserve to be treated as equal members of French society."[7] The mutability of referents in common usage in France today highlights the confused state of affairs. For example, "If we review the main terms currently in use, notably in the media, we come up with the following typology, based on territorial, ethnic, religious, and temporal criteria. . . . In all there are around thirty different appellations, riddled with fallacies, contradictions, and ambiguities embodying the unease of the Republic vis-à-vis 'citizens' who are not like 'us'" (Begag, *Ethnicity and Equality*, 19–21). What is more, as Etienne Balibar has shown, organizing official rhetoric around the figure of the "foreigner" (étranger)—whereby the "immigrant" comes to function as signifier for a broad range of cultural, political, and social issues—is particularly problematic since "The less the social problems of the 'immigrants', or the social problems which massively affect immigrants, are specific, the more their existence is made responsible for them."[8] This is additionally complicated by the fact that such designations are applied even "to a whole category of people who have never migrated (the 'second' and 'third generation')."[9] Pascal Blanchard, Nicolas Bancel, and Sandrine Lemaire have argued that during the colonial period, ideals of liberty and equality that were in principle fundamental to the French Republic were strategically adopted within a more strictly "culturalist discourse," whereas in fact "racial inequality is at the heart of the colonial republican mechanism."[10] Attempts to deracialize the colonial project and adopt a more culturalist agenda allowed for the *civilizing mission* while simultaneously deferring assimilation indefinitely—this type of colonial discourse informs to this day official thinking on the question of immigration in France in which the incompatibility of cultural practices is cited in relation to *French* values.

In the literal and metaphorical transition from *beur* to *banlieue* writing, both descriptive categories nevertheless share numerous points of commonality, foremost among which is the question of reception. "Their writings," as Hargreaves has argued, "are still to a large extent ignored by cultural elites in France. Far from celebrating rootlessness, one of the main driving forces behind their work is to stake a place for themselves within French society" (*Immigration and identity*, 172). Having said this, there have been numerous developments on the French literary scene that suggest things may be changing. There is of course a long history of recuperation by the publishing establishment in France around the tradition of francophone writing. Pascale Casanova in *The World Republic of Letters* underlined how

> The position of Francophone writers, on the other hand, is paradoxical if not tragic as well. Since for them Paris is not merely the capital of world literary space, as historically it has been for writers everywhere, but also the very source of the political and/or literary domination under which they labor. . . . Making matters worse, the power of Paris is still more domineering and more keenly felt by Francophone writers for being incessantly denied in the name of the universal belief in the universality of French letters and on behalf of the values of liberty promoted and monopolized by France itself.[11]

This tenuous relationship with the French literary establishment has been the subject of two separate, though interrelated manifestos published in 2007.

The first, signed by forty-four writers of French expression (including Tahar Ben Jelloun, Maryse Condé, Ananda Devi, Edouard Glissant, Alain Mabanckou, Anna Moï, Boualem Sansel, Brina Svit, and Abdourahman A. Waberi), initially appeared on March 16, 2007, in *Le Monde* newspaper, under the title "Pour une 'littérature-monde' en français" (Toward a world literature in French).[12] This manifesto denounced the reductive dimension of the nationalizing imperative whereby literary production remains inseparable from the ideological component of *francophonie* as a hegemonic state-sponsored organization in which cultural particularities are reduced or ignored. The call for a French-style *world literature* similar to its Anglophone counterpart across the Channel (globalized by international writers such as J. M. Coetzee, Nadine Gordimer, Kazuo Ishiguro, Ben Okri, Caryl Phillips, Salman Rushdie, Wole Soyinka, and so forth) is increasingly understood as a prerequisite for accommodating the new contours of literature *in* French. Having said this, the claims and demands made in "Toward a World Literature in French"—as legitimate as they may have been—failed to include a single *beur* or *banlieue* author in their "constellation."[13]

The debates triggered by the call for a *world literature in French* become all the more relevant when one situates them in the broader context of postcolonial France. Questions of recognition and claims for incorporation are in fact far more widespread than this manifesto may suggest, and questions of social (in) visibility have been at the forefront of political discussions, especially since the 2005 French riots and uprisings. In the same year as the call for a *world literature in French* reverberated, a collective of ten young ethnic minority authors, artists, musicians, and rappers published another manifesto entitled "Qui fait la France?"[14] An anthology of essays and short-stories, *Chroniques d'une société annoncée,* written by the founding members, was published in September 2007 by the Editions Stock.[15] This manifesto provides a kind of blueprint for what I have described as *new writing for new times,* alongside a rejection of the centripetal force of the hegemonic center. For example, seemingly ill-equipped to judge and historiographically locate Faïza Guène's extremely successful first novel, *Kiffe kiffe demain* (Just like tomorrow, 2004), critics soon began to describe her as the "Sagan des banlieues" (after the well-known French writer who had received much critical acclaim some fifty years earlier upon publication of her novel *Bonjour Tristesse,* when she was, like Guène, also a teenager).[16] Guène is strongly opposed to this comparison, stating that "I don't want to be the Sagan of the housing projects.... That's a bit much. I don't want to be called the Arab girl from the suburbs who had a tough life and made good because I don't think I had a tough life."[17] What we have here then is not simply an evolution or reformulation of *beur* literature (or an extension of traditional *French* literature), but rather the birth of a new kind of writing.

The "collective" is grouped under the rubric "qui fait la France," adhering to a statement aimed at an inclusive and constructive notion of demographic belonging, and prompting readers to reflect on the question "Qui fait la France" (Who makes/up France?), but at the same time a suggestive play on words whereby the "qui fait" sounds like the neologism "kiffer" that has entered into public discourse and means "to love/be crazy about something or someone," in this case claiming "to love/be crazy about France." It is thus a questioning of belonging, but simultaneously a statement of intention (and desire) to belong to the mainstream and be a part of the French Republic:

> *Because* the literature we believe in . . . is the exact opposite of today's selfish, egotistical and small-minded literature that is merely an outlet for bourgeois dispositions.... *Because* we remain convinced that writing, today more than ever, cannot remain confined, spineless, ingratiating, but should on the contrary become engaged, combative and ferocious. *Because* we refuse to remain spectators to human suffering, the victims of which are the most vulnerable, downtrodden, and invisible members of our society.... *Because* since we have been categorized as *banlieues* writers, etymologically the site of ban, we want to invest the cultural field, transcend frontiers and thereby recuperate the space that has been confiscated and that is rightly ours. (www.quifaitlafrance.com)

The constitutive nature of French-other relations were thus insisted upon, alongside an explicit and unambiguous call for social inclusion and belonging. The common denominator among these young artists and activists—no longer organized as merely *beurs* or black authors, but rather across ethnic lines—is that they are for the most part residents of the *banlieues.* This manifesto called for the implementation of a strategy that would allow for a demoralized generation to celebrate the potentialities of a multicultural France, as fully-fledged partners in the project of building a new kind of country:

> *Because* we believe that France is a modern country in which co-existence can occur by opening people's minds, through the recognition of common suffering, and the narration of its diversity and imaginary. . . . *Because* this country, our country, has all it needs to become exemplary again, as long as it accepts itself as it is rather than as it was; *We,* artists, have decided to join forces and to work together against inequality and injustice; *We,* the children of a plural France, want to promote this diversity which is an asset and an opportunity for tomorrow. . . . *We,* a composite of mixed identities, *we* are joining forces in the struggle for equal rights and respect for all, above and beyond geographic origins and social conditions; *We,* citizens from here and elsewhere, open to the world and its richness, intend to fight against the shameful prejudices that have fossilized our country and undermined our ability to live together. . . . *We,* the children of the Republic, want to be participants in spreading the power of its message, its inspirational power, and in translating its values and principles into action. . . . *Together,* we exist. (www.quifaitlafrance.com)

The tone of this manifesto is all the more remarkable given that so much of the analysis concerning the 2005 riots blamed either the unwillingness of ethnic minorities to integrate into French society or alternatively the system itself for ineffective integration policies. In fact, this manifesto provides an affirmation by the "invisibles of the French Republic" that they constitute not so much a threat—their arguments do, after all, express adherence to republican ideals—but rather, and somewhat paradoxically, an asset to France as members of a plural society.[18]

Not surprisingly, this emerging category of *banlieue* writing exposes social injustice and inequality and, in doing so, effectively records the realities of a part of French society that had previously been either ignored or reductively *represented* by outsiders. Works thus reflect many of the problems intrinsic to those urban areas in which a disadvantaged global underclass resides, such as violence, over-representation in prisons, high unemployment rates, poverty, and so on, but also introduce universal themes such as family relations, love, and friendship. Titles are indicators of various shared concerns, such as race and identity (Habiba Mahany, *Je kiffe ma race,* 2008, Thomté Ryam, *Banlieue noire,* 2006, Jean-Éric Boulin, *Supplément au roman national,* 2006 and *La Question Blanche,* 2008), discrimination and the lack of opportunity (Karim Amellal, *Discriminez-moi. Enquête sur nos inégalités,* 2005, Ahmed Djouder, *Désintégra-*

tion, 2006), violence (Mohamed Razane, *Dit violent,* 2006, Aymeric Patricot, *Azima la rouge,* 2006), social uprising (Mabrouk Rachedi, *Le poids d'une âme,* 2006), law and policing (Akli Tadjer, *Bel-Avenir,* 2006), adolescence and youth culture (Faïza Guène, *Kiffe kiffe demain,* 2004, *Du rêve pour les oufs,* 2006, Rachid Djaïdani, *Boumkœur,* 2000 and *Viscéral,* 2007, Dembo Goumane, *Dembo Story,* 2006), and schooling (Houda Rouane, *Pieds-Blancs,* 2006).[19] These works have garnered considerable recognition, some achieving bestseller status in mainstream bookstores (Djaïdani, Guène, Tadjer) while also contributing to what one might describe as a *democratization of readership* given that these authors have been able to bring their personal stories to a larger segment of French society while also attracting a new generation of readers to their texts.

Faïza Guène has been inspirational in this regard. Born in 1985, her novels have already been translated into over twenty languages—her work is a long way from the *beur* generation authors, and her tone is confrontational while also successfully combining humor in her insightful commentary on French society: "It was school that signed me up to see her [the social worker]. The teachers, when they weren't on strike I mean, decided I was shut down or depressed or something and needed help. Maybe they've got a point. Who gives a shit? I go. It's free" (Guène, *Just Like Tomorrow,* 1). Her assessment of the French authorities' commitment to achieving social equality and opportunities for social mobility in a more general manner, "It's like a film script and we're the actors. Trouble is, our scriptwriter's got no talent. He's never heard of happily ever after" (Guène, *Just Like Tomorrow,* 11), is nevertheless tempered by a refusal to embrace the downbeat and pessimistic register of many earlier works and a newfound optimism can be traced through a willingness to engage with society.

The French *banlieues* are genuinely global, though ironically of course located at the periphery of major French cities. The struggle for incorporation and the process of rethinking the homogeneity of French society has begun; whether or not the French authorities accept the challenge this represents remains to be seen. But writers, intellectuals, and social activists will surely continue to contribute to the project of defining the coordinates of postcolonial France in ways that will more accurately reflect its complicated history, while making sure that mechanisms are put into place that will ensure that newly dismantled centers are not accompanied by new peripheries. *Banlieue* authors offer a privileged perspective on the "invisibles" in French society, and attempt to alter public consciousness and perceptions. Their works also articulate a sociological reality that remains otherwise defined only by reductive external projections and representations that circulate in print media and on television, in which violence and delinquency are foregrounded at the service of *and* in order to legitimatize harsher legislation and government responses.[20] As Achille Mbembe has shown, "As in the United States the conflation of extreme poverty and delinquency, and then of delinquency and threats to insecurity, makes it possible to criminalize a part of the population and to 'racialize' social problems, which can then be presented as insoluble except through penal institutions."[21]

The "quifaitlafrance" collective's "call for an alternative idea of literature and of France" coincides with the wider call for inclusion and recognition. Indeed, such demands for incorporation proved to be completely at odds with the exclusionary policies associated with Nicolas Sarkozy's term in office (2007–2012) and his much-repeated claim that one should "love France" or elect to leave. Sarkozy insisted on a presupposed and necessary love for France that was of course completely absurd from a legal point of view, but also clearly aimed at immigrant populations who did not fit in to his monolithic view of France. For the members of the collective, it is rather the potentiality of a constitutive interpretation of French history that is stressed, "*Because* this country, our country, has all it needs to become exemplary again, as long as it accepts itself as it is rather than as it was; *We,* artists, have decided to join forces and to work together against inequality and injustice; *We,* the children of a plural France, want to promote this diversity which is an asset and an opportunity for tomorrow" (www.quifaitlafrance.com). By contrast, Sarkozy implicitly subscribed to the notion of social hierarchies under the aegis of the French nation, since for him some "French" people are *more* French than others.[22]

The question of social hierarchies is of course absolutely key to the project of the collective. As Nicolas Bancel, Pascal Blanchard, and Françoise Vergès demonstrate in *La République coloniale,* "becoming French," in the conventional discourse of French republicanism, "means relinquishing all that differentiates—regional language, religion, a desire for autonomy. The Republic is one and indivisible, and cannot accept any breach of this principle."[23] Historically, the idea that some were "more" citizens than others was confirmed in 1946 when the French authorities created the distinct category of "colonial citizenship." Thus, for the members of the collective, their manifesto was less about challenging the Republic than seeking *access* to it.[24] Of course, the circumstances are further complicated by the fact that these artists were overwhelmingly born in France, have never migrated, yet still find themselves reminded of their status in French society as descendants of colonized subjects, views that reaffirm a legacy of subjugation.[25]

At this juncture, I propose to bring some of these questions to bear on the novels of Faïza Guène. The author herself is all the more interesting because she actually complicates any discussion of *beur* and *banlieue* writing. She was born in 1985 in Bobigny (France) to Algerian parents; her father arrived in France in 1952 and her mother in 1981. If the *beur* are the children of North African immigrants (or second-generation North Africans), then she is by definition a *beurette* (the feminine form of *beur*). However, she is technically (or chronologically) of the *rebeu* generation (backslang often used to designate the third generation or the children of the *beur*), in the sense that she grew up during the 1990s whereas the main wave of the second generation had by then reached adulthood. This is of course significant, since her concerns are anchored in the late-twentieth and early-twenty-first century, and informed by the circumstances of her life in the Courtillières project located at the northeast periphery of Paris in Seine-Saint-Denis.

In addition to her two novels, *Kiffe kiffe demain* and *Du rêve pour les oufs* (Dreams from the endz), she has also made several short films and documentaries to which we shall turn our attention later in this chapter.[26] Her novels have been exceptionally well received and were immediately translated worldwide; by comparison, Azouz Begag's bestselling first novel, *Le gône du Châaba* (The shantytown kid), was only translated into English in 2007, over twenty years after it was first published.[27] What, one may ask, is the particular appeal of these works written by a young Algerian *and* French woman? One answer may well reside in the increased attention that has been granted to marginalized urban populations. Sociologist Loïc Wacquant has convincingly demonstrated how the French *banlieue* is by no means a unique phenomenon: "*Ghetto* in the United States, *banlieue* in France, *quartieri periferici* (or *degradati*) in Italy, *problemområde* in Sweden, *favela* in Brazil, *villa miseria* in Argentina, *rancho* in Venezuela: North American, Western European and Latin American societies all have a special term in their topographic repertory with which to designate these stigmatized spaces that occupy the lowest hierarchical rank in their metropolises."[28] But other factors—beyond the literary and linguistic qualities of the works themselves—have surely contributed to the interest generated by Guène's work: a concerted effort to avoid the kind of "misérabilisme" (sordid realism) that had defined so much *beur* writing; a commitment to accessibility and to reaching out to new audiences; an assumption of responsibility concerning the choice of themes and populations represented; and finally an alternative perspective on the cultural and social circumstances of the *banlieue.*

In an interview with Caroline Carisoni, Guène claimed: "Contemporary literature is made out to be this mystical thing you have to be initiated into. I want to make it accessible. My books have been read by people who had never picked up a book before."[29] This demystification of the act of writing—and therefore *also* of the French literary establishment itself—is accompanied by a concerted effort (one that is echoed by the "quifaitlafrance" collective) to counter false perceptions and representations of the environment in which she grew up: "I realized something important, which is that not many people from my background, with my social and cultural origins, are represented in the media or have a voice. I got this opportunity, and now I realize I don't have the right to pass it up. It's rare for someone to speak out, especially in a field that's not normally reserved for people like us."[30] Indeed, a cursory glance at some of the works that claim to provide *authoritative* accounts of *banlieue* life or of Islam (the two are indistinguishable in this context) in France—Souad with Marie-Thérèse Cuny, *Brûlée vive* (2003), Jamila Aït-Abbas, *La Fatiha: née en France, mariée de force en Algérie* (2003), and Samira Bellil, *Dans l'enfers des tournantes* (2003)—reveal the prevalence and popularity of sensationalist narratives about minority women, narratives that in turn sustain recuperative culturalist agendas.[31] Guène does not deny the existence of problems; rather, she shows how these exist *alongside* other experiences. Countering negative perceptions and stereotypes of *banlieue* populations is, however, a Sisyphean task.

One of the pioneering elements of Guène's work concerns her refusal to embrace the departure or escape narrative that was so central to *beur* texts. Mehdi Charef's now classic work, *Le thé au harem d'Archi Ahmed* (Tea in the harem), is indicative of that trend, organized around the central protagonist's repeated attempts to *get out* from the housing project.[32] Thus, when Hargreaves argues that "[w]hat distinguishes this third generation is that, unlike the first two, it has never known anything other than the ethnically stigmatized environment into which it was born, and many of its members are convinced that there is no hope of their ever escaping from the banlieues,"[33] he is insisting on the figurative dimension (in which *getting out* primarily concerns social mobility and inclusion), whereas for the *beurs* this quest was literal. Guène is repeatedly asked if her literary success has allowed her to leave the *banlieue.* But for Guène, this question betrays the logic she is determined to deconstruct and points to those misguided oversimplifications of *banlieue* life disseminated by outsiders who adhere to depictions and portrayals with which she refuses to identity: "I have no desire to leave now. If leaving symbolizes success, then the implication is that staying would be a failure,"[34] and "I don't agree with this Manichean view of the *banlieue* that places the good on one side, the exceptions to the rule on a pedestal, and then the hoodlums on the other to be excoriated."[35] In fact, this is precisely the view that was promoted by President Sarkozy. In his "Discours de Grenoble" in July 2010, he claimed that "[t]here are residents in these neighborhoods [the housing projects] who are desperate to get out."[36] Having said this, one should stress that Guène's work does not disguise the harsh realities associated with living in underprivileged communities in France. On the contrary, equilibrium is achieved between an engagement with social realities and an insistence upon the quotidian aspect of family living, along with the various trials and tribulations, joys and disappointments associated with this life. The topography is unmistakably that of the *banlieue,* and the spatial configuration that of the "block" (*Just Like Tomorrow,* 83), where the "caretaker doesn't give a shit about our flats.... There was piss and spit in the lift, plus it stank, but at least it was working" (*Just Like Tomorrow,* 29), and "It was grey outside, the same color as the concrete of the tower blocks and there was a fine drizzle, like God was spitting on us" (*Just Like Tomorrow,* 62). In *Du rêve pour les oufs,* the main character Ahlème (a twenty-four-year-old woman who moved to France in 1992 after her mother's assassination in Algeria), describes her environment in the following terms:

> I'm surrounded by all these screwball housing blocks that hem in our lives here, our noises and smells. I'm standing alone, in the middle of their wacky architecture, their garish colors, their mad shapes that have cradled our illusions for so long. The days are over when running water and electricity were enough to camouflage the injustices, and the shanty towns are far away. I'm standing proud and thinking about a whole heap of stuff. What's happened in our endz these past few weeks has stirred up the whole world press, but after a few clashes between youths and the police, everything's calmed down again. What can the carcasses of burnt-out cars do to change anything, when an army of fanatics is trying to silence us? (*Dreams from the Endz,* 22–23)[37]

This passage is significant for two reasons. On the one hand, Ahlème invokes the "bidonvilles" (shanty towns) in which an earlier generation of ethnic minorities had lived (as was documented in several *beur* texts)—thereby indicting the authorities for their failure to improve the socioeconomic state of affairs—and at the same time, she alludes to the 2005 riots that are at once the expression of growing irritation, exasperation, dejection, and despondency in the face of a hostile republic. In an essay on the subject of the 2005 riots,

"The Republic and Its Beast: On the Riots in the French *Banlieues*," Achille Mbembe addressed the manner in which participatory citizenship has effectively been denied to ethnic minorities as substantiated by their treatment at the hands of the authorities: "This treatment and these forms of humiliation, which were once tolerated only in the colonies, are now resurfacing in the metropolis itself, during sweeps and raids in the *banlieues,* they are applied not only to aliens—illegal immigrants and refugees—but increasingly to French citizens of African decent or the descendants of former African slaves" ("The Republic and Its Beast," 51–52).

The connection between the Republic and republican ideals in *Kiffe kiffe demain* is not of course arbitrary. Indeed, the French State functions metonymically for the Republic and suffuses the narrative: fifteen-year-old Doria attends public school, a range of state mechanisms mobilize in order to allocate her a social worker (symbolic agent of integration), and even her poverty is paradoxically inseparable from the state through the benefits she receives. In explaining, as Guène's insightful protagonist does, the necessity to—"think twice about everything I'm saying. Can't say a single word in slang or young people's language, even if that's the best way of getting her to understand how I'm feeling" (*Just Like Tomorrow,* 165)—she actually underscores the more crucial issue that is at the heart of this communicative barrier. This concerns the disconnect between, on the one hand, those who reside in the *banlieues* and, on the other, those located in mainstream French society, and concurrently the attributes and characteristics accorded to those insiders by a range of constructs generated by outsiders. Naturally, the challenge for the *banlieue* writer consists in altering these distorted assessments.

While attending civics class, Doria comments on the difficult relationship *banlieue* youth entertain with the actual practice of citizenship and the lack of representation: "The guy's got to fight just to survive each day, so you can forget about being a good citizen. . . . If things worked out better for him, maybe he'd shift his arse and vote. Except I don't really see who'd represent him. . . . When I'm eighteen, I'll vote. You never get a chance to speak out round here. So when you've got it, you grab it" (*Just Like Tomorrow,* 87–88). This is a problem that has been much discussed since the 2005 riots, and which Laurent Mucchielli has commented upon: "Access to citizenship poses a particular challenge to the descendants of immigrants since they feel unrecognized, stigmatized, even rejected by French society; they don't feel represented by the authorities and therefore find themselves unable to build independent collective actions that are sustainable and non-violent, in contrast to uprisings that are nothing but merely fleeting emotional outburst."[38] Nevertheless, the text Guène published prior to the riots confronts this realization, and Doria embraces a programmatic component in the conclusion to the novel through a form of engaged citizenship: as exemplified by the protagonist Doria's concluding statement: "I'll lead the uprising on the Paradise estate. . . . It will be a smart revolution with nobody getting hurt, and we'll all rise up to make ourselves heard" (*Just Like Tomorrow,* 178–179). Doria is able to consider, lightheartedly, her newfound optimism and "forts élans républicains" (*Kiffe kiffe demain,* 193 [I'm getting way too political, *Just Like Tomorrow,* 179]). There is of course an element of cynicism tempering her optimism, but the fact remains that "Maintenant, kif-kif demain je l'écrirais différemment. Ça serait kiffe kiffe demain" (*Kiffe kiffe demain,* 192 [But now I'd say it differently. I'd say just *like* tomorrow, *Just Like Tomorrow,* 192]).

Ironically, one of the criticisms leveled at the rioters in 2005 concerned precisely the lack of coordination: "One of the most striking features of the disturbances was their lack of political leadership. No spokespeople emerged, no list of demands was put forward nor did any meetings or negotiations take place between rioters and police or politicians" (Hargreaves, *Multi-Ethnic France,* 135). Even though racial advocacy groups, such as the Conseil représentatif des associations noires (CRAN) and the Indigènes de la République have remained active, immigration reform and integration policy have contributed to mounting feelings of disenchantment among ethnic minorities and escalating contempt for the authorities. Guène published *Kiffe kiffe demain* in 2004 and the shift to the Right that France has experienced since that time means that she would be unlikely to reach the same conclusions today.

Abandoning the repetition and formulaic component of her quotidian existence on the Paradise Estate in favor of something more positive, "Guène's title," Sarah Adams shows, "means both 'different day, same shit' and 'perhaps I might just *like* tomorrow'" (*Just Like Tomorrow,* 182). Yet, it is this playfulness, irony, and judicious use of humor that allows Guène to tackle the multifaceted social issues that confront the *banlieue.* Humor permeates her descriptions of the people she comes into contact with, from the social worker who is "old, ugly and she smells of Quit Nits shampoo" (*Just Like Tomorrow,* 1), and the school principal, "He's fat, he's stupid, and when he opens his mouth it smells of cheap wine, plus he smokes a pipe. At the end of the school day, his big sister picks him up from the main gates in a red Skoda. So he's kind of got a credibility problem when he wants to make out he's boss" (*Just Like Tomorrow,* 5). Similarly, thinking about her life and future, Doria remarks: "Fate stinks. It's a pile of shit because you've got no control over it. Basically, whatever you do you'll always be screwed" (*Just Like Tomorrow,* 11). But, subsequently, her pragmatic response reveals a philosophical approach to life that is refreshing: "We worry about the future but what's the point? We might not even have one" (*Just Like Tomorrow,* 14). Television is omnipresent in her life—"When we did the Middle Ages with Mr. Werbert, my geography teacher from last year, he told us how stained glass windows in churches were like the poor person's Bible for people who couldn't read. I reckon these days it's the TV that's the poor person's Koran" (*Just Like Tomorrow,* 141). Television provides contact with another world, one to which she is able to escape without nevertheless ignoring the harsh realities of her life: "It wasn't like in the films. It was like in real life" (*Just Like Tomorrow,* 53–54). At times, an element of pathos pervades the narrative, particularly when the subject of poverty arises: when Doria and her mother visit the Eiffel Tower (itself a product of the Universal Exposition of 1889, and symbol of imperial glory and republican *grandeur*) but cannot afford to go up it, or when she equates her appearance with that of "Cosette" in Victor Hugo's *Les Misérables* (*Just Like Tomorrow,* 116).

Somewhat paradoxically, the French government during Sarkozy's presidency continued to insist that immigrants demonstrate the ability to support themselves and find "adequate housing." Yet this image of the nondescript, unexceptional, ordinary *étranger,* the figure of the "invisible" marginal citizen—the *ouf*—found in Guène's writings, is often, *already,* a French citizen residing *in* France. During the colonial era, schoolchildren learned that their ancestors were Gauls, and in 2005 the French National Assembly voted the "Loi Fillon" that made it obligatory for schoolchildren to learn *La Marseillaise.* But these gestures were and continue to be futile when the foundations to the Republic—*liberty, equality, fraternity*—are applied unevenly. As the Rap artist H-Magnum has claimed, "We're not given the same chance, in spite of the fact that we learn the same things, we don't have the same France . . . children of immigrants and in spite of our skills, France spits on us" (*Plafond de verre*). *Banlieue* writers provide invaluable insights on a dimension of French society that would otherwise remain either invisible or subject to stereotypical representations.

Before I explore Faïza Guène's short films and how these have contributed to improving our appreciation and understanding of the French *banlieues,* I will briefly discuss film genres. As François Niney has pointed out, "*Entre les murs* (2008, The Class) by Laurent Cantet, is a paradocumentary in which the subjects concerned by the film play themselves in order to reconstitute the 'reality' of a High School class," and served to underscore the complex ways in which fiction and reality were being *documented* today and how the division between filmic genres had become increasingly complicated by rapid technological innovation.[39] Strictly-speaking, "*a 'documentary'* distinguishes itself because it refers to a specific document, or form of documentation, that is either visual or audiovisual: *a documentary* then is a film (or a video) as opposed to a fiction film, a distinction similar to the one we may draw between an essay and a novel" (Niney, *Le documentaire,* 15–16). As well, "Most French-language dictionaries along with the vocabulary used to discuss cinema tend to define documentaries with reference to two principle features: its didactic quality and its opposition to fiction that would cover the opposition between the real and imaginary" (Niney, *Le documentaire,* 16). However, the indiscriminate recourse to such terms as "showing real events" and "referring to the real" (Niney, *Le documentaire,* 17) to designate events or features of *all* forms of film has served to further complicate the process of categorizing film productions.

Given their specific objective of *documenting* the cultural, economic, political, and social realities of the *banlieues,* the short films by Faïza Guène that are under consideration here compel viewers to reflect simultaneously on the subjects explored and the effectiveness—and therefore the social function—of the camera itself as a tool. Relying as they do on diverse evidentiary modes, testimonies, and privileged ethnographic informers, Guène has said, "Beyond the fact that these are creative works, works of fiction, these films offer an opportunity to better understand aspects of the lives of adolescents of my generation and from my social milieu" (Guène, "Personal communication"), these films engage in a dialogue between the center and the periphery.

The French *banlieues* have received considerable attention—on the subject of religion and gender roles,[40] comparative urban policies,[41] ethnicity, race and class,[42] social mobility,[43] police repression[44]—and we are today better equipped thanks to these historical and sociological analyses to understand cultural and social dynamics in these urban spaces and also to identity reductive characterizations of these. However, as new generations of researchers have gained scholarly legitimacy as a result of extensive fieldwork in the *banlieues,* it remains of crucial importance to determine what can be gained by connecting these findings and observations with the *internal* productions. For, as Alec Hargreaves demonstrated with reference to the *beurs,* they were "the first to write from *within* the immigrant community itself" (*Immigration and Identity,* 4, emphasis added).[45] Ultimately, these cultural practitioners provided a perspective on France that was not available elsewhere. The documentary component—albeit mediated via fiction—was integral to the genealogy of production, recording an aspect of French society that might not have otherwise been available.

The focus on sociological elements complicated the reception of literary works within a highly institutionalized literary establishment, and *beur* authors were often heavily criticized for this. Furthermore, the critiques these writers articulated against failed assimilationist and integrational measures and policies were also construed as calling into question accepted norms and attributes. As Ahmed Boubeker has argued, "Of course, the struggle may well seem questionable when faced with the watchmen of traditional France [vieille France]. . . . But the fact remains that during the 1980s and 1990s, a symbolic revolution occurred: immigration became a key element in discussions on identity as it imposed itself as a component of French society."[46] Relative newcomers to the cultural scene elected to investigate subjects anchored in personal experience, but also to address how these communities were represented. Therefore, when one attempts to categorize films, as François Niney has shown, distinctions between *fiction* and *reality* have not always been that obvious, given that "both fiction and documentary are films, and they each have recourse to a cinematographic language," so that one has to consider "the relationship between the person filming and the person being filmed" and "the relationship between the situations and events (diegesis)," and ultimately recognize that "fiction just like the documentary is founded on *prises de vues réelles* . . . that transform real and chronicle time into narrative" (*Le documentaire,* 62). The decision to engage with dominant society was partially the result of growing awareness of discrimination and the advances that had been made thanks to social activism and mobilization.[47] In an interview pertaining to the role played by the organization DiverCité, Boualam Azahoum remarked, "Of course there are problems that are specific to some neighborhoods, but some of these problems can be attributed to social, economic, cultural, and historical contexts. There are variations that can be attributed to different local histories, but problems are for the most part the same. . . . The challenge has been to pool together our resources so as overcome these problems and to better understand the changes we are experiencing."[48] Thus, aligning oneself with the momentum in place and working toward improving the circulation of ideas and images *out* of the *banlieues* necessarily means foregrounding the dual components of representation—on the one hand, tracing the positive developments that had resulted from enhanced political consciousness and advocacy, and on the other emphasizing the benefits of coordinating efforts aimed at achieving more accurate representations of the *banlieues* themselves. Such measures would entail a direct confrontation with colonial history and postcolonial realities, and with an analysis of the social and political mechanisms responsible for producing inequality.[49]

The transcoloniality of these questions may seem obvious, but they remain contested issues in French society today. "The concept of integration," as Pierre Tevanian has shown, "was brandished in this way by the colonial State as a concession designed to contain the colonized population and suppress their claims for equality and later self-determination. . . . This suppression of the question of equality finds its continuity in the public debate as it stands today."[50] Some historians have been slightly less inclined to accept the linearity of these colonial legacies, arguing that in order to "achieve a more global and less mechanical understanding of the colonial experience in the present compels us to pay attention to power relations that are necessarily temporary in nature given the fact that they are constantly reallocated."[51] However, the "colonial precedent"[52] appears incontrovertible, and as Hafid Gafaiti maintains, the fact nevertheless remains that "[t]he French colonial authorities produced an ethnic discourse that would serve as the basis of and justification for their policies. Along with economic and political factors that determine the development of immigration in France, this discourse shaped the representation of North African immigrants within France. . . . The new status of immigrants, and of their children in particular, designated as the second generation, led to what are currently exacerbated tensions within the French social fabric and to an increasing racism and discourse of exclusion."[53] Nowhere, arguably, have these transcolonial links been more convincingly present than in the images found on television, whereby the "images that do feature on screen tend to be neocolonial in character, presenting migrants and their descendants as alien to the national community and/or as the beneficiaries of paternalistic condescension" (Hargreaves, "Gatekeepers and Gateways," 96). Also, "A qualitative assessment of television shows in fact reveals that both the positive and negative stereotypes produced are consistent in reducing non-whites to their 'origins,' essential constituents of their foreignness in French society."[54]

In 1997, Alec Hargreaves published an insightful study of postcolonial minorities and French television in which he remarked that the "Heavy capital cost involved in television production and marketing do not make it easy for minority groups to take an active role as program-makers and suppliers" ("Gatekeepers and Gateways," 96). Since that time, technological evolution has democratized access to production (digital cameras) and distribution (on the Internet), and young people have capitalized on these digital and technological advances. In turn, this has translated into greater minority participation and therefore visibility. In a 2008 article in *Le Monde,* "Les cités s'emparent de la caméra" (The housing estates get hold of movie cameras), Pascale Krémer indicated how creativity abounds in the *banlieues*—"The tools of the trade, digital cameras and editing software have been democratized, along with a drastic drop in prices and substantial improvement in user-friendliness," and "Sold in DVD format, but more significantly distributed free of charge on Internet sites, some of which resemble web-TV networks, on video blogs or on video sharing service websites like Dailymotion. . . . No matter what final outlet is chosen for the films, along with diverse forms of organization (informal collectives, associations, or workshops in cultural centers)."[55] The potential of filmmaking was also partially addressed in the 2007 manifesto "quifaitlafrance," and when later that year the edited volume *Chroniques pour une société annoncée* was published, the authors announced that "All the royalties from this book will go to the association and be earmarked for projects made by the people who live in these underprivileged neighborhoods."[56] The primary concern of the collective has been to reject stereotypes and false characterizations of the *banlieues,* and accordingly to counter these by registering accurate accounts of France's cultural, economic, ethnic, and social diversity: "*because* we refuse to allow the public space, that only intellectual resource where a society can reflect on itself, to be wasted on empty debates, systematic derision, superficial discourses, and the indefatigable staging of the ruling class."[57]

In Faïza Guène's 2006 novel, *Du rêve pour les oufs,* the twenty-four-year-old main character Ahlème reflects on her circumstances, concluding "I'm standing proud and thinking about a whole heap of stuff" (*Dreams from the Endz,* 23) and much like Guène herself, resolving to be proactive.[58] The aim of writers and filmmakers could be summarized as examples of concerted action, whereby "[e]xasperated by the same old stereotypes the television networks feed them on the *banlieues,* the young people who live there have seized the power media has to offer" (Krémer, "Les cités s'emparent de la caméra," 24). Theirs is a cathartic action, an "endeavor that offers therapeutic benefits to their self-image, so as to counter the image offered in the media. . . . Assuming a position behind the camera, they are able to reappropriate their image" (Krémer, "Les cités s'emparent de la caméra," 25). The question of visibility is therefore twofold, allowing populations that occupy an otherwise marginal status to be noticed by dominant society, and rendering conspicuous a broad range of social issues that necessarily question and place under pressure republican ideals and values. For, as Carrie Tarr has demonstrated, "Films from the cinemas of the periphery tell a different story [and provide] the potential to articulate exclusion and double consciousness in a way that challenges the hegemony of French culture."[59] Historically at least, this is a recent phenomenon, for until 1999

> The ways in which non-white minorities and the new configurations of the French nation were represented in the collective imaginary had not been addressed explicitly. . . . Up until 1998, French television was pretty much a reflection of the French republican model: in the name of the principle of equality between individuals, it was assumed to be "indifferent to differences," in other words it did not take into consideration differences between individuals and groups in order to avoid threatening the unity of the nation by juxtaposing "communities" based on "race," ethnicity, gender, religion. The perverse consequence of this "indifference to differences" was indifference to discrimination. (Macé, "Postcolonialité et francité," 391–392)

The project of documenting the *banlieues,* the principles, rationale, and logistics of obtaining an *eye* into the contemporary postcolonial context and of obtaining a view from within that could then be juxtaposed with external projections was advanced by the creation of numerous associations and groups in the *banlieues*—partially as a response to the multiple uprisings that had occurred during the 1990s in such Parisian *banlieues* as Sartrouville, Garges-lès-Gonesse, Mantes-la-Jolie, and Nanterre. Different associations and organizations,[60] web-TV networks,[61] internet sites,[62] and youth organizations were set up. As Pascale Krémer has underlined, these are "documentaries and fictions, mostly, that ring true" ("Les cités s'emparent de la caméra," 27). On some sites, such as www.les-engraineurs.org, most films are accessible and can be downloaded, the objective being above all to "Encourage new voices to emerge from these so-called problem areas [quartiers sensibles] by developing small scale or more ambitious audiovisual projects."[63] Films thus address a broad range of important issues, including gender roles and expectations, poverty, family values, education, school, youth culture, disillusionment, language, and Islam. Omnipresent are concerns with delinquency, the nationalistic and xenophobic tendencies of the far right, police brutality and harassment, and increased monitoring and surveillance of the *banlieues.* Documenting these harsh realities also entails demystifying external projections. As Guy Gauthier has shown, films and documentaries assume multiple forms, ranging from an "immersion in everyday life," "the authenticity that comes from testimony," or "documentary fiction."[64] Over time, documentaries have evolved, but what has remained constant is the imperative of constructing a narrative, of directing and guiding the viewer, of communicating ideas and positions; ultimately though, the objective is to sustain a relationship to a given reality. "Documentaries," Guy Gauthier has shown, "have defined themselves in terms of their relationship to life, something that allows them to affirm their uniqueness; in relation to fiction, by trying to exploit its gigantic shadow; in relation to various techniques that can either be foregrounded or in turn relegated to a secondary position by the essential question of authenticity" (*Le documentaire un autre cinéma,* 206).

In addition to being a best-selling author, Faïza Guène has also proven particularly adept at making short films. She collaborated with the *engraineurs* group, founded originally as a direct response to media representations of the *banlieues:* "We did not recognize ourselves in the images of our lives we found in the media, and so we made our own images" (Guène, "Personal communication"). For Guène,

> Making short-films was really a pretext for stimulating debates in different forums, and the films themselves focused on current issues while also being centered on the daily lives of young people; this provided me with all kinds of opportunities to engage in discussions with the pupils I met with in various schools. They identified with many of the issues we explored, and film was a particularly useful medium in helping them relate and share their opinions. My feeling is that these short-films were more of a pedagogic tool, an almost sociological approach, more than they were works of cinematography. Certainly I believe a quite different approach than my novels. ("Personal communication")

Cited in Mohamed Ridha Bouguerra's and Sahiba Bouguerra's *Histoire de la littérature du Maghreb: littérature francophone,* Guène has indicated how "My parents were alive during the war in Algeria, and experienced the events of October 1961 in Paris. They don't want to be a nuisance. But we were born here and we refuse to keep quiet."[65] This realization provided the motivation for her documentary *Mémoires du 17 octobre* (with Bernard Richard 2002, 17 mins.). Inspired by Jean-Luc Einaudi's important and controversial book published in 1991, *La bataille de Paris: 17 octobre* 1961, on the massacre of several hundred Algerians (and physical injury to several thousand others) that took place in Paris in October 1961, Guène's documentary stands today as an important contribution to the process of establishing and recognizing—as well as memorializing—some of the more disquieting aspects of French-Algerian contact and history.[66]

The documentary brings together a number of first hand testimonies by individuals (Algerian workers, demonstrators, journalists, photographers, bystanders, and organizers) who witnessed the violent response by the police to a peaceful demonstration organized by Algerian workers and pro-FLN supporters against the imposition of a curfew that limited circulation in the city and prevented workers from getting to night-shifts at various factories. Georges Azenstarck, then a staff photographer at the Communist newspaper *L'Humanité,* was on assignment at the time: "I was there. I witnessed events first hand." Such statements—made in the documentary—proved crucial when he testified before the French courts to support Jean-Luc Einaudi's accusation that Maurice Papon (the former chief of the Paris police) had been responsible for the organization of the October 1961 massacres. On the evening of October 17, 1961, Algerian workers congregated at the Place de l'Opéra in Paris. According to the documentary, the evidence gathered corroborates claims pertaining to the peaceful goals of the demonstration and confirms that the organizers had implemented a set of safety and precautionary measures. All the eyewitness accounts thus contradict the official version of events. Monique Hervo, for example, claims that "I've always said it, the police were firing on demonstrators, I was there," statements substantiated by Ahmed Touil: "I saw it with my own eyes." His brother Omar Touil has also asserted that the events of October 17 were to be inscribed in a broader pattern of police harassment, whereby "[t]here were constant *roundups*" (emphasis added), and Monique Hervo described the alarming accounts of Algerians being lynched and tortured in the woods of Boulogne and Vincennes to the western and eastern perimeter of the capital: "We were living under conditions of total arbitrariness. . . . Effectively a reign of terror that could only lead to demonstrations, with the curfew imposed following Papon's direct orders. So for me, October 17 remains something awful, but the days and the months that preceded that day were just as bad."[67] Guène's documentary examines one of the most problematic chapters in Algerian-French history, revealing the constitutive nature of the apparatus of contemporary identity-formation. It is to these themes, among others, that the short-films under consideration turn their attention. Likewise, these provide alternative accounts of life in the *banlieues* that challenge those available in what may be considered official outlets.

Mathieu Kassovitz's 1995 film *La haine* includes a sequence during which a television news crew pulls up in a *banlieue* housing estate seeking live footage of urban youth commenting on their role in the previous night's violent uprising and clash with the police. Rather than providing the journalist with the kind of predetermined answers she hopes for, one of the main characters, Hubert, shouts out "This isn't Thoiry!" Much in the same way as one would visit Thoiry (a wildlife animal park located on the outskirts of Paris), the journalist in question remains within the confines of her vehicle, keeping a safe distance—and thereby causing offense—from the *wild* youth she encounters. As I will argue, *Sale réput'* (2002, 14 mins., Bad Rep'), a short film to which Faïza Guène contributed, operates intertextually with the kind of conclusion Kassovitz is drawing in terms of media perceptions of *banlieue* youth. In *Sale réput'*, a journalist (Carole, played by Isabelle Carré) is given the assignment of following up on a news story about rival gangs fighting in the neighborhood around La Défense. Rather than going to La Défense, she opts instead to visit the peaceful Courtillières estate located at the opposite perimeter of Paris in Pantin where she has a contact. For her, one must assume, *banlieue* spaces are interchangeable, perhaps defined by varying degrees of violence, but essentially sharing common signifiers. One can comprehend this perception, given that "By inventing for all intents and purposes an enemy and in making fear of this enemy into the cornerstone of everyday life and culture, the objective has been to accord legitimacy to the role of the authorities as the enforcers of protection and security."[68]

As with the scene from Kassovitz's film alluded to earlier, the journalist in question begins to ask loaded questions that have to do with gang activity, violence, and so on. Initially, the respondents challenge the premise of her questions:

RESPONDENT #1: When people see us hanging around in groups, they're afraid. But we aren't going to harm anybody.

CAROLE: *Where does this fear come from?*

RESPONDENT #2: They get all these ideas from the TV. From politics. All they hear about is delinquency, violence in the *banlieues*.

However, these responses prove unsatisfactory because they don't conform to the narrative she is endeavoring to construct and are therefore not newsworthy. (This is made even more apparent in some of the footage that was cut from the final edit, in which Carole states, "I didn't get the footage I needed"). She therefore seeks out other interviewees and eventually obtains the kind of response she has been looking for from a teenage girl named Rachida:

CAROLE: Are you OK answering a few questions?

RACHIDA: Yeah, no problem.

At this moment the film switches to the evening televised news program on which we learn that young people in the *banlieues* settle differences with weapons that are stored in no less than an "armurerie" (armory). The journalist's "fact-checking" mission to *a banlieue* thus proves successful in terms of the kind of audience expectations they have created through sensationalized news coverage, but grossly inaccurate in terms of the *reality* on the ground.

As Ernesto Oña comments (a young man interviewed by Pascale Krémer for her *Le Monde* article on *banlieue* filmmaking), "After 2005 [the social uprisings and riots], we agreed that was enough, that we wouldn't allow ourselves to be spoken of in this hurtful, violent way! Henceforth, voices would be heard from the inside" (Krémer, "Les cités s'emparent de la caméra," 25). Although *Sale réput'* was released several years before the 2005 uprisings, the film was a response to prevalent assumptions about the *banlieues.* As Krémer has shown, outsiders "are only interested in spectacular images that reinforce their prejudicial views, those eternal stereotypes on the *banlieues* and the people who live there—a world apart, characterized by violence, delinquency, and suffering, and populated by rappers, drug dealers, rapists and hooded fundamentalists" ("Les cités s'emparent de la caméra," 26).

There are of course consequences for running stories such as these. In the case of *Sale réput',* the footage screened on television results in—or serves to justify—a toughening of police controls in their neighborhood. Adult residents express their concern with *correcting* such negative characterizations by contacting the media, but of course one knows only too well that such attempts would prove futile. The "sale réput'"—or "bad rep'"—corresponds to accepted opinions about the *banlieue,* enabling an apparently inescapable cycle of violence, the kind of "tautology of fear"[69] we examined in chapter 3 to trigger a heightened police presence which in turn prompts further anger, resistance, and oppositionality. The fatigue with such images and ongoing discussions as to how best to represent oneself also culminates in further disillusionment. As Ahmed Boubeker has written "They are nothing more nor less than caricatures of a sham alienness that reinforces an unhealthy taste for the sensational even while appeasing the conscience. With no place of recognition to hang their hats, these new barbarians in the news do not even have the extenuating circumstance of being the offspring of generations of poverty and oppression. For under the state of emergency of monstrosity or subhuman barbarism, they are emptied of all social meaning, deprived of any experience proper to them."[70]

In both *beur* and *banlieue* films, boredom—and therefore the consequences of limited activity and opportunity—has become a common feature. In *Le bon à rien* (2001, 11 mins., Good for nothing), written by Faïza Guène, three teenage boys are seen resting on the grass outside one of the neighborhood projects. True to the title of the film—*Le bon à rien,* literally "good for nothing"—two of them decide to go shoplifting. In a later scene, one of the young men (Brahim) has now returned home where his mother is struggling to interrupt endless hours of computer gaming. "I'm ashamed of you," she interjects, pressuring him to get up and find work. His offhand response, "In any case, I'm a good for nothing," reveals the extent to which he has appropriated this label. However, faced with his mother's ultimatum that he either find work or leave home, the camera now marks Brahim's decision to respond to the challenge with a transition from the domestic space of the home to the public one where we observe Brahim in front of the Intérim employment agency scrutinizing job announcements. The agency's promotional statement, prominently displayed in the front window—"Et si j'essayais l'intérim?"—confronts Brahim with the existential choice between action—"What if I tried Interim" *or* "What if I gave Interim a chance?"—and the status quo. Realizing that Intérim's list only contains specialized job offerings, Brahim makes his way to the local Agence nationale pour l'emploi (ANPE) office. At first he seems reluctant to enter the building—his hesitation might even imply a concern that others witness him crossing the threshold into what is, effectively, a government agency. At the very moment when he has built up the courage to enter, another man exiting the building tells him not to waste his time since the minimum requirement for the positions they have available is the BAC + 3 (i.e., three years of post-secondary education).

Not surprisingly, as Brahim is left wandering the area, he comments, "It sucks around here." He does make one additional attempt to find a job at the local auto shop, but when his alarm clock fails to wake him up the following morning for the agreed upon 8:30 start, he realizes it is not worth arriving late and attempting to convince his employer to give him another chance. Disheartened, downhearted, he wanders the streets until he happens upon a young black boy drowning, unable to get out of the canal into which he has fallen. Brahim hesitates and then decides that he will not intervene (interestingly enough, another version of the film explored an ending in which Brahim runs to the boy's rescue). His unwillingness to act operates metaphorically, pointing to a form of social paralysis whereby he has been told or made to feel on so many occasions that he is a "good for nothing" that he most likely feels incapable of rescuing the drowning boy, much in the same way that no figure of authority (either an adult or the French State itself) has been able to save him, or afforded him the skills and training to save himself from his own social drowning. The inadequacies of the broader infrastructure are exposed, shown to be intrinsic to government agencies and inseparable from the emptiness of political rhetoric, producing overwhelming obstacles and barriers to social mobility and perpetuating marginality and inequality. The impact is most powerfully felt in the home environment where a precarious relationship exists between the hopes, aspirations, and expectations of parents, the demands of the French State, and the autonomy of the children.

In *RTT* (2002, 11 mins.), written and directed by Faïza Guène, a single mother (Zohra, played by the author's own mother Kadra Guène) of three children who works the evening shift as an office cleaner takes a day off work (through the "Réduction du temps de travail" policy [reduced work hours]) in order to be able to attend a parent-teacher conference at the school's request. At the meeting she discovers the extent of her eldest son's (Mehdi) absenteeism—the school has sent out multiple letters, but Mehdi and his sister (Naïma) have thus far successfully intercepted the mail so that the letters from the school do not reach their intended recipient. The teacher remarks, "We don't see you very often at these meetings," and Zohra informs him that this is because "I work evenings." Throughout *RTT* the viewer becomes aware of the precarious situation in which the family lives: the children are asleep when Zohra returns from work, they live in a housing project, and their finances are limited. The interaction between Zohra and the teacher is all the more interesting because her usage of French is familiar, often grammatically incorrect, and the level of proficiency limited (she speaks for the most part in Arabic with her children, and they in turn respond in French): "All I'm interested in is my son's success." What pains her in discovering that her seventeen-year-old son has abandoned school is both that he has relinquished an individual opportunity—"What a waste; all this time I thought he was studying, working" (expressed in Arabic with subtitles in French)—as well as implicated the rest of the family because of his selfish behavior—"and get me out of this misery his father left us in." Rafik, the youngest child, accompanies her to the meeting. Rather than recognizing Mehdi's poor judgment, he interprets this instead as an injustice toward him: "Mehdi doesn't go to school so I don't see why I should have to?" His mother assumes parental authority, highlighting that Mehdi's choices are not to be emulated: "Be quiet. Do you want to end up like him, is that it?" The family argument that ensues when Zohra returns home serves to bring into the open conflicting views of domestic responsibility. Mehdi offers his mother some money, stating, "Well I've also had enough of watching my mother humiliate herself," apparently clarifying his determination to assume responsibility for the household even if this entails operating outside the strict confines of the system (the unidentified source of the money he offers his mother remains subject to interpretation). *RTT* ends with a powerful visual sequence, during which Naïma and Mehdi are filmed walking along a path that leads them out of the housing estate. Eventually the path bifurcates; the former elects to follow the path to school, while the latter heads off in the other direction. However, the outcome is left deliberately ambiguous: societal expectations call for conformity by adhering to uniform standards of mobility provided by educational advancement, yet it remains difficult to trust their application given the inequitable allocation of resources to *banlieue* schools, such that a feeling of helplessness lingers, coupled with the inescapable downward economic and social obstacles and pressures. Metaphors of imprisonment—inescapability, rigid class structures, tradition, and so on—are all too familiar.

In *La zonzonnière* (2001, 8 mins.), Faïza Guène uses the slang term for a prison, "zonzon," whose variations on the noun form include "zonzonnier" and "zonzonnière" to indicate the male and female form of "prisoner" or "inmate." In this case, as with *Rien que des mots* (2003, 27 mins., Nothing but words), the attention has shifted to complex gender dynamics in Muslim households. In *La zonzonnière,* teenage Fatima has been skipping school and both her father and brother (Farid) step in. First her father, who in harsh terms (speaking in Arabic), asserts his authority over her and restricts her movements henceforth between home and school: "I'm your father, yes or no? So listen to what I'm saying. I make the rules around here, I'm in charge!" And then her brother tells her, clarifying gender roles, "You're here to help Mom and your little sisters." Initially, the father's response and frustration upon learning of his daughter's behavior may be understandable, but an additional point is being made here relating to the anxiety young women experience as they seek to negotiate or reconcile expectations at home with those demands that are being made outside. Likewise, in *Rien que des mots,* Laïla feels compelled to hide her activities and interests from her parents. When she returns home after dark one evening, her mother (played by Kadra Guène) informs her that "Since your Dad went back to Algeria, you've been nothing but trouble." Also, the homeostasis she has disrupted will be restored: "Just you wait until he comes back. He'll put you straight!" Subtitles afford access to the non-Arabophone viewer, who will subsequently discover that the family will provide stability by pursuing a planned marriage for Laïla in Algeria. The emphasis on maintaining order and abiding by parental appraisals of cultural and social standards filter into the broader community. This is persuasively displayed in *Rumeurs* (2003,

8 mins., Rumors)—co-written by Faïza Guène and Sonia Chikh, and directed by Faïza Guène—when a young black boy from the *banlieue* neighborhood observes "the Chafri girl" (played by Faïza Guène herself) during an excursion into the center of Paris walking along the banks of the Seine River talking to a white man. This triggers several discussions between protagonists *back* in the *banlieue* about gender roles, Islam, immigrant women and those in the Maghreb; the questionable actions and behavior of "the Chafri girl" persist in acquiring negative overtones as the rumor spreads and provides the occasion for the community to come together against a shared detractor. Disobedience and failure to follow convention are now met with such statements as "Do you want to end up like that Chafri girl? People talk about her all day long!" and "Everyone in the neighborhood says she's dating a Parisian," and in the entrance to her building graffiti now reads "Chafri's a slut." The dénouement exposes the potential dangers of collective ignorance as we discover that the "Chafri girl" has in actuality been working on a homework assignment, conducting a survey that required interviewing subjects outside of her neighborhood.

The tenuous relationship between the center and the periphery and between the inside and the outside is of course a subjective one. Similarly, *banlieue* artists might very well reject or question the pertinence of such a label. Yet, what remains relevant is the commitment to meet head on those images that circulate in the media, in political discourse, and elsewhere, which aim at essentializing and stigmatizing the behavior of underprivileged members of society. The term "immigrant" continues to operate metonymically for all kinds of twenty-first-century problems in French society, but the authorities refuse to acknowledge (and are therefore incapable of correcting economic and social dissymmetry) that ethnicity itself remains a foundational element of discrimination: "Our government can hardly admit that the problem does not lie with immigration as such, but rather the immigration policies they have adopted."[71]

10

Decolonizing France

NATIONAL LITERATURES, *WORLD LITERATURE*, AND *WORLD IDENTITIES*

Identity is similar to an outfit you wear throughout life. You, however, expect us to wear a uniform. But you know how dangerous uniforms can be! I want to be able to change my outfits and even my look, to never have to be the same, because I would find that boring, and I don't want to have to take up position behind some kind of symbolic barbed wire that would separate me from others. I refuse to accept real or metaphoric walls.

—*Ananda Devi*[1]

Nevertheless, culture almost always flourishes in the margins, because the perspective on the center, the seat of power and of glory, is always more penetrating from the periphery.

—*Juan Goytisolo*[2]

The field of *Francophone studies* has allowed for the improved contextualization of the colonial and postcolonial era in France while also broadening the reception of creative and critical works produced by hexagonal and non-hexagonal writers. Yet, in the same way that recent discussions in France on postcolonial studies have often ignored advances made in other cultural and political contexts on these issues, *national* intellectuals have also tended to obfuscate the significance of existing international contributions and research. A number of important questions therefore need to be further explored in light of the publication in 2007 of the Manifesto "Pour une 'littérature-monde' en français" (Toward a world literature in French).[3] How might a *world litera-*

ture in French paradoxically serve to re-affirm the centrality of *Francophonie* as a hegemonic/monolithic force? Given that "[t]he global status of France and the French language remains tenaciously rooted in French colonial history and its outgrowths: *Francophonie* and *la Françafrique*" (Miller, "The Slave Trade, *La Françafrique,* and the Globalization of French," 251), this remains of primary concern.[4] What cultural, economic, political, and social differences/similarities can be located within alternative spheres of linguistic influence? What might the criteria for exclusion/inclusion be in an expanded version of the Manifesto? How do the more substantive claims correlate with other aesthetic and political conceptualizations of literary production? And finally, to what degree can these debates be situated within the framework of ethnic mobilization, identity formation, and cultural globalization?

The anthology, *Pour une littérature-monde,* published in 2007, brought together a broad range of critically acclaimed writers, with multiple *national* origins whose production reflects the diversity of French-language writing today.[5] Closer scrutiny of the anthology serves to highlight the multiple levels at which authors are connected: for the most part, they do not reside in their place of birth, in many cases *became* French nationals, and are thus separated by numerous factors from *homegrown* authors. The majority publishes almost exclusively in France; narratives generally adhere to topographic *Francophone* sites—in France (including of course the DOM-TOM), former colonial territories, or in other French-speaking areas of the world. However, "One sign of change in recent years," Christopher L. Miller writes, "has been a new global turn taken by certain African writers. . . . Numerous authors have taken at least a few steps beyond the borders of the Hexagon, sending their characters on forays to other states of the European Union."[6] As diverse as the modes of expression may be, the fact nevertheless remains that the central—perhaps even the only point of unification—concerns the "partage," the sharing of the French language, a reality further complicated by the foundational statement of the Organisation internationale de la Francophonie (OIF) whereby "The [OIF] is an institution founded on the basis of a shared language (French) and shared values," with a mandate to work toward the promotion of "the French language and cultural and linguistic diversity."[7] Yet, the signatories of the Manifesto articulate the following claims:

> Let's be clear: the emergence of a consciously affirmed, transnational world-literature in the French language, open to the world, signs the death certificate of so-called *francophonie.* No one speaks or writes "francophone." *Francophonie* is

> a light from a dying star. . . . With the center placed on an equal plane with other centers, we're witnessing the birth of a new constellation, in which language freed from its exclusive pact with the nation, free from every other power hereafter but the powers of poetry and the imaginary, will have no other frontiers but those of the spirit. ("Toward a World Literature in French," 56, translation altered)

In other words, residential, territorial, and diasporic factors serve to delineate a complex colonial-national-postcolonial-*Francophonie* cartography that places the category of the "monde" (world) and/or "global" dimension under pressure—while also blurring the distinction between "écrire en français" (writing in French) and "un écrivain français" (a French writer).

When Michel Le Bris invokes in the anthology, "The end of that particular kind of Francophonie and the emergence of a world-literature in French," the obvious question that arises concerns which "Francophonie" he has in mind.[8] Whose "world" are we talking about? Are we concerned with those who *govern* or those who are *governed,* for those who *govern* without concern for/the consent of the *governed,* those who circulate or those who remain landlocked at the periphery, or for that matter those who attempt perilous ocean crossings or internal migrations? Those who sit in camps and detention centers, those who have no residency papers, in other words those who have no voice? Obioma Nnaemeka has underscored the distinction between the French term *mondialisation* and the English term *globalization: "La mondialisation,* derived from *le monde* with its double meaning of the physical world (materiality) and people (humanity), captures both the materiality and humanity of globalization. The humanity that is at best minimized and at worst ignored in the discourse and practice of globalization in general takes center stage in discourses and practices that I see evolving in Africa."[9] Broadening the parameters of the discussion to include alternative spheres of discourse can assist us in understanding the French language context.

The break from/interment of "Francophonie" is accompanied in the anthology by the celebration of *world* authors who have been recognized in Britain as evidence of a vibrant *world literature* elsewhere. The politics of reception in the Anglophone world has succeeded, for the most part, in disentangling itself from an imperial history and neo-imperial pressures associated with the realm of the Commonwealth—there are, for example, no remnants of empire to be found (unlike in the Académie française) in the guise of *Anglophonie* officers patrolling the English language. However, while it is important to underscore how *Anglo-World literature* has been useful to comparative cultural analysis, this category has not itself been undisputed. Kenyan author Ngùgì wa Thiong'o has been the most forceful critic of this apparatus, arguing in *Decolonizing the Mind: The Politics of Language in African Literature* that: "The choice of language and the use to which language is put is central to a people's definition of themselves in relation to their natural and social environment, indeed in relation to the entire universe. . . . Unfortunately writers who should have been mapping paths out of that linguistic encirclement of their continent also came to be defined and to define themselves in terms of the languages of imperialist imposition."[10] The decolonization Ngùgì wa Thiong'o evokes has also been an institutional challenge, one that has mobilized postcolonial studies and Francophone studies to contest the limits and limitations of French Studies, thereby fostering critical paradigms that have contributed to the dismantling of those hierarchies that structured the *canon* alongside various *centers* and *peripheries.* Recourse to the category "Francophone" in the United States and United Kingdom (among other places), inaugurated a framework that allowed for the idea of a *world/global* literature in French, a historical precursor therefore to the *littérature-monde* invoked in the anthology. Indeed, ambiguity lingers in terms of the usage that is made in the Manifesto of the categories "Francophone" and "Francophonie"—for to be a "Francophone author" in the Anglo-scholarly context is to be associated with an affirmative category. As the Congolese novelist and playwright Sony Labou Tansi was famous for saying: "I write in French because that is the language in which the people I speak for were raped, that is the language in which I myself was raped. I remember my virginity. . . . One must say that if between myself and French there is anyone who is in a position of strength, it is not French, but I. I have never had recourse to French, it is rather French that has had recourse to me."[11] In fact, the objective has been to redefine the tenuous relationship between the center and the periphery, and important collective volumes have suggested new ways in which these constitutive historical relationships can provide greater inclusivity.[12] Thus, pronouncements of the kind made by French intellectuals such as Michel Le Bris, who claims to have coined the term "Littérature-monde" in 1992 ("Pour une littérature-monde en français," 24), tend to be formulated in a critical vacuum, reinventing wheels by largely ignoring a wealth of insights and perspectives on French culture already developed in the Anglophone world. These also fail to take into account the work performed by those *internal* scholars who have endeavored to decentralize (decolonize) the French institutional landscape, highlighting "colonial fracture."[13] The disciplinary realignment and reconfiguration of French studies in the United States coincided with such critical advances and have partially reversed academic dissymmetries; to a large degree today, French departments *need* Francophone studies. Some *national* scholars in the embryonic field of hexagonal postcolonial studies have been attentive to the "sociocultural contexts from which these literatures have emerged, . . . evaluating the situation of French in the world today by taking into account colonialism" and signaling the ways in which Anglophone postcolonial theory can be incorporated to the analysis of the French experience and context given that "Postcolonial studies emphasize the plurality of the French language, bereft of any obvious center."[14] Not surprisingly, the signatories do not embrace a common position on the concrete and symbolic objective of the Manifesto and the essays selected in the anthology confirm this.

Michel Le Bris's conceptualization of the term "Francophone" as a potentially marginalizing category rather than as an affirmative one is fallacious in the context of the Anglophone Academy. When, in arguing his point, Le Bris speaks of: "writers of French language expression that we still refer to (not for much longer, I venture) as 'Francophones'" (Le Bris, "Pour une littérature-monde en français," 32), something is actually *lost in translation* here as we navigate between English and French and the respective symbolic spaces occupied by the referents "Francophonie" and "Francophone." The suggestion that such distinctions are no longer necessary (and by extension therefore that "Francophone studies" has outlived its initial purpose) might seem to point to a leveling of the playing field. Yet, the issue has never been exclusively about *incorporating* Francophone authors to the curriculum but rather more importantly about rethinking the ways in which cultural inquiries are conducted, acknowledging how such an approach would simultaneously account for the history of exclusion *and* provide for the improved contextualization of the French language experience in the world. This objective continues to face institutional resistance and marketing and publishing strategies still disproportionately impact *world literature in French* in the *global south*. Back in 1997, having identified a new trend whereby numerous Francophone authors (Tahar Ben Jelloun, Patrick Chamoiseau, Andreï Makine, Amin Maalouf, and Ahmadou Kourouma) were being granted increasing critical recognition in the Parisian literary establishment in the form of major literary prizes (the Goncourt and the Renaudot), the *New York Times* published an article exploring this dynamic.[15] When a decade later this phenomenon became still more visible with the successes between 2006 and 2008 of Alain Mabanckou, Nancy Huston, Jonathan Littell, Tierno Monénembo, and Atiq Rahimi, there was journalistic talk of the "death of French culture."[16] Yet, while public figures continue to promote a mythic interpretation of French national identity, unstoppable transformations in the coordinates of the cultural landscape have been provided by vibrant global production that exceeds the narrow parameters of a monolithic historical interpretation of human relations—changes also much in evidence in the rap, hip hop, and urban art originating in the French *banlieues* neighborhoods, arguably those sites at which interaction and interchange between global populations are the most pronounced.

Writers such as Sony Labou Tansi sought to break away from the restrictive nature of the French language, disfiguring and dismantling syntax and form in order to articulate the nature of postcolonial power relations. Likewise, the emergence of national literatures in postcolonial Africa served to question the pertinence of independence borders and the nationalist agendas of postcolonial leaders. This dimension is all the more important in order to gauge the validity of the shift to the global that is the post-national framework. Dany Laferière emphasized this in his novel *Je suis un écrivain japonais* (I am a Japanese writer), claiming that "I couldn't care less about identity. . . . I did this [i.e., wrote a book with such a title] to show that there are no borders . . . I'd had enough of cultural nationalisms."[17]

Michel Le Bris was right to recognize the potential pitfalls of relinquishing French usage of the category "Francophone" in favor of "littérature-monde" if the latter merely served to reproduce the limitations of the former. However, suggesting that "these authors [i.e., Francophone authors] are *also* French authors" ("Pour une littérature-monde en français," 45) is on the one hand only partially correct—some of the signatories have in fact *become* French nationals—but the more significant element is ignored here, namely that which concerns the all-important difference between the consanguineous *écrivains français* (French writers) and the linguistic fraternity circumscribed by the denominator *écrire en français* (writing *in* French). Remaining attentive to the separation of literary production from nationalist demands is crucial, precisely because the objective has not been to reaffirm French hegemony but rather to indicate the numerous ways in which it has been displaced by the Francophone component. The decoupling of signifiers is a prerequisite for the goal of bringing "an end to an imperialist understanding of language" (Le Bris, "Pour une littérature-monde en français," 45) to become attainable. Abdourahman Waberi has argued that the whole point is precisely to "undo the suffocating knot" that supposedly binds together French as a language, a *race* and a nation, that is, citing Achille Mbembe, to "denationalize the French language."[18] For Alain Mabanckou, this represents a crucial matter: "In the end, saying that a Francophone author enriches or saves a language is far from being a compliment. Such remarks set up a relationship of subordination in which Francophone literature ends up being considered purely for its social function, for what it brings to the French language. . . . Why does the French language require surveillance, night watchmen?"[19]

Toward a World Literature in French has not paid sufficient attention to the fact that the authors included are almost exclusively published in Paris. While denouncing the centrifugal force of the Latin Quarter publishing industry, the collected anthology underexplores the importance of Quebec as a Francophone zone, as well as national micropublishing outlets in certain African countries (the Ivory Coast, Morocco, and Senegal). A point worth emphasizing though is that the products of the micro-national sector do not essentially circulate *out* of that context much in the same way that the works of the *littérature-monde* authors, because of prohibitive costs and inadequate purchasing power, do not circulate *in*. Thus, *world literature* in English, edited and published in *markets* as diverse as Australia, Canada, South Africa, the United Kingdom, the United States, and so on, may still privilege *first-world* consumers, but is nevertheless more inclusive when one considers that *world literature in French* is *not* read by the *world*. This observation further highlights the economic dissymmetry that disproportionately impacts those populations living in the *global south*.

Ngùgì wa Thiong'o has recently turned his attention to this problem: "The middle class prefers the European linguistic screen that keeps it worlds apart from the people. In all other societies, writers, keepers of memories, and carriers of national discourse use the languages of their communities; but the postcolonial intellectuals prefer to express communal memories in foreign languages, which, in the end, means sharing those communal memories with the foreign owners of the languages or among themselves as a foreign-language-speaking elite."[20] Thus, subjected to the lingering hegemonic forces of the Latin Quarter publishing monopoly, socioeconomic and sociocultural Francophone zones have only limited counterparts to offer in comparison to global Anglophone publication. Attempts to redress this imbalance by introducing specialized series such as Gallimard's *Continents noirs* or Hatier's *Monde Noir,* while introducing new voices, perpetuate hierarchies associated with the politics of reception and aesthetic classification. Calling for greater representation and inclusion in the Latin Quarter misses the point. The center is not transformed when the margins are mainstreamed. Change will come through a decentralization of those sites of production, publication, and dissemination, and by reassessing the economics of consumer/reader(ship) and textual circulation, that is by "connecting to the languages the actors in the social drama of change actually speak" (Ngùgi wa Thiong'o, *Something Torn and New,* 56) while also recognizing that the migration *of* and *into* other languages is an indistinguishable component of globalization. Naturally, this raises important questions concerning the claims of the Manifesto given that for the most part these were not accompanied by a programmatic component. Unlike Pascal Blanchard, Nicolas Bancel, and Sandrine Lemaire, who have argued that "The objective is to situate France's colonial past in the context of national thought and historiography, so as to produce perspectives that will render intelligible postcolonial circumstances,"[21] the Manifesto maintains that "We're witnessing the birth of a new constellation" ("Toward a World Literature in French," 56). However, the selection process—and here lies the shortsightedness of the project—ignores (arguably deploying its own restrictive set of aesthetic criteria to its definition of canonical *world literature*), as we saw in the previous chapter, the entire corpus of *beur* and *banlieue* literature, representatives of which had formulated demands for greater inclusivity in their own manifesto "quifaitlafrance?"[22]

The *Etonnants Voyageurs* literary festival initiative improved the circulation and visibility of authors who write *in* French—shifting attention away from the restrictive family portrait that had previously only included *national* authors.[23] The challenge therefore comes from finding new and innovative ways of extricating the festival from complex patronage structures and reliance on various French governmental agencies. This would allow for the convergence of both literary aspirations *and* a more self-reflexive component—one that would seek to incorporate international scholarship on France and the Francophone world (alongside internal efforts that seek to accord increasing acceptance and legitimacy in France to postcolonial studies) without perceiving of such external evaluations as intrusive but rather as integral and constitutive elements of more expansive inquiries on global diversity and cultural exchange. All of these considerations can serve to highlight the complexity of claims for a *world literature* in which global dissymmetries figure as the most compelling evidentiary modes of contemporary contact and exchange. Clearly, the shelves of the library of a *world literature in French* will continue to be arranged.

The opportunity to broaden some of the objectives of the Manifesto came after Éric Besson launched the *National Identity Debate* in 2009. On that occasion, as we saw in chapter 3, he proposed a *patriotic* reading list, precisely the kind of historiography the Manifesto had endeavored to revise. History—one is often told—can provide us with all kinds of interesting insights on contemporary issues. To this end, a speech delivered by Sir Winston Churchill to the Congress of Europe on May 7, 1948, remains surprisingly pertinent to current E.U. debates: "We need not waste our time in disputes about who originated this idea of United Europe. There are many valid modern patents. There are many famous names associated with the revival and presentation of this idea, but we may all, I think, yield our pretensions to Henry of Navarre, King of France, who, with his great Minister Sully, between the years 1600 and 1607, labored to set up a permanent committee representing the fifteen—now we are sixteen—leading Christian States of Europe."[24] As we have seen repeatedly throughout this book, there have been disquieting manifestations of nationalist sentiment in the E.U. zone; arguably, nowhere else has this been more evident than in France during the *National Identity Debate.* What are the implications of a debate of this kind for contemporary France and for rethinking colonial history, and how might these questions connect to the actual process of studying/teaching France and the Francophone world today?[25] As institutions of higher education worldwide are forced to (re)consider the role of language study in the *era of globalization* and as *national* departmental boundaries are increasingly collapsing into broader curricular structures—comparative, crosscultural, intercultural, postcolonial, transcultural, and transnational—language study remains inextricably linked to shifts in geopolitics, and the need for competence in language and cultural analysis proficiency has perhaps never been greater.

Likewise, historical developments and historiographic transformations have in turn challenged and redefined the parameters of twenty-first-century notions of Frenchness.[26] We have considered how various decrees and policies have influenced these debates: the "Taubira Law" (2001), whereby "The French Republic recognizes the Atlantic slave trade and the slave trade in the Indian Ocean as a crime against humanity, as well as slavery perpetrated from the 15th century onwards in the Americas and the Caribbean, in the Indian Ocean and in Europe, against African, Amerindian, Malagasy and Indian populations";[27] the controversial "Debré Law" (2005) which included a section underlining "the need for school programs to highlight positive aspects of the French overseas presence, notably in North Africa"; how the issue of "repentance" has galvanized intellectuals (Bruckner, Lefeuvre); the terrain of colonial "fracture" and postcolonial "rupture" (Bancel, Blanchard, Coquery-Vidrovitch, Mbembe, Vergès) and the diametrically opposed *camps* in postcolonial studies (Amselle, Bayart).[28] To this end, the publication in 2010 of *Je est un autre. Pour une identité-monde*—what could be considered the follow-up volume to the 2007

Manifesto—provides an excellent opportunity to address some of these questions.

Éric Besson's own short book on the subject of national identity, *Pour la Nation,* is presented as an attempt to "contribute to the debate that is taking place on our 'national identity.'"[29] However, as the Collective "Pour un véritable débat" (Towards a real debate) has insisted, what is really needed is a debate that would explore the tenuous relationship between "Identité nationale" (national identity) and "histoire coloniale" (colonial history), since "[t]he 'debate on national identity' is but the most recent avatar in a much larger conflict that opposes two visions of France."[30] The comprehensive website set up by the Ministry of Immigration, Integration, National Identity and Co-Development for the purposes of the *National Identity Debate* provided a strong indication as to the terms of the discussion and the manner in which it was framed. In turn, the rationale informing the contents of this archival resource connects in significant ways with current debates in the field of French studies that have involved complex negotiations between, on the one hand, those who adhere to traditional methodological approaches to literary analysis and linguistic training and, on the other, those who have embraced more global and interdisciplinary models of intercultural inquiry.[31]

This is particularly true given that the website offers a suggested reading list that is divided into "Les auteurs classiques" (classical authors) running from the sixteenth to the twentieth century and including Joachim Du Bellay (*Les Regrets*), Charles-Louis de Montesquieu (*De l'Esprit des Lois*), Nicolas de Condorcet (*Cinq mémoires sur l'instruction publique*), Chateaubriand (*Mémoires d'Outre-tombe*), Victor Hugo (*Discours sur la liberté de l'enseignement* and *Les Châtiments*), Alphonse De Lamartine (*Histoire de la Révolution de 1848*), Jules Michelet (*Tableau de la France*), Jules Ferry (*De l'égalité d'éducation*), Ernest Renan (*Qu'est-ce qu'une nation?*), Jean Jaurès ("Aux instituteurs et institutrices"), Charles Peguy ("Notre Jeunesse"), and "Les auteurs contemporains" (contemporary authors), which include Max Gallo (*Fier d'être français* and *L'âme de la France: une histoire de la nation des origines à nos jours*), Daniel Lefeuvre and Michel Renard (*Faut-il avoir honte de l'identité nationale?*), Théodore Zeldin (*Histoires des passions françaises*), Fernand Braudel (*L'identité de la France*), Michel Winock ("Les nationalismes français"), and Dominique Schnapper (*Qu'est-ce que la citoyenneté?*).[32] As we saw earlier, the criteria for inclusion (and therefore also for exclusion) on this civic education list are *not* ideologically neutral. The appeal of Maurice Barrès' particular brand of nationalist and patriotic fervor evidenced in the trilogy *Le Roman de l'énergie natio-*

nale he began in 1897 resonated well with Besson's construal of the possibilities and potentialities of a *national identity debate.* As the collective "Towards a Real Debate" argued: "We all know only too well that the way in which a question is asked, the context and the presuppositions that are made often determine the response.... The French must honor France, its flag, its great men, its national anthem, its glorious past, and embrace values of generosity and open-mindedness; ... in other words, a return to a nationalism of symbols, a narrow-minded and exclusionary model, one which of course will fail to attend to the most pressing contemporary questions."[33] Besson may very well claim that the *National Identity Debate* offers the potential for productive dialogue on complex social issues—but these claims are undermined by the substance of official rhetoric. The question of *national identity* in twenty-first-century France cannot be decoupled from colonial history; this historical legacy is an incontestable and incontrovertible module of *postcolonial* France. Instead, responding to very real electoral pressures (midterm legislative elections) and the need to appeal to extreme right-wing voters, which the Union pour un Mouvement Populaire (UMP) had successfully lured away from the Front National in the 2007 general election by mainstreaming their policy objectives on such questions as immigration, Besson opted instead to "stay away from these ticklish subjects and focus instead on the original principles of the Nation's 'founding fathers,' updated in this instance by the zealous guardians of national pride."[34] These concerns, therefore, have teaching and pedagogic implications. If the imperative is to provide a more comprehensive understanding of French history and of France today, to contextualize cultural, political, and social debates and issues, then Besson's antiquated and nostalgic "biography" of France—one that is disconnected from realities on the ground—necessarily falls short of that aspiration.

Naturally, these *identity* questions must be inscribed in the broader context of shifting, rapidly mutating global identities, those associated with the "liquid modernity" evoked by Zygmunt Bauman.[35] The French authorities have endeavored to reconcile the imperative to *globalize* with the simultaneous objective of preserving accepted parameters of national identity—arguably the kind of interpretation of *Frenchness* and French history that provided the organizing principles and rationale for Pierre Nora's influential multi-volume project, *Les lieux de mémoire,* in which he attempted to define French *memory* according to carefully selected historical events and symbols.[36] Thinking on the question of identity has evolved considerably as a result of globalization—conceptualizations of nations, arguments, and concerns made in different times by such thinkers as Fernand Braudel (*L'identité de la France*), Eugen Weber (*Peasants into Frenchmen*), and Ernest Gellner (*Nations and Nationalism*) have been updated by new paradigms in theorizations by Bauman, Ernesto Laclau (*La guerre des identités*), and so forth, and in turn redeployed in order to assist with the analysis of specific circumstances, such as "French identity" (Patrick Weil, *Qu'est-ce qu'un français?*), "European identity" (Anne-Marie Thiesse, *La Création des identités nationales*), extreme right-wing agendas (Peter Davies, *The National Front in France*), or for that matter more utilitarian uses of the "national" (Gérard Noiriel, *A quoi sert l'identité "nationale"?*).[37] Not only have these developments over the last few decades radically altered the sociological and cultural components of "identity" studies, but these have also been addressed within the francophone sphere by French and francophone postcolonial thinkers such as Edouard Glissant and Patrick Chamoiseau in their respective writings on *antillanité, créolité,* and the *tout-monde*—ideas and concepts that in turn have necessarily infused the formulations of authors of the *littérature-monde* and *identité-monde* group. Not surprisingly, therefore, the developing discussion of these complex identity questions is likely to have a substantial impact on the ways in which French (France *and* the francophone world) will need to be taught, and what kinds of contextual references will be called upon and incorporated to the process of delivering accurate representations of contemporary France.[38]

The two anthologies, *Pour une littérature-monde* and *Je est un autre. Pour une identité-monde,* in introducing to the French landscape notions of "world literature" and "world identities," relate in compelling ways with the *National Identity Debate.* This is especially true in the case of the latter because it constitutes a direct engagement with the debate, responding in many ways to widespread criticism of the narrow conceptualization of a *World Literature in French* found in the Manifesto. As Michel Le Bris ironically suggests, "'Je est un autre.' I'm not sure our minister had this famous phrase in mind when he launched his debate on 'national identity.'"[39] As has been repeatedly stated, several major French literary prizes were awarded to foreign-born writers in 2006, namely the Goncourt to Jonathan Littell (*Les Bienveillantes*), the Renaudot to Alain Mabanckou (*Mémoires de porc-épic*), and the Femina to Nancy Huston (*Lignes de faille*). For the signatories of the Manifesto, this merely confirmed "[w]hat the literary milieu already knew without admitting it: the center, from which supposedly radiated a franco-French literature, is no longer the center. Until now, the *center,* although less and less frequently, had its absorptive capacity that forced authors who came from elsewhere to rid themselves of their foreign trappings before melting in the crucible of the French language and its *national history:* the *center,* these Fall prizes tell us, is henceforth everywhere, at the four corners of the world" ("Toward a World Literature in French," 54, emphasis added). The signifiers, "center" and "national history," which I have highlighted in the above passage, are a direct attempt at tackling and putting into question prevalent political thought. The attempt (albeit a relatively precautious one) in the Manifesto to broaden the parameters of the discussion explicitly operates in conjunction with those calls that have been made for greater diversity and incorporation *into* the French Republic. In actuality, the kind of *mythic* France that Besson has in mind has only ever existed in distorted *dominant* imaginaries (which does not mean of course that such constructs do not resonate in powerful ways with sizeable elements of French society), and so *littérature-monde* provides an alternative space in which *official libraries* (repositories for national narratives) find themselves displaced, marginalized, within the newly delineated parameters of a *world* in which *identities* are formed according to constitutive principles in contradistinction to those exemplified in the narrow confines of Besson's imaginary.

Earlier in this chapter I critiqued some of arguments made by the *littérature-monde* Manifesto. For example, when the claim is made that "[w]ith the center placed on an equal plane with other centers, we're witnessing the birth of a new constellation, in which language freed from its exclusive pact with the nation, free from every other power hereafter but the powers of poetry and the imaginary, will have no other frontiers but those of the spirit," my feeling was that the full implications of what was at stake in rethinking the relationship and power dynamic between the "center" and the "periphery" had been under-exploited (Towards a World Literature in French," 56). However, unlike Besson's restricted schema, *Littérature-monde* remains nevertheless an opportunity for open and reciprocal exchange, and *Identité-monde* advances that project by taking up the challenge of situating "France's colonial past in the context of national thought and historiography, so as to produce perspectives that will render intelligible postcolonial circumstances."[40]

The *identité-monde* volume brings together, as it had previously with *littérature-monde,* a diverse range of authors with different relationships to France *and* to the French language—Ananda Devi, Alain Mabanckou, Anna Moï, Wilfried N'Sondé, Leïla Sebbar, Abdourahman Waberi, Jean-Marie Laclavetine, Azouz Begag, Juan Goytisolo, and Kebir Ammi. Some were signatories of the Manifesto itself and others have joined the lively discussion in the latest chapter in this undertaking, exemplifying in their texts Michel Le Bris's and Jean Rouaud's words in the preface, whereby "as multi-layered beings" we are "required to invent for ourselves a *world-identity*" that "cannot be reduced to this fiction of *national identity*."[41] Contributions reflect on the role of literature and the capacity of creative endeavors to go beyond the dictates of government ideologues, and contemplate on the multifarious ways in which inter-relationality (the je" and the "autre," "self" and the "other") are established and fostered, and how in turn these contrast sharply with Besson's inclination to "have us think in terms of categories such as the stable, the Nation-State, territories, borders, the opposition between exterior-interior, families, communities, identities, *concepts*" (Le Bris, "Lisez Rimbaud," *Je est un autre,* 25). Literature (more specifically, the novel) thus emerges as something "open, as opposed to concepts," that can be juxtaposed with the inertia and monolithism offered by Besson, as "a fluid space in which the experience of reversibility between the inside and the outside, the dispossession and the recomposition of self unfolds" (Le Bris, "Lisez Rimbaud," *Je est un autre,* 26).

Dismantling and deconstructing the kinds of myths that inform Besson's (among others of course) motionless characterization of French history and understanding of cultural and social dynamics in France today, will necessarily entail acknowledging the existence and role of a hegemonic discourse and then repudiating such mentalities. As Achille Mbembe has demonstrated, "The various histories of slavery and the history of different forms of colonization confirm that these institutions were veritable manufacturers of difference. In each and every case, difference was the result of a complex process of abstraction, objectification and hierarchization."[42] These are of course *identitarian* questions; in other words, they oblige us to ponder the definition of the "je" and the "autre," to question the structure of the "us" and the "them," and to consider the (pre)conditions for constitutive formations that cultivate proximity rather than distance. Without explicitly "naming it, the debate keeps returning to the theme of immigration," as Pascal Blanchard has emphasized, and "The question is not 'What is it to be French,' but rather what is the place in citizenship for those labeled as 'visible minorities' who are the inheritors of this colonial past (in other words, can the *natives* of yesterday be *citizens* today?)."[43] As Wilfried N'Sondé contends, "The ethno-identitarian machine has become a deadly poison. . . . It has a tendency to regionalize and to persist in confining art and people to the arbitrariness of geography. To use questionable criteria in order to divide and categorize, driving us gradually further away from the essence of being and magic of words."[44]

To this end, articulations made on the subject of *identité-monde* might begin to provide solutions to these uncertainties; this is certainly the case when Kebir Ammi maintains that "my identity is merely that of the other, because when I set out to discover others on my travels and in books, it is myself that I continue to discover. This identity can help us in building, I dare to believe, the only fortress that is worthwhile, that of the mind, to protect oneself from barbarism."[45] Clearly though, a France in which such relationships with identity are possible is yet to be built; as Alain Mabanckou reminds us, "I dreamed of another France, the France that I am waiting for."[46] Instead, Besson and other government representatives sought to usher in a "*uniform* society" in which one has "turned this Other into society's public enemy," an outdated concept that can be attributed to a "minority clinging to an outmoded idea of the nation, not to say of *identity*"[47] that no longer corresponds to twenty-first-century conditions. Just as *littérature-monde* had stipulated the need for a "language freed from its exclusive pact with the nation," when Philippe Forest writes that "Linguistic identity is hardly better than national identity. No authentic work seeks to define itself with either of those in mind,"[48] this must be understood as a denunciation of insular interpretations of Frenchness.

Throughout this book we have explored various facets of the soul searching taking place in metropolitan France. This relates in concrete ways to the kinds of questions departments of French/francophone studies are being confronted with today, particularly in countries in which French is not an official language. In order to improve our understanding of France and to achieve an open and inclusive interpretation of Frenchness, of the French colonial past and of its spectral presence in contemporary society, and of the larger francophone world, curricula need to be adapted. Concerted effort will have to be made to bring together and into dialogue analyses of France both *inside* and *outside* the Hexagon that are influenced by postcolonial theory, and contemporary debates surrounding identity, history and memory.[49] Such methodological adaptations promise to reveal not so much the "death of French culture" (as alluded to earlier with reference to Donald Morrison's provocative article), but instead the coordinates of genuinely vibrant and truly globalized site(s) of cultural, political, and social production. As Dominick LaCapra argued in an essay entitled "Reconfiguring French Studies," such transformations will entail:

> The movement or expansion of the field of interest from literature to culture, society, and history, including francophone cultures, societies, and histories. With this shift the civilization course is no longer a makeshift course delegated to an overly gullible, unguardedly good-natured, insufficiently high-powered, or otherwise theory-impaired colleague. It becomes a truly demanding undertaking that epitomizes the entire problem of expanding the field from a study of literature in

> the restricted sense to a concern with culture in a broader anthropological, theoretical, and historical sense. . . . In other words the civilization course or text becomes an exemplary site for an attempt to rearticulate and reframe the field of French studies and critically explore the demanding problem of the interaction among theory, criticism, historiography, ethnography.[50]

The kind of prerequisite "movement" or "expansion" alluded to above exists in diverse scholarship in such fields as francophone studies, museum studies, migration studies, memory studies, francophone/postcolonial studies, but also of course in studies of popular culture, film, and sport.[51] These critical and curricular modifications have of course *already* translated into curricular enrichment, allowed for genuinely cross/inter/pluridisciplinary connections to be established with various university constituencies as well as numerous entities beyond the Academy, and aligned learning outcomes with the wider intellectual and political significance of the modern world. At a time when concerted efforts are being made by governments to restrict and limit definitions of identity and difference to biological considerations (through DNA testing, fingerprinting, saliva samples),[52] the corresponding effort at achieving accurate historical contextualization, as Andrew Delbanco has argued, "requires students to become informed about the past and the present—to learn, that is, something substantial about history, science, and contemporary society in order to bring that knowledge to bear on unforeseeable challenges of the future."[53] Spanish author Juan Goytisolo has perhaps most effectively recapitulated this predicament, warning that "the obsession with purity" is "symptomatic of decadence and ill-health."[54]

NOTES

Introduction

1. Achille Mbembe, *Sortir de la grande nuit. Essai sur l'Afrique décolonisée* (Paris: Editions La Découverte), 93.

2. Linton Kwesi Johnson, "New Word Hawdah," *Selected Poems* (London: Penguin, 2006), 103. The poem features a complex interplay between "word" and "world," terms that are both contained in the "brand new langwidge a barbarity."

3. See, for example, Patrick Williams, "Roads to Freedom: Jean-Paul Sartre and Anti-Colonialism," in *Postcolonial Thought in the French-Speaking World,* ed. Charles Forsdick and David Murphy (Liverpool: Liverpool University Press, 2009), 147–156.

4. See, for example, Laurent Dubois, "Haunting Delgrès," *Radical History Review* 78 (2000): 166–177, and his book *A Colony of Citizens: Revolution and Slave Emancipation in the French Caribbean, 1787–1804* (Chapel Hill: University of North Carolina Press, 2004); Nick Nesbitt, *Voicing Memory: History and Subjectivity in French Caribbean Literature* (Charlottesville: University of Virginia Press, 2003); and Daniel J. Walkowitz and Lisa Maya Knauer, eds. *Contested Histories in Public Space* (Durham, NC: Duke University Press, 2009).

5. http://olympedegouges.wordpress.com/qui-sommes-nous/, first published in *Le Monde* (8 March 2007).

6. Herman Lebovics, *Mona Lisa's escort: André Malraux and the Reinvention of French Culture* (Ithaca, NY: Cornell University Press, 1999), ix.

7. See, www.culture.gouv.fr. See Jacques Rigaud and Olivier Duhamel, "De l'utilité d'un ministre pour la culture, l'exemple de Jacques Duhamel," *débat,* 164 (March–April 2011): 27–36.

8. See Loïc Wacquant, ed. *Pierre Bourdieu and Democratic Politics: The Mystery of Ministry* (Cambridge, UK: Polity Press, 2005).

9. See "Décret n° 2010–1444 du 25 novembre 2010 relatif aux attributions du ministre de l'intérieur, de l'outre-mer, des collectivités territoriales et de l'immigration," http://www.legifrance.gouv.fr/affichTexte.do;jsessionid=?cidTexte=JORFTEXT000023137326&dateTexte=&oldAction=rechJO&categorieLien=id.

10. See Herman Lebovics, *Bringing the Empire Back Home: France in the Global Age* (Durham, NC: Duke University Press, 2004), and Robert Aldrich, *Vestiges of the Colonial Empire in France: Monuments, Museums and Colonial Memories* (London: Palgrave Macmillan, 2005).

11. See Bancel, Nicolas, Pascal Blanchard, Gilles Boëtsch, Éric Deroo, Sandrine Lemaire, and Charles Forsdick, eds. *Human Zoos: From the Hottentot Venus to Reality Shows*

(Liverpool: Liverpool University Press, 2009), and *Museums in Postcolonial Europe,* ed. Dominic Thomas (London: Routledge, 2009).

12. See www.debatidentitenationale.fr.

13. See, for example, Charles Tshimanga, Didier Gondola, and Peter J. Bloom, eds. *Frenchness and the African Diaspora: Identity and Uprising in Contemporary France* (Bloomington: Indiana University Press, 2009).

14. This project never came to fruition during Sarkozy's first term in office, and since he was voted out of office on May 6, 2012, he will not leave behind landmark cultural projects in the way that several of his predecessors did.

15. Christopher L. Miller, *Blank Darkness: Africanist Discourse in French* (Chicago: University of Chicago Press, 1985), 246.

16. Catherine Coquery-Vidrovitch, *La Découverte de* l'Afrique (Paris: Editions René Julliard, 1965), William B. Cohen, *The French Encounter with Africans: White Response to Blacks, 1530–1880* (Bloomington: Indiana University Press, 1980), and Valentin Y. Mudimbe, *The Idea of Africa* (Bloomington and Indianapolis: Indiana University Press, 1994).

17. Paul Gilroy, "Foreword: Migrancy, Culture, and a New Map of Europe," in *Blackening Europe: The African American Presence,* eds. Heike Raphael-Hernandez (London: Routledge, 2004), xiv.

18. Orhan Pamuk, *The Museum of Innocence,* trans. Maureen Freely (New York: Alfred A. Knopf, 2009), 73.

19. Edward W. Said, *Culture and Imperialism* (New York: Alfred A. Knopf, 1993), xx.

20. Pap Ndiaye, *La condition noire. Essai sur une minorité française* (Paris: Editions Calmann-Lévy, 2008), 178–179.

21. Nicolas Bancel, Pascal Blanchard, and Françoise Vergès, *La République coloniale* (Paris: Editions Albin Michel, 2003), 30.

22. Marie NDiaye, *Trois femmes puissantes* (Paris: Editions Gallimard, 2009).

23. Camille Polloni and Pierre Siankowski. "Éric Raoult s'attaque à Marie Ndiaye et invente un "devoir de réserve" pour les prix Goncourt," http://www.lesinrocks.com/actualite/actu-article/article/eric-raoult-sattaque-a-marie-ndiaye-et-invente-un-devoir-de-reserve-pour-les-prix-goncourt/. November 10, 2009.

24. See Pascal Blanchard and Ruth Ginio, "Révolution coloniale: le mythe colonial de Vichy (1940–1944)," in *Culture coloniale en France. De la Révolution française à nos jours,* eds. Pascal Blanchard, Nicolas Bancel, and Sandrine Lemaire (Paris: CNRS Editions, 2008), 369–384.

25. Olivier Adam, *A l'abri de rien* (Paris: Editions de l'Olivier, 2007) Jean-Pierre Améris, *Maman est folle* (Escazal Films, 2007); and Philippe Lioret, *Welcome* (Nord-Ouest Films, 2009).

26. See Luc Legoux, "La réorganisation mondiale de l'asile," in *L'asile au Sud,* eds. Luc Cambrézy, Smaïn Laacher, Véronique Lassailly-Jacob and Luc Legoux (Paris: Editions La Dispute, 2008), 9–22, and Smaïn Laacher, *Après Sangatte . . . Nouvelles immigrations, nouveaux enjeux* (Paris: Editions La Dispute, 2002).

27. "La démocratie phobique ou comment se soustraire aux analogies embarrassantes," in *Cette France-là,* Vol. 2 (Paris: Editions La Découverte, 2010), 418.

28. Jocelyne Dakhlia, "La France dedans dehors," *Ligne* 25 (2008): 173.

29. www.quifaitlafrance.com.

30. Achille Mbembe, "Figures of the Multiplicity: Can France Reinvent its Identity?" in *Frenchness and the African Diaspora: Identity and Uprising in Contemporary France,* trans. Jean Marie Todd, eds. Tshimanga, Gondola, and Bloom, 65.

31. "Pour une 'littérature-monde' en français," *Le Monde,* (March 16, 2007): 1–3; "Toward a World Literature in French," trans. Daniel Simon, *World Literature Today* 83.2 (March–April 2009): 54–56.

32. Pascal Blanchard, Nicolas Bancel, and Sandrine Lemaire, eds. *La fracture coloniale: La société française au prisme de l'héritage colonial* (Paris: Editions La Découverte, 2005), 30. See also and Nicolas Bancel, Pascal Blanchard, Françoise Vergès, Achille Mbembe, and Florence Bernault, eds. *Ruptures postcoloniales: Les nouveaux visages de la société française* (Paris: Editions La Découverte, 2010).

33. Achille Mbembe, "Provincializing France?" trans. Janet Roitman, *Public Culture* 23.1 (2011): 112.

34. Michel Le Bris and Jean Rouaud, eds. *Je est un autre: Pour une identité-monde.* (Paris: Editions Gallimard, 2010).

1. Museology and Globalization

1. Susan Vogel, "Always True to the Object, in Our Fashion," in *Exhibiting Cultures: The Poetics and Politics of Museum Display,* eds. Ivan Karp and Steven S. Lavine (Washington, DC: Smithsonian, 1991), 191.

2. See Nicolas Bancel, Pascal Blanchard, Gilles Boëtsch, Eric Deroo, Sandrine Lemaire, and Charles Forsdick, eds. *Human Zoos: From the Hottentot Venus to Reality Shows* (Liverpool: Liverpool University Press, 2009); and Jennifer A. González, *Subject to Display: Reframing Race in Contemporary Installation Art* (Boston: MIT Press, 2008).

3. Nicolas Bancel and Pascal Blanchard, "La colonisation: du débat sur la guerre d'Algérie au discours de Dakar," in *Les Guerres de mémoires: La France et son histoire. Enjeux politiques, controverses historiques, stratégies médiatiques,* eds. Pascal Blanchard and Isabelle Veyrat-Masson (Paris: Editions La Découverte, 2008), 140. See also Catherine Coquio, ed. *Retour du colonial: disculpation et réhabilitation de l'histoire coloniale* (Nantes: Librairie l'Atalante, 2008); and Patrick Weil, "Politique de la mémoire: l'interdit de la commémoration," in *Liberté, égalité, discriminations: 'l'identité nationale' au regard de l'histoire* (Paris: Editions Grasset & Fasquelle, 2008), 165–209.

4. Michaela Giebelhausen, "Architecture *is* the Museum," in *New Museum Theory and Practice,* ed. Janet Marstine (Oxford: Blackwell, 2006), 41–63.

5. Carol Duncan, "Art Museums and the Ritual of Citizenship," in *Exhibiting Cultures: The Poetics and Politics of Museum Display,* eds. Ivan Karp and Steven S. Lavine (Washington, DC: Smithsonian Books, 1991), 89.

6. Panivong Norindr, "*La Plus Grande France:* French Cultural Identity and Nation Building under Mitterrand," in *Identity Papers,* eds. Steven Ungar and Tom Conley (Minneapolis: University of Minnesota Press, 1996), 234–235.

7. Annie E. Coombes, "Museums and the Formation of National and Cultural Identities," in *Museum Studies: An Anthology of Contexts,* ed. Bettina Messias Carbonell (Oxford: Blackwell Publishing, 2004), 232.

8. Roger G. Kennedy, "Some Thoughts about National Museums at the End of the Century," in *Museum Studies,* ed. Carbonell, 304.

9. Robert Aldrich, *Vestiges of the Colonial Empire in France. Monuments, Museums and Colonial Memories* (New York: Palgrave Macmillan, 2005), 6.

10. Jean-Loup Amselle, *Rétrovolutions. Essais sur les primitivismes contemporains* (Paris: Editions Stock, 2010), 189.

11. Susan Crane, "Memory, Distortion, and History in the Museum," in *Museum*

Studies, ed. Carbonell, 320. See also Coombes, "Museums and the Formation of National and Cultural Identities."

12. Hilde S. Klein, *The Museum in Transition: A Philosophical Perspective* (Washington, DC: Smithsonian, 2000), 42.

13. Anne-Christine Taylor, "Les vies d'un objet de musée," TDC, *Le musée du quai Branly,* 918 (June 15, 2006), 9. On museographic practices, see Françoise Lionnet, "The Mirror and the Tomb: Africa, Museums, and Memory," *African Arts* 34.3 (Autumn 2001): 50–59.

14. Andrew McClellan, "Museum Studies Now," in *Spectacle and Display,* eds. Deborah Cherry and Fintan Cullen (Oxford: Blackwell Publishing, 2008), 92.

15. Tony Bennett, "Exhibition, Difference, and the Logic of Culture," in *Museum Frictions: Public Cultures/Global Transformations,* eds. Ivan Karp, Corinne A. Kratz, Lynn Szwaja, and Tomás Ybarra-Frausto (Durham, NC: Duke University Press, 2007), 46. See also Corinne Kratz, and Ciraj Rassool, "Remapping the Museum," in *Museum Frictions,* eds. Karp, Kratz, Szwaja, and Ybarra-Frausto, 347–356.

16. Pascal Blanchard, Nicolas Bancel and Sandrine Lemaire, eds. *La fracture coloniale: La société française au prisme de l'héritage colonial* (Paris: Editions La Découverte, 2005).

17. Aldrich, "Le musée colonial impossible," in *Culture post-coloniale 1961–2006: Traces et mémoires coloniales en France,* eds. Pascal Blanchard and Nicolas Bancel (Paris: Editions La Découverte, 2005), 97. See also Sarah Frohning Deleporte, "Trois musées, une question, Une République," in *La fracture coloniale,* eds. Blanchard, Bancel, and Lemaire, 105–111.

18. See Gail Anderson, ed. *Reinventing the Museum: Historical and Contemporary Perspectives on the Paradigm Shift* (Lanham: AltaMira Press, 2004); Janet Marstine, ed. *New Museum Theory and Practice* (Oxford: Blackwell, 2006); Donald Preziosi and Claire Farago, eds. *Grasping the World: The Idea of the Museum* (Aldershot, UK: Ashgate Publishing Limited, 2004).

19. www.icom.org, emphasis mine.

20. See Terence M. Duffy, "Museums of 'Human Suffering' and the Struggle for Human Rights," in *Museum Studies,* ed. Carbonell, 117–122.

21. www.quaibranly.fr.

22. See Herman Lebovics, *Bringing the Empire Back Home: France in the Global Age* (Durham, NC: Duke University Press, 2004).

23. Jacques Chirac, "Speech by M. Jacques Chirac, President of the Republic, at the opening of the Quai Branly Museum," http://www.ambafrance-uk.org/Speech-by-M-Jacques-Chirac,7357.html (June 20, 2006).

24. See James Clifford, "Quai Branly in Process," *October 120* (2007), 3–23; Sally Price, *Paris Primitive: Jacques Chirac's Museum on the Quai Branly* (Chicago: Chicago University Press, 2007); Susan Vogel, "Des ombres sur la Seine: L'art africain, l'obscurité et le musée du quai Branly," *Le moment du Quai Branly, le débat* 147 (2007): 178–192.

25. Karen Margolis, "Missing: Germany's Immigration Museum," http://www.mut-gegen-rechte-gewalt.de/eng/news/missing-germanys-immigration-museum (April 3, 2008). Consulted April 10, 2009.

26. See www.histoire-immigration.fr.

27. Jacques Toubon, "La place des immigrés dans la construction de la France," in *Mission de préfiguration du Centre de ressources et de mémoires de l'immigration,* Jacques Toubon (Paris: La Documentation Française, 2004), 9. See also Nancy L. Green, "A French Ellis Island? Museums, Memory and History in France and the United States," *History Workshop Journal* 63 (2007), 239–253.

28. www.liverpoolmuseums.org.uk.

29. www.empiremuseum.co.uk.

30. www.africamuseum.be.

31. See Ellen W. Sapega, "Remembering Empire/Forgetting the Colonies: Accretions of Memory and the Limits of Commemoration in a Lisbon Neighborhood," *History & Memory* 20.2 (2008): 18–38.

32. See Catherine Brice, "Monuments: pacificateurs ou agitateurs de mémoires," in *Les Guerres de mémoires,* eds. Blanchard and Veyrat-Masson, 199–208.

33. See Alexandra Poli, Jonna Louvrier, and Michel Wieviorka, "Introduction," *La Cité Nationale de l'Histoire de l'Immigration: Quels publics ? Hommes et Migrations* 1267 (2007): 10–25.

34. Eilean Hooper-Greenhill, "Changing values in the Art Museum: Rethinking Communication and Learning," in *Museum Studies,* ed. Carbonell, 572. See also Danielle Rice, "Museums: Theory, Practice, and Illusion," in *Art and its Publics: Museum Studies at the Millenium,* ed. Andrew McClellan (Oxford: Blackwell Publishing, 2003), 77–95.

35. See Emmanuel de Roux, "Un public nouveau pour le Quai Branly," www.lemonde.fr (June 1, 2007).

36. See Mark O'Neill, "The good enough visitor," in *Museums, Society, Equality,* ed. Richard Sandell (London: Routledge, 2002), 24–40.

37. Andrew Newman and Fiona McLean, "Architectures of inclusion: museums, galleries and inclusive communities," in *Museums, Society, Equality,* ed. Sandell, 65.

38. See Ali Behdad, *A Forgetful Nation: On Immigration and Cultural Identity in the United States* (Durham: Duke University Press, 2005).

39. www.newamericansmuseum.org.

40. Julia M. Klein, "One part history, two parts shrine," *New York Times* (March 19, 2009).

41. Norindr: "*La Plus Grande France:* French Cultural Identity and Nation Building under Mitterrand" in *Identity Papers,* eds. Ungar and Conley, 234.

42. Dominic Thomas, *Black France: Colonialism, Immigration, and Transnationalism* (Bloomington: Indiana University Press), 2007.

43. Daniel Lefeuvre, *Pour en finir avec la repentance coloniale* (Paris: Editions Flammarion, 2006); Pascal Bruckner, *La tyrannie de la pénitence. Essai sur le masochisme occidental* (Paris: Editions Grasset & Fasquelle, 2006); and Blanchard, Bancel, and Lemaire, eds. *La fracture coloniale.*

44. See Julio Godoy, "How beautiful was my colony," Inter Press Service News Agency, http://ipsnews.net/africa/nota.asp?idnews=34672. Consulted September 15, 2006.

45. Alice Conklin, *A Mission to Civilize: The Republican Ideal of Empire in France and West Africa, 1895–1930* (Stanford, CA: Stanford University Press, 1997), 131. See also Hans-Jürgen Lüsebrink, "Acculturation coloniale et pédagogie interculturelle -l'œuvre de Georges Hardy," in *Sénégal-Forum: Littérature et Histoire,* ed. Papa Samba Diop (Frankfurt, Germany: IKO Verlag, 1995), 113–122.

46. Lebovics, "The Dance of the Museums," *Bringing the Empire Back Home,* 151.

47. See Nélia Dias, "Le musée du quai Branly: une généalogie," *Le moment du Quai Branly,* 65–79.

48. For an official account of all these questions, see Stéphane Martin's book (the director of the Quai Branly Museum), *Musée du Quai Branly. Là où dialoguent les cultures* (Paris: Editions Gallimard, 2011).

49. Robert Goldwater, "The Development of Ethnological Museums," in *Museum Studies: An Anthology of Contexts,* ed. Carbonell, 136. For Ivan Karp, "Cross-cultural ex-

hibitions present such stark contrasts between what we know and what we need to know that the challenge of reorganizing our knowledge becomes an aspect of exhibition experience," "Culture and Representation," in *Exhibiting Cultures,* eds. Karp and Lavine, 22. See also several recent works on these questions: Barbara Kirshenblatt-Gimblett, *Destination Culture: Tourism, Museums, and Heritage* (Berkeley: University of California Press, 1998); Gustavo Buntinx, ed. *Museum Frictions: Public Cultures/Global Transformations* (Durham: Duke University Press, 2006); and Elizabeth Edwards, Chris Gosden, and Ruth Phillips, eds. *Sensible Objects: Colonialism, Museums and Material Culture* (Oxford: Berg, 2006).

50. See also Maureen Murphy, "L'Afrique au cœur des ténèbres parisiennes: du pavillon des Sessions au musée du quai Branly," in *De l'imaginaire au musée. Les arts d'Afrique à Paris et à New York (1931–2006)* (Dijon: Les presses du réel, 2009), 289–323.

51. Marc Augé, *Oblivion,* trans. Marjolijn de Jager (Minneapolis: University of Minnesota Press, 2004).

52. Bogumil Jewsiewicki, "La mémoire est-elle soluble dans l'esthétique?" *Le moment du Quai Branly,* 174–177. The structural, ideological, and organizational principles that inform museum collections are incisively addressed by Lara Kriegel in "After the Exhibitionary Complex: Museum Histories and the Future of the Victorian Past," *Victorian Studies* 48.4 (Summer 2006): 681–704.

53. These measures naturally further exacerbate the "colonial fracture" that has been so convincingly put into evidence by Blanchard, Bancel, and Lemaine.

54. See also Sally Price, "The Art of Darkness," *Paris Primitive,* 150–168. For Bogumil Jewsiewicki, this has resulted in a process of "décontextualisation" and "déhistoricisation," "La mémoire est-elle soluble dans l'esthétique," *Le moment du Quai Branly,* 176.

55. Bancel and Blanchard, "Mémoire coloniale: Résistances à l'émergence d'un débat," in *Culture post-coloniale,* eds. Blanchard and Bancel, 35.

56. James Clifford, *Routes: Travel and Translation in the Late Twentieth Century* (Cambridge, MA: Harvard University Press, 1997), 204.

57. Voir Achille Mbembe, "La république désœuvrée: La France à l'ère post-coloniale," *le débat,* 137 (November–December 2005): 159–175.

58. See also Etienne Balibar, *We, the People of Europe: Reflections on Transnational Citizenship,* trans. James Swenson (Princeton, NJ: Princeton University Press, 2004).

59. Tomke Lask, "Introduction," in *Museums, Collections, Interpretations: Rethinking the Construction of Meanings and Identities,* ed. Tomke Lask, *Civilisations,* 52.2 (2005): 18.

60. Jean-Pierre Mohen, "Musée du Quai Branly: actualité et devenir: entretien croisé avec Jean-Pierre Mohen et Dominic Thomas," in *Le retour du colonial,* ed. Nicolas Bancel, *Cultures du Sud* (May–July 2007), 42. The museum's director, Stéphane Martin, remains unequivocal in his defense of the "official" position: "We only display objects from our collection. This means that we have decided . . . to avoid offering a particular historical take or assuming any kind of ideological posture," Stéphane Martin (Interview), "Un musée pas comme les autres," *Le moment du Quai Branly,* 19.

61. Naturally, a diametrically opposed discourse exists. See for example Bernard Müller, "Faut-il restituer les butins des expéditions coloniales," *Le Monde Diplomatique* (July 2007): 20–21; and Bernard Dupaigne, *Le Scandale des arts premiers la véritable histoire du quai Branly* (Paris: Editions Mille et une nuits, 2006).

62. Susan A. Crane, "Memory, Distortion, and History in the Museum," in *Museum Studies,* ed. Carbonell, 320.

63. Deleporte, "Trois musées, une question," in *La fracture coloniale,* eds. Blanchard, Bancel, and Lemaire, 108.

64. Gilles Labarthe, "Histoires brouillées," *Le Courrier: Un quotidien suisse d'information et d'opinion* (June 24, 2006), www.lecourrier.ch. Consulted on January 3, 2007.

65. See also Véronique De Rudder, ed. *L'Inégalité raciste. L'universalité républicaine à l'épreuve* (Paris: Presses Universitaires de France, 2000).

66. Benoît de L'Estoile, "L'oubli de l'héritage colonial," *Le moment du Quai Branly,* 99.

67. In fact, as Lebovics has stated, "The museum will show what it owns, the accumulation of French history . . . French law . . . makes state property inalienable. No claim that an object from a community or a relative was taken improperly, illicitly, or impiously will be honored" (Lebovics, *Bringing the Empire Back Home,* 162).

68. Olivier Le Cour Grandmaison, "Sur la réhabilitation du passé colonial de la France," in *La fracture coloniale,* eds. Blanchard, Bancel, and Lemaire, 126.

69. Emmanuel de Roux, "Un public nouveau pour le Quai Branly." www.lemonde.fr (June 1, 2007).

70. See www.quaibranly.fr/index.php?id=diaspora.

71. See http://www.quaibranly.fr/en/programmation/exhibitions/last-exhibitions/planete-metisse-to-mix-or-not-to-mix.html.

72. See for example the action taken in the French Département d'outre-mer (DOM) by the Collective "Lyannaj kont pwofitasion" (Union Against Exploitation): http://www.lkp-gwa.org//). Their published manifesto included Patrick Chamoiseau and Edouard Glissant as signatories: *Manifeste pour les "produits" de Haute Nécessité* (Paris: Editions Galaade, 2009).

73. Nicolas Sarkozy, "Discours: Cérémonie d'hommage solennel de la Nation à Aimé Césaire," http://www.elysee.fr/president/les-actualites/discours/2011/discours-ceremonie-d-hommage-solennel-de-la.11063.html (April 6, 2011).

74. See also the documentary by Pascal Blanchard and Éric Deroo, *Zoos humains* (Bâtisseurs de mémoire, Cités télévision, Films du Village, Arte France, 2002).

75. Nicolas Bancel, "L'exposition des Outre-mer au Jardin d'Acclimatation est un scandale," *Le Monde* (March 29, 2011): http://www.lemonde.fr/idees/article/2011/03/28/l-exposition-des-outre-mer-au-jardin-d-acclimatation-est-un-scandale_1497533_3232.html.

76. See "Invitation au Jardin des Outre-mer," http://www.2011-annee-des-outre-mer.gouv.fr/actualites/345/invitation-au-jardin-des-outre-mer.html?date=20110627 (April 9, 2011). This site also includes a PDF of Marie-Luce Penchard's official letter to CMPHE President, Françoise Vergès.

77. Françoise Vergès, *Rapport de la mission sur la mémoire des expositions ethnographiques et coloniales,* http://www.ladocumentationfrancaise.fr/rapports-publics/114000663/index.shtml (November 15, 2011), consulted May 9, 2012, and Nicolas Bancel, "Les oubliés du Jardin d'Acclimatation," *Le Monde* (January 27, 2012): http://www.lemonde.fr/idees/article/2012/01/27/les-oublies-du-jardin-d-acclimatation_1635204_3232.html.

78. An earlier exhibition, "Kréyol factory," had been held at the Parc de la Villette in Paris (April 7–July 5, 2009), curated by Yolande Bacot in collaboration with Claude Archambault and Christian Coq. Inspired by Stuart Hall's influential work on Afro-Caribbean identities, "Kréyol Factory" interrogated "the complexities of reflecting on identity in a historical framework, processes of creolization, and the impact of globalization," www.kreyolfactory.com/exposition/parcours_de_l_exposition.html. See also *Kréyol factory: Des artistes interrogent les identités créoles* (Paris: Editions Gallimard, 2009).

79. Pascal Blanchard, Gilles Boëtsch and Nanette Jacomijn Snoep, "Human Zoos. The Invention of the Savage," in *Human Zoos: The Invention of the Savage,* eds. Pascal Blanchard, Gilles Boëtsch and Nanette Jacomijn Snoep (Paris: Musée du Quai Branly and Arles: Actes Sud, 2011), 26.

80. The exhibition was a remarkable success, attracting several hundred thousand visitors.

81. An International colloquium on "Human Zoos" was also held January 24–25, 2012.

82. See Catherine Coquery-Vidrovitch, "Le musée du Quai Branly ou l'histoire oubliée," in Adame Ba Konaré, ed. *Petit précis de remise à niveau sur l'histoire africaine à l'usage du président Sarkozy* (Paris: Editions La Découverte, 2008), 125–137.

83. See Carole Barjon, "La métamorphose de Monsieur Claude Guéant," *Nouvel Observateur* (March 24, 2011).

2. *Object/Subject Migration*

1. Jennifer A. González, *Subject to Display: Reframing Race in Contemporary Installation Art* (Boston: The MIT Press, 2008), 5.

2. www.histoire-immigration.fr.

3. See Vincent Duclert, "L'Etat et les historiens," *Regards sur l'actualité,* 325 (November 2006): 5–15.

4. See Migration museums map: http://www.migrationmuseums.org/web/index.php?page=map.

5. UNESCO-IOM Migration Museums Initiative: http://www.migrationmuseums.org/web/.

6. Press Dossier, http://www.histoire-immigration.fr/upload/file/ext_media_fichier_342_dossier_presse.pdf, 18.

7. Jacques Toubon, "La place des immigrés dans la construction de la France," *Mission de préfiguration du Centre de ressources et de mémoires de l'immigration* (Paris: La Documentation Française, 2004): 9.

8. Robert Aldrich, "Remembrances of Empires Past," *Journal of Multidisciplinary International Studies* 7.1 (January 2010), http://epress.lib.uts.edu.au/ojs/index.php/portal/article/view/1176/1640, 6.

9. Marie Poinsot, "Convaincre tous les publics," *La Cité Nationale de l'Histoire de l'Immigration: Quels publics?, Hommes et Migrations,* 1207 (2007): 1. On the question of the evolution, over time, of this imaginary, see Benoît de l'Estoile, "Étranges reflets dans la vitrine," *Télérama horizons,* no. 4 (April 2011): 24–27.

10. Michel Wieviorka, "Inscrire l'immigration dans le récit national," *La Cité Nationale de l'Histoire de l'Immigration: Quels publics?,* 8–9.

11. www.icom.museum/definition.html.

12. Alexandra Poli, Jonna Louvrier, and Michel Wieviorka, "Introduction," *La Cité Nationale de l'Histoire de l'Immigration: Quels publics?,* 12. Nancy L. Green, "A French Ellis Island? Museums, Memory and History in France and the United States," *History Workshop Journal* 63 (2007): 239–253.

13. Hélène Lafont-Couturier, "Les coulisses d'une collection en formation," *La Cité Nationale de l'Histoire de l'Immigration: Une collection en devenir, Hommes et Migrations,* 1267 (2007): 9.

14. Panivong Norindr, "*La Plus Grande France:* French Cultural Identity and Nation Building under Mitterrand," in *Identity Papers: Contested Nationhood in Twentieth-Century France,* eds. Steven Ungar and Tom Conley (Minneapolis: University of Minnesota Press, 1996), 234.

15. Fabrice Grognet, "Quand 'l'étranger' devient patrimoine français," *La Cité Nationale de l'Histoire de l'Immigration: Une collection en devenir,* 29.

16. Mary Stevens, "Designing Diversity: The Visual Identity of the Cité nationale de l'histoire de l'immigration (National Museum of Immigration), "http://www.susdiv.org/uploadfiles/ED2007-056.pdf (December 2007), 1–2.

17. Florence Bernault, "Colonial Syndrome: French Modern and the Deceptions of History," in *Frenchness and the African Diaspora: Identity and Uprising in Contemporary France,* eds. Charles Tshimanga, Didier Gondola, and Peter J. Bloom (Bloomington: Indiana University Press, 2009), 141.

18. CNHI Research Council, "Immigration et identité nationale: une association inacceptable," http://www.ldh-toulon.net/spip.php?article2047.

19. Nicolas Sarkozy, "Diversity Speech," http://www.elysee.fr/documents/index.php?mode=cview&cat_id=7&press_id=2142&lang=fr (December 17, 2007), 10.

20. See Pascal Blanchard and Isabelle Veyrat-Masson, eds., *Les Guerres de mémoires: La France et son histoire. Enjeux politiques, controverses historiques, stratégies médiatiques* (Paris: Editions La Découverte, 2008); Gilles Manceron, "La loi: régulateur ou acteur des guerres de mémoires?" in *Les Guerres de mémoires,* eds. Blanchard and Veyrat-Masson, 241–251; and Patrick Weil, "Politique de la mémoire: l'interdit de la commémoration," *Liberté, égalité, discriminations: 'l'identité nationale' au regard de l'histoire* (Paris: Grasset & Fasquelle, 2008), 165–209.

21. See Blanchard, Bancel, and Lemaire, eds. *La fracture coloniale,* 2007.

22. See Edouard Glissant, *Mémoires des esclavages: La fondation d'un Centre national pour la mémoire des esclavages et leurs abolitions* (Paris: Editions Gallimard, 2007); and Françoise Vergès, "La mémoire de l'esclavage et la loi," *La mémoire enchaînée: Questions sur l'esclavage* (Paris: Editions Albin Michel, 2006), 105–148.

23. See Benjamin Stora, *La gangrène et l'oubli. La mémoire de la guerre d'Algérie* (Paris: Editions La Découverte, 1992).

24. See Benoît Falaize and Françoise Lantheaume, "Entre pacification et reconnaissance: les manuels scolaires et la consurrence des mémoires," in *Les Guerres de mémoires,* eds. Blanchard and Veyrat-Masson, 177–186; and Gilles Boëtsch, "L'université et la recherche face aux enjeux de mémoire: le temps des mutations," in *Les Guerres de mémoires,* eds. Blanchard and Veyrat-Masson, 187–198.

25. Maureen Murphy, "Le CNHI au Palais de la Porte Dorée," in *La Cité Nationale de l'Histoire de l'Immigration: Une collection en devenir,* 46–48.

26. Maureen Murphy, *Un Palais pour une cité: Du musée des colonies à la Cité nationale de l'histoire de l'immigration* (Paris: Réunion des musées nationaux, 2007), 27.

27. Robert Aldrich, "Le musée colonial impossible," in *Culture post-coloniale 1961–2006: Traces et mémoires coloniales en France,* eds. Pascal Blanchard and Nicolas Bancel, eds. (Paris: Editions Autrement, 2005), 84–85.

28. Mary Stevens, "Still the family secret? The representation of colonialism in the Cité nationale de l'histoire de l'immigration," *African and Black Diaspora: An International Journal* 2 (July 2009): 245 and 252.

29. Nicolas Bancel and Pascal Blanchard, "Incompatibilité: la CNHI dans le sanctuarire du colonialisme français," in *La Cité Nationale de l'Histoire de l'Immigration: Une collection en devenir,* 126.

30. See www.indigenes-republique.fr.

31. *Comité pour la mémoire de l'esclavage, Mémoires de la traite négrière, de l'esclavage et de leurs abolitions* (Paris: Editions La Découverte, 2005), 11.

32. On museographic choices, see Hélène Lafont-Couturier (the former director of the CNHI), "Le musée national de l'histoire de l'Immigration: un musée sans collection," *Museum International*, 233/234 (2007), 42–48, and *La Cité Nationale de l'Histoire de l'Immigration. Guide l'exposition permanente* (Editions CNHI/ Hommes et migrations, 2010).

33. Isabelle Renard, "Lorsque l'art contemporain interroge l'histoire," *La Cité Nationale de l'Histoire de l'Immigration: Une collection en devenir*, 21.

34. Leïla Sebbar, *Parle mon fils, parle à ta mère* (Paris: Editions Stock, 1984).

35. See Yamina Benguigui, *Inch-Allah Dimanche*, www.filmmovement.com; Azouz Begag, *Le gône du Châaba* (Paris: Editions du Seuil, 1986); and Alec G. Hargreaves, *Immigration and Identity in beur fiction: Voices from the North African Community in France* (Oxford: Berg, 1991). To date, the focus on literature at the CNHI has been limited to a handful of recorded interviews with francophone authors such as François Cheng, Tahar Ben Jelloun, Milan Kundera, and Andreï Makine.

36. The free handout and map of the CNHI entitled *Cité guide* (City Guide) makes a similar point: "Through an interactive presentation which calls upon the demands of history and the emotion of eyewitness accounts, images, archive documents, objects which were part of the lives of some of these individuals and ancient and contemporary works of art also provide an insight into this world."

37. "United Nations High Commissioner for Refugees," http://www.unhcr.org/cgi-bin/texis/vtx/asylum?page=home.

38. Hervé Lemoine, "La Maison de l'Histoire de France": Pour la création d'un centre de recherche et de collections permanentes dédié à l'histoire civile et militaire de la France (April 16, 2008).

39. Nicolas Sarkozy, "Vœux aux acteurs de la Culture," http://www.culture.gouv.fr/culture/actualites/conferen/albanel/prculture09.pdf (January 13, 2009), 16.

40. Tzvetan Todorov, "A bas le multiculturalisme!" *Télérama horizons* 4 (April 2011): 50–51.

41. Olivier Le Cour Grandmaison, *La République impériale: Politique et racisme d'état* (Paris: Editions La Découverte, 2009), 372.

42. Nicolas Bancel and Herman Lebovics, "Building the History Museum to Stop History: Nicolas Sarkozy's New Presidential Museum of French History," *French Cultural Studies* 22.4 (November 2011): 279.

3. *Sarkozy's Law*

1. Patrick Rambaud, *Chronique du règne de Nicolas Ier* (Paris: Editions Grasset & Fasquelle, 2008), 13–15.

2. Edouard Glissant and Patrick Chamoiseau, *Quand les murs tombent: l'identité nationale hors-la-loi* (Paris: Editions Galaade, 2007), 7–9.

3. Delphine Coulin, *Samba pour la France* (Paris: Editions du Seuil, 2011), 27.

4. Max Frisch, "United Nations Convention on Human Rights," http://portal.unesco.org/shs/en/files/2874/11163348401InfoKit_en.pdf/InfoKit%2Ben.pdf (2003), 1. Consulted August 12, 2010.

5. Two government reports were commissioned in 2008 to explore the question of "diversity" in contemporary France. See Simone Veil, "Comité de reflexion sur le préambule de la Constitution: Rapport au Président de la République" (December 2008), and Michel Wieviorka, *La diversité: Rapport à la Ministre de l'Enseignement supérieur et*

de la Recherche (Paris: Editions Robert Laffont, 2009). President Sarkozy also appointed Yazid Sabeg as High Commissioner for Diversity. Sabeg established an expert Comité pour la mesure et l'évaluation des discriminations (COMEDD), and at the same time, another group made up of eminent scholars challenged the usage of ethnic statistics in France (the CARSED, Commission alternative de réflexion sur les "statistiques ethniques" et les "discriminations"). See CARSED, *Le retour de la race: Contre les "statistiques ethniques"* (La Tour d'Aigues: Editions de l'Aube, 2009).

6. Alain Badiou/Alain Finkielkraut, *L'explication. Conversation avec Aude Lancelin* (Paris: Nouvelles Editions Lignes, 2010), 25 and 23, respectively (emphasis added).

7. Éric Fassin, *Démocratie précaire. Chroniques de la déraison d'État* (Paris: Editions La Découverte, 2012), 266.

8. Alessandro Dal Lago's "Tautology of Fear" is summarized here for the purposes of the analysis. See *Non-Persons: The Exclusion of Migrants in a Global Society,* trans. Marie Orton (Milan, Italy: IPOC Press, 2009), 85.

9. Gérard Noiriel, *A quoi sert "l'identité nationale"* (Marseille: Editions Agone, 2007), 146. See Abdellali Hajjat, *Les frontières de l'identité nationale: L'injonction à l'assimilation en France métropolitaine et coloniale* (Paris: Editions La Découverte, 2012) and the documentary by Valérie Osouf, *L'identité nationale* (Granit Films, 2012).

10. Alexis Spire, *Accueillir ou reconduire. Enquête sur les guichets de l'immigration* (Paris: Editions Raison d'Agir, 2008), 91. See also Annamaria Rivera, trans. Michaël Gasperoni, *Les dérives de l'universalisme. Ethnocentrisme et islamophobie en France et en Italie* (Paris: Editions La Découverte, 2010), Laurent Mucchielli, *L'invention de la violence. Des peurs, des chiffres et des faits* (Paris: Editions La Découverte, 2011), and Cette France-là, *Sans-papiers et préfets. La culture du résultat en portraits* (Paris: Editions La Découverte, 2012).

11. Éric Fassin, *Démocratie précaire. Chroniques de la déraison d'État* (Paris: Editions La Découverte, 2012), 96.

12. See www.svr-migration.de. See also the Federal Government Commissioner for Migration, Refugees and Integration (Die Beauftragte der Bundesregierung für Migration, Flüchtlinge und Integration), www.bundesregierung.de.

13. "L'intégration: ça marche," *La France sait-elle encore intégrer les immigrés?* Report to the Prime Minister (April 12, 2011), 21–32. See also the publications of the Office français de l'immigration et de l'intégration, http://www.ofii.fr/article.php3.

14. See Vincent Tiberj, *La crispation hexagonale. France fermée contre France plurielle, 2001–2007* (Paris: Collection Fondation Jean Jaurès/Plon, 2008).

15. Sarkozy's positions on "integration" and "religion" were already a component of a book he published (with Thibauld Collin and Philipe Verdin), *La République, les religions, l'espérance* (Paris: Éditions du Cerf, 2004).

16. Alec G. Hargreaves, *Multi-Ethnic France: Immigration, Politics, Culture and Society* (New York: Routledge, 2007), 2.

17. Etienne Balibar, "Is There a 'Neo-Racism'," in *Race, Nation, Class: Ambiguous Identities,* eds. Etienne Balibar and Immanuel Wallerstein (London: Verso, 1991), 21.

18. See, for example, Didier Fassin and Éric Fassin, eds. *De la question sociale à la question raciale: Représenter la société française* (Paris: Editions La Découverte, 2006).

19. Pierre Tevanian, *Le ministère de la peur. Réflexions sur le nouvel ordre sécuritaire* (Paris: Editions L'Esprit frappeur, 2003), 9–10, Pierre Tevanian and Sylvie Tissot, *Dictionnaire de la lepénisation des esprits* (Paris: Editions L'Esprit frappeur, 2002), 270–297, and Noiriel, *A quoi sert "l'identité nationale"*, 2. See also Pierre Tevanian, *La République du mépris. Les métamorphoses du racisme dans la France des années Sarkozy* (Paris: Editions La Découverte, 2007).

20. See Monique Chemillier-Gendreau, *L'injustifiable. Les politiques françaises de l'immigration* (Paris: Editions du Seuil, 1998).

21. See Azouz Begag, "*C'est quand il y en a beaucoup." Nouveaux périls identitaires français* (Paris: Editions Belin, 2011). Indeed, an analogous discourse in Germany can certainly help us better understand the publishing success and appeal of Thilo Sarrazin's racist bestseller *Deutschland Schafft Sich Ab: Wie wir under Land aufs Spiel setzen* [Germany Abolishes Itself: How We are Putting Our Country at Risk] (Munich: DVA, 2010).

22. Jérôme Valluy, *Rejet des exilés. Le grand retournement du droit d'asile* (Bellecombe-en-Bauges: Editions du Croquant, 2009), 23.

23. Alain Ruscio, in his book *Y'a bon les colonies? La France sarkozyste face à l'histoire coloniale, à l'identité nationale et à l'immigration* (Paris: Le Temps des Cerises, 2011), has traced the manner in which this xenophobic discourse is now commonly employed by politicians, intellectuals, and in the media.

24. German Marshall Fund, "Transatlantic Trends—immigration," http://trends.gmfus.org/immigration/doc/TTI2010_English_Key.pdf (2010), 12.

25. Dominique Reynié, *Populismes: la pente fatale* (Paris: Editions Plon, 2011), 231–232. See also the E.U. barometer that measures public opinion in the European Union: "Europeans' perception on the state of the economy," http://ec.europa.eu/public_opinion/archives/eb/eb75/eb75_en.pdf, (August 2011), 1–25.

26. See Charles Tshimanga, Didier Gondola, and Peter J. Bloom, eds. *Frenchness and the African Diaspora: Identity and Uprising in Contemporary France* (Bloomington: Indiana University Press, 2009).

27. See Lilian Thuram et al., *Appel pour une République multiculturelle et postraciale, Respect Mag*, 10 (January–March 2010) [http://www.respectmag.com/appel-pour-une-république-multiculturelle-et-postraciale] and "Identité nationale et passé colonial. Pour un véritable débat," http://www.achac.com/?O=204 (December 24, 2009).

28. Pascal Blanchard, Nicolas Bancel and Sandrine Lemaire, eds. *La fracture coloniale: La société française au prisme de l'héritage colonial* (Paris: Editions La Découverte, 2005) and Nicolas Bancel, Pascal Blanchard, Achille Mbembe, Françoise Vergès, and Florence Bernault, eds. *Ruptures post-coloniales: Les nouveaux visages de la société-francaise* (Paris: Editions La Découverte, 2010); Rama Yade-Zimet, *Noirs de France* (Paris: Editions Calmann-Lévy, 2007); Gaston Kelman, *Je suis noir et je n'aime pas le manioc* (Paris: Max Milo Editions, 2003), *Au-delà du Noir et du Blanc* (Paris: Max Milo Editions, 2005), *Parlons enfants de la patrie* (Paris: Max Milo Editions, 2007); Jean-Baptiste Onana, *Sois-nègre et tais-toi* (Nantes: Editions du Temps, 2007); Patrick Lozès, *Nous les noirs de France* (Paris: Editions Danger Public, 2007); Claude Ribbe, *Les Nègres de la République* (Monaco: Editions Alphée, 2007); Pap Ndiaye, *La condition noire: Essai sur une minorité ethnique française* (Paris: Editions Calmann-Lévy, 2008); Christiane Taubira, *Egalité pour les exclus: La politique face à l'histoire et à la mémoire coloniale* (Paris: Editions du Temps Présent, 2009); Rokhaya Diallo, *Racisme: Mode d'emploi* (Paris: Editions Larousse, 2011); Pascal Blanchard, Sylvie Chalaye, Éric Deroo, Dominic Thomas, and Mahamet Timera, *La France noire. Trois siècles de présences des Afriques, des Caraïbes, de l'océan Indien, et d'Océanie* (Paris: Editions La Découverte, 2011), and Alain Mabanckou, *Le Sanglot de l'Homme Noir* (Paris: Editions Fayard, 2012).

29. See, for example, Mary Dewhurst Lewis, *The Boundaries of the Republic: Migrant Rights and the Limits of Universalism in France, 1918–1940* (Stanford: Stanford University Press, 2007).

30. See, for example, Patrick Charaudeau, *Entre populisme et peopolisme. Comment Sarkozy a gagné!* (Paris: Librairie Vuibert, 2008).

31. See www.immigration.gouv.fr. Public debates and activism have also shaped opposition to the creation of this ministry. The Collectif pour la suppression du ministère de l'identité nationale remained active in monitoring the activities of the ministry, a website was devoted to this task (www.anticolonial.org), Thomas Lacoste directed a documentary on the question (*Ulysse Clandestin*, www.labandepassante.org), and "No Sarkozy Day" was held on March 27, 2010, to protest the existence of the ministry. Publications denounced the troubling link between "national identity" and "immigration" (Agnès Maillot, *Identité nationale et immigration. La liaison dangereuse* [Paris: Les carnets de l'Info, 2008]), and Claude Liauzu hinted at the Orwellian overtones (readers of Orwell's *1984* will remember that "the Ministry of Love betrays and kills, the Ministry of Peace wages war, the Ministry of Truth tells lies") in an article entitled "Ministère de l'hostilité," *Le Monde diplomatique* (July 2007): 28.

32. *Les Orientations de la politique de l'immigration* (Paris: La Documentation Française, 2007). Similar documents were published by this ministry until 2010, and subsequently by other official bodies. See Secrétariat général du comité interministériel de contrôle de l'immigation, *Rapport annuel: Les orientations de la politique de l'immigration et de l'intégration* (Paris: Direction de l'information légale et administrative, 2011) and Claude Guéant, "Les résultats de la politique migratoire," (10 January 10, 2012). The British government has recently started the process of overhauling the U.K.'s immigration system in an effort to "improve" control of migration.

33. See the new "organigramme" (organizational chart) for the French Ministry of the Interior: http://www.interieur.gouv.fr/sections/a_l_interieur/le_ministere/organisation/organigramme/downloadFile/attachedFile/ORGANIGRAMME_12_janvier_2011.pdf?nocache=1312296771.03. In the U.K., since 1999, shifting concerns and governmental agendas and priorities have been reflected in the repeated "renaming" of the Ministry of State to include asylum, borders, citizenship, community-cohesion, immigration, and counter-terrorism.

34. See, for example, Elsa Camiscioli, *Reproducing the French Race: Immigration, Intimacy, and Embodiment in the Early Twentieth Century* (Durham: Duke University Press, 2009).

35. Rocard is of course attributing the status of "misère" to what we might call today a global underclass. I have translated this notion by adopting the English title of Pierre Bourdieu et al.'s influential book, *The Weight of the World: Social Suffering in Contemporary Society*, trans. Priscilla Parkhurst, Susan Emanuel, Joe Johnson, and Shoggy T. Waryn (Stanford: Stanford University Press, 2000) [first pub. 1993].

36. See Laurent Mucchielli, "Faire du chiffre: le 'nouveau management de la sécurité'," Laurent Mucchielli, ed. *La frénésie sécuritaire. Retour à l'ordre et nouveau contrôle social* (Paris: Editions La Découverte, 2008), 99–112, and Serge Slama, "Politique d'immigration: un laboratoire de la frénésie sécuritaire," in *La frénésie sécuritaire*, ed. Mucchielli, 64–76.

37. Nicolas Sarkozy, "Discours sur la nation," http://sites.univ-provence.fr/veronis/Discours2007/transcript.php?n=Sarkozy&p=2007-03-09 (March 9, 2007). One should note that the French parliament voted unanimously May 21, 2001, to recognize France's role in the Atlantic slave trade and slavery as crimes against humanity. The relevant law is known as "Loi Taubira" after its *rapporteuse*, the Deputy from French Guiana, Christiane Taubira.

38. Brice Hortefeux, "Ma vision de l'identité nationale," *Libération* (July 27, 2007): 20. See also Laetitia Van Eeckhout, "Brice Hortefeux à la tête d'un grand ministère de l'immigration incluant l'identité nationale," *Le Monde* (May 19, 2007).

39. For the version adopted by the National Assembly, see "Projet de loi relatif à la

maîtrise de l'immigration, à l'intégration et à l'asile," http://www.assemblee-nationale.fr/13/ta/ta0026.asp (September 19, 2007). In the U.K., Cellmark is contracted to the U.K. Foreign and Commonwealth Office U.K. visas scheme. See http://www.cellmark.co.uk/dna_testing/immigration_dna_testing.php. In the United States, rules and guidelines have been developed to govern the use of DNA testing to support immigration applications. See http://www.dnacenter.com/international/immigration/immigration-test-embassy.html.

40. "La technologie du soupçon: tests osseux, tests de pilosité, tests ADN," in *Cette France-là*, Vol. 1 (Paris: Editions La Découverte, 2009), 159.

41. Achille Mbembe, "Provincializing France?" trans. Janet Roitman, *Public Culture* 23.1 (2011): 92. These arguments are also developed in his "Le long hiver impérial français," *Sortir de la grande nuit. Essai sur l'Afrique décolonisée* (Paris: Editions La Découverte, 2010), 121–171.

42. See "Missions and Role," http://www.immigration.gouv.fr/spip.php?page=dossiers_det_org&numrubrique=311&numarticle=1331. This official translation has been slightly altered.

43. See Éric Fassin, "'Immigration et délinquance': la construction d'un problème entre politique, journalisme et sociologie," *Cités: Philosophie, Politique, Histoire* 46 (2011): 69–85.

44. See Brice Hortefeux's speech delivered at the 8th conference of the Council of European Ministers in charge of immigration questions in Kiev, Russian Federation: "Migrations économiques, cohésion sociale et développement: vers une approche intégrée," http://www.coe.int/t/dg3/migration/Ministerial_Conferences/8th%20conference/Speeches/Inaugural%20Session%20-%20II%20-%20Introductory%20speech%20by%20Mr%20Hortefeux_fr.pdf (4–5 September, 2008), 5–7. Numerous critics and observers have argued that a "brain drain" is occurring and negatively impacting African economies. See, for example, Angela Balakrishnan and Pui-Guan Man, "The best move out so the rest lose out," *The Guardian*, (July 20, 2007): 21. Furthermore, the economic shortcomings of such development policies have been criticized. Saskia Sassen, for example, has convincingly shown how the "[promotion of] growth in the migrant-sending countries by encouraging direct foreign investment and export-oriented international development assistance, in the belief that raising economic opportunities in the developing world will deter emigration [. . .] seems to have had precisely the opposite effect," *Globalization and Its Discontents: Essays on the New Mobility of People and Money* (New York: The New Press, 1998), 34.

45. Nathalie Kotlok, "Une politique migratoire au service du développement des pays africains?" in *Les migrations subsahariennes*, ed. Patrick Gonin. Special dossier, *Hommes et Migrations*, 1286–1287 (July–October 2010): 277.

46. Communication from the Commission to the Council, the European Parliament, the European Economic and Social Committee and the Committee of the Regions, *Third Annual Report on Migration and Integration* (September 11, 2007), 3.

47. "Towards a Common European Union Migration Policy," http://ec.europa.eu/justice_home/fsj/immigration/integration/fsj_immigration_integration_en.htm (September 2007).

48. See Directive 2008/115/EC of the European Parliament and of the Council of 16 December 2008 on common standards and procedures in Member States for returning illegally staying third-country nationals, http://eur-lex.europa.eu/LexUriServ/LexUriServ.do?uri=OJ:L:2008:348:0098:0107:EN:PDF (2008).

49. Catherine Wihtol de Wenden, *L'Immigration en Europe* (Paris: La Documentation Française, 1997), 27.

50. Didier Bigo, "Contrôle migratoire et libre circulation en Europe," in *L'enjeu mondial. Les migrations,* eds. Christophe Jaffrelot and Christian Lequesne (Paris: Presses de la Fondation Nationale des Sciences Politiques, 2009), 165.

51. Violaine Carrère, "Sangatte et les nasses aux frontières de l'Europe," *Ceras—revue,* Projet 272 (2002), http://www.ceras-projet.com/index.php?id=1764.

52. "European Pact on Immigration and Asylum," Document 13440/08. http://www.immigration.gouv.fr/IMG/pdf/Plaquette_EN.pdf (October 15–16, 2008), 2.

53. Claire Rodier, "Europe et migrations: la gestion de l'inquiétude. L'exemple de la directive 'retour'," in *Douce France. Rafles, rétentions, expulsions,* ed. Olivier Le Cour Grandmaison (Paris: Editions du Seuil, 2009), 261.

54. See map in Jacques Huntzinger, "La Méditerranée d'une rive à l'autre," *Questions Internationales* 36 (2009): 9.

55. Évelyne Ritaine, "Des migrants face aux murs d'un monde frontière," in *L'enjeu mondial,* eds. Jaffrelot and Lequesne, 158. Frontex is the *Agence européenne pour la gestion de la coopération opérationnelle aux frontières extérieures,* a specialized and independent-body tasked to coordinate the operational cooperation between Member States in the field of border security. See http://www.frontex.europa.eu/.

56. Claire Rodier, "Aux marges de l'Europe: la construction de l'inacceptable," in *Le retour des camps: Sangatte, Lampedusa, Guantanamo,* eds. Olivier Le Cour Grandmaison, Gilles Lhuilier and Jérôme Valluy (Paris: Editions Autrement, 2007), 138. See also Jean-Robert Henry, "Sarkozy, the Mediterranean and the Arab Spring," *Contemporary French and Francophone Studies: Sites* 16.3 (June 2012): 405–415.

57. Catherine Wihtol de Wenden, "Immigration: une politique contradictoire," *Esprit* 11, 339 (2007): 83; and Michèle Tribalat, *Les Yeux grands fermés. L'immigration en France* (Paris: Editions Denöel, 2010).

58. Marc Bernardot, "Rafles et internement des étrangers: les nouvelles guerres de capture," in *Douce France,* ed. Le Cour Grandmaison, 64.

59. Cette France-là, "Eléments de langage. Trois rhétoriques pour un même acharnement," *Xénophobie d'en haut. Le choix d'une droite éhontée* (Paris: Editions La Découverte, 2012), 29.

60. Monique Chemillier-Gendreau, "Interview," *Diasporiques* 2 (2008): 10–18.

61. See www.debatidentitenationale.fr.

62. "Projet de loi relatif à l'immigration," http://www.immigration.gouv.fr/IMG/pdf/DP20100401ProjLoi.pdf. April 1, 2010, 1–36. I have summarized the key components.

63. Didier Fassin, "Frontières extérieures, frontières intérieures," in *Les nouvelles frontières de la société française,* ed. Didier Fassin (Paris: Editions La Découverte: 2010), 6.

64. See Sophie Duchesne, "Quelle identité européenne?" *Cahiers français* 342 (2008): 17–21.

65. Norbert Elias and John L. Scotson, *Logiques de l'exclusion* (Paris: Editions Fayard, 1997) [first pub. 1965].

66. See Gérard Noiriel, *Immigrations, antisémitisme et racisme en France (XIXe–XXe siècles)* (Paris: Editions Fayard, 2007).

67. Joël Roman, "La question de l'identité nationale n'est pas taboue!," *Diasporiques* 2 (2008): 24.

68. Mathieu Rigouste, *L'ennemi intérieur. La généalogie coloniale et militaire de l'ordre sécuritaire dans la France métropolitaine* (Paris: Editions La Découverte, 2009).

69. See also Loïc Wacquant, *Punir les pauvres. Le nouveau gouvernement de l'insécurité sociale* (Marseille: Editions Agone, 2004).

70. Olivier Le Cour Grandmaison, "Xénophobie d'état et politique de la peur," *Lignes* 26 (May 2008): 24. See also Valluy, "L'Empire du rejet: xénophobie de gouvernement et

politiques antimigratoires entre Europe et Afrique," in *Douce France,* ed. Le Cour Grandmaison, 121–143.

71. See http://www.debatidentitenationale.fr/bibliotheque/.

72. See www.medipart.fr.

73. See www.arretezcedebat.com.

74. Cited in Le Cour Grandmaison, ed. *Douce France,* 292. See also "Lettre de Mission," http://www.immigration.gouv.fr/spip.php?page=dossiers_them_org&numrubrique=341 (March 31, 2009).

75. Éric Besson, "Le débat sur l'identité nationale," www.youtube.com/ministereimmigration#p/u/8/lkNPlgOv-YU.

76. Published interview with Marc Vignaud, www.lepoint.fr/actualites-societe/2009-12-02/interview-gallo-en-chaque-francais-il-y-a-un-etranger/920/0/400886 (December 2, 2009).

77. Éric Besson, "Faire connaître et partager l'identité nationale," www.debatidentitenationale.fr/propositions-d-eric-besson/faire-connaitre-et-partager-l.html (October 31, 2009).

78. Éric Besson, "Valoriser l'identité nationale," www.debatidentitenationale.fr/propositions-d-eric-besson/valoriser-l-identite-nationale.html (October 31, 2009).

79. Laurence de Cock, Fanny Madeline, Nicolas Offenstadt, and Sophie Wahnich, "Introduction," in *Comment Nicolas Sarkozy écrit l'histoire de France,* eds. Laurence de Cock, Fanny Madeline, Nicolas Offenstadt, and Sophie Wahnich (Marseille: Editions Agone, 2008), 15–19.

80. Olivier Le Cour Grandmaison, *La République impériale: Politique et racisme d'État* (Paris: Editions Fayard, 2009), 372.

81. See www.debatidentitenationale.fr/bibliotheque/.

82. See, for example, Max Gallo, *Fier d'être français* (Paris: Editions Fayard, 2006) and *L'âme de la France. Une histoire de la nation des origines à nos jours* (Paris: Editions Fayard, 2007), and Daniel Lefeuvre's and Michel Renard's *Faut-il avoir honte de l'identité nationale?* (Paris: Editions Larousse, 2008).

83. Nicolas Sarkozy, "Un nouvel avenir pour notre agriculture," http://www.elysee.fr/president/mediatheque/videos/2009/octobre/un-nouvel-avenir-pour-notre-agriculture.4967.html (October 27, 2009).

84. Frantz Fanon, *The Wretched of the Earth,* trans. Richard Philcox (New York: Grove Press, 2004 [first pub. 1961]), 9.

85. Éric Besson, "Débat sur l'identité nationale," http://www.assemblee-nationale.fr/13/cri/2009–2010/20100079.asp#ANCR200900000093–00745 (December 8, 2009).

86. Albin Wagener, *Le débat sur "l'identité nationale." Essai à propos d'un fantôme* (Paris: Editions L'Harmattan, 2010), 21 and 22.

87. For in-depth analysis of questionnaire responses pertaining to the "elements that make up national identity" (values, universalism, history language, culture, territory, and so forth) see Wagener, *Le débat sur "l'identité nationale",* 34–44.

88. Somewhat paradoxically, given their opposition to the E.U., both Jean-Marie and Marine Le Pen are elected members of the European Parliament. In this capacity, they are able to influence inter-governmental and supranational policy-making that can in turn shape French laws and policies.

89. See www.defendonsnoscouleurs.fr.

90. Marine Le Pen, "Face à l'anomie, redonner un sens," http://www.frontnational.com/?p=4143#more-4143 (March 2, 2010).

91. Alain Badiou, Interview with Frédéric Taddéï, "De quoi Sarkozy est-il le nom?" http://www.ldh-toulon.net/spip.php?article2403 (December 9, 2007). See also his ar-

ticle, "Le racisme des intellectuels," *Le Monde* (May 5, 2012), http://www.lemonde.fr/election-presidentielle-2012/article/2012/05/05/le-racisme-des-intellectuels-par-alain-badiou_1696292_1471069.html.

92. Nicolas Sarkozy, "Discours de Grenoble sur la sécurité et l'immigration," http://www.elysee.fr/president/les-actualites/discours/2010/discours-de-m-le-president-de-la-republique-a.9399.html (July 30, 2010).

93. Nicolas Bancel, "La brèche. Vers la radicalisation des discours publiques," *Mouvements* 1 (2011): 13.

94. Herman Lebovics, *True France: The Wars Over Cultural Identity, 1900–1945* (Ithaca: Cornell University Press, 1992).

95. Alain Badiou, *De quoi Sarkozy est-il le nom?* (Paris: Nouvelles Editions Lignes, 2007), 113.

96. See also his article, Claude Guéant, "Quelle France pour demain?" *Le Monde,* (May 31, 2011).

97. Patrick Simon, "Nationalité et sentiment national," in *Trajectoires et origines. Enquête sur la diversité des populations en France* [Documents de travail 168], eds. Cris Beauchemin, Christelle Hamel and Patrick Simon, http://www.ined.fr/fichier/t_telechargement/35196/telechargement_fichier_fr_dt168.13janvier11.pdf, (October 2010), 122.

98. See, for example, Thierry Blin, *L'invention des sans-papiers* (Paris: Presses Universitaires de France, 2010) and Valluy, *Rejet des exilés.*

99. Available at www.europarl.europa.eu/comparl/libe/elsj/charter/art05/default_en.htm#6.

100. Hugo Brady, *EU Migration Policy,* www.cer.org.uk/pdf/briefing_813.pdf (2008), 27.

101. Fabrizio Gatti, "I was a slave in Puglia," http://espresso.repubblica.it/dettaglio/I%20was%20a%20slave%20in%20Puglia/1373950 (September 4, 2006).

102. Nicolas Sarkozy, "Discours du Président de la République à Toulon," http://www.elysee.fr/president/les-actualites/discours/2011/discours-du-president-de-la-republique-a-toulon.12553.html (December 1, 2012).

103. See Jocelyne Dakhlia, "La France dedans dehors," *Lignes* 25 (March 2008): 160–176.

104. "E.U. Warns France of Action over Roma," http://www.bbc.co.uk/news/world-europe-11437361 (September 29, 2010).

105. On this issue, see *Multiple discrimination, Roma Rights: Journal of the European Roma Rights Centre* 2 (2009), Tony Gatlif, "Tsiganes, Gitans, Manouches. La fin du voyage," *Ravages* 5 (April 2011): 30–45, Claude Cahn and Elspeth Guild, "Recent Migration of Roma in Europe," OSCE High Commissioner on National Minorities, Council of Europe Commissioner for Human Rights (December 10, 2008), 1–86, and Jean-Pierre Dacheux and Bernard Delemotte, *Roms de France, Roms en France. Le peuple du* voyage (Montreuil: Editions Cédis, 2010).

106. Michel Bart, "Evaluations des campements élicites," http://www.france-info.com/IMG/pdf/7/f/6/Circulaire_du_5aout_2010.pdf (August 5, 2010), 1.

107. Éric Fassin, "Pourquoi les Roms?" *Lignes* 35 (June 2011): 120. See also Etienne Balibar, "Racisme et politique communautaire: les Roms," *Lignes* 34 (February 2011): 135–144.

108. See, for example, William Easterly, "Foreign Aid for Scoundrels," *New York Review of Books,* (November 25, 2010): 37–38.

109. Europe has been and remains actively complicit in the destitution of large parts of Africa, but the defenders of Fortress Europe cannot directly govern the behavior of the people they exclude. As Philippe Bernard has shown, "In spite of all the obstacles,

xenophobia and expulsions, when one considers the multiple forms of migration, Africans emerge as the most mobile inhabitants of the planet," "L'autre immigration africaine," *Le Monde* (June 26, 2008), 2.

110. Catherine Coquery-Vidrovitch, *Enjeux politiques de l'histoire coloniale* (Marseille: Editions Agone 2009), 168.

111. Cited in Ibrahima Signaté, *Med Hondo: Un cinéaste rebelle* (Paris: Editions Présence Africaine, 1994), 72.

112. Azouz Begag, *Ethnicity and Equality: France in the Balance,* trans. Alec G. Hargreaves (Lincoln: University of Nebraska Press, 2007), 19.

113. Etienne Balibar, "Racism and Crisis," in *Race, Nation,* Class, eds. Balibar and Wallerstein, 220.

114. Tahir Abbas, "Recent Developments to British Multicultural Theory, Polity and Practice: The Case of British Muslims," *Citizenship Studies* 9.2 (May 2005): 154.

115. Jacques Chirac, http://www.youtube.com/watch?v=eERFYd1DuDE (1991). Emphasis added.

116. Azouz Begag, *Un mouton dans la baignoire* (Paris: Editions Fayard, 2007), 9.

117. Patrick Weil, *How to be French: Nationality in the Making Since 1789,* trans. Catherine Porter (Durham: Duke University Press, 2008), 29.

118. Faïza Guène, *Du rêve pour les oufs* (Paris: Hachette Littératures, 2006); *Dreams from the Endz,* trans. Sarah Adams (London: Chatto & Windus, 2008), 43.

119. Olivier Le Cour Grandmaison "Xénophobie d'état et politique de la peur," *Lignes 26* (May 2008): 24.

120. Anne-Marie Thiesse, *La création des identités nationales. Europe XVIIIe–XIXe* (Paris: Editions du Seuil, 2001).

4. *Africa, France, and Eurafrica in the Twenty-First Century*

1. "Address at the University Cheikh Anta Diop," http://www.africaresource.com/index.php?option=com_content&view=article&id=437%3Athe-unofficial-english-translation-of-sarkozys-speech&catid=36%3Aessays-a-discussions&Itemid=346 (July 26, 2007). Translation slightly altered.

2. Cheikh Hamidou Kane, *Ambiguous Adventure,* trans. Katherine Woods (Exeter: Heinemann Educational Books, Ltd., 1963), 48.

3. "On ne s'improvise pas en diplomate": http://www.lemonde.fr/idees/article/2011/02/22/on-ne-s-improvise-pas-diplomate_1483517_3232.html (February 23, 2011). Consulted February 24, 2011.

4. Henri Brunschwig, *Le partage de l'Afrique noire* (Paris: Editions Flammarion, 1971), 101.

5.Nicolas Sarkozy, "Discours à Toulon," http://mouveuropeprovence.free.fr/serendipity/index.php%3F/archives/17-Discours-Nicolas-Sarkozy-a-Toulon,-Mercredi-7-fevrier-2007.html.&ie=UTF-8&oe=UTF-8-Discours-Nicolas-Sarkozy-a-Toulon,-Mercredi-7-fevrier-2007.html (February 7, 2007).

6. For French policy on African immigration, see Jacques Barou, "La politique française vis-à-vis de l'immigration africaine," in *De l'Afrique à la France. D'une génération à l'autre,* ed. Jacques Barou (Paris: Armand Colin, 2011), 39–64.

7. Daniel Bourmaud, "La nouvelle politique africaine de la France à l'épreuve," *Esprit* 317 (August–September 2005): 17–27.

8. Catherine Coquery-Vidrovitch, *Petite histoire de l'Afrique. L'Afrique au sud du Sahara de la préhistoire à nos jours* (Paris: Editions La Découverte, 2011), 212.

9. Jean-Pierre Dozon, *Frères et sujets. La France et l'Afrique en perspective* (Paris: Editions Flammarion, 2003), 343.

10. On January 26, 2012 the Ivory Coast's new president, Alassane Ouattara, made an official state visit to France. In the words of a Ouattara advisor, "Nothing would have been possible without the friendship and personal support of Nicolas Sarkozy." Cited in Thomas Hofnung, "Ouattara et Sarkozy, les copains d'abord," *Libération* (January 26, 2012), 8.

11. This particular parade added itself to a long list of prior similar displays of African soldiers in France, such as those held to commemorate different historical turns in 1899, 1918, 1939, and 1989 on the occasion of the French bicentennial. It might be worth noting that the ostentatious practices of African leaders—and the tolerance of these by the French authorities—have been subjected to increasing scrutiny in recent years, as the front page headline on July 28, 2011, of *Libération* newspaper confirms: "Bien mal acquis: La France complice."

12. See Jean-Pierre Dozon, "L'État franco-africain," *Les Temps modernes* 620–621 (August-November 2002): 261–288 and "Une décolonisation en trompe-l'œil (1956–2006)," in *Culture coloniale en France. De la Révolution à nos jours,* eds. Pascal Blanchard, Nicolas Bancel, and Sandrine Lemaire (Paris: CNRS Editions, 2008), 537–544.

13. François-Xavier Verschave, *De la Françafrique à la Mafiafrique* (Brussels, Belgium: Editions Tribord, 2004), 9. See also Thomas Deltombe, Manuel Domergue and Jacob Tatsitsa, *Kamerun! Une guerre cachée aux origines de la Françafrique, 1948–1971* (Paris: Editions La Découverte, 2011).

14. Achille Mbembe, "Provincializing France?" trans. Janet Roitman, *Public Culture* 23.1 2011): 89, and see also "Le long hiver impérial français," *Sortir de la grande nuit. Essai sur l'Afrique décolonisée* (Paris: Editions La Découverte, 2010), 121–171.

15. Patrick Benquet, *Françafrique, 50 années sous le sceau du secret* (Paris: Compagnie des phares et balises, 2010).

16. Achille Mbembe, "At the Edge of the World: Boundaries, Territoriality, and Sovereignty in Africa," trans. Steven Rendall, in *Globalization,* ed. Arjun Appadurai (Durham: Duke University Press, 2001), 29.

17. See Catherine Coquery-Vidrovitch, "Colonisation, coopération, partenariat. Les différentes étapes (1950–2000)," in *Étudiants africains en France (1951–2001),* ed. Michel Sot (Paris: Editions Karthala, 2002), 29–48.

18. François-Xavier Verschave and Philippe Hauser, *Au mépris des peuples: Le néocolonialisme franco-africain* (Paris: Editions la Fabrique, 2004), 7.

19. Sylvain Touati, "French Foreign Policy in Africa: Between *pré-carré* and Multilaterialism," The Royal Institute of International Affairs, http://www.chathamhouse.org/sites/default/files/public/Research/Africa/bnafrica0207.pdf (2007), 11–12.

20. Christopher L. Miller, "The Slave Trade, *La Françafrique,* and the Globalization of French," in *French Global: A New Approach to Literary History,* eds. Christie McDonald and Susan Rubin Suleiman (New York: Columbia University Press, 2010), 241.

21. "La cellule africaine de l'Elysée," http://reseaugaribaldi.info/wp-content/uploads/2011/05/La-cellule-africaine-de-lElysée.pdf (2011), 4.

22. François-Xavier Verschave, *La Françafrique. Le plus long scandale de la République* (Paris: Editions Stock, 1998), 86.

23. See Patrick Benquiet's documentary, *Françafrique, 50 années sous le sceau du secret* (Paris: Compagnie des phares et balises, 2010).

24. See Pierre Péan, *L'Homme de l'Ombre* (Paris: Editions Fayard, 1990), and Kaye Whiteman, "The man who ran Françafrique," *National Interest* 49 (Fall 1997), as well as

Foccart's multi-volume publications published between 1997 and 2001, *Journal de l'Élysée* (Paris: Editions Fayard/Jeune Afrique) and *Foccart parle,* interviews with Philippe Gaillard, two volumes (Paris: Editions Fayard/Jeune Afrique, 1995 and 1997). See also Samuël Foutoyet, *Nicolas Sarkozy ou la Françafrique décomplexée* (Brussels, Belgium: Éditions Tribord, 2009), 22–23, and François-Xavier Verschave, *Noir Chirac. Secret et impunité* (Paris: Editions des Arènes, 2002).

25. Mongo Béti, In *Main basse sur le Cameroun, Autopsie d'une décolonisation* (Paris: François Maspéro, 1972) and *La France contre l'Afrique. Retour au Cameroon* (Paris: Editions La Découverte, 2006) [first pub. 1993]. See also François Gèze, "L'héritage colonial au cœur de la politique étrangère française," in *La fracture coloniale: La société française au prisme de l'héritage colonial,* eds. Pascal Blanchard, Nicolas Bancel, and Sandrine Lemaire (Paris: Editions La Découverte, 2005), 155–163.

26. Odile Tobner, "Préface," Béti, *La France contre l'Afrique,* 216.

27. See, for example, Jean-Paul Gourévitch, *L'Afrique, le fric, la France* (Paris: Editions Le Pré aux Clercs, 1997) and Michel Pinçon et Monique Pinçon-Charlot, *Le président des riches. Enquête sur l'oligarchie dans la France de Nicolas Sarkozy* (Paris: Editions la Découverte, 2010). See also Renaud Lecadre, "Les grandes manœuvres de Bolloré dans le port de Conakry," *Libération* (July 29, 2011): 14, and Gilles Labarthe, *Sarko l'Africain* (Paris: Editions Hugo & Cie, 2011).

28. François-Xavier Verschave, *Noir silence. Qui arrêtera la Françafrique* (Paris: Editions les Arènes, 2000), 557.

29. See, for example, the web-site of the Association Survie, that is devoted to monitoring "la françafrique," notably the activities of the Groupe Bolloré: http://survie.org/francafrique/?lang=fr. See also the activities of the group "Stop françafrique": http://www.stop-francafrique.com/, François-Xavier Verschave, *Noir Chirac. Secret et impunité* (Paris: Editions des Arènes, 2002), and Gilles Labarthe with Xavier-François Verschave, *L'or africain. Pillages, trafics et commerce international* (Marseille: Editions Agone, 2007). For a satirical attempt at addressing the question of "la françafrique," see Grégory Jarry and Otto T., *Petite histoire des colonies françaises. Tome 4: La Françafrique* (Poitiers: Editions Flblb, 2011).

30. See Claude Wauthier, *Quatre Présidents et l'Afrique. De Gaulle, Pompidou, Giscard d'Estaing, Mitterrand* (Paris: Editions du Seuil, 1995). See also Odile Tobner, "La vision de l'Afrique chez les présidents de la Cinquième République française," in *L'Afrique répond à Sarkozy: Contre le discours de Dakar,* ed. Makhily Gassama (Paris: Editions Philippe Rey, 2008), 509–523.

31. François Mitterrand, "Discours de La Baule," http://www.rfi.fr/actufr/articles/037/article_20103.asp (June 20, 1990).

32. Charles de Gaulle, "Discours de Brazzaville," http://www.charles-de-gaulle.org/pages/temp/en/the-man/home/speeches/speech-made-by-general-de-gaulle-at-the-opening-of-the-brazzaville-conference-on-january-30th-1944..php?searchresult=1&sstring=Brazzaville (January 30, 1944).

33. Nicolas Sarkozy, "Discours de Cotonou," http://discours.vie-publique.fr/notices/063001811.html (19 May, 2006).

34. Nicolas Sarkozy, "Discours sur la nation," http://www.gauchemip.org/spip.php?article2702 (March 9, 2007). Nigerian writer, Uzodinma Iweala, has formulated a harsh critique of Western "concern" for Africa, deconstructing the dynamic between "nurture" and "exploitation." See his article "Cessez de vouloir 'sauver' l'Afrique!," *Le Monde,* (29–30 July, 2007): 13.

35. Achille Mbembe, "Nicolas Sarkozy's Africa," trans. Melissa Thackway, http://www

.africaresource.com/index.php?option=com_content&view=article&id=376:a-critique-of-nicolas-sarkozy&catid=36:essays-a-discussions&Itemid=346 (August 8, 2007).

36. Achille Mbembe, "L'intarissable puit aux fantasmes," in *L'Afrique de Sarkozy: Un déni de l'histoire,* ed. Jean-Pierre Chrétien. (Paris: Editions Karthala, 2008), 122.

37. Éric Fassin, *Démocratie précaire. Chroniques de la déraison d'État* (Paris: Editions La Découverte, 2012), 111.

38. Christopher L. Miller, *Blank Darkness: Africanist Discourse in French* (Chicago and London: University of Chicago Press, 1985), Valentin Y. Mudimbe, *The Idea of Africa* (Bloomington: Indiana University Press, 1994), and Achille Mbembe, *On the Postcolony* (Berkeley: University of California Press, 2001).

39. See, for example, Didier Gondola, *L'Africanisme: la crise d'une illusion* (Paris: Editions L'Harmattan, 2007) and Catherine Coquery-Vidrovitch, *Enjeux politiques de l'histoire coloniale* (Marseille: Editions Agone, 2009).

40. *Aimé Césaire: The Collected Poetry,* ed. Clayton Eshleman and Annette Smith (Berkeley and Los Angeles: University of California Press, 1983), 64–66.

41. See also "Henri Guaino: Le gourou du Président," *Le Nouvel Observateur,* 2245 (November 15–21, 2007).

42. Henri Guaino, "L'homme africain et l'histoire, par Henri Guaino," *Le Monde,* http://www.lemonde.fr/idees/article/2008/07/26/henri-guaino-toute-l-afrique-n-a-pas-rejete-le-discours-de-dakar_1077506_3232.html (June 28, 2008).

43. Georg W. F. Hegel, *Philosophy of History,* trans. John Sibree (New York: American Dome Library Company, 1902 [first pub. 1822]). See also Patricia Purtschert, "On the limit of spirit: Hegel's racism revisited," *Philosophy & Social Criticism* 36 (November 2010): 1039–1051.

44. See, for example, André Julien Mbem, *Nicolas Sarkozy à Dakar. Débats et enjeux autour d'un discours* (Paris: Editions L'Harmattan, 2007).

45. Jean-Pierre Chrétien, "Le discours de Dakar. Le poids idéologique d'un 'africanisme' traditionnel," *Esprit* 339 (November 2007): 173.

46. Adame Ba Konaré, ed. *Petit précis de remise à niveau sur l'histoire africaine à l'usage du président Sarkozy* (Paris: Editions La Découverte, 2008).

47. Laurence de Cock, Fanny Madeline, Nicolas Offenstadt, and Sophie Wahnich, eds. *Comment Nicolas Sarkozy écrit l'histoire de France* (Marseille: Editions Agone, 2008), 32.

48. Mwatha Musanji Ngalasso, "*Je suis venu vous dire . . .* Anatomie d'un discours néocolonial en langue de caoutchouc," in *L'Afrique répond à Sarkozy,* ed. Gassama, 326.

49. Laurence de Cock, "Afrique," in *Comment Nicolas Sarkozy écrit l'histoire de France,* eds. de Cock, Madeline, Offenstadt, and Wahnich, 30–31. See also Pierre Boilley, "Les visions françaises de l'Afrique et des Africains," in *Petit précis de remise à niveau sur l'histoire africaine,* ed. Konaré, 113–123. See also Cilas Kemedjio, "The Western Anticolonialist of the Postcolonial Age: The Reformist Syndrome and the Memory of Decolonization in (Post-) Imperial French Thought," in *Remembering Africa,* ed. Elisabeth Mudimbe (Portsmouth: Heinemann, 2002), 32–55, and Charles Thomas Kounkou, "L'ontologie négative de l'Afrique. Remarques sur le discours de Nicolas Sarkozy à Dakar," *Cahiers d'études africaines,* 50 (2–3–4), 198–200 (2010), 755–770.

50. Bogumil Jewsiewicki, "Le refus de savoir est un refus de reconnaissance," in *Petit précis de remise à niveau sur l'histoire africaine,* ed. Konaré, 141.

51. Touati, "French Foreign Policy in Africa," 16.

52. See "Africa-EU Strategic Partnership," www.africa-eu-partnership.org/partnerships/africa-eu-strategic-partnership (29–30 November, 2010). See also Ian Taylor, *International Relations of Sub-Saharan Africa* (New York: Continuum, 2010). On the various

trade agreements between the E.U. and Africa, see Demba Moussa Dembélé, "Méconnaissance ou provocation délibérée," in *L'Afrique répond à Sarkozy,* ed. Makhily Gassama, 87–122.

53. See, for example, the Africa-EU Migration, Mobility and Employment (MME) Partnership, launched in Lisbon: http://www.africa-eu-partnership.org/node/1744/ (in December 2007).

54. See, for example, the "Discours à Toulon." Guaino has also attempted to clarify these policy objectives, calling upon people to "Stop rehashing the past and let's focus, together, on the future. This future has a name: Eurafrica, and the Union for the Mediterranean is the first stage," "L'homme africain et l'histoire," *Le Monde.*

55. Discours au Cap, http://www.cellulefrancafrique.org/Le-discours-de-Sarkozy-au-Cap.html (February 28, 2008) and https://pastel.diplomatie.gouv.fr/editorial/actual/ae12/bulletin.asp?liste=20100601.html (May 31, 2010).

56. Isidore Ndaywel È Nziem, "L'Union pour la Méditerranée: un projet pour diviser l'Afrique et tourner le dos à la Francophonie," in *Petit précis de remise à niveau sur l'histoire africaine,* ed. Konaré, 273 and 275.

57. Nicolas Sarkozy, "Discours à Toulon," http://mouveuropeprovence.free.fr/serendipity/index.php?/archives/17http://www.google.com/search?client=safari&rls=en&q=http://mouveuropeprovence.free.fr/serendipity/index.php%3F/archives/17-Discours-Nicolas-Sarkozy-a-Toulon,-Mercredi-7-fevrier-2007.html.&ie=UTF-8&oe=UTF-8-Discours-Nicolas-Sarkozy-a-Toulon,-Mercredi-7-fevrier-2007.html (February 7, 2007).

58. Jean-Loup Amselle, *Rétrovolutions, Essais sur les primitivismes contemporains* (Paris: Editions Stock, 2010), 47.

59. Nicolas Sarkozy, "Discours de Tanger sur le projet de l'Union de la Méditerranée," http://www.ambafrance-uk.org/Discours-du-President-Sarkozy-sur.html (October 23, 2007). See also "Discours de Dakar et de Tanger: Les deux Afriques de Sarkozy," http://www.lefaso.net/spip.php?article24161&rubrique7 (October 25, 2007). A comparative analysis of speeches delivered in other regions of the world also provide interesting insights on the Sarkozy administration's ways of conceptualizing diverse cultural political, and social spaces. See, for example, Charles Forsdick, "Sarkozy in Port-au-Prince," *French Studies* Bulletin 32.118 (2011): 4–8.

60. Olivier Le Cour Grandmaison, "Apologie du colonialisme, usages de l'histoire et identité nationale: sur la rhétorique de Nicolas Sarkozy," in *Petit précis de remise à niveau sur l'histoire africaine,* ed. Konaré, 166 and 168.

61. Xavier Harel and Thomas Hofnung, *Le scandale des biens mal acquis. Enquête sur les milliards volés de la françafrique* (Paris: Editions La Découverte, 2011), 211 and 15.

62. Angelique Chrisafis, "France impounds African autocrats' 'ill-gotten gains,'" *The Guardian* (February 6, 2012).

63. See Bolya, *L'Afrique, le maillon faible* (Paris: Editions Le Serpent à Plumes, 2002), Aminata Traoré, *Le viol de l'imaginaire* (Arles: Actes Sud, Paris: Editions Fayard, 2002), *L'Afrique dans un monde sans frontières* (Arles: Actes Sud, 1999), *Lettre au Président des Français à propos de la Côte d'Ivoire et de l'Afrique en général* (Paris: Editions Fayard, 2005), and more recently, Moussa Konaté, *L'Afrique noire est-elle maudite* (Paris: Editions Fayard, 2010).

64. One should note that these conclusions have not been shared by all observers. For example, Stephen Smith, author of *Négrologie: pourquoi l'Afrique meurt* (Paris: Editions Calmann-Lévy, 2003), has shifted the blame away from France in his assessment of postcolonial Africa, whereas Gaston Kelman offered a form of apologia for Sarkozy's Da-

kar speech in his book *Les hirondelles du printemps africains* (Paris: Editions Jean-Claude Lattès, 2008). Smith's book was denounced as racist by Boubacar Boris Diop, Odile Tobner and François-Xavier Verschave, *Négrophobie* (Paris: Editions les Arènes, 2005). For an analysis of the blame attributed to corrupt governance, see Rosa Amelia Plumelle-Uribe, "Vous avez dit indépendance," in *50 ans après, quelle indépendance pour l'Afrique,* ed. Makhily Gassama (Paris: Editions Philippe Rey, 2010), 483–507. See also Pierre Péan, *L'argent noir. Corruption et sous-développement* (Paris: Editions Fayard, 1988), and more recently, William Easterly, "Foreign Aid for Scoundrels," *New York Review of Books* (November 25, 2010): 37–38. See also Achille Mbembe, "Enterrons la Françafrique," http://www.africapresse.com/politique/achille-mbembe-enterrons-la-francafrique/11/12/2010/ (December 11, 2010).

5. *From mirage to image*

1. Derek Walcott, "The Lost Empire," *White Egrets* (London: Faber and Faber, 2010), 37.

2. See Valentin Y. Mudimbe, ed. *The Surreptitious Speech:* Présence Africaine *and the Politics of Otherness, 1947–1987* (Chicago: Chicago University Press, 1992); Bennetta Jules-Rosette, *Black Paris: The African Writers' Landscape* (Urbana: University of Illinois Press, 1998); Dominic Thomas, *Black France: Colonialism, Immigration, and Transnationalism* (Bloomington: Indiana University Press, 2007); Manthia Diawara, *In Search of Africa* (Cambridge: Harvard University Press, 2000) and *We Won't Budge: An African exile in the World* (New York: Basic *Civitas* Books, 2003); Susan Peabody and Tyler Stovall, eds. *The Color of Liberty: Histories of Race in France* (Durham: Duke University Press, 2003); and Madeleine Dobie and Rebecca Saunders, eds. *France in Africa/Africa in France, Comparative Studies of South Asia, Africa, and the Middle East* 26.2 (2006).

3. I am borrowing the term "francocentrism" from Christopher L. Miller, *Nationalist and Nomads: Essays on Francophone African literature and Culture* (Chicago: University of Chicago Press, 1998), 62. See also Pascal Casanova, *The World Republic of Letters,* trans. M. B. DeBevoise (Cambridge: Harvard University Press, 2004) for a discussion of the role Paris has played as a cultural capital.

4. Manthia Diawara, *African Cinema: Politics and Culture* (Bloomington: Indiana University Press, 1992). Similar conclusions are to be found in Joseph Gugler, *African Film: Re-Imagining a Continent* (Bloomington: Indiana University Press, 2003); and Kenneth W. Harrow, *Postcolonial African Cinema: From Political Engagement to Postmodernism* (Bloomington: Indiana University Press, 2007).

5. See Peter J. Bloom, "The State of French Cultural Exceptionalism: The 2005 Uprisings and the Politics of Visibility," in *French and the African Diaspora. Identity and Uprising in Contemporary France,* eds. Charles Tschimanga, Didier Gondola, and Peter J. Bloom (Bloomington: Indiana University Press, 2009), 227–247.

6. See also the documentary on the memorialization of slavery in France by Arnaud Ngatcha and Jérôme Sesquin, *Noirs, l'identité au coeur de la question noire* (Jackie Bastide Production, France 5, France 3, Tabo Films, Arno Production, 2006).

7. See, for example, Édouard Mills-Affif, *Filmer les immigrés, les représentations audiovisuelles de l'immigration à la télévision française (1960–1986)* (Brusells, Belgium: De Boeck, 2004). Other regions of the former French Empire have also provided the subject of films in recent years, such as Régis Wargnier, *Indochine* (Bac Films, 1992), Jean-Jacques Annaud, *L'Amant* (TF1 Vidéo, 1992), and Pierre Schoendoerffer, *Diên Biên Phú* (AMLF, 1992).

8. On educational policy, see Alice Conklin, *A Mission to Civilize: The Republican Ideal of Empire in France and West Africa, 1895–1930* (Stanford: Stanford University Press, 1997); Hans-Jürgen Lüsebrink, "Acculturation coloniale et pédagogie interculturelle—l'œuvre de Georges Hardy," *Sénégal-Forum: Littérature et Histoire,* ed. Papa Samba Diop (Frankfurt, Germany: IKO Verlag, 1995), 113–122; and Georges Hardy, *Une conquête morale, L'enseignement en A.O.F.* (Paris: Armand Colin, 1917).

9. Paulin S. Vieyra, *Le cinéma africain* (Paris: Editions Présence Africaine, 1969), 40.

10. Peter Bloom, *French Colonial Documentary: Mythologies of Humanitarianism* (Minneapolis: University of Minnesota Press, 2008), 128.

11. David Murphy and Patrick Williams, *Postcolonial African Cinema: Ten Directors* (Manchester: Manchester University Press, 2007), 11.

12. Cameroonian filmmaker Jean-Marie Teno addressed these questions, audience expectations, and the challenges of a globalized cinema, notably during a roundtable discussion, "The Artist as Critic, The Academic as Intellectual," Wellesley College, April 19, 2008. See also Nwachukwu Frank Ukadike, *Black African Cinema* (Berkeley: University of California Press, 1994).

13. See Gary Wilder, *The French Imperial Nation State: Negritude and Colonial Humanism between the Two World Wars* (Chicago: University of Chicago Press, 2005); Jennifer Anne Boittin, *Colonial Metropolis: The Urban Grounds of Anti-Imperialism and Feminism in Interwar Paris* (Lincoln: University of Nebraska Press, 2010); and Brent Hayes Edwards, *The Practice of Diaspora: Literature, Translation, and the Rise of Black Internationalism* (Cambridge: Harvard University Press, 2003).

14. Clément Tapsoda, "Portrait de Paulin S. Vieyra (1925–1987): *l'homme à la casquette,*" in *Afrique 50: Singularités d'un cinéma pluriel,* ed. Catherine Ruelle (Paris: Editions L'Harmattan, 2005), 294.

15. Paulin S. Vieyra, 1956–1957. "Quand le cinéma français parle au nom de l'Afrique noire," *Présence Africaine,* 11 (1956–1957): 142–145: "Propos sur le cinéma africain," *Présence Africaine* 22 (1958): 106–117; and "Responsabilités du cinéma dans la formation d'une conscience nationale," *Présence africaine* 27–28 (1959): 303–313.

16. "Seminar on 'The Role of the African Film-Maker in Rousing an Awareness of Black Civilization', Ouagadougou, April 8–13, 1974," in *Cinemas of the Black Diaspora: Diversity, Dependence, and Oppositionality,* ed. Michael T. Martin (Detroit: Wayne State University Press, 1995), 474.

17. Olivier Barlet, *African Cinemas: Decolonizing the Gaze,* trans. Chris Turner (London: Zed Books, 2000), 268–269. See also Femi Okiremuete Shaka, "Film Production Structures and Sponsorship Policies in Francophone Africa," in *Modernity and the African Cinema: A Study in Colonialist Discourse, Postcoloniality, and Modern African Identities* (Trenton: Africa World Press, 2004), 301–328.

18. Madeleine Cottenet-Hage, "*Decolonizing Images:* Soleil O *and the Cinema of Med Hondo,*" in *Cinema, Colonialism, Postcolonialism: Perspectives from the French and Francophone Worlds,* ed. Dina Sherzer (Austin: University of Texas Press, 1996), 175.

19. Carrie Tarr, "French Cinema and Post-Colonial Minorities," in *Post-Colonial Cultures in France,* eds. Alec G. Hargreaves and Mark McKinney (London: Routledge, 1997), 60.

20. Melissa Thackway, *Africa Shoots Back: Alternative Perspectives in Sub-Saharan Francophone: Alternative Perspectives* (Bloomington: Indiana University Press, 2003), 1.

21. Melissa Thackway, "Images d'immigrés," *Cinémas africains, une oasis dans le désert,* ed. Samuel Lelièvre, *CinémAction* 106 (2003): 50.

22. See also for example Mark A. Reid, "Producing African Cinema in Paris," in *Cinemas of the Black Diaspora,* ed. Martin, 346–353.

23. Other films could also have been considered, such as François Reichenbach, *Un Coeur gros comme ça* (Production Pierre Braunberger, 1962), Maurice Delbez, *Un Gosse de la butte* (Les Films de mai, 1964), or Jacques Krier, *Ouvriers noirs de Paris* (Institut National de l'Audiovisuel, INA, 1964).

24. For a comprehensive account of the conditions of African students in France during this time period, see Fabienne Guimont, *Les étudiants africains en France: 1950–1965* (Paris: Editions L'Harmattan, 1997).

25. See Pierre Nora, *Realms of Memory: Rethinking the French Past,* trans. Arthur Goldhammer (New York: Columbia University Press, 1996).

26. Melissa Thackway, "Filming the Immigrant Experience: Francophone African cinema in Europe," in *Africa Shoots Back,* 121.

27. Lieve Spaas, *The Francophone Film: A Struggle for Identity* (Manchester: Manchester University Press, 2001), 173.

28. Camara Laye, *L'enfant noir* (Paris: Editions Plon, 1953); Cheikh Hamidou Kane, *L'aventure ambiguë* (Paris: Editions Julliard, 1961).

29. The importance of African Americans in Paris at this historical juncture has been explored by Tyler Stovall, *Paris Noir: African Americans in the City of Lights* (New York: Houghton Mifflin Company, 1996); Michel Fabre, *From Harlem to Paris: Black American Writers in France, 1840–1980* (Urbana: University of Illinois Press, 1991); and Alain Mabanckou, *Lettre à Jimmy* (Paris: Editions Fayard, 2007).

30. Françoise Pfaff, "Africa from Within: The Films of Gaston Kaboré and Idrissa Ouedraogo as Anthropological Sources," *African Experiences of Cinema,* eds. Imruh Bakari and Mbye B. Cham (London: British Film Institute, 1996), 225.

31. Madeleine Cottenet-Hage, "Images of France in Francophone African Films (1978–1998)," *Focus on African Films,* ed. Françoise Pfaff (Bloomington: Indiana University Press, 1998), 112.

32. Pierre Bourdieu, *Masculine Domination* (Stanford: Stanford University Press, 2001), 101.

33. Didier Gondola, "Dream and Drama: The Search for Elegance among Congolese Youth," *African Studies Review* 42.1 (1999): 31.

34. Alec G. Hargreaves, *Multi-Ethnic France: Immigration, Politics, Culture and Society* (London: Routledge, 2007), 24–25.

35. Citation from Inoussa Ousseini's film *Paris c'est joli* (1974, 23 minutes).

36. Mireille Rosello, *Postcolonial Hospitality: The Immigrant as Guest* (Stanford: Stanford University Press, 2001), 38–39.

37. Alain Mabanckou, *Bleu, Blanc, Rouge* (Paris: Présence Africaine, 1998), 132.

38. Lydie Moudileno, "La fiction de la migration: manipulation des corps et des récits dans *Bleu blanc rouge* d'Alain Mabanckou," *Présence Africaine* 163–164 (2001): 187.

39. See, for example, Manthia Diawara, "Toward a Regional Imaginary in Africa," *The Cultures of Globalization,* eds. Fredric Jameson and Masao Miyoshi (Durham: Duke University Press, 1998), 103–124.

40. Michael T. Martin, "Framing the 'Black' in Black Diasporic Cinemas," in *Cinemas of the Black* Diaspora, ed. Martin, 9.

41. Elisabeth Lequeret, "Un aller simple pour Paris," in *Afrique 50: Singularités d'un cinéma pluriel,* ed. Catherine Ruelle (Paris: Editions L'Harmattan, 2005), 215.

42. Dina Sherzer, "Introduction," in *Cinema, Colonialism,* Postcolonialism, ed. Sherzer, 10.

43. Paul Gilroy, *There Ain't No Black in the Union Jack: The Cultural Politics of Race and Nation* (Chicago: University of Chicago Press, 1987, 57); and *Black Britain: A Photographic History* (London: Saqi Books/Getty Images, 2007), 23.

44. See also Adrian Fielder, "Poaching on Public Space: Urban Autonomous Zones in French *Banlieue* Films," in *Cinema and the City: Film and Urban Societies in a Global Context,* eds. Mark Shiel and Tony Fitzmaurice (Oxford: Blackwell, 2001), 270–281.

45. See, for example, Guy Hennebelle and Roland Schneider, eds. *Cinémas métis: de Hollywood aux films beurs, CinémAction* 56 (July 1990).

46. Françoise Pfaff, "The films of Med Hondo An African filmmaker in Paris," *Jump Cut: A Review of Contemporary Media* 31 (1986): 44.

47. Quoted in Ibrahima Signaté, *Med Hondo: Un cinéaste rebelle* (Paris: Editions Présence Africaine, 1994), 75.

48. Carrie Tarr, "French Cinema and Post-Colonial Minorities," in *Post-Colonial Cultures in France,* eds. Hargreaves and McKinney, 61.

49. Azouz Begag and Ahmed Beneddif, *Ahmed de Bourgogne* (Paris: Editions du Seuil, 2001); Madjiguène Cissé, *Parole de sans-papiers* (Paris: Editions La Dispute/Sinédit, 1999); Ababacar Diop, *Dans la peau d'un sans-papiers* (Paris: Editions du Seuil, 1997). See also Mireille Rosello, "Representing Illegal Immigrants in France: From *clandestins* to *l'affaire des sans-papiers de Saint-Bernard,*" *Journal of European Studies* 38 (1998): 137–151.

50. Olivier Barlet, "Les nouveaux films d'Afrique sont-ils africains?" in *Cinémas africains, une oasis dans le désert,* ed. Samuel Lelièvre, *CinémAction* 106 (2003): 43–49.

51. See, for example, the documentary by Rafaelle Ventura and Samir Abdallah, *La Ballade des sans-papiers* (Agence IM'media/Les Yeux ouverts, 1996).

52. Mathilde Blottière, "Des visas pour l'image," *Télérama horizons, Etrangers. Une obsession européenne* 4 (April 2011): 66. Monique Crouillère has provided a comprehensive typology of African film production in her article "Cinéma africain et immigration," in *Images et mirages des migrations dans les littératures et les cinémas d'Afrique francophone,* eds. Françoise Naudillon and Jean Ouédraogo (Montréal, Québéc: Mémoire d'encrier, 2011), 11–30.

53. Gilles de Maistre, *La Citadelle Europe* (Lost in Transit, Tetra Media, 2003), Eliane De Latour, *Les Oiseaux du ciel* (Birds of Heaven, Les Films de Cinéma, Autonomous Limited, 2006), Sylvestre Amoussou, *Africa paradis* (Metis/Koffi Productions, 2007), and Olivier Masset-Depasse, *Illégal* (O'brother Distribution, 2010).

54. Etienne Balibar, *We, the People of Europe: Reflections on Transnational Citizenship* (Princeton: Princeton University Press, 2004), 111.

55. See also Laurent Dubois, "Republic at Sea: On the margins of the New Europe," *Transition* 79 (1999): 64–79.

56. Ousmane Sembene, "Black Girl," trans. Ellen Conroy Kennedy, *Under African Skies: Modern African Stories,* ed. Charles R. Larson (New York: The Noonday Press, 1997), 47.

57. Med Hondo, "The Cinema of Exile," in *Cinemas of the Black Diaspora,* ed. Martin (Detroit: Wayne State University Press, 1995), 343. For Françoise Pfaff, *Les bicots-nègres vos voisins* is an "intricate political film, it demonstrates how French neocolonialism exploits migrant labor and exerts a cultural imperialism over their minds," "The films of Med Hondo," 45.

58. Quoted in Signaté, *Med Hondo,* 75. See also Med Hondo, "What is Cinema for Us," in *African Experiences of Cinema,* eds. Bakari and Cham, 39–41.

59. Didier Daeninckx, *Lumière noire* (Paris: Editions Gallimard, 1987).

60. This subject has also featured in sub-Saharan African novels, such as Abdourahman A. Waberi's *Transit* (Paris: Editions Gallimard, 2003).

61. See also Guido Convents, *Images et Démocratie: Les Congolais face au cinéma et à l'audiovisuel: Une histoire politico-culturelle du Congo des Belges jusqu'à la République*

Démocratique du Congo [1896–2006] (Holsbeek, Belgium: Afrika Film Festival, 2006), 359–364.

62. The Senegalese novelist Fatou Diome adopts a similar position in her novel *Le ventre de l'Atlantique* (Paris: Editions Anne Carrière, 2003).

63. Sheila Petty, "Postcolonial geographies: Landscape and Alienation in *Clando*," in *Cinema and Social Discourse in Cameroon*, ed. Alexie Tcheuyap, *Bayreuth African Studies* 69 (2005): 170.

64. Moussa Sene Absa, *Ainsi meurent les anges* (California Newsreel, 2001) and Cheik Doukouré, *Paris selon Moussa* (Bako Productions, 2002).

65. Alain Gomis, *L'Afrance* (Mille et une Productions, 2001). Sathya Rao, "Mythologies et mythoscopies de l'exil dans les cinémas africain francophone et de la postcolonie," in *Images et mirages des migrations dans les littératures et les cinémas d'Afrique francophone*, eds. Naudillon and Ouédraogo, 111 and 114.

66. S. Pierre Yaméogo, *Moi et mon blanc* (Dunia Productions/Les films de l'espoir, 2003).

67. Éric Deroo and Pascal Blanchard, *Paris couleurs* (Image et Compagnie, France 3, France 5, 2005).

68. Medhi Kabara and Régis Chaoupa, *Diaspora. La communauté noire en France* (Diaspora Communication, 2006), Emmanuelle Bisou and Fabienne Kanor, *Jambé Dlo, une histoire antillaise* (Mat Films, 2008), Amélie Brumet and Philippe Goma, *Des Noirs et des hommes* (Les Films Grains de Sable, 2009), and Juan Gélas and Pascal Blanchard, *Noirs de France de 1889 à nos jours: une histoire de France* (Compagnie Phares et Balises, INA, l'Acsé/France Television, TV5, and LCP, 2011).

6. *The "Marie NDiaye Affair," or the Coming of a Postcolonial évoluée*

1. Chinua Achebe, *The Education of a British Protected Child* (New York: Alfred A. Knopf, 2009), 117–118.

2. Marie NDiaye, *Trois femmes puissantes* (Paris: Editions Gallimard, 2009). See "Toward a World Literature in French," trans. Daniel Simon, *World Literature Today* 83.2 (March–April 2009): 54–56.

3. www.indigenes-republique.fr.

4. www.debatidentitenationale.fr.

5. Michel Le Bris and Jean Rouaud, eds. *Pour une littérature-monde* (Paris: Editions Gallimard, 2007). Three writers contributed to the Gallimard volume who had not signed the manifesto: Eva Almassy (Hungarian-born), Chahdortt Djavann (born in Iran), and Fabienne Kanor (Martinican).

6. René Maran, *Batouala: véritable roman nègre* (Paris: Editions Albin Michel, 1921).

7. See www.prix-litteraires.net/goncourt_liste.php and www.prix-litteraires.net/renaudot_liste.php. The Editions Gallimard launched a new series in 2000 called *Continents Noirs* that has published a broad range of "Black" authors. The problem with this particular series though is that several authors—Patrick Chamoiseau, Ananda Devi, etc.—have subsequently been published in the prestigious "série blanche" (the White Series), thus setting up an in-house distinction that is not to be found in other noted publishing houses, such as Actes Sud, Grasset, or the Seuil. Furthermore, the recent signing away from the Seuil to Gallimard in January 2010 of Alain Mabanckou has rendered such distinctions between authors all the more apparent.

8. Lydie Moudileno, "Fame, Celebrity, and the Conditions of Visibility of the Post-

colonial Writer," in *Francophone Sub-Saharan African Literature in Global Contexts,* eds. Alain Mabanckou and Dominic Thomas, *Yale French Studies* 120 (2011): 70.

9. Nicki Hitchcott, *Calixthe Beyala: Performances of Migration* (Liverpool: Liverpool University Press, 2006), 30.

10. Beverley Ormerod and Jean-Marie Volet, *Romancières africaines d'expression française: le sud du Sahara* (Paris: Editions L'Harmattan, 2004).

11. Nicki Hitchcott, *Women Writers in Francophone Africa* (Oxford: Berg, 2000), 24.

12. Dominic Thomas, "Daniel Biyaoula: Exile, Immigration, and Transnational Cultural productions," in *Immigrant Narratives in Contemporary France,* eds. Susan Ireland and Patrice J. Proulx (Westport: Greenwood Press, 2001), 167.

13. Fatou Diome, *La préférence nationale* (Paris: Editions Présence Africaine, 2001), *Le ventre de l'Atlantique* (Paris: Editions Anne Carrière, 2003), *Kétala* (Paris: Editions Flammarion, 2006), *Inasouvies* (Editions Flammarion, 2008), and *Celles qui attendent* (Paris: Editions Flammarion, 2010).

14. Nicki Hitchcott, "Calixthe Beyala: Prizes, Plagiarism, and 'Authenticity'," in *Textual Ownership in Francophone African Literature,* eds. Alec G. Hargreaves, Nicki Hitchcott, and Dominic Thomas, *Research in African Literatures* 37.1 (Spring 2006): 105. One should note that Senegalese novelist Aminata Sow Fall's *L'appel des arènes* (Dakar: Les Nouvelles Editions Africaines, 1982) was short-listed for the Prix Goncourt in 1982.

15. The allusion is to Pascale Casanova's *The World Republic of Letters,* trans. M. B. DeBevoise (Cambridge: Harvard University Press, 2004).

16. Nelly Kaprièlian, Interview with Marie Ndiaye, "Écris et tais-toi," *les inrockuptibles* 729 (18–24 November, 2009): 10. It should be noted that the author's preferred spelling of her name, NDiaye, is sometimes incorrectly rendered as Ndiaye, as in the title and text of the interview with Kaprièlian.

17. Nelly Kaprièlian, Dossier littéraire, "Marie Ndiaye: aux prises avec le monde," *Les inrockuptibles* 716 (August 18–24, 2009): 29.

18. Alain Mabanckou, "La francophonie," *Balma info.* 41 (April 2009): 13.

19. See Charles Tshimanga, Didier Gondola, and Peter J. Bloom, eds. *Frenchness and the African Diaspora: Identity and Uprising in Contemporary France* (Bloomington: Indiana University Press, 2009).

20. Lucie Clair, Interview, "La discrète empathie," *Le Matricule des anges: Le mensuel de la littérature contemporaine* 107 (October 2009): 26–29.

21. Lucie Clair, "Tenir tête," *Le Matricule des anges: Le mensuel de la littérature contemporaine* 107 (October 2009): 25.

22. Gérard Noiriel, *A quoi sert "l'identité nationale"* (Marseille: Editions Agone, 2007), 95–96.

23. Alec G. Hargreaves, "Testimony, Co-Authorship, and Dispossession among Women of Maghrebi Origin in France," in *Textual Ownership in Francophone African Literature,* eds. Hargreaves, Hitchcott, and Thomas, 45.

24. Dominic Thomas, *Black France: Colonialism, Immigration, and Transnationalism* (Bloomington: Indiana University Press, 2007), 116.

25. Susan Sontag, *Regarding the Pain of Others* (New York: Penguin, 2003).

26. Abdourahman A. Waberi, *Aux États-Unis d'Afrique* (Paris: Editions Jean-Claude Lattès, 2006), Laurent Gaudé, *Eldorado* (Arles: Actes Sud, 2006), J.R. Essomba, *Le paradis du Nord* (Paris: Editions Présence Africaine, 1996), Antoine Matha, *Épitaphe* (Paris: Editions Gallimard, 2009), Fatou Diome, *Le ventre de l'Atlantique* (Paris: Editions Anne Carrière, 2003), Alain Mabanckou, *Bleu-Blanc-Rouge* (Paris: Editions Présence Africaine,

1998), and Mahi Binebine, *Cannibales: Traversée dans l'enfer de Gibraltar* (Paris: Editions Fayard, 1999).

27. Éric Raoult, www.youtube.com/watch?v=lN_Yh4AHB5I (November 10, 2009), emphasis added.

28. Yun Sun Limet, "Analyse d'un sous-texte," http://remue.net/spip.php?article3433 (November 11, 2009).

29. Gaston Kelman, *Je suis noir et je n'aime pas le manioc* (Paris: Max Milo Editions, 2003).

30. Grégoire Leménager, http://bibliobs.nouvelobs.com/20091111/15823/marie-ndiaye-en-appelle-a-mitterrand-et-maintient-ses-propos-apres-le-texte-grotesque (November 11, 2009).

31. Frédéric Mitterrand, http://www.lemonde.fr/politique/article/2009/11/12/frederic-mitterrand-ne-souhaite-pas-arbitrer-la-polemique-ndiaye-raoult_1266002_823448.html (November 12, 2009).

32. Cited in Olivier Le Cour Grandmaison, ed. *Douce France: Rafles, Rétentions, Expulsions* (Paris: Editions du Seuil/RESF, 2009), 292. See also "Lettre de Mission," March 31, 2009, PDF file available at: http://www.immigration.gouv.fr/spip.php?page=dossiers_them_org&numrubrique=341, 6.

33. National Assembly. file:///Users/cdhuser/Desktop/French%20history/Assemblee.Debate.webarchive. For further indication as to Éric Besson's particular conception of the national space in this debate, see Éric Besson, *Pour la nation* (Paris: Editions Grasset & Fasquelle: 2009).

34. Éric Besson, "Faire connaître et partager l'identité nationale," http://www.debatidentitenationale.fr/propositions-d-eric-besson/faire-connaitre-et-partager-l.html (October 31, 2009).

35. Besson, "Valoriser l'identité nationale," http://www.debatidentitenationale.fr/propositions-d-eric-besson/valoriser-l-identite-nationale.html (October 31, 2009).

36. See, for example, http://lci.tf1.fr/politique/2009–11/fillon-se-paye-rama-yade-et-guaino-5518589.html.

37. Jacqueline Rémy, ed. *Comment je suis devenu français* (Paris: Editions du Seuil, 2007).

38. "Fillon se paye Rama Yade et Guaino," http://www.lepost.fr/article/2009/11/25/1808877_rama-yade-et-ses-racines-senegalaises-2-deputes-ump-attaquent.html (November 3, 2009).

39. François Soudan, "Rama Yade: 'Sarkozy, les Africains et moi'," *Jeune Afrique,* http://www.jeuneafrique.com/Article/ARTJAJA2511p022–029-bis.xm10/france-interview-rama-yade-secretaire-d-etatrama-yade-sarkozy-les-africains-et-moi.html (February 25, 2009).

40. Pap Ndiaye, *La condition noire: Essai sur une minorité ethnique française* (Paris: Editions Calmann-Lévy, 2008).

41. Ndiaye, ""Les sœurs," *La condition noire,* 9–15.

42. Catherine Coquery-Vidrovitch, *Enjeux politiques de l'histoire coloniale* (Marseille: Agone, 2009), 163.

43. A publication record available on his web-site: http://www.ehess.fr/cena/membres/ndiaye_pub.hhtml.

44. Nicolas Bancel, Pascal Blanchard, and Françoise Vergès, *La République coloniale: Essai sur une utopie* (Paris: Editions Albin Michel, 2003),122–123.

45. Faïza Guène: "Voice of the People," interview with Sarah Adams, *The Guardian,* (May 10, 2006), http://www.guardian.co.uk/society/2006/may/10/books.socialexclusion.

46. See Achille Mbembe, "The Republic and Its Beast: On the Riots in the French *Banlieues*," in *Frenchness and the African Diaspora,* eds. Tshimanga, Gondola, and Bloom, 47–69.

47. Lucie Clair, "Écrire, quoi d'autre?" *Le Matricule des anges: Le mensuel de la littérature contemporaine* 107 (October 2009): 22.

48. "Nous exigeons la suppression du ministère de l'Identité nationale et de l'Immigration," http://www.liberation.fr/societe/0101606559-nous-exigeons-la-suppression-du-ministere-de-l-identite-nationale-et-de-l-immigration (December 4, 2009).

7. The Euro-Mediterranean

1. Chinua Achebe, *The Education of a British Protected Child* (New York: Alfred A. Knopf, 2009), 157.

2. Dany Laferrière, *L'Enigme du retour* (Paris: Editions Grasset & Fasquelle, 2009), 43.

3. "Communication on Migration," http://www.statewatch.org/news/2011/may/eu-com-migration-com-248–11.pdf, (May 4, 2011), 3.

4. Of course, the question of migration on the African continent is of crucial importance, particularly since it exceeds, quantitatively, African emigration towards the E.U. See Christophe Daum and Isaïe Dougnon, eds. *L'Afrique en mouvement,* special dossier, *Hommes et Migrations* 1279 (May-June 2009): 4–164, and Patrick Gonin, ed. *Les migrations subsahariennes,* Special dossier, *Hommes et Migrations* 1286–1287 (July–October 2010); 4–278.

5. See, for example, Didier Fassin, "Frontières extérieures, frontières intérieures," in *Les nouvelles frontières de la société française,* ed. Didier Fassin (Paris: Editions la Découverte, 2010), 5–24.

6. Paul Gilroy, "Foreword: Migrancy, Culture, and a New Map of Europe," in *Blackening Europe: The African American Presence,* ed. Heike Raphael-Hernandez (London: Routledge, 2004), xi. As William Brown has shown, "exploitation is necessary for Europe's conception of itself as a powerful center, but if formerly this exploitation took place in the invisible colonies, now, in the imperial era [. . .], such exploitation also takes place *elsewhere within* Europe," "Negotiating the Invisible," in *Moving People, Moving Images: Cinema and Trafficking in the New Europe,* eds. William Brown, Dina Iordanova and Leshu Torchin (St. Andrews: St Andrews Film Studies Publishing, 2010), 28–29.

7. Pap Ndiaye, *La condition noire. Essai sur une minorité française* (Paris: Editions Calmann-Lévy, 2008), 178–179.

8. "Migration policy from Control to Governance," http://www.opendemocracy.net/people-migrationeurope/militarising_borders_3735.jsp (July 12, 2006). Consulted on May 13, 2010.

9. Achille Mbembe, "At the Edge of the World: Boundaries, Territoriality, and Sovereignty in Africa," trans. Steven Rendall, in *Globalization,* ed. Arjun Appadurai (Durham: Duke University Press, 2001), 40. It is also worth noting the historical geopolitical importance of the Mediterranean; certainly it provided the framework for Fernand Braudel's thinking and writing, a dimension Claude Liauzu explored in his *Colonisation, migrations, racismes. Histoires d'une passeurs de civilisations* (Paris: Editions Syllepse, 2009). Sarkozy reasserted his commitment to the Musée des civilisations de l'Europe et de la Méditerranée, http://www.musee-europemediterranee.org/fr/Musee-Le-projet, in his speech, "Vœux aux acteurs de la Culture," delivered in Nîmes January 13, 2009, http://www.culture.gouv.fr/culture/actualites/conferen/albanel/prculture09.pdf, 2.

10. Etienne Balibar, *We, The People of Europe? Reflections on Transnational Citizenship,* trans. James Swenson (Princeton: Princeton University Press, 2004).

11. See Vincent Geisser, "Adieu Bonaparte, bonjour Nicolas!," http://oumma.com/Adieu-Bonaparte-bonjour-Nicolas (November-December 2008).

12. Virginie Lydie, *Traversée interdite! Les harragas face à l'Europe forteresse* (Le Pré Saint-Gervais: Editions le passager clandestin, 2011), 14. See also Constantin Stephanou, "'Union européenne' et 'Union pour la Méditerranée': Des projets politiques concurrents ou complémentaire?" in *Euro-Méditerranée: Histoire d'un futur,* ed. Ali Sedjari (Paris: Editions L'Harmattan, 2010), 131–136, Abdelkhaleq Berramdane, "L'émergence d'une politique européenne commune d'immigration et son externalisation progressive," in *La politique européenne d'immigration,* eds. Abdelkhaleq Berramdane and Jean Rossetto (Paris: Editions Karthala, 2009), 39–59, and Gérard-François Dumont, "La politique d'immigration de l'Union européenne: une stratégie volontaire ou contrainte?" in *La politique européenne d'immigration,* eds. Berramdane and Rossetto, 11–31.

13. The European Commission (Home Affairs), has also published two documents that address migration, mobility and security: "A partnership for democracy and shared prosperity for democracy and shared prosperity with the Southern Mediterranean," http://eeas.europa.eu/euromed/docs/com2011_200_en.pdf (March 8, 2011), 1–17, and "A dialogue for migration, mobility and security with the southern Mediterranean countries," http://ec.europa.eu/home-affairs/news/intro/docs/110524/292/1_EN_ACT_part1_v12.pdf (May 24, 2011), 1–13.

14. "Third Annual Report on Migration and Integration," http://europa.eu/rapid/pressReleasesAction.do?reference=MEMO/07/351&format=HTML&aged=1&language=EN&guiLanguage=en (September 11, 2007). See also "Towards a common European Union migration policy," http://ec.europa.eu/home-affairs/policies/immigration/immigration_intro_en.htm, and Emmanuel Bribosia and Andrea Rea, *Les Nouvelles Migrations, un enjeu européen* (Brussels, Belgium: Editions Complexe, 2001).

15. See for example Rachid Chaabita, ed. *Migration clandestine africaine vers l'Europe. Un espoir pour les uns, un problème pour les autres* (Paris: Editions L'Harmattan, 2010) and Stéphane de Tapia, *The Euro-Mediterranean migration system* (Strasbourg: Editions du Conseil de l'Europe, 2008).

16. "A Common immigration policy for Europe: principles, actions and tools," http://europa.eu/rapid/pressReleasesAction.do?reference=MEMO/08/402&format=HTML&aged=0&language=EN&guiLanguage=en (June 17, 2008).

17. "European Pact on Migration and Asylum," Document document 13440/08, http://www.immigration.gouv.fr/IMG/pdf/Plaquette_EN.pdf (October 15–16, 2008), 4.

18. "Final statement—Barcelona Process: Union for the Mediterranean," http://www.aer.eu/fileadmin/user_upload/MainIssues/International_Solidarity/2009/Final_Statement_Mediterranean_Union_EN.pdf (3–4 November, 2008), 1.

19. "Irregular immigration," http://ec.europa.eu/home-affairs/policies/immigration/immigration_illegal_en.htm. See also Isabel Schäfer, "Politiques migratoires et identitaires de l'Union européenne dans l'espace euro-méditerranéen," Hybrid European-Muslim Identity-Models (HEYMAT), *Heymat Working Paper Nr. 01/2010,* http://www.heymat.hu-berlin.de/heymat-workingpaper (December 2010).

20. Breyten Breytenbach, "On Progress," in *Notes from the Middle of the World* (Chicago: Haymarket Books, 2009), 91.

21. The focus here is primarily provided by the francophone context but a broad range of works in other languages has also explored analogous questions. See for example Eduardo Iglesias, *Tarifa: L'auberge de l'Allemand* [Tarifa, la venta del alemán, 2004],

trans. William Soler (Lyon: Rouge Inside, 2011) and Erri de Luca, *Solo andata* (Milan, Italy: Feltrinelli, 2005).

22. Hakim Abderrezak, "'Burning the Sea': Clandestine Migration Across the Strait of Gibraltar in Francophone Moroccan 'Illiterature,'" *Contemporary French & Francophone Studies: Sites* 13.4 (September 2009): 461.

23. Mireille Rosello, *Postcolonial Hospitality: The Immigrant as Guest* (Stanford: Stanford University Press, 2001), 137. Recent studies point to the growing scholarly attention for films focusing on migration. See Najib Redouane, *Clandestins dans le texte maghrébin de langue française* (Paris: Editions L'Harmattan, 2008), Yosefa Loshitzky, *Screening Strangers: Migration and Diaspora in Contemporary European Cinema* (Bloomington: Indiana University Press, 2010), and William Brown, Dina Iordanova and Leshu Torchin, eds., *Moving People, Moving Images: Cinema and Trafficking in the New Europe* (St. Andrews: St Andrews Film Studies Publishing, 2010).

24. The acclaimed German video artist Marcel Odenbach produced a short-film exploring the question of oceanic migration: "Im Schiffbruch nicht schwimmen können" (The shipwrech cannot swim, 2011, 8.10 minutes), Copenhagen Video Kunst Festival, 9–26 February, 2012.

25. Ursula Biemann, "Writing Video—Writing the World: Videogeographies as Cognitive Medium," http://www.escholarship.org/uc/item/5542borw, *Transit* 4.1 (2008): 3. Consulted May 3, 2010.

26. Terms adopted, respectively, by Jacques Chevrier, Bennetta Jules-Rosette and Léonora Miano.

27. Saul Taylor, "Barriers and Barrios: Melilla," *Monocle* 28.3 (2009): 55–59. See also Laurent Dubois, "Republic at Sea: On the margins of the new Europe," *Transition* 79 (1999): 64–79.

28. Omar Ba, *Soif d'Europe: Témoignage d'un clandestin* (Paris: Editions du Cygne, 2008), Serge Daniel, *Les routes clandestines: L'Afrique des immigrés et des passeurs* (Paris: Editions Hachette Littératures, 2008), Fabrizio Gatti, *Bilal sur la route des clandestins,* trans. Jean-Luc Defromont (Paris: Editions Liana Levi, 2008), and Emmanuel Bribosia and Andrea Rea, *Les nouvelles migrations, un enjeu européen* (Brussels, Belgium: Editions Complexe, 2001). Costa-Gavras, *L'Eden à l'ouest* (K. G. Productions, Pathé, France 3, 2009). See also the following films: Gilles de Maistre, *La Citadelle Europe* (Lost in Transit, Tetra Media, 2003), Eliane De Latour, *Les Oiseaux du ciel* (Birds of Heaven, Les Films de Cinéma, Autonomous Limited, 2006), Olivier Masset-Depasse, *Illégal* (Belgium: O'Brother Distribution, 2010), and Nicolas Provost, *L'Envahisseur* (Belgium: O'Brother Distribution, 2011). The term "harraga" (burning), refers to "the common practice of burning identification documents before undertaking the sea crossing in order to avoid repatriation," Abderrezak, "'Burning the Sea,'" 463.

29. Christopher L. Miller, *Nationalist and Nomads: Essays on Francophone African literature and Culture* (Chicago: University of Chicago Press, 1998), 62.

30. Bernard Dadié, *Un nègre à Paris* (Paris: Editions Présence Africaine, 1959); *An African in Paris,* trans. Karen Hatch (Urbana: University of Illinois Press, 1994), 3.

31. Alain Mabanckou and Christophe Merlin, *L'Europe depuis l'Afrique* (Paris: Editions Naïve, 2009), 7.

32. Salim Jay, *Tu ne traverseras pas le détroit* (Paris: Editions Fayard, 2001), 10.

33. Juan Goytisolo, "Défense de l'hybridité ou La pureté, mère de tous les vices," trans. Jean-Marie Laclavetine, in *Je est un autre. Pour une identité-monde,* eds. Michel Le Bris and Jean Rouaud (Paris: Editions Gallimard, 2010), 215.

34. Jean-Philippe Stassen, "Les visiteurs de Gibraltar," XXI (January-March 2008): 157.

35. Tahar Ben Jelloun, *Partir* (Paris: Editions Gallimard, 2006), 179.

36. Laila Lalami, *Hope and Other Dangerous Pursuits* (Chapel Hill: Algonquin Books, 2005), 1.

37. Laurent Gaudé, *Eldorado* (Arles: Actes Sud, 2006); *Eldorado,* trans. Adriana Hunter (San Francisco: MacAdam/Cage, 2008), 180.

38. J. R. Essomba, *Le Paradis du Nord* (Paris: Editions Présence Africaine, 1996), 13.

39. Abdourahman Waberi, *Transit* (Paris: Editions Gallimard, 2003), 55 and 137–138.

40. Abasse Ndione, *Mbëkë mi: A l'assaut des vagues de l'Atlantique* (Paris: Editions Gallimard, 2008), 11.

41. See also Philippe Basabose, "Partir et conquérir: les apories du nouvel ordre mondial," in *Images et mirages des migrations dans les littératures et les cinémas d'Afrique francophone,* eds. Françoise Naudillon and Jean Ouédraogo (Montréal, Québéc: Mémoire d'encrier, 2011), 119–138.

42. Mahi Binebine, *Cannibales: Traversée dans l'enfer de Gibraltar* (La Tour d'Aigues: Editions de l'Aube, 2005 [first pub. 1999]); *Welcome to paradise,* trans. Lulu Norman (London: Granta Books, 2003), 46–47.

43. Claire Rodier, "Aux marges de l'Europe: la construction de l'inacceptable," in *Le retour des camps: Sangatte, Lampedusa, Guantanamo,* eds. Olivier Le Cour Grandmaison, Gilles Lhuilier and Jérôme Valluy (Paris: Editions Autrement, 2007), 138.

44. Abdourahman Waberi, *Aux Etats-Unis d'Afrique* (Paris: Editions Jean-Claude Lattès, 2006); *In the United States of Africa,* trans. David and Nicole Ball (Lincoln: University of Nebraska Press, 2009).

45. Christopher L. Miller, *The French Atlantic Triangle: Literature and Culture of the Slave Trade* (Durham: Duke University Press, 2008). In her novel *Blonde Roots* (London: Penguin, 2008), British-Nigerian writer Bernardine Evaristo reimagines a similar history in which African masters control the transatlantic slave trade, and in Sylvestre Amoussou's film, *Africa paradis* (Metis/Koffi Productions, 2007), Africa has become by 2040 the center of economic dynamism.

8. Into the European "Jungle"

1. Aravind Adiga, *White Tiger* (London: Atlantic Books, 2008), 3.

2. Roland Barthes, "African Grammar," *The Eiffel Tower and Other Mythologies,* trans. Richard Howard (Berkeley: University of California Press, 1997), 103.

3. Marguerite Abouet and Clément Oubrerie, *Aya de Yopougon* (Paris: Editions Gallimard, 2008), 1.

4. Claire Rodier, "Europe et migrations: la gestion de l'inquiétude. L'exemple de la directive 'retour'," in *Douce France. Rafles, rétentions, expulsions,* eds. Olivier Le Cour Grandmaison (Paris: Editions du Seuil, 2009), 260.

5. United Nations Convention on Human Rights, http://portal.unesco.org/shs/en/files/2874/11163348401InfoKit_en.pdf/InfoKit%2Ben.pdf, 5. Consulted August 12, 2010.

6. See Luc Legoux, "La réorganisation mondiale de l'asile," in *L'asile au Sud,* eds. Luc Cambrézy, Smaïn Laacher, Véronique Lassailly-Jacob, and Luc Legoux (Paris: Editions La Dispute, 2008), 9–22, and Smaïn Laacher, *Après Sangatte . . . Nouvelles immigrations, nouveaux enjeux* (Paris: Editions La Dispute, 2002).

7. "International Convention on the Protection of the Rights of All Migrant Workers and Members of Their Families," http://www.un.org/documents/ga/res/45/a45r158.htm (2003). Consulted August 12, 2010.

8. *A New Framework Strategy for Multilingualism,* http://ec.europa.eu/education/policies/lang/doc/com596_en.pdf (November 22, 2005), 3.

9. See Claude Truchot, "Le régime linguistique des institutions de l'Union européene: le droit . . . et la pratique," *Questions Internationales* 36 (2009): 94–101 and *Europe: l'enjeu linguistique* (Paris: La Documentation Française, 2009).

10. Claire Kramsch, "Grammar Games and Bilingual Blends," PMLA 124.3 (2009): 894.

11. Analogous phenomena have been observed in other contexts, as the work of Jean-Pierre Faye has shown: "Langages totalitaires: Fascistes et nazis," *Cahiers internationaux de sociologies* 36 (1964): 75–100.

12. "La démocratie phobique ou comment se soustraire aux analogies embarrassantes," in *Cette France-là,* Vol. 2 (Paris: Editions La Découverte, 2010), 418.

13. Michel Agier, *Le couloir des exilés. Être étranger dans un monde commun* (Bellecombe-en-Bauges: Editions du Croquant, 2011), 55 and 68. See also Michel Agier, *Gérer les indésirables. Des camps de réfugiés au gouvernement humanitaire* (Paris: Editions Flammarion, 2008).

14. "The Schengen *acquis,*" Official Journal of the European Communities, http://eur-lex.europa.eu/LexUriServ/LexUriServ.do?uri=OJ:L:2000:239:0001:0473:EN:PDF (2000), 15.

15. See Giorgio Agamben, *State of Exception,* trans. Kevin Attell (Chicago: University of Chicago Press, 2005) and Alessandro Dal Lago, *Non-Persone: L'esclusione dei migranti in una società globale, interzone* (Milan: Feltrinelli, 1999).

16. See Abdelkhaleq Berramdane and Jean Rossetto, eds. *La Politique européenne de l'immigration* (Paris: Editions Karthala, 2009); and Didier Fassin, "Frontières extérieures, frontières intérieures," in *Les nouvelles frontières de la société française,* ed. Didier Fassin (Paris: Editions La Découverte, 2010), 5–24.

17. See http://eurovoc.europa.eu/drupal/?cl=en. See also, for example, Jean-Paul Betbèze and Jean-Dominique Giuliani, *Les 100 mots de l'Europe* (Paris: Presses Universitaires de France, 2011), and Sylvie Aprile and Stéphane Dufoix, *Les mots de l'immigration* (Paris: Editions Belin: 2009).

18. Pierre Tevanian, *La République du mépris. Les métamorphoses du racisme dans la France des années Sarkozy* (Paris: Editions la Découverte, 2007), 11.

19. Sophie Dulucq, Jean-François Klein and Benjamin Stora, *Les mots de la colonisation* (Toulouse: Presses Universitaires du Mirail, 2008), 5, Pierre Tevanian, *Le ministère de la peur. Réflexions sur le nouvel ordre sécuritaire* (Paris: Editions L'Esprit frappeur, 2003), 9–10. See also *Dictionnaire critique du "Sarkozysme," Lignes* 33 (October 2010), and Pierre Tevanian and Sylvie Tissot, *Dictionnaire de la lepénisation des esprits* (Paris: Editions L'Esprit frappeur, 2002).

20. Alexis Spire, *Accueillir ou reconduire. Enquête sur les guichets de l'immigration* (Paris: Editions Raison d'Agir, 2008), 65.

21. Éric Fassin, *Démocratie précaire. Chroniques de la déraison d'État* (Paris: Editions La Découverte, 2012), 98.

22. Bertrand Cassaigne, "Des camps pour les migrants, urgence et suspicion," *Ceras—revue,* Projet no. 308, http://www.ceras-projet.com/index.php?id=3472 (2009). Consulted August 12, 2010.

23. See Marc Isaacs. *Calais, la dernière frontière* (Andana Films, 2003), Sandrine Driv-

ers and Flora Galuchot, *D'une rive à l'autre,* in *Je de mémoire* (Paris: La Médiathèque des trois mondes, [2002]), Jonathan Le Fourn and Andreï Schtakleff, *L'exil et le royaume* (L'Harmattan/Red Star Cinema, 2009), Yann Perreau and Thomas Dutter, *Clandestin, mon semblable, mon frère* (France Culture, 2003); Jean-Pierre Améris, *Maman est folle* (Escazal Films, 2007); Philippe Lioret, *Welcome* (Nord-Ouest Films, 2009); Jean Rolin, *Terminal Frigo* (Paris: P.O.L., 2005); Olivier Adam, *A l'abri de rien* (Paris: Editions de l'Olivier, 2007); and Sylvain George, *Qu'ils reposent en révolte (Des figures de guerre I)* (Noir Production/Independencia Distribution, 2010).

24. See Saul Taylor, "Barriers and Barrios: Melilla," *Monocle 28* 3 (2009): 55–59.

25. Violaine Carrère, "Sangatte et les nasses aux frontières de l'Europe," *Ceras—revue,* Projet no. 272. http://www.ceras-projet.com/index.php?id=1764 (2002).

26. Philippe Eurin, *La Jungle de Calais. Misère et solidarité* (Paris: L'Harmattan, 2010).

27. See Jane Freedman, *Immigration and Insecurity in France* (Aldershot, UK: Ashgate, 2004); and Smaïn Laacher, *Des étrangers en situation de "transit" au Centre d'Hébergement et d'Accueil d'Urgence Humanitaire de Sangatte* (Paris: CNRS-EHESS, 2002).

28. See Romain Liagre and Frédéric Dumont, "Sangatte: vie et mort d'un centre de réfugiés," *Annales de Géographie* 114 (2005): 93–112.

29. Après Sangatte: l'occultation des inexpulsables," in *Cette France-là,* Vol. 1 (Paris: Editions La Découverte, 2009), 199.

30. Jérôme Equer, *La jungle. Calais, un déshonneur européen* (Paris: Editions Jean-Paul Rocher, 2011), 14–15.

31. See Marc Bernardot, "Les mutations de la figure du camp," in *Le retour des camps: Sangatte, Lampedusa, Guantanamo,* eds. Olivier Le Cour Grandmaison, Gilles Lhuilier and Jérôme Valluy (Paris: Editions Autrement, 2007), 37.

32. See Michel Agier, "Le camp comme limite et comme espace politique," Carolina Kobelinsky and Chowra Makaremi, eds. *Enfermés dehors. Enquêtes sur le confinement des étrangers* (Bellecombe-en-Bauges: Editions du Croquant, 2009), 27–40.

33. See Trevor Paglen, *Blank Spots on the Map* (New York: Dutton, 2009).

34. See Wendy Brown, *Murs: Les murs de séparation et le déclin de la souveraineté étatique* (Paris: Editions Les Prairies Ordinaires, 2009) and Claude Quétel, *Murs. Une Autre histoire des hommes* (Paris: Editions Perrin, 2012).

35. Giorgio Agamben, *State of Exception,* trans. Kevin Attell (Chicago: University of Chicago Press, 2005).

36. See Olivier Brossat, "L'espace-camp et l'exception furtive," *Lignes* 26 (2008): 5–22.

37. See Violaine Carrère, "Sangatte: un toit pour les fantômes," *Hommes et Migrations* 1238 (2002): 13–22; Henri Courau, *Ethnologie de la* Forme-camp *de Sangatte. De l'exception à la régulation* (Paris: Editions des Archives Contemporaines, 2007); Marc Bernardot, *Camps d'étrangers* (Bellecombe-en-Bauges: Editions du Croquant, 2008); and Le Cour Grandmaison, Lhuilier and Valluy, eds. *Le retour des camps.*

38. "*The encampment* in Europe and around the Mediterranean Sea," http://migreurop.org (2009).

39. See Carolina Kobelinsky and Chowra Makaremi, eds., *Enfermés dehors. Enquêtes sur le confinement des étrangers* (Bellecombe-en-Bauges: Editions du Croquant, 2009).

40. Évelyne Ritaine, "Des migrants face aux murs d'un monde frontière," in *L'enjeu mondial. Les migrations,* eds. Christophe Jaffrelot and Christian Lequesne (Paris: Presses de la Fondation Nationale des Sciences Politiques, 2009), 163.

41. See Olivier de Bruyn, Interview with director Philippe Lioret, "Calais, c'est notre frontière mexicaine à nous," http://www.rue89.com/la-bande-du-cine/2009/03/10/philippe-lioret-calais-est-notre-frontiere-mexicaine (2009); and Vincent Bocher, "Au-

tour de Welcome," *Ceras—revue,* Projet no. 311, http://www.ceras-projet.com/index.php?id=3862 (2009).

42. Vincent Lindon, "Débat sur les migration," http://www.paperblog.fr/2330480/sangatte-detruit-la-jungle-de-calais-aneantie-violences-arretes-deporteset-demain/ (2009)

43. Marc Bernardot, "Rafles et internement des étrangers: les nouvelles guerres de capture," in *Douce France,* ed. Le Cour Grandmaison, 57.

44. Éric Besson, "Éric Besson propose cinq mesures pour renforcer l'action de l'Union Européenne contre l'immigration irrégulière," http://www.immigration.gouv.fr/spip.php?page=comm&id_rubrique=306&id_article=1794 (2009).

45. Éric Besson, "Calais: le démantèlement des filières clandestines se poursuit," http://www.immigration.gouv.fr/spip.php?page=comm&id_rubrique=306&id_article=1854 (2009). Consulted August 2010.

46. Éric Besson, "Calais: Eric Besson annonce la fermeture de la 'jungle' avant la semaine prochaine," http://www.immigration.gouv.fr/spip.php?page=comm&id_rubrique=306&id_article=1790 (2009).

47. Éric Besson, "Demantèlement de la 'jungle' à Calais: point de situation du 28 septembre 2009," http://www.immigration.gouv.fr/spip.php?page=comm&id_rubrique=306&id_article=1812 (2009).

48. Éric Besson, "Présentation du projet de loi relatif à l'immigration," http://www.immigration.gouv.fr/IMG/pdf/DP20100401ProjLoi.pdf (April 1, 2010), 2.

49. Éric Besson, "Demantèlement de la 'jungle' à Calais: Point de situation," http://www.immigration.gouv.fr/spip.php?page=dossiers_det_res&numrubrique=427&numarticle=1811 (September 28, 2010).

50. Coordination française pour le droit d'asile (CFDA), *La loi des "jungles." La situation des exilés sur le littoral de la Manche et de la Mer du Nord,* http://cfda.rezo.net/download/Rapport_CFDA_092008.pdf (September 2008), 1–186.

51. See also Coordination française pour le droit d'asile (CFDA), "The Law of the 'Jungle': The Situation of Exiles on the shore of the Channel and the North Sea: Recommendations," http://cfda.rezo.net/download/The%20law%20of%20Jungles%20recommendations%2009%2008.pdf (September 2008), 2.

52. Andrea Rea, "Laisser circuler, laisser enfermer: les orientations paradoxales d'une politique migratoire débridée en Europe," in *Enfermés dehors. Enquêtes sur le confinement des étrangers,* eds. Carolina Kobelinsky and Chowra Makaremi (Bellecombe-en-Bauges: Editions du Croquant, 2009), 265.

53. Catherine Wihtol de Wenden, "La crise de l'asile," in *Allers-Retours,* eds. Abdellatif Chaouite and Marie Virolle (Paris: Téraèdre Publishing /Revues Plurielles, 2008), 161.

54. Didier Bigo, "Contrôle migratoire et libre circulation en Europe," in *L'enjeu mondial,* eds. Jaffrelot and Lequesne, 167.

55. On this subject, see "Délit de solidarité: la réalité," *Plein droit: La revue du GISTI* 83 (2009): 1–8; and Mireille Rosello, *Postcolonial Hospitality: The Immigrant as Guest* (Stanford: Stanford University Press, 2001).

56. See for example Jean-Luc Nancy, *Identités* (Paris: Éditions Galilée, 2010).

57. Ryszard Kapuscinski, *The Other* (London: Verso, 2008), 45–46.

58. See Jürgen Habermas, *Europe: The Faltering project* (Cambridge, UK: Polity Press, 2009).

59. Jocelyne Dakhlia, "La France dedans dehors," *Lignes* 25 (2008): 173.

60. Caryl Phillips, "Strangers in a Strange Land," *Color Me English: Migration and Belonging Before and After 9/11* (New York: The New Press, 2011), 288.

61. Pierre Tevanian, "Le legs colonial," in *Une mauvaise décolonisation: La France: de l'Empire aux émeutes des quartiers populaires,* eds. Georges Labica, Francis Arzalier, Olivier Le Cour Grandmaison, Pierre Tevanian, and Saïd Bouamama (Paris: Le Temps des Cerises, 2007), 64.

62. See Le Théâtre du Soleil, http://www.theatre-du-soleil.fr/caravan/index.shtml.

63. Ariane Mnouchkine, *Le Dernier Caravansérail* (Odyssées) (Théâtre du Soleil, Bel Air Media, Arte video/Bel Air Classiques, 2006).

64. Françoise Lauwaert, "Comme une écaille sur le mur: A propos de 'Le Dernier caravansérail (Odyssées)', un spectacle en deux parties du Théâtre du Soleil," *Civilisations* 56.1–2 (2007): 168.

65. Judith Miller, "New Forms for New Conflicts: Thinking About Ariane Mnouchkine and Tony Kushner," *Contemporary Theatre Review* 16.2 (2006): 214.

66. Patricia Krus, "Postcolonial Performance," *Ariel: A Review of International Literature* 38.1 (2007): 125.

9. *Documenting the Periphery*

1. These lyrics are from the title track "Plafond de verre" [Glass ceiling] of Ivorian rapper H-Magnum's CD *Rafales,* released in 2009. In the original French, the lyrics are "On n'a pas les mêmes chances, on a pas la même France." In order to maintain the rhyme scheme in the English translation, one is required to abandon the plural form of "chances" which operates in the French where the final consonant is not pronounced.

2. www.quifaitlafrance.com.

3. Alec G. Hargreaves, *Immigration and Identity in beur fiction: Voices from the North African Community in France* (Oxford: Berg, 1991), 1–3. Similar factors are included in Michel Laronde's analysis, whereby "the term *beur* should be understood both in its ethnic sense (novels written by the *Beurs*) and expanded to a dialectic sense: one that *speaks* to the situation of young Maghrebis in contemporary French society," *Autour du roman beur: Immigration et identité* (Paris: Editions L'Harmattan, 1993), 6.

4. See Bennetta Jules-Rosette, *Black Paris: The African Writers' Landscape* (Urbana: University of Illinois Press, 1998); Lydie Moudileno, *Parades postcoloniales: La fabrication des identités dans le roman congolais* (Paris: Editions Karthala, 2006); and Dominic Thomas, *Black France: Colonialism, Immigration, and Transnationalism* (Bloomington: Indiana University Press, 2007). Furthermore, Romuald-Blaise Fonkoua's attempt to circumscribe the corpus of *banlieue* authors through national, geographic, gender, age, and thematic considerations encounters similar challenges to those raised by Hargreaves and Laronde, among others. See Romuald-Blaise Fonkoua, "Ecrire la banlieue: la littérature des 'invisibles'," in *Le retour du colonial,* ed. Nicolas Bancel, *Cultures du Sud* 165 (April–June 2007): 89–96.

5. Ousmane Sembene, *Le docker noir* (Paris: Editions Présence Africaine, 1956); "La noire de . . . ," *Voltaïque* (Paris: Editions Présence Africaine, 1962); Ousmane Socé, *Mirages de Paris* (Paris: Nouvelles Editions Latines, 1937); and Bernard Dadié, *Un nègre à Paris* (Paris: Editions Présence Africaine, 1959).

6. See for example Thomté Ryam, *Banlieue noire* (Paris: Editions Présence Africaine, 2006); Insa Sané, *Sarcelles-Dakar* (Paris: Editions Sarbacane, 2006); Houda Rouane, *Pieds-blancs* (Paris: Editions Philippe Rey, 2006); Ahmed Djouder, *Désintégration* (Paris: Editions Stock, 2006); and Didier Mandin, *Banlieue Voltaire* (Paris: Editions Desnel, 2006). See also Naïma Yahi, "L'immigré dans la fiction, des années soixante à nos jours,"

in *Immigrances: L'immigration en France au XXème siècle,* eds. Benjamin Stora and Emile Temine (Paris: Hachette, 2007), 275–298.

7. Azouz Begag, *Ethnicity and Equality: France in the Balance* (Lincoln: University of Nebraska Press, 2007), 24.

8. Etienne Balibar, "Racism and Crisis, Etienne Balibar and Immanuel Wallerstein, eds. *Race, Nation, Class: Ambiguous Identities* (London: Verso, 1991), 220.

9. Lorenzo Prencipe, "Médias et immigration: un rapport difficile," *Migrations Société* 14. 81–82 (May–August 2002): 140.

10. Pascal Blanchard, Nicolas Bancel, and Sandrine Lemaire, "Les origines républicaines de la fracture coloniale," in *La fracture coloniale: La société française au prisme de l'héritage colonial,* eds. Pascal Blanchard, Nicolas Bancel, and Sandrine Lemaire (Paris: Editions La Découverte, 2005), 38–37.

11. Pascale Casanova, *The World Republic of Letters,* trans. M. B. DeBevoise (Cambridge: Harvard University Press, 2004), 124.

12. "Pour une 'littérature-monde' en français," *Le Monde des livres* (March 16, 2007): 2. See also "Toward a World Literature in French," trans. Daniel Simon, *World Literature Today* 83.2 (March–April 2009): 54–56.

13. Azouz Begag was invited to participate before the manifesto was published but was too busy with ministerial matters to be able to do so. Had he been able to do so, *beur* and *banlieue* literature would still of course have been underrepresented.

14. Also published as "Manifeste par le collectif *Qui fait la France?*" *Les inrockuptibles* 614 (September 4, 2007): 18.

15. *Chroniques d'une société annoncée* (Paris: Editions Stock, 2007). Authors include Karim Amellal, Khalid El Bahji, Jean-Éric Boulin, Faïza Guène, Dembo Goumane, Habiba Mahany, Samir Ouazen, Mabrouk Rachedi, Mohamed Razane, and Thomté Ryam.

16. Faïza Guène, *Kiffe kiffe demain* (Paris: Hachette Littératures, 2004); *Just Like Tomorrow,* translated by Sarah Adams (London: Definitions, 2006); and Françoise Sagan, *Bonjour tristesse* (Paris: Editions Julliard, 1954).

17. Elaine Sciolino, "From Paris Suburbs, A Different Voice," *New York Times,* (October 26, 2004). See also Lydie Moudileno on this question in relation to the Congolese author Sony Labou Tansi, "Magical Realism: 'Arme miraculeuse' for the African Novel?" in *Textual Ownership in Francophone African Literature,* eds. Alec G. Hargreaves, Nicki Hitchcott, and Dominic Thomas, *Research in African Literatures* 37.1 (Spring 2006): 28–41.

18. Achille Mbembe, "The Republic and Its Beast: On the Riots in the French *Banlieues,*" trans. Jean Marie Todd, in *Frenchness and the African Diaspora: Identity and Uprising in Contemporary France,* eds. Charles Tshimanga, Didier Gondola, and Peter J. Bloom (Bloomington: Indiana University Press, 2009), 47–69.

19. Habiba Mahany, *Je kiffe ma race* (Paris: Editions Jean-Claude Lattès, 2008); Thomté Ryam, *Banlieue noire* (Paris: Editions Présence Africaine, 2006); Jean-Éric Boulin, *Supplément au roman national* (Paris: Editions Stock, 2006) and *La Question Blanche* (Paris: Editions Stock, 2008); Karim Amellal, *Discriminez-moi. Enquête sur nos inégalités* (Paris: Editions Flammarion, 2005); Ahmed Djouder, *Désintégration* (Paris: Editions Stock, 2006); Mohamed Razane, *Dit violent* (Paris: Editions Gallimard, 2006); Aymeric Patricot, *Azima la rouge* (Paris: Editions Flammarion, 2006); Mabrouk Rachedi, *Le poids d'une âme* (Paris: Editions Jean-Claude Lattès, 2006); Akli Tadjer, *Bel-Avenir* (Paris: Editions Flammarion, 2006); Rachid Djaïdani, *Boumkœur* (Paris: Editions du Seuil, 2000) and *Viscéral* (Paris: Editions du Seuil, 2007); Dembo Goumane, *Dembo Story* (Paris:

Editions Hachette, 2006); and Houda Rouane, *Pieds-Blancs* (Paris: Editions Philippe Rey, 2006).

20. See for example Azouz Begag's dismantling of Paul Smaïl's *Vivre me tue* (Paris: Editions Balland, 1997), a text written under a false name in an attempt to simulate an authentic voice on ethnic minorities, "Of Imposture and Incompetence: Paul Smaïl's *Vivre me tue*," in *Textual Ownership in Francophone African Literature,* eds. Hargreaves, Hitchcott, and Thomas, *Research in African Literatures,* 55–71. For an account of positive contributions from the banlieues, see Marc Hatzfeld, *La culture des cités: Une énergie positive* (Paris: Editions Autrement, 2006).

21. Achille Mbembe, "Figures of the Multiplicity: Can France Reinvent its Identity?" in *Frenchness and the African* Diaspora, eds. Tshimanga, Gondola, and Bloom, 65. See also Loïc Wacquant, "The response by the authorities to poverty and collective violence varies from country to country. . . . They range from the *criminalization of misery* and of precarious populations at one extreme, to the *politicization of the problem* in the form of a renegotiation of social and economic rights at the other," *Parias urbains: Ghetto, banlieues, état* (Paris: Editions La Découverte, 2006), 39.

22. See also David Blatt, "Immigrant politics in a republican nation," in *Post-Colonial Cultures in France,* eds. Alec G. Hargreaves and Mark McKinney (London: Routledge, 1997), who has argued that "The increased political saliency of immigration issues helped revive a traditional French discourse on integration and the nation-state that insists on the preservation of republican principles of undifferentiated citizenship and a firm rejection of any public recognition of ethnic or cultural identities," 40–41.

23. Nicolas Bancel, Pascal Blanchard, and Françoise Vergès, *La République Coloniale: Essai sur une utopie* (Paris: Editions Albin Michel, 2003), 122–123.

24. See for example Evelyne Ribert, *Liberté, égalité, carte d'identité: les jeunes issus de l'immigration et l'appartenance nationale* (Paris: Editions La Découverte, 2006); and on the question of equal opportunities, Hargreaves, "Politics and public policy," *Multi-Ethnic France,* 165–203.

25. See Pierre Tevanian, "Le legs colonial," in *Une mauvaise décolonisation: La France: de l'Empire aux émeutes des quartiers populaires,* eds. Georges Labica, Francis Arzalier, Olivier Le Cour Grandmaison, Pierre Tevanian, and Saïd Bouamama (Paris: Le Temps des Cerises, 2007), 64.

26. Faïza Guène, *Du rêve pour les oufs* (Paris: Hachette Littératures, 2006); *Dreams from the Endz,* trans. Sarah Adams (London: Chatto & Windus, 2008). See also the short story "Je suis qui je suis," *Chroniques pour une société annoncée* (Paris: Editions Stock, 2007).

27. Azouz Begag, *Le gône du Chââba* (Paris: Editions du Seuil, 1986); and *The Shantytown Kid,* trans. Naïma Wolf and Alec G. Hargreaves (Lincoln: University of Nebraska Press, 2007).

28. Loïc Wacquant, *Parias urbains: Ghetto, banlieues, état,* 5. See also Mike Davis, *Planet of Slums* (London: Verso, 2006).

29. Caroline Carisoni, "Faïza, dans un monde de oufs," *Les Clès* 676 (September 7–13, 2006).

30. Statement made to her English translator, Sarah Adams. See "Voice of the People," *The Guardian,* (May 10, 2006).

31. Such texts might include Souad with Marie-Thérèse Cuny, *Brûlée vive* (Paris: Oh! Editions, 2003); Jamila Aït-Abbas, *La Fatiha: née en France, mariée de force en Algérie* (Paris: Editions Michel Lafon, 2003); and Samira Bellil, *Dans l'enfers des tournantes* (Paris: Editions Denöel, 2003). In turn, Fadela Amara's, *Ni Putes Ni Soumises* (Paris: Edi-

tions La Découverte, 2003), has emerged as an important advocacy group for women's rights. On the question of sensationalism, see Hargreaves, "Testimony, Co-Authorship and Dispossession Among Women of Maghrebi Origin in France," in *Textual Ownership in Francophone African Literature*, eds. Hargreaves, Hitchcott and Thomas, *Research in African Literatures*, 42–54; and Dominic Thomas, "Rhetorical Mediations of Slavery" and "Afro-Parisianism and African Feminisms," *Black France*, 114–130 and 131–154.

32. Mehdi Charef, *Le thé au harem d'Archi Ahmed* (Paris: Editions Mercure de France, 1983); *Tea in the Harem*, trans. Ed Emery (London: Serpent's Tail, 1989).

33. Hargreaves, "Translator's Introduction," Begag, *Ethnicity and Equality*, 9.

34. Cited in V. Mo, "Sa banlieue de A à Z," *Le Parisien* (August 23, 2006): 10.

35. Vincent Mongaillard, "Faïza Guène, plume du bitume," Sa banlieue de A à Z," *Le Parisien* (August 23, 2006): 10.

36. Nicolas Sarkozy, "Discours de Grenoble," http://www.elysee.fr/president/les-actualites/discours/2010/discours-de-m-le-president-de-la-republique-a.9399.html (July 30, 2010).

37. Tyler Stovall has carefully illustrated how "the interweaving of colonialism and postcolonialism, like that of race and class, constitutes an important characteristic of French identity in the twentieth century as a whole," "From Red Belt to Black Belt: Race, Class, and Urban Marginality in Twentieth-Century Paris," in *The Color of Liberty: Histories of Race in France*, eds. Susan Peabody and Tyler Stovall (Durham: Duke University Press, 2003), 363. For a recent sociological study of the Courtillières, see Trica Keaton, *Muslim Girls and the Other France: Race, Identity Politics, and Social Exclusion* (Bloomington: Indiana University Press, 2006). See also Fatimata Wane's and Didier Gondola's documentary on the Cité Pont-de-Créteil at Saint-Maur-des-Fossés, a banlieue located to the east of Paris: *Transient Citizens* (*Les citoyens de l'avion*, DVD documentary, 2006).

38. Laurent Mucchielli, "Les émeutes de novembre 2005: les raisons de la colère," in *Quand les banlieues brûlent . . . Retour sue les émeutes de novembre 2005*, eds. Laurent Mucchielli and Véronique Le Goaziou (Paris: Editions La Découverte, 2006), 35. See also Yann Moulier Boutang, *La révolte des banlieues ou les habits nus de la République* (Paris: Editions Amsterdam, 2005); and Christophe Soullez, *Les violences urbaines* (Toulouse: Les Editions Milan, 2006).

39. François Niney, *Le documentaire et ses faux-semblants* (Paris: Editions Klincksieck, 2009), 11.

40. Keaton, *Muslim Girls and the Other France.*

41. Loïc Wacquant, "Banlieues françaises et ghettos noir américain: de l'amalgame à la comparaison," *French Politics and Society* 10.4 (1992): 81–103, and *Parias urbains.*

42. Stovall, "From Red Belt to Black Belt," 351–369.

43. Didier Fassin, eds. *Les nouvelles frontières de la société française* (Paris: Éditions La Découverte, 2010).

44. Le Cour Grandmaison, ed. *Douce France.*

45. See also Hedi Dhoukar, "Les thèmes du cinéma beur," *CinémAction/Hommes et Migrations* 56 (1990): 152–160.

46. Ahmed Boubeker, "La 'petite histoire' d'une génération d'expérience: Du Mouvement beur aux banlieues de l'islam," in *Histoire politique des immigrations (post)coloniales. France, 1920–2008*, eds. Ahmed Boubeker and Abdellali Hajjat (Paris: Editions Amsterdam, 2008), 192.

47. Hargreaves, "Minority ethnic identification and mobilization," in *Multi-Ethnic France*, 75–139.

48. Boualam Azahoum, Interview, "L'expérience de DiverCité: Entretien avec Boualam

Azahoum," in *Histoire politique des immigrations (post)*coloniales, eds. Boubeker and Hajjat, 203.

49. Driss Maghraoui, "French Identity, Islam and North Africans: Colonial Legacies, Postcolonial Realities," in *French Civilization and Its Discontents: nationalism, colonialism, race,* eds. Tyler Stovall and Georges Van Den Abbeele (Lanham: Lexington Books, 2003), 213–234.

50. Pierre Tevanian, "Le legs colonial," in *Une mauvaise décolonisation,* eds. Labica, Arzalier, Le Cour Grandmaison, Tevanian, and Bouamama, 64–65.

51. Emmanuelle Saada, "Un racisme de l'expansion. Les discriminations raciales au regard des situations coloniales," in *De la question sociale à la question raciale. Représenter la société francaise,* eds. Didier Fassin and Éric Fassin (Paris: Editions la Découverte, 2006), 71.

52. Françoise Masure, "Des Français paradoxaux. L'expérience de la naturalisation des enfants de l'immigration maghrébine," in *Les nouvelles frontières de la société française,* ed. Fassin, 568.

53. Hafid Gafaiti, "Nationalism, Colonialism, and Ethnic Discourse in the Construction of French Identity,'" in *French Civilization and Its Discontents,* eds. Stovall and Van Den Abbeele, 201–208.

54. Eric Macé, "Postcolonialité et francité dans les imaginaires télévisuels de la nation," in *Ruptures postcoloniales: Les nouveaux visages de la société française,* eds. Nicolas Bancel, Pascal Blanchard, Françoise Vergès, Achille Mbembe, and Florence Bernault (Paris: Editions La Découverte, 2010), 298.

55. Pascale Krémer, "Les cités s'emparent de la caméra," *Le Monde* 2 (Supplement), 207 (February 2, 2008): 24.

56. www.quifaitlafrance.com/content/blogcategory/26/58/.

57. www.quifaitlafrance.com.

58. See Adams "Voice of the People," *The Guardian.*

59. Carrie Tarr, "French Cinema and Post-Colonial Minorities," in *Post-Colonial Cultures in France,* eds. Hargreaves and McKinney, 73–79.

60. www.citeart.free.fr.

61. www.icetream.com.

62. Such as www.regards@banlieue.org and www.enattendantdemain.org.

63. See www.les-engraineurs.org.

64. Guy Gathier, *Le documentaire un autre cinéma* (Paris: Editions Armand Colin, 2008), 207, 208, and 212.

65. Mohamed Ridha Bouguerra and Sahiba Bouguerra, *Histoire de la littérature du Maghreb: littérature francophone* (Paris: Editions Ellipses, 2010), 148.

66. Jean-Luc Einaudi, *La bataille de Paris: 17 octobre 1961* (Paris: Editions du Seuil, 1991). See also his article, "Le crime: violence coloniale en métropole (1954–1961)," in *Culture coloniale en France. De la Révolution française à nos jours,* eds. Pascal Blanchard, Nicolas Bancel, and Sandrine Lemaire (Paris: CNRS Editions, 2008), 471–479.

67. Monique Hervo, speaking in Faïza Guène's and Bernard Richard's *Mémoires du 17 octobre* (2002, 17 mins.).

68. Achille Mbembe, "Figures du Multiple: La France peut-elle réinventer son identité?" *Le Messager,* 2005 (Article available at http://www.europe-solidaire.org/spip.php?article4898).

69. Alessandro Dal Lago, *Non-Persons: The Exclusion of Migrants in a Global Society,* trans. Marie Orton (Milan, Italy: IPOC Press, 2009), 85.

70. Ahmed Boubeker, "Outsiders in the French Melting Pot: The Public Construc-

tion of Invisibility for Visible Minorities," trans. Jane Marie Todd, in *Frenchness and the African* Diaspora, eds. Tshimanga, Gondola, and Bloom (Bloomington: Indiana University Press, 2009), 77.

71. "La crise de la politique d'immigration," in *Cette France-là,* Vol. 2 (Paris: Editions La Découverte, 2010), 7.

10. Decolonizing France

1. Ananda Devi, "Flou identitaire," in *Je est un autre. Pour une identité monde,* eds. Michel Le Bris and Jean Rouaud (Paris: Editions Gallimard, 2010), 184.

2. Juan Goytisolo, "Défense de l'hybridité ou La pureté, mère de tous les vices," trans. Jean-Marie Laclavetine, in *Je est un autre,* eds. Le Bris and Rouaud, 206–207.

3. "Pour une 'littérature-monde' en français," *Le Monde des livres* (March 16, 2007): 2. See also "Toward a World Literature in French," trans. Daniel Simon, *World Literature Today* 83.2 (March–April 2009): 54–56. The full French version of the text is available at: http://www.etonnants-voyageurs.com/spip.php?article1574.

4. See, for example, "La Francophonie dans le monde 2006–2007," http://www.francophonie.org/IMG/pdf/La_francophonie_dans_le_monde_2006-2007.pdf, (2007), 1–329.

5. Michel Le Bris and Jean Rouaud, eds. *Pour une littérature-monde* (Paris: Editions Gallimard, 2007).

6. Christopher L. Miller, "The Slave Trade, *La Françafrique,* and the Globalization of French," in *French Global: A New Approach to Literary History,* eds. Christie McDonald and Susan Rubin Suleiman (New York: Columbia University Press, 2010), 251.

7. www.francophonie.org.

8. Michel Le Bris, "Pour une littérature-monde en français," in *Pour une littérature-monde,* eds. Le Bris and Rouaud, 24.

9. Obioma Nnaemeka, "Nego-Feminism: Theorizing, Practicing, and Pruning Africa's Way," *Signs: Journal of Women in Culture and Society* 29.2 (Winter 2004): 371.

10. Ngùgì wa Thiong'o, *Decolonizing the Mind: The Politics of Language in African Literature* (London: Heinemann, 1986), 4–5.

11. Ifé Orisha, "Sony Labou Tansi face à douze mots," *Equateur* 1 (October–November 1986): 30.

12. See Charles Forsdick and David Murphy, eds. *Francophone Postcolonial Studies* (London: Arnold, 2003); and Anne Donadey and H. Adlai Murdoch, eds. *Postcolonial Theory and Francophone Literary Studies* (Gainesville: University Press of Florida, 2005).

13. See Pascal Blanchard, Nicolas Bancel, and Sandrine Lemaire, eds. *La fracture coloniale: La société française au prisme de l'héritage colonial* (Paris: Editions La Découverte, 2005).

14. Jean-Marc Moura, "Les influences et permanences coloniales dans le domaine littéraire," in *Culture post-coloniale 1961–2006: Traces et mémoires coloniales en France,* eds. Pascal Blanchard and Nicolas Bancel (Paris: Editions Autrement, 2006), 172–173 and *Littératures francophones et théorie postcoloniale* (Paris: Presses Universitaires de France, 2007), 7.

15. See Alan Riding, "Neocolonialists Seize the French Language: An Invading Legion of Foreign Writers Is Snapping Up the Medals," *New York Times,* (October 8, 1997).

16. See Donald Morrison, "The Death of French Culture," *Time Magazine* (November 21, 2007).

17. Dany Lafferière, *Je suis un écrivain japonais* (Paris: Editions Grasset & Fasquelle, 2008), 197–198.

18. Abdourahman A. Waberi, "Ecrivains en position d'entraver," in *Pour une littérature-monde,* eds. Le Bris and Rouaud, 72.

19. Alain Mabanckou, "Le chant de l'oiseau migrateur," in Michel Le Bris and Jean Rouaud, eds., *Pour une littérature-monde* (Paris: Editions Gallimard, 2007), 59–60.

20. Ngùgì wa Thiong'o, *Something Torn and New: An African Renaissance* (New York: Basic Civitas Books, 2009), 56.

21. Pascal Blanchard, Nicolas Bancel and Sandrine Lemaire, "La fracture coloniale: une crise française," in *La fracture coloniale,* 30.

22. See www.quifaitlafrance.com.

23. See, for example, Anna Moï, *Espéranto, désespéranto. La francophonie sans les français* (Paris: Editions Gallimard, 2006).

24. An argument developed in *The Guardian* newspaper by James Meek in relation to Turkey's candidacy for European Union membership, "What is Europe?" (December 17, 2004), 2.

25. See, for example, Catherine Coquery-Vidrovitch, *Enjeux politiques de l'histoire coloniale* (Marseille: Éditions Agone, 2009); Catherine Coquio, ed. *Retours du colonial: Disculpation et réhabilitation de l'histoire coloniale* (Nantes: L'Atalante, 2008); and Olivier Le Cour Grandmaison, *La République impériale: Politique et racisme d'état* (Paris: Editions La Découverte, 2009).

26. See, for example, Dominic Thomas, *Black France: Colonialism, Immigration, and Transnationalism* (Bloomington: Indiana University Press, 2007); Pap Ndiaye, *La condition noire. Essai sur une minorité francaise* (Paris: Editions Calmann-Lévy, 2008); and Charles Tshimanga, Didier Gondola, and Peter J. Bloom, eds. *Frenchness and the African Diaspora: Identity and Uprising in Contemporary France* (Bloomington: Indiana University Press, 2009).

27. "Textes de lois relatifs à la mémoire et à l'histoire," in *La colonisation, la loi et l'histoire,* eds. Claude Liauzu and Gilles Manceron (Paris: Editions Syllepse, 2006), 164–165.

28. Blanchard, Bancel, Sandrine Lemaire, eds. *La fracture coloniale;* Nicolas Bancel, Pascal Blanchard, Françoise Vergès, Achille Mbembe, and Florence Bernault, eds. *Ruptures postcoloniales: Les nouveaux visages de la société française* (Paris: Editions La Découverte, 2010); Jean-François Bayart, *Les études postcoloniales. Un carnaval académique* (Paris: Editions Karthala, 2010); and Jean-Loup Amselle, *L'Occident décroché: Enquête sur les postcolonialismes* (Paris: Editions Stock, 2008).

29. Éric Besson, *Pour la Nation* (Paris: Editions Grasset & Fasquelle, 2009), 11.

30. Pascal Blanchard, "L'identité, l'historien et le passé colonial: le trio impossible," in *Je est un autre,* eds. Le Bris and Rouaud, 124; and "Towards a Real Debate: National Identity and Colonial History," trans. Dominic Thomas, http://www.achac.com/?O=204, February 14, 2010, 1–7.

31. See Donadey and Murdoch, eds. *Postcolonial Theory and Francophone Literary Studies;* Forsdick and Murphy, eds. *Francophone Postcolonial Studies;* Forsdick and Murphy, eds. *Postcolonial Thought in the French-Speaking World* (Liverpool: Liverpool University Press, 2009); and Farid Laroussi and Christopher L. Miller, eds. *The Challenge of Expanding Horizons, Yale French Studies* 103 (2003).

32. See www.debatidentitenationale.fr/bibliotheque/.

33. "Pour un véritable débat," www.achac.com/?O=204, 2.

34. Blanchard, "L'identité, l'historien et le passé colonial: le trio impossible," in *Je est un autre,* eds. Le Bris and Rouaud, 126.

35. Zygmunt Bauman, *Liquid Modernity* (Cambridge, UK: Polity Press, 2000).

36. Pierre Nora, *Les lieux de mémoire* (Paris: Editions Gallimard, 1984–1992).

37. Fernand Braudel, *L'identité de la France: les hommes et les choses* (Paris: Editions Flammarion, 1990); Eugen Weber, *Peasants into Frenchmen: The Modernization of France* (Cambridge: Harvard University Press, 1977); Ernest Gellner, *Nations and Nationalism* (Ithaca: Cornell University Press, 1983); Ernesto Laclau, *La guerre des identités. Grammaire de l'émancipation* (Paris: Editions La Découverte, 2000); Patrick Weil, *Qu'est-ce qu'un francais? Histoire de la nationalité française depuis la Révolution* (Paris: Editions Grasset & Fasquelle, 2002); Anne-Marie Thiesse, *La Création des identités nationales: Europe* xxvllle–xxe (Paris: Editions du Seuil, 2001); Peter Davies, *The National Front in France: Ideology, Discourse and Power* (London: Routledge, 1999); and Gérard Noiriel, *A quoi sert l'identité "nationale"* (Marseille: Editions Agone, 2007).

38. See also Maxim Silverman, *Deconstructing the Nation: Immigration, Racism and Citizenship in Modern France* (London: Routledge, 1992); Rogers Brubaker, *Citizenship and Nationhood in France and Germany* (Cambridge: Harvard University Press, 1992); and Tyler Stovall and Georges Van Den Abbeele, eds., *French Civilization and its Discontents: Nationalism, Colonialism, Race* (Lanham: Lexington Books, 2003).

39. Michel Le Bris, "Lisez Rimbaud," in *Je est un autre,* eds. Le Bris and Rouaud, 11.

40. Pascal Blanchard, Nicolas Bancel and Sandrine Lemaire, "La fracture coloniale: une crise française," in *La fracture coloniale,* 30.

41. Le Bris and Rouaud, "Avant-propos," *Je est un autre,* eds. Le Bris and Rouaud, 9, emphasis added.

42. Achille Mbembe, "Pièce d'identité et désirs d'apartheid," in *Je est un autre,* eds. Le Bris and Rouaud, 119.

43. Pascal Blanchard: "L'identité, l'historien et le passé colonial: le trio impossible," in *Je est un autre,* eds. Le Bris and Rouaud, 126 and 125.

44. Wilfried N'Sondé, "Ethnidentité," in *Je est un autre,* eds. Le Bris and Rouaud, 100.

45. Kebir Ammi, "Mon identité, celle de l'autre," in *Je est un autre,* eds. Le Bris and Rouaud, 193.

46. Alain Mabanckou, "Le sang, le sol, la souche," in *Je est un autre,* eds. Le Bris and Rouaud, 39.

47. Mabanckou, "Le sang, le sol, la souche," in *Je est un autre,* eds. Le Bris and Rouaud, 39, 40 and 43.

48. Philippe Forest, "Notre âme n'est jamais une," in *Je est un autre,* eds. Le Bris and Rouaud, 74.

49. See, for example, Laurent Dubreuil (éd.), *Faut-il être postcolonial?,* Special issue of *Labyrinthe: Atelier Interdisciplinaire* 24 (Paris: Editions Maisonneuve & Larose, 2006); Achille Mbembe, "La république désœuvrée: la France à l'ère post-coloniale," *Le Débat,* 137 (November–December 2005): 159–175; Achille Mbembe and Nicolas Bancel, "De la pensée postcoloniale," *Cultures du Sud* 165 (April–June 2007): 83–92; and Marie-Claude Smouts, ed. *La Situation postcoloniale: Les* postcolonial studies *dans le débat français* (Paris: Presses de Sciences Po, 2007).

50. Dominick LaCapra, "Reconfiguring French Studies," in *History and Reading: Tocqueville, Foucault, French Studies* (Toronto: University of Toronto Press, 2000), 193–194.

51. See, for example, Herman Lebovics, *Bringing the Empire Back Home: France in*

the Global Age (Durham: Duke University Press, 2004); Robert Aldrich, *Vestiges of the Colonial Empire in France: Monuments, Museums and Colonial Memories* (London: Palgrave Macmillan, 2005); Dominic Thomas, ed. *Museums in Postcolonial Europe* (London: Routledge, 2009); Pascal Blanchard and Isabelle Veyrat-Masson. eds. *Les Guerres de mémoires: La France et son histoire. Enjeux politiques, controverses historiques, stratégies médiatiques* (Paris: Editions la Découverte, 2008); Gary Wilder, *The French Imperial Nation State: Negritude and Colonial Humanism between the Two World Wars* (Chicago: University of Chicago Press, 2005); Jennifer Anne Boittin, *Colonial Metropolis: The Urban Grounds of Anti-Imperialism and Feminism in Interwar Paris* (Lincoln: University of Nebraska Press, 2010); Jill Forbes and Michael Kelly, eds. *French Cultural Studies: An Introduction* (Oxford: Oxford University Press, 1995); Nicholas Hewitt, ed. *The Cambridge Companion to Modern French Culture* (Cambridge: Cambridge University Press, 2003); Kristin Ross, *Fast Cars, Clean Bodies: Decolonization and the Reordering of French Culture* (Boston: MIT Press, 1996); Alec G. Hargreaves and Mark McKinney, eds. *Post-Colonial Cultures in France* (London: Routledge, 1997); and Laurent Dubois, *Soccer Empire: The World Cup and the Future of France* (Berkeley: University of California Press, 2010).

52. See, for example, "La technologie du soupçon: tests osseux, tests pilosité, tests ADN," in *Cette France-là* (Paris: Editions La Découverte, 2009), 157–159.

53. Andrew Delbanco, "Scandals of Higher Education," *New York Review of Books,* (29 March 2007): 46.

54. Goytisolo, "Défense de l'hybridité ou La pureté, mère de tous les vices," in *Je est un autre,* eds. Le Bris and Rouaud, 213.

BIBLIOGRAPHY

Abbas, Tahir. "Recent Developments to British Multicultural Theory, Polity and Practice: The Case of British Muslims." *Citizenship Studies* 9.2 (May 2005): 153–166.

Abderrezak, Hakim. "'Burning the Sea': Clandestine Migration across the Strait of Gibraltar in Francophone Moroccan 'Illiterature.'" *Contemporary French & Francophone Studies: Sites* 13.4 (September 2009): 461–469.

Abouet, Marguerite, and Clément Oubrerie. *Aya de Yopougon.* Paris: Editions Gallimard, 2008.

Absa, Moussa Sene. *Ainsi meurent les anges.* California Newsreel, 2001.

Achebe, Chinua. *The Education of a British-Protected Child.* New York: Alfred A. Knopf, 2009.

Adam, Olivier. *A l'abri de rien.* Paris: Editions de l'Olivier, 2007.

Adams, Sarah. "Voice of the People." *The Guardian,* May 10, 2006.

Adiga, Aravind. *White Tiger.* London: Atlantic Books, 2008.

Agamben, Giorgio. *State of Exception.* Trans. Kevin Attell. Chicago: University of Chicago Press, 2005.

Agier, Michel. *Le couloir des exilés. Être étranger dans un monde commun.* Bellecombe-en-Bauges: Editions du Croquant, 2011.

———. "Le camp comme limite et comme espace politique." In *Enfermés dehors. Enquêtes sur le confinement des étrangers,* eds. Carolina Kobelinsky and Chowra Makaremi, 27–40. Bellecombe-en-Bauges: Editions du Croquant, 2009.

———. *Gérer les indésirables. Des camps de réfugiés au gouvernement humanitaire.* Paris: Editions Flammarion, 2008.

Aït-Abbas, Jamila. *La Fatiha: née en France, mariée de force en Algérie.* Paris: Michel Lafon, 2003.

Aldrich, Robert. "Le musée colonial impossible." In *Culture post-coloniale 1961–2006: Traces et mémoires coloniales en France,* ed. Pascal Blanchard and Nicolas Bancel, 83–91. Paris: Editions La Découverte, 2005.

———. "Remembrances of Empires Past." *Journal of Multidisciplinary International Studies* 7.1 (January 2010): http://epress.lib.uts.edu.au/ojs/index.php/portal/article/view/1176/1640, 1–19.

———. *Vestiges of the Colonial Empire in France. Monuments, Museums and Colonial Memories.* New York: Palgrave Macmillan, 2005.

Amara, Fadela. *Ni Putes Ni Soumises.* Paris: Editions La Découverte, 2003.

Amellal, Karim. *Discriminez-moi. Enquête sur nos inégalités,* Paris: Editions Flammarion, 2005.

Améris, Jean-Pierre. *Maman est folle.* Escazal Films, 2007.

Ammi, Kebir. "Mon identité, celle de l'autre." In *Je est un autre. Pour une identité-monde,* eds. Michel Le Bris and Jean Rouaud, 187–193. Paris: Editions Gallimard, 2010.

Amoussou, Sylvestre. *Africa paradis.* Metis/Koffi Productions, 2007.

Amselle, Jean-Loup. *L'Occident décroché: Enquête sur les postcolonialismes.* Paris: Editions Stock, 2008.

———. *Rétrovolutions. Essais sur les primitivismes contemporains.* Paris: Editions Stock, 2010.

Anderson, Gail, ed. *Reinventing the Museum: Historical and Contemporary Perspectives on the Paradigm Shift.* Lanham: AltaMira Press, 2004.

Annaud, Jean-Jacques. *L'Amant.* TF1 Vidéo, 1992.

Aprile, Sylvie, and Stéphane Dufoix. *Les mots de l'immigration.* Paris: Editions Belin, 2009.

Augé, Marc. *Oblivion.* Trans. Marjolijn de Jager. Minneapolis: University of Minnesota Press, 2004.

Azahoum, Boualam. Interview. "L'expérience de DiverCité: Entretien avec Boualam Azahoum." In *Histoire politique des immigrations (post)coloniales. France, 1920–2008,* eds. Ahmed Boubeker and Abdellali Hajjat, 201–206. Paris: Editions Amsterdam, 2008.

Ba, Omar. *Soif d'Europe: Témoignage d'un clandestin.* Paris: Editions du Cygne, 2008.

Badiou, Alain. *De quoi Sarkozy est-il le nom?* Paris: Nouvelles Editions Lignes, 2007.

———. Interview with Frédéric Taddéï. "De quoi Sarkozy est-il le nom? http://www.ldh-toulon.net/spip.php?article2403. December 9, 2007.

———. "Le racisme des intellectuels." *Le Monde,* May 5, 2012. http://www.lemonde.fr/election-presidentielle-2012/article/2012/05/05/le-racisme-des-intellectuels-par-alain-badiou_1696292_1471069.html.

Badiou, Alain, and Alain Finkielkraut. *L'explication. Conversation avec Aude Lancelin.* Paris: Nouvelles Editions Lignes, 2010.

Balakrishnan, Angela, and Pui-Guan Man. "The Best Move Out So the Rest Lose Out." *The Guardian,* July 20, 2007, 21.

Balibar, Etienne. "Le droit de cité ou l'apartheid?" In *Sans-papiers: l'archaïsme fatal,* eds. Etienne Balibar, Monique Chemillier-Gendreau, Jacqueline Costa-Lascoux and Emmanuel Terray, 89–116. Paris: Editions La Découverte, 1999.

———. "Is There a 'Neo-Racism.'" In *Race, Nation, Class: Ambiguous Identities,* eds. Etienne Balibar and Immanuel Wallerstein, 17–28. London: Verso, 1991.

———. "Racism and Crisis." In *Race, Nation, Class: Ambiguous Identities,* eds. Etienne Balibar and Immanuel Wallerstein, 217–227. London: Verso, 1991.

———. "Racisme et politique communautaire: les Roms." *Lignes* 34 (February 2011): 135–144.

———. *We, the People of Europe: Reflections on Transnational Citizenship.* Trans. James Swenson. Princeton, N.J.: Princeton University Press, 2004.

Bancel, Nicolas. ed., *Le retour du colonial. Cultures du Sud* 165 (April–June 2007).

———. "La brèche. Vers la radicalisation des discours publiques." *Mouvements* 1 (2011): 13–28.

———. "L'exposition des Outre-mer au Jardin d'Acclimatation est un scandale" *Le Monde,* March 29, 2011. http://www.lemonde.fr/idees/article/2011/03/28/l-exposition-des-outre-mer-au-jardin-d-acclimatation-est-un-scandale_1497533_3232.html.

———. "Les oubliés du Jardin d'Acclimatation" *Le Monde,* January 27, 2012. http://www.lemonde.fr/idees/article/2012/01/27/les-oublies-du-jardin-d-acclimatation_1635204_3232.html.

Bancel, Nicolas, and Pascal Blanchard. "La colonisation: du débat sur la guerre d'Algérie au discours de Dakar." In *Les Guerres de mémoires: La France et son histoire. Enjeux politiques, controverses historiques, stratégies médiatiques,* eds. Pascal Blanchard and Isabelle Veyrat-Masson, 137–154. Paris: Editions La Découverte, 2008.

———. "Incompatibilité: la CNHI dans le sanctuarire du colonialisme français." *La Cité Nationale de l'Histoire de l'Immigration: Une collection en devenir, Hommes et Migrations* 1267 (2007): 112–127.

———. "Mémoire coloniale: Résistances à l'émergence d'un débat." In *Culture postcoloniale 1961–2006: Traces et mémoires coloniales en France,* eds. Pascal Blanchard and Nicolas Bancel, 22–41. Paris: Editions La Découverte, 2005.

Bancel, Nicolas, Pascal Blanchard, Gilles Boëtsch, Éric Deroo, Sandrine Lemaire, and Charles Forsdick, eds. *Human Zoos: From the Hottentot Venus to Reality Shows.* Liverpool: Liverpool University Press, 2009.

Bancel, Nicolas, Pascal Blanchard, and Françoise Vergès. *La République coloniale: Essai sur une utopie.* Paris: Editions Albin Michel, 2003.

Bancel, Nicolas, Pascal Blanchard, Françoise Vergès, Achille Mbembe, and Florence Bernault, eds. *Ruptures postcoloniales: Les nouveaux visages de la société française.* Paris: Editions La Découverte, 2010.

Bancel, Nicolas, and Herman Lebovics. "Building the History Museum to Stop History: Nicolas Sarkozy's New Presidential Museum of French History." *French Cultural Studies* 22.4 (November 2011): 271–288.

Barjon, Carole. "La métamorphose de Monsieur Claude Guéant." *Nouvel Observateur,* March 24, 2011.

Barlet, Olivier. *African Cinemas: Decolonizing the Gaze.* Trans. Chris Turner. London: Zed Books, 2000.

———. "Les nouveaux films d'Afrique sont-ils africains?" *Cinémas africains, une oasis dans le désert.* Edited by Samuel Lelièvre. *CinémAction* 106 (2003): 43–49.

Barou, Jacques. "La politique française vis-à-vis de l'immigration africaine." In *De l'Afrique à la France. D'une génération à l'autre,* ed. Jacques Barou, 39–64. Paris: Editions Armand Colin, 2011.

Bart, Michel. "Evaluations des campements élicites." http://www.france-info.com/IMG/pdf/7/f/6/Circulaire_du_5aout_2010.pdf. August 5, 2010, 1–7.

Barthes, Roland. "African Grammar." *The Eiffel Tower and Other Mythologies.* Trans. Richard Howard, 103–109. Berkeley: University of California Press, 1997.

Basabose, Philippe. "Partir et conquérir: les apories du nouvel ordre mondial." In *Images et mirages des migrations dans les littératures et les cinémas d'Afrique francophone,* eds. Françoise Naudillon and Jean Ouédraogo, 119–138. Montréal, Québéc: Mémoire d'encrier, 2011.

Bauman, Zygmunt. *Liquid Modernity.* Cambridge, UK: Polity Press, 2000.

Bayart, Jean-François. *Les études postcoloniales. Un carnaval académique.* Paris: Editions Karthala, 2010.

———. "The 'Social Capital' of the Felonious State." In *The Criminalization of the State in Africa,* eds. Jean-François Bayart, Stephen Ellis, and Béatrice Hibou, 32–48. Oxford: James Currey and Bloomington: Indiana University Press, 1999.

Begag, Azouz. "*C'est quand il y en a beaucoup.*" *Nouveaux périls identitaires français.* Paris: Editions Belin, 2011.

———. *Ethnicity and Equality: France in the Balance.* Trans. Alec G. Hargreaves. Lincoln: University of Nebraska Press, 2007.

———. *Le gône du Châaba.* Paris: Editions du Seuil, 1986.

———. *The Shantytown Kid.* Trans. Naïma Wolf and Alec G. Hargreaves. Lincoln: University of Nebraska Press, 2007.
———. *Un mouton dans la baignoire.* Paris: Editions Fayard, 2007.
Begag, Azouz, and Ahmed Beneddif. *Ahmed de Bourgogne.* Paris: Editions du Seuil, 2001.
Behdad, Ali. *A Forgetful Nation: On Immigration and Cultural Identity in the United States.* Durham, NC: Duke University Press, 2005.
Bellil, Samira. *Dans l'enfers des tournantes.* Paris: Editions Denöel, 2003.
Ben Jelloun, Tahar. *Partir.* Paris: Editions Gallimard, 2006.
Benguigui, Yamina. *Inch-Allah Dimanche,* 2001. www.filmmovement.com.
Bennett, Tony. "Exhibition, Difference, and the Logic of Culture." In *Museum Frictions: Public Cultures/Global Transformations,* eds. Ivan Karp, Corinne A. Kratz, Lynn Szwaja, and Tomás Ybarra-Frausto, 46–69. Durham, NC: Duke University Press, 2007.
Benquet, Patrick. *Françafrique. 50 années sous le sceau du secret.* Paris: Compagnie des phares et balises, 2010.
Bernard, Philippe. "L'autre immigration africaine." *Le Monde,* June 26, 2008, 2.
Bernardot, Marc. *Camps d'étrangers.* Bellecombe-en-Bauges: Editions du Croquant, 2008.
———. "Les mutations de la figure du camp." In *Le retour des camps: Sangatte, Lampedusa, Guantanamo,* eds. Olivier Le Cour Grandmaison, Gilles Lhuilier, and Jérôme Valluy, 42–55. Paris: Editions Autrement, 2007.
———. "Rafles et internement des étrangers: les nouvelles guerres de capture." In *Douce France. Rafles, rétentions, expulsions,* ed. Olivier Le Cour Grandmaison, 45–71. Paris: Editions du Seuil, 2009.
Bernault, Florence. "Colonial Syndrome: French Modern and the Deceptions of History." In *Frenchness and the African Diaspora: Identity and Uprising in Contemporary France,* eds. Charles Tshimanga, Didier Gondola, and Peter J. Bloom, 120–145. Bloomington: Indiana University Press, 2009.
Berramdane, Abdelkhaleq. "L'émergence d'une politique européenne commune d'immigration et son externalisation progressive." In *La politique européenne d'immigration,* eds. Abdelkhaleq Berramdane and Jean Rossetto, 39–59. Paris: Editions Karthala, 2009.
Berramdane, Abdelkhaleq, and Jean Rossetto, eds. *La politique européenne de l'immigration.* Paris: Editions Karthala, 2009.
Besson, Éric. "Calais: Éric Besson annonce la fermeture de la 'jungle' avant la semaine prochaine." http://www.immigration.gouv.fr/spip.php?page=comm&id_rubrique=306&id_article=1790. 2009.
———. "Calais: le démantèlement des filières se poursuit." http://www.immigration.gouv.fr/spip.php?page=comm&id_rubrique=306&id_article=1854. 2009.
———. "Débat sur l'identité nationale." http://www.assemblee-nationale.fr/13/cri/2009-2010/20100079.asp#ANCR200900000093-00745. December 8, 2009.
———. "Le débat sur l'identité nationale." www.youtube.com/ministereimmigration#p/u/8/lkNPlgOv-YU. Consulted January 12, 2010.
———. "Démantèlement de la 'jungle' à Calais: point de situation du 28 septembre 2009." http://www.immigration.gouv.fr/spip.php?page=comm&id_rubrique=306&id_article=1812. 2009.
———. "Éric Besson propose cinq mesures pour renforcer l'action de l'Union Européenne contre l'immigration irrégulière." http://www.immigration.gouv.fr/spip.php?page=comm&id_rubrique=306&id_article=1794. 2009.

———. "Faire connaître et partager l'identité nationale." http://www.debatidentitenationale.fr/propositions-d-eric-besson/faire-connaitre-et-partager-l.html. October 31, 2009.

———. *Pour la nation.* Paris: Editions Grasset, 2009.

———. "Projet de loi relatif à l'immigration." http://www.immigration.gouv.fr/IMG/pdf/DP20100401ProjLoi.pdf. April 1, 2010, 1–36.

———. "Valoriser l'identité nationale." http://www.debatidentitenationale.fr/propositions-d-eric-besson/valoriser-l-identite-nationale.html. October 31, 2009.

Besson, Luc. *Banlieue 13.* Europa Corp, TF1 Films Production, Canal +, 2004.

Betbèze, Jean-Paul, and Jean-Dominique Giuliani. *Les 100 mots de l'Europe.* Paris: Presses Universitaires de France, 2011.

Béti, Mongo. *La France contre l'Afrique: Retour au Cameroun.* Paris: Editions La Découverte, 2006 [first pub. 1993].

———. *Main basse sur le Cameroun: Autopsie d'une décolonisation.* Paris: Editions La Découverte, 2003 [first pub. 1972].

Biemann, Ursula. "Writing Video—Writing the World: Videogeographies as Cognitive Medium." http://www.escholarship.org/uc/item/5542b0rw. *Transit* 4.1 (2008). Consulted May 3, 2010.

"Bien mal acquis: La France complice." *Libération,* July 28, 2011, 1–4.

Bigo, Didier. 2009. "Contrôle migratoire et libre circulation en Europe." In *L'enjeu mondial. Les migrations,* eds. Christophe Jaffrelot and Christian Lequesne, 165–176. Paris: Presses de la Fondation Nationale des Sciences Politiques, 2009.

Binebine, Mahi. *Cannibales: Traversée dans l'enfer de Gibraltar.* La Tour d'Aigues: Editions de l'Aube, 2005 [first pub. 1999].

———. *Welcome to Paradise.* Trans. Lulu Norman. London: Granta Books, 2003.

Bisou, Emmanuelle, and Fabienne Kanor. *Jambé Dlo, une histoire antillaise.* Mat Films, 2008.

Blanchard, Pascal. "L'identité, l'historien et le passé colonial: le trio impossible." In *Je est un autre. Pour une identité-monde,* eds. Michel Le Bris and Jean Rouaud, 123–137. Paris: Editions Gallimard, 2010.

Blanchard, Pascal, and Nicolas Bancel. "De l'indigène à l'immigré, le retour du colonial." *Hommes et Migrations* 1207 (May–June 1997): 100–13.

Blanchard, Pascal, Nicolas Bancel, and Sandrine Lemaire, eds. *La fracture coloniale: La société française au prisme de l'héritage colonial.* Paris: Editions La Découverte, 2005.

———. "La fracture coloniale: une crise française." In *La fracture coloniale: La société française au prisme de l'héritage colonial,* eds. Pascal Blanchard, Nicolas Bancel, and Sandrine Lemaire, 9–30. Paris: Editions La Découverte, 2005.

———. "Les origines républicaines de la fracture coloniale." In *La fracture coloniale: La société française au prisme de l'héritage colonial,* eds. Pascal Blanchard, Nicolas Bancel, and Sandrine Lemaire, 33–43. Paris: Editions La Découverte, 2005.

Blanchard, Pascal, Gilles Boëtsch, and Nanette Jacomijn Snoep. "Human Zoos. The Invention of the Savage." In *Human Zoos: The Invention of the Savage,* eds. Pascal Blanchard, Gilles Boëtsch, and Nanette Snoep, 20–53. Paris: Musée du Quai Branly and Arles: Actes Sud, 2011.

Blanchard, Pascal, Sylvie Chalaye, Éric Deroo, Dominic Thomas, and Mahamet Timera. *La France noire. Trois siècles de présences des Afriques, des Caraïbes, de l'océan Indien, et d'Océanie.* Paris: Editions La Découverte, 2011.

Blanchard, Pascal, and Éric Deroo. *Zoos humains.* Bâtisseurs de mémoire, Cités télévision, Films du Village, Arte France, 2002.

Blanchard, Pascal, and Ruth Ginio. "Révolution coloniale: le mythe colonial de Vichy (1940–1944)." In *Culture coloniale en France. De la Révolution française à nos jours,* eds. Pascal Blanchard, Nicolas Bancel, and Sandrine Lemaire, 369–384. Paris: CNRS Editions, 2008.
Blanchard, Pascal, and Isabelle Veyrat-Masson, eds. *Les Guerres de mémoires: La France et son histoire. Enjeux politiques, controverses historiques, stratégies médiatiques.* Paris: Editions La Découverte, 2008.
Blatt, David. "Immigrant Politics in a Republican Nation." In *Post-Colonial Cultures in France,* eds. Alec G. Hargreaves and Mark McKinney, 40–55. London: Routledge, 1997.
Blin, Thierry. *L'invention des sans-papiers.* Paris: Presses Universitaires de France, 2010.
Bloom, Peter. *French Colonial Documentary: Mythologies of Humanitarianism,* Minneapolis: University of Minnesota Press, 2008.
———. "The State of French Cultural Exceptionalism: The 2005 Uprisings and the Politics of Visibility." In *French and the African Diaspora. Identity and Uprising in Contemporary France,* eds. Charles Tschimanga, Didier Gondola, and Peter J. Bloom, 227–247. Bloomington: Indiana University Press, 2009.
Blottière, Mathilde. "Des visas pour l'image." *Télérama horizons* 4 (April 2011): 66–71.
Bocher, Vincent. "Autour de Welcome." *Ceras—revue,* Projet no. 311. http://www.ceras-projet.com/index.php?id=3862. 2009.
Boëtsch, Gilles. "L'université et la recherche face aux enjeux de mémoire: le temps des mutations." In *Les Guerres de mémoires: La France et son histoire. Enjeux politiques, controverses historiques, stratégies médiatiques,* eds. Pascal Blanchard and Isabelle Veyrat-Masson, 187–198. Paris: Editions La Découverte, 2008.
Boilley, Pierre. "Les visions françaises de l'Afrique et des Africains." In *Petit précis de remise à niveau sur l'histoire africaine à l'usage du président Sarkozy,* ed. Adame Ba Konaré, 113–123. Paris: Editions La Découverte, 2008.
Boittin, Jennifer Anne. *Colonial Metropolis: The Urban Grounds of Anti-Imperialism and Feminism in Interwar Paris.* Lincoln: University of Nebraska Press, 2010.
Bolya. *L'Afrique, le maillon faible.* Paris: Le Serpent à Plumes, 2002.
Boubeker, Ahmed. "Outsiders in the French Melting Pot: The Public Construction of Invisibility for Visible Minorities." Trans. Jane Marie Todd. In *Frenchness and the African Diaspora: Identity and Uprising in Contemporary France,* eds. Charles Tshimanga, Didier Gondola, and Peter J. Bloom, 70–88. Bloomington: Indiana University Press, 2009.
———. "La 'petite histoire' d'une génération d'expérience: Du Mouvement beur aux banlieues de l'islam." In *Histoire politique des immigrations (post)coloniales. France, 1920–2008,* eds. Ahmed Boubeker and Abdellali Hajjat, 179–192. Paris: Editions Amsterdam, 2008.
Bouchareb, Rachid. *Indigènes.* Tessalit Productions, Kiss Films, France Cinéma, 2006.
Bouguerra, Mohamed Ridha, and Sahiba Bouguerra. *Histoire de la littérature du Maghreb: littérature francophone.* Paris: Ellipses, 2010.
Boulin, Jean-Eric. *Supplément au roman national,* Paris: Editions Stock, 2006.
———. *La Question Blanche,* Paris: Editions Stock, 2008.
Bourdieu, Pierre. *Masculine Domination.* Stanford: Stanford University Press, 2001.
Bourdieu, Pierre, et al. *The Weight of the World: Social Suffering in Contemporary Society.* Trans. Priscilla Parkhurst, Susan Emanuel, Joe Johnson, and Shoggy T. Waryn. Stanford: Stanford University Press, 2000 [first pub. 1993].

Bourmaud, Daniel. "La nouvelle politique africaine de la France à l'épreuve." *Esprit* 317 (August–September 2005): 17–27.
Boyle, T. Coraghessan. 1995. *The Tortilla Curtain.* New York: Penguin Books.
Brady, Hugo. *EU Migration Policy.* www.cer.org.uk/pdf/briefing_813.pdf. 2008, 1–20.
Braudel, Fernand. *L'identité de la France: les hommes et les choses.* Paris: Editions Flammarion, 1990.
Breytenbach, Breyten. "On Progress." *Notes from the Middle of the World,* 85–93. Chicago: Haymarket Books, 2009.
Bribosia, Emmanuel, and Andrea Rea. *Les nouvelles migrations, un enjeu européen.* Brussels, Belgium: Editions Complexe, 2001.
Brice, Catherine. "Monuments: pacificateurs ou agitateurs de mémoires." In *Les Guerres de mémoires: La France et son histoire. Enjeux politiques, controverses historiques, stratégies médiatiques,* eds. Pascal Blanchard and Isabelle Veyrat-Masson, 199–208. Paris: Editions La Découverte, 2008.
Brossat, Olivier. "L'espace-camp et l'exception furtive." *Lignes* 26 (2008): 5–22.
Brown, Wendy. *Murs: Les murs de séparation et le déclin de la souveraineté étatique.* Paris: Les Prairies Ordinaires, 2009.
Brown, William. "Negotiating the Invisible." In William Brown, Dina Iordanova and Leshu Torchin, eds., *Moving People, Moving Images: Cinema and Trafficking in the New Europe,* 16–48. St. Andrews: St Andrews Film Studies Publishing, 2010.
Brown, William, Dina Iordanova, and Leshu Torchin, eds. *Moving People, Moving Images: Cinema and Trafficking in the New Europe.* St. Andrews: St Andrews Film Studies Publishing, 2010.
Brubaker, *Citizenship and Nationhood in France and Germany.* Cambridge: Harvard University Press, 1992.
Bruckner, Pascal. *La tyrannie de la pénitence. Essai sur le masochisme occidental.* Paris: Editions Grasset, 2006.
Brumet, Amélie, and Philippe Goma. *Des Noirs et des hommes.* Les Films Grains de Sable, 2009.
Brunschwig, Henri. *Le partage de l'Afrique noire.* Paris: Editions Flammarion, 1971.
Buntinx, Gustavo, ed. *Museum Frictions: Public Cultures/Global Transformations.* Durham, NC: Duke University Press, 2006.
Cahn, Claude, and Elspeth Guild. "Recent Migration of Roma in Europe." OSCE High Commissioner on National Minorities, Council of Europe Commissioner for Human Rights. December 10, 2008, 1–86.
Caligaris, Nicole, and Eric Pessan, eds. *Il me sera difficile de venir te voir: Correspondances littéraires sur les conséquences de la politique française d'immigration.* La Roque d'Anthéron: Vents d'ailleurs, 2008.
Camara, Laye. *L'enfant noir.* Paris: Editions Plon, 1953.
Camiscioli, Elsa. *Reproducing the French Race: Immigration, Intimacy, and Embodiment in the Early Twentieth Century.* Durham, NC: Duke University Press, 2009.
Cantet, Laurent. *Entre les murs.* Haut et Court, France 2 cinéma, Canal+, 2008.
Carisoni, Caroline. "Faïza, dans un monde de oufs." *Les Clès* 676 (September 7–13, 2006).
Carrère, Violaine. "Sangatte et les nasses aux frontières de l'Europe." *Ceras—revue,* Projet no. 272. http://www.ceras-projet.com/index.php?id=1764 (2002).
———. "Sangatte: un toit pour les fantômes." *Hommes et Migrations* 1238 (2002): 13–22.
CARSED. *Le retour de la race: Contre les "statistiques ethniques."* La Tour d'Aigues: Editions de l'Aube, 2009.

Casanova, Pascale. *The World Republic of Letters.* Trans. M. B. DeBevoise. Cambridge: Harvard University Press, 2004.
Cassaigne, Bertrand. "Des camps pour les migrants, urgence et suspicion." *Ceras—revue,* Projet no. 308. http://www.ceras-projet.com/index.php?id=3472. 2009.
"La cellule africaine de l'Elysée." http://reseaugaribaldi.info/wp-content/uploads/2011/05/La-cellule-africaine-de-lElysée.pdf. 2011, 1–13.
Cette France-là. "Après Sangatte: l'occultation des inexpulsables." In *Cette France-là,* Vol. 1, 198–204. Paris: Editions La Découverte, 2009.
———. "La crise de la politique d'immigration." In *Cette France-là.* Vol. 2. Paris: Editions La Découverte, 2010, 3–7.
———. "La démocratie phobique ou comment se soustraire aux analogies embarrassantes." In *Cette France-là.* Vol. 2. Paris: Editions La Découverte, 2010, 418–422.
———. "Eléments de langage. Trois rhétoriques pour un même acharnement." *Xénophobie d'en haut. Le choix d'une droite éhontée.* Paris: Editions La Découverte, 2012, 27–47.
———. *Sans-papiers et préfets. La culture du résultat en portraits.* Paris: Editions La Découverte, 2012.
———. "La technologie du soupçon: tests osseux, tests de pilosité, tests ADN." In *Cette France-là,* Vol. 1. Paris: Editions La Découverte, 2009, 157–159.
Chaabita, Rachid, ed. *Migration clandestine africaine vers l'Europe. Un espoir pour les uns, un problème pour les autres.* Paris: Editions L'Harmattan, 2010.
Charaudeau, Patrick. *Entre populisme et peopolisme. Comment Sarkozy a gagné!* Paris: Librairie Vuibert, 2008.
Charef, Mehdi. *Le thé au harem d'Archi Ahmed.* Paris: Editions Mercure de France, 1983.
———. *Tea in the Harem.* Trans. Ed Hemery. London: Serpent's Tail, 1989.
Chemillier-Gendreau, Monique. 2008. Interview. *Diasporiques* 2 (2008): 10–18.
———. *L'injustifiable. Les politiques françaises de l'immigration.* Paris: Editions du Seuil, 1998.
Chirac, Jacques. "Address by Jacques Chirac, President of the Republic, at the opening of the Quai Branly Museum." http://www.ambafrance-uk.org/Speech-by-M-Jacques-Chirac,7357.html. June 20, 2006, 1–6.
Choay, Françoise. "Un nouveau Luna Park était-il nécéssaire?" "Le moment du Quai Branly." *Le Débat* 147 (November–December 2007): 57–64.
Chrétien, Jean-Pierre. "Le discours de Dakar. Le poids idéologique d'un 'africanisme' traditionnel." *Esprit* 339 (November 2007): 163–181.
Chrisafis, Angelique. "France impounds African autocrats' 'ill-gotten gains'." *The Guardian,* February 6, 2012.
Chroniques pour une société annoncée. Paris: Editions Stock, 2007.
Cissé, Madjiguène. *Parole de sans-papiers.* Paris: Editions La Dispute/Snédit, 1999.
Clair, Lucie. "Écrire, quoi d'autre?" *Le Matricule des anges: Le mensuel de la littérature contemporaine* 107 (October 2009): 20–24.
———. Interview. "La discrète empathie." *Le Matricule des anges: Le mensuel de la littérature contemporaine* 107 (October 2009): 26–29.
———. "Tenir tête." *Le Matricule des anges: Le mensuel de la littérature contemporaine,* 107 (October 2009): 25.
Clifford, James. "Quai Branly in Process." *October* 120 (Spring 2007): 3–23.
———. *Routes: Travel and Translation in the Late Twentieth Century.* Cambridge, MA: Harvard University Press, 1997.
Cohen, William B. *The French Encounter with Africans: White Response to Blacks, 1530–1880.* Bloomington: Indiana University Press, 1980.

CNHI Research Council. "Immigration et identité nationale: une association inacceptable." http://www.ldh-toulon.net/spip.php?article2047.

Comité pour la mémoire de l'esclavage, Mémoires de la traite négrière, de l'esclavage et de leurs abolitions. Paris: Editions La Découverte, 2005.

"A Common Immigration Policy for Europe: Principles, Actions, and Tools." http://europa.eu/rapid/pressReleasesAction.do?reference=MEMO/08/402&format=HTML&aged=0&language=EN&guiLanguage=en. June 17, 2008.

Conklin, Alice. *A Mission to Civilize: The Republican Ideal of Empire in France and West Africa, 1895–1930.* Stanford, CA: Stanford University Press, 1997.

Convents, Guido. *Images et Démocratie: Les Congolais face au cinéma et à l'audiovisuel: Une histoire politico-culturelle du Congo des Belges jusqu'à la République Démocratique du Congo (1896–2006)*, 359–364. Holsbeek, Belgium: Afrika Film Festival, 2006.

Coombes, Annie E. "Museums and the Formation of National and Cultural Identities." In *Museum Studies: An Anthology of Contexts*, ed. Bettina Messias Carbonell, 231–246. Oxford: Blackwell Publishing, 2004.

Coordination française pour le droit d'asile (CFDA). *La loi des "jungles." La situation des exilés sur le littoral de la Manche et de la Mer du Nord.* http://cfda.rezo.net/download/Rapport_CFDA_092008.pdf. September 2008, 1–186.

———. *The Law of the "Jungle": The Situation of Exiles on the shore of the Channel and the North Sea: Recommendations.* http://cfda.rezo.net/download/The%20law%20of%20Jungles%20recommendations%2009%2008.pdf. September 2008, 1–4.

Costa-Gavras. *L'Eden à l'ouest.* K. G. Productions, Pathé, France 3, 2009.

Cottenet-Hage, Madeleine. "Decolonizing Images: Soleil O *and the Cinema of Med Hondo.*" In *Cinema, Colonialism, Postcolonialism: Perspectives from the French and Francophone Worlds*, ed. Dina Sherzer, 173–187. Austin: University of Texas Press, 1996.

———. "Images of France in Francophone African Films (1978–1998)." In *Focus on African Films*, ed. Françoise Pfaff, 107–123. Bloomington: Indiana University Press, 1998.

Coquery-Vidrovitch, Catherine. "Colonisation, coopération, partenariat. Les différentes étapes (1950–2000)." In *Étudiants africains en France (1951–2001)*, ed. Michel Sot, 29–48. Paris: Editions Karthala, 2002.

———. *La Découverte de* l'Afrique. Paris: Editions René Julliard, 1965.

———. *Enjeux politiques de l'histoire coloniale.* Marseille: Editions Agone, 2009.

———. "Le musée du Quai Branly ou l'histoire oubliée." In *Petit précis de remise à niveau sur l'histoire africaine à l'usage du président Sarkozy*, ed. Adame Ba Konaré, 125–137. Paris: Editions La Découverte, 2008.

———. *Petite histoire de l'Afrique. L'Afrique au sud du Sahara de la préhistoire à nos jours.* Paris: Paris: Editions La Découverte, 2011.

Coquio, Catherine, ed. *Retour du colonial: disculpation et réhabilitation de l'histoire coloniale.* Nantes: Librairie l'Atalante, 2008.

Costa-Gavras. 2009. *L'Eden à l'ouest.* K. G. Productions, Pathé, France 3.

Coulin, Delphine. *Samba pour la France.* Paris: Editions du Seuil, 2011.

Courau, Henri. *Ethnologie de la* Forme-camp *de Sangatte. De l'exception à la régulation.* Paris: Editions des Archives Contemporaines, 2007.

Crane, Susan A. "Memory, Distortion, and History in the Museum." In *Museum Studies: An Anthology of Contexts*, ed. Bettina Messias Carbonell, 318–334. Oxford: Blackwell Publishing, 2004.

Crouillère, Monique. "Cinéma africain et immigration." In *Images et mirages des migrations dans les littératures et les cinémas d'Afrique francophone*, eds. Françoise Naudillon and Jean Ouédraogo, 11–30. Montréal, Québéc: Mémoire d'encrier, 2011.

Dacheux, Jean-Pierre, and Bernard Delemotte. *Roms de France, Roms en France. Le peuple du* voyage. Montreuil: Editions Cédis, 2010.

Dadié, Bernard. *An African in Paris.* Trans. Karen Hatch. Urbana: University of Illinois Press, 1994.

———. *Un nègre à Paris.* Paris: Editions Présence Africaine, 1959.

Daeninckx, Didier. *Lumière noire.* Paris: Editions Gallimard, 1987.

Dakhlia, Jocelyne. "La France dedans dehors." *Lignes* 25 (March 2008): 160–176.

Dal Lago, Alessandro. *Non-Persone: L'esclusione dei migranti in una società globale, interzone.* Milan, Italy: Feltrinelli, 1999.

———. *Non-Persons: The Exclusion of Migrants in a Global Society.* Trans. Marie Orton. Milan, Italy: IPOC Press, 2009.

Daniel, Serge. *Les routes clandestines: L'Afrique des immigrés et des passeurs.* Paris: Hachette Littératures, 2008.

Daum, Christophe, and Isaïe Dougnon, eds. *L'Afrique en mouvement,* special dossier, *Hommes et Migrations* 1279 (May–June 2009): 4–164.

Davies, Peter. *The National Front in France: Ideology, Discourse and Power.* London: Routledge, 1999.

Davis, Mike. *Planet of Slums.* London: Verso, 2006.

De Bruyn, Olivier. Interview with director Philippe Lioret. "Calais, c'est notre frontière mexicaine à nous." http://www.rue89.com/la-bande-du-cine/2009/03/10/philippe-lioret-calais-est-notre-frontiere-mexicaine, 2009.

De Cock, Laurence. "Afrique." In *Comment Nicolas Sarkozy écrit l'histoire de France,* eds. Laurence de Cock, Fanny Madeline, Nicolas Offenstadt, and Sophie Wahnich, 30–32. Marseille: Editions Agone, 2008.

———. "Introduction." In *Comment Nicolas Sarkozy écrit l'histoire de France,* eds. Laurence de Cock, Fanny Madeline, Nicolas Offenstadt, and Sophie Wahnich, 15–19. Marseille: Editions Agone, 2008.

De Cock, Laurence Fanny Madeline, Nicolas Offenstadt, and Sophie Wahnich, eds. *Comment Nicolas Sarkozy écrit l'histoire de France.* Marseille: Editions Agone, 2008.

"Décret n° 2010–1444 du 25 novembre 2010 relatif aux attributions du ministre de l'intérieur, de l'outre-mer, des collectivités territoriales et de l'immigration." http://www.legifrance.gouv.fr/affichTexte.do;jsessionid=?cidTexte=JORFTEXT000023137326&dateTexte=&oldAction=rechJO&categorieLien=id.

De Gaulle, Charles. "Discours de Brazzaville." http://www.charles-de-gaulle.org/pages/temp/en/the-man/home/speeches/speech-made-by-general-de-gaulle-at-the-opening-of-the-brazzaville-conference-on-january-30th-1944..php?searchresult=1&sstring=Brazzaville. January 30, 1944.

De Latour, Eliane. *Les Oiseaux du ciel.* Les Films de Cinéma, Autonomous Limited, 2006.

Delbanco, Andrew. "Scandals of Higher Education." *New York Review of Books,* March 29, 2007, 45–46.

Delbez, Maurice. *Un Gosse de la butte.* Les Films de mai, 1964.

Deleporte, Sarah Frohning. "Trois musées, une question, une République." In *La fracture coloniale: La société française au prisme de l'héritage colonial,* eds. Pascal Blanchard, Nicolas Bancel, and Sandrine Lemaire, 105–111. Paris: Editions La Découverte, 2005.

De L'Estoile, Benoît. "L'oubli de l'héritage colonial." *Le Débat* 147 (November–December 2007): 91–99.

———. "Étranges reflets dans la vitrine." *Télérama horizons* 4 (April 2011): 24–27.

"Délit de solidarité: la réalité." *Plein droit: La revue du GISTI* 83 (2009): 1–8.

Deltombe, Thomas, Manuel Domergue, and Jacob Tatsitsa. *Kamerun! Une guerre cachée aux origines de la Françafrique, 1948–1971*. Paris: Editions La Découverte, 2011.

De Luca, Erri. *Solo andata*. Milan, Italy: Feltrinelli, 2005.

De Maistre, Gilles. *La Citadelle Europe*. Tetra Media, 2003.

Dembélé, Demba Moussa. "Méconnaissance ou provocation délibérée." In *L'Afrique répond à Sarkozy: Contre le discours de Dakar*, ed. Makhily Gassama, 87–122. Paris: Editions Philippe Rey, 2008.

Deroo, Éric, and Pascal Blanchard. *Paris couleurs*. Image et Compagnie, France 3, France 5, 2005.

De Roux, Emmanuel. "Un public nouveau pour le Quai Branly." www.lemonde.fr, June 1, 2007.

De Rudder, Véronique, ed. *L'Inégalité raciste. L'universalité républicaine à l'épreuve*. Paris: Presses Universitaires de France, 2000.

De Tapia, Stéphane. *The Euro-Mediterranean migration system*. Strasbourg: Editions du Conseil de l'Europe, 2008.

Devi, Ananda. "Flou identitaire." In *Je est un autre. Pour une identité-monde*, eds. Michel Le Bris and Jean Rouaud, 179–186. Paris: Editions Gallimard, 2010.

Diallo, Rokhaya. *Racisme: Mode d'emploi*. Paris: Editions Larousse, 2011.

Dias, Nélia. "Le musée du quai Branly: une généalogie." *Le Débat* 147 (November–December 2007): 65–79.

Diawara, Manthia. *African Cinema: Politics and Culture*. Bloomington: Indiana University Press, 1992.

———. *In Search of Africa*. Cambridge: Harvard University Press, 2000.

———. "Toward a Regional Imaginary in Africa." In *The Cultures of Globalization*, eds. Fredric Jameson & Masao Miyoshi, 103–124. Durham, NC: Duke University Press, 1998.

———. *We Won't Budge: An African exile in the World*. New York: Basic Civitas Books, 2003.

Dictionnaire critique du "Sarkozysme." Lignes 33 (October 2010).

Diome, Fatou. *Celles qui attendent*. Paris: Editions Flammarion, 2010.

———. *Inasouvies*. Editions Flammarion, 2008.

———. *Kétala*. Paris: Editions Flammarion, 2006.

———. *La préférence nationale*. Paris: Editions Présence Africaine, 2001.

———. *Le ventre de l'Atlantique*. Paris: Editions Anne Carrière, 2003.

Diop, Ababacar. *Dans la peau d'un sans-papiers*. Paris: Editions du Seuil, 1997.

Diop, Boubacar Boris, Odile Tobner, and François-Xavier Verschave. *Négrophobie*. Paris: Editions les Arènes, 2005.

Directive 2008/115/EC of the European Parliament and of the Council of 16 December 2008 on common standards and procedures in Member States for returning illegally staying third-country nationals. http://eur-lex.europa.eu/LexUriServ/LexUriServ.do?uri=OJ:L:2008:348:0098:0107:EN:PDF. December 16, 2008.

"Discours de Dakar et de Tanger: Les deux Afriques de Sarkozy." http://www.lefaso.net/spip.php?article24161&rubrique7. October 25, 2007.

Djaïdani, Rachid. *Boumkœur*. Paris: Editions du Seuil, 2000.

———. *Viscéral*. Paris: Editions du Seuil, 2007.

Djouder, Ahmed. *Désintégration*. Paris: Editions Stock, 2006.

Dobie, Madeleine, and Rebecca Saunders, eds. *France in Africa/Africa in France. Comparative Studies of South Asia, Africa, and the Middle East* 26.2 (2006).

Donadey, Anne, and H. Adlai Murdoch, eds. *Postcolonial Theory and Francophone Literary Studies*. Gainesville: University Press of Florida, 2005.

Doukouré, Cheik. *Paris selon Moussa.* Bako Productions, 2002.

Dozon, Jean-Pierre. *Frères et sujets. La France et l'Afrique en perspective.* Paris: Editions Flammarion, 2003.

———. "L'État franco-africain." *Les Temps modernes* 620–621 (August-November 2002): 261–288.

———. "Une décolonisation en trompe-l'œil (1956–2006)." In *Culture coloniale en France. De la Révolution à nos jours,* eds. Pascal Blanchard, Nicolas Bancel, and Sandrine Lemaire, 537–544. Paris: CNRS Editions, 2008.

Dhoukar, Hedi. "Les thèmes du cinéma beur." *CinémAction/Hommes et Migrations 56* (1990): 152–160.

Drivers, Sandrine, and Flora Galuchot. "D'une rive à l'autre." In *Je de mémoire.* Paris: La Médiathèque des trois mondes, 2002.

Dubois, Laurent. *A Colony of Citizens: Revolution and Slave Emancipation in the French Caribbean, 1787–1804.* Chapel Hill: University of North Carolina Press, 2004.

———. "Haunting Delgrès." *Radical History Review* 78 (2000): 166–177.

———. "Republic at Sea: On the margins of the New Europe." *Transition* 79 (1999): 64–79.

———. *Soccer Empire: The World Cup and the Future of France.* Berkeley: University of California Press, 2010.

Dubreuil, Laurent. *L'empire du langage: Colonies et francophonie.* Paris: Editions Hermann, 2008.

———. ed. *Faut-il être postcolonial?* Special issue of *Labyrinthe: Atelier Interdisciplinaire* 24. Paris: Editions Maisonneuve & Larose, 2006.

Duchesne, Sophie. "Quelle identité européenne?" *Cahiers français* 342 (2008): 17–21.

Duclert, Vincent. "L'Etat et les historiens." *Regards sur l'actualité* 325 (November 2006): 5–15.

Duffy, Terence M. "Museums of 'Human Suffering' and the Struggle for Human Rights." In *Museum Studies: An Anthology of Contexts,* ed. Bettina Messias Carbonell, 117–122. Oxford: Blackwell Publishing, 2004.

Dulucq, Sophie, Jean-François Klein, and Benjamin Stora. *Les mots de la colonisation.* Toulouse: Presses Universitaires du Mirail, 2008.

Dumont, Gérard-François. "La politique d'immigration de l'Union européenne: une stratégie volontaire ou contrainte?" In *La politique européenne d'immigration,* eds. Abdelkhaleq Berramdane and Jean Rossetto, 11–31. Paris: Editions Karthala, 2009.

Duncan, Carol. "Art Museums and the Ritual of Citizenship." In *Exhibiting Cultures: The Poetics and Politics of Museum Display,* eds. Ivan Karp and Steven S. Lavine, 88–103. Washington, DC: Smithsonian, 1991.

Dupaigne, Bernard. *Le Scandale des arts premiers: la véritable histoire du quai Branly.* Paris: Editions Mille et une nuits, 2006.

Easterly, William. "Foreign Aid for Scoundrels." *New York Review of Books,* November 25, 2010, 37–38.

Edwards, Brent Hayes. *The Practice of Diaspora: Literature, Translation, and the Rise of Black Internationalism.* Cambridge, MA: Harvard University Press, 2003.

Edwards, Elizabeth, Chris Gosden, and Ruth Phillips, eds. *Sensible Objects: Colonialism, Museums and Material Culture.* Oxford: Berg, 2006.

Einaudi, Jean-Luc. "Le crime: violence coloniale en métropole (1954–1961)." In *Culture coloniale en France. De la Révolution française à nos jours,* eds. Pascal Blanchard, Nicolas Bancel, and Sandrine Lemaire, 471–479. Paris: CNRS Editions, 2008.

———. *La bataille de Paris: 17 octobre 1961.* Paris: Editions du Seuil, 1991.

Elalamy, Youssouf Amine. 2001. *Les clandestins.* Vauvert: Editions Au Diable Vauvert, 2001.

Elias, Norbert, and John L. Scotson. *Logiques de l'exclusion.* Paris: Editions Fayard, 1997 [first pub. 1965].

"The *encampment* in Europe and around the Mediterranean Sea." http://migreurop.org. 2009.

Equer, Jérôme. *La jungle. Calais, un déshonneur européen.* Paris: Editions Jean-Paul Rocher, 2011.

Essomba, J.R. *Le paradis du Nord.* Paris: Editions Présence Africaine, 1996.

Eurin, Philippe. *La Jungle de Calais. Misère et solidarité.* Paris: Editions L'Harmattan, 2010.

"E.U. Warns France of Action over Roma." http://www.bbc.co.uk/news/world-europe-11437361. September 29, 2010.

European Union. "Africa-EU Migration, Mobility and Employment (MME) Partnership." http://www.africa-eu-partnership.org/node/1744/. December 2007.

———. "Africa-EU Strategic Partnership." www.africa-eu-partnership.org/partnerships/africa-eu-strategic-partnership. November 29–30, 2010.

———. "Communication on Migration." http://www.statewatch.org/news/2011/may/eu-com-migration-com-248-11.pdf. May 4, 2011, 1–25.

———. "A dialogue for migration, mobility and security with the southern Mediterranean countries" http://ec.europa.eu/home-affairs/news/intro/docs/110524/292/1_EN_ACT_part1_v12.pdf. May 24, 2011, 1–13.

———. "European Pact on Immigration and Asylum." Document 13440/08. http://www.immigration.gouv.fr/IMG/pdf/Plaquette_EN.pdf. October 15–16, 2008, 1–10.

———. "Europeans' perception on the state of the economy." http://ec.europa.eu/public_opinion/archives/eb/eb75/eb75_en.pdf. August 2011, 1–25.

———. "A partnership for democracy and shared prosperity for democracy and shared prosperity with the Southern Mediterranean." http://eeas.europa.eu/euromed/docs/com2011_200_en.pdf. March 8, 2011, 1–17.

Evaristo, Bernardine. *Blonde Roots.* London: Hamish Hamilton, 2008.

Fabre, Michel. *From Harlem to Paris: Black American Writers in France, 1840–1980.* Urbana and Chicago: University of Illinois Press, 1991.

Falaize, Benoît, and Françoise Lantheaume. "Entre pacification et reconnaissance: les manuels scolaires et la consurrence des mémoires." In *Les Guerres de mémoires: La France et son histoire. Enjeux politiques, controverses historiques, stratégies médiatiques,* eds. Pascal Blanchard and Isabelle Veyrat-Masson, 177–186. Paris: Editions La Découverte, 2008.

Fall, Aminata Sow. *L'appel des arènes.* Dakar: Les Nouvelles Editions Africaines, 1982.

Fanon, Frantz. *The Wretched of the Earth.* Trans. Richard Philcox. New York: Grove Press, 2004 [first pub. 1961].

Fassin, Didier. "Frontières extérieures, frontières intérieures." In *Les nouvelles frontières de la société française,* ed. Didier Fassin, 5–24. Paris: Editions La Découverte: 2010.

———. ed. *Les nouvelles frontières de la société française.* Paris: Editions La Découverte, 2010.

Fassin, Didier, and Éric Fassin, eds. *De la question sociale à la question raciale: Représenter la société française.* Paris: Editions la Découverte, 2006.

Fassin, Éric. *Démocratie précaire. Chroniques de la déraison d'État.* Paris: Editions La Découverte, 2012.

———. "'Immigration et délinquance': la construction d'un problème entre politique, journalisme et sociologie." *Cités: Philosophie, Politique, Histoire* 46 (2011) 69–85.

———. "Pourquoi les Roms?" *Lignes* 35 (June 2011): 115–122.
Faye, Jean-Pierre. "Langages totalitaires: Fascistes et nazis." *Cahiers internationaux de sociologies* 36 (1964): 75–100.
Fielder, Adrian. "Poaching on Public Space: Urban Autonomous Zones in French *Banlieue* Films." In *Cinema and the City: Film and Urban Societies in a Global Context,* eds. Mark Shiel and Tony Fitzmaurice, 270–281. Oxford: Blackwell, 2001.
"Fillon se paye Rama Yade et Guaino." http://www.lepost.fr/article/2009/11/25/1808877_rama-yade-et-ses-racines-senegalaises-2-deputes-ump-attaquent.html. November 3, 2009.
"Final statement—Barcelona Process: Union for the Mediterranean." http://www.aer.eu/fileadmin/user_upload/MainIssues/International_Solidarity/2009/Final_Statement_Mediterranean_Union_EN.pdf. 3–4. November, 2008, 1–22.
Foccart, Jacques. *Foccart parle.* Interviews with Philippe Gaillard. Vols. I–II. Paris: Editions Fayard/Jeune Afrique, 1995 and 1997.
———. *Journal de l'Élysée.* Vols. I-V. Paris: Editions Fayard/Jeune Afrique, 1997–2001.
Foix, Alain. *Noir de Toussaint Louverture à Barack Obama.* Paris: Galaade Editions, 2009.
Fonkoua, Romuald-Blaise. "Ecrire la banlieue: la littérature ds 'invisibles.'" In *Le retour du colonial,* ed. Nicolas Bancel, *Cultures du Sud* 165 (April–June 2007): 89–96.
Forbes, Jill, and Michael Kelly, eds. *French Cultural Studies: An Introduction.* Oxford: Oxford University Press, 1995.
Forest, Philippe. "Notre âme n'est jamais une." In *Je est un autre. Pour une identité-monde,* eds. Michel Le Bris and Jean Rouaud, 67–79. Paris: Editions Gallimard, 2010.
Forsdick, Charles, and David Murphy, eds. *Francophone Postcolonial Studies.* London: Arnold, 2003.
———. Eds. *Postcolonial Thought in the French-Speaking World.* Liverpool: Liverpool University Press, 2009.
Forsdick, Charles. "Sarkozy in Port-au-Prince." *French Studies* Bulletin 32.118 (2011): 4–8.
Foutoyet, Samuël. *Nicolas Sarkozy ou la Françafrique décomplexée.* Brussels, Belgium: Editions Tribord, 2009.
"La Francophonie dans Le Monde, 2006–2007." http://www.francophonie.org/IMG/pdf/La_francophonie_dans_le_monde_2006-2007.pdf. 2007, 1–329.
Freedman, Jane. *Immigration and Insecurity in France.* Aldershot, UK: Ashgate, 2004.
Frisch, Max. "United Nations Convention on Human Rights." http://portal.unesco.org/shs/en/files/2874/11163348401InfoKit_en.pdf/InfoKit%2Ben.pdf. 2003.
Frontext. http://www.frontex.europa.eu/.
Gafaiti, Hafid. "Nationalism, Colonialism, and Ethnic Discourse in the Construction of French Identity.'" In *French Civilization and Its Discontents: nationalism, colonialism, race,* eds. Tyler Stovall and Georges Van Den Abbeele, 189–212. Lanham: Lexington Books, 2003.
Gallo, Max. *L'âme de la France. Une histoire de la nation des origines à nos jours.* Paris: Editions Fayard, 2007.
———. *Fier d'être français.* Paris: Editions Fayard, 2006.
Gassama, Makhily, ed. *L'Afrique répond à Sarkozy: Contre le discours de Dakar.* Paris: Editions Philippe Rey, 2008.
———. *50 ans après, quelle indépendance pour l'Afrique?* Paris: Editions Philippe Rey, 2010.
Gauthier, Guy. *Le documentaire un autre cinéma.* Paris: Editions Armand Colin, 2008.
Gatlif, Tony. "Tsiganes, Gitans, Manouches. La fin du voyage." *Ravages* 5 (April 2011): 30–45.

Gatti, Fabrizio. *Bilal sur la route des clandestins.* Trans. Jean-Luc Defromont. Paris: Editions Liana Levi, 2008.

———. "I was a slave in Puglia." http://espresso.repubblica.it/dettaglio/I%20was%20a%20slave%20in%20Puglia/1373950. September 4, 2006.

Gaudé, Laurent. *Eldorado.* Arles: Actes Sud, 2006.

———. *Eldorado.* Trans. Adriana Hunter. San Francisco: MacAdam/Cage, 2008.

Gauthier, Guy. *Le documentaire un autre cinéma.* Paris: Editions Armand Colin, 2008.

Geisser, Vincent. "Adieu Bonaparte, bonjour Nicolas!" http://oumma.com/Adieu-Bonaparte-bonjour-Nicolas. November-December 2008.

Gélas, Juan, and Pascal Blanchard. *Noirs de France de 1889 à nos jours: une histoire de France.* Compagnie Phares et Balises, INA, l'Acsé/France Television, TV5, and LCP, 2011.

Gellner, Ernest. *Nations and Nationalism.* Ithaca, NY: Cornell University Press, 1983.

George, Sylvain. *Qu'ils reposent en révolte (Des figures de guerre I).* Noir Production/Independencia Distribution, 2010.

German Marshall Fund. "Transatlantic Trends—immigration." http://trends.gmfus.org/immigration/doc/TTI2010_English_Key.pdf. 2010, 1–43.

Gèze, François. "L'héritage colonial au cœur de la politique étrangère française." In *La fracture coloniale: La société française au prisme de l'héritage colonial,* eds. Pascal Blanchard, Nicolas Bancel, and Sandrine Lemaire, 155–163. Paris: Editions La Découverte, 2005.

Giebelhausen, Michaela. "Architecture *is* the Museum." In *New Museum Theory and Practice,* ed. Janet Marstine, 41–63. Oxford: Blackwell, 2006.

Gilou, Thomas. *Black Mic Mac.* DVD Studiocanal, 1986.

Gilroy, Paul. *Black Britain: A Photographic History.* London: Saqi Books/Getty Images, 2007.

———. "Foreword: Migrancy, Culture, and a New Map of Europe." In *Blackening Europe: The African American Presence,* ed. Heike Raphael-Hernandez, xi–xxii. London: Routledge, 2004.

———. *There Ain't No Black in the Union Jack: The Cultural Politics of Race and Nation.* Chicago: University of Chicago Press, 1987.

Glissant, Edouard. *Mémoires des esclavages: La fondation d'un Centre national pour la mémoire des esclavages et leurs abolitions.* Paris: Editions Gallimard, 2007.

Glissant, Edouard, and Patrick Chamoiseau. *Quand les murs tombent. L'identité nationale hors-la-loi.* Paris: Galaade Editions, 2007.

Godoy, Julio. "How beautiful was my colony." Inter Press Service News Agency, http://ipsnews.net/africa/nota.asp?idnews=34672. Consulted September 15, 2006.

Golan, Tamar. "A Certain Mystery: How can France do everything that it does in Africa-and get away with it?" *African Affairs* 80.318 (January 1981): 3–11.

Goldberg, Daniel. "Proposition de loi visant à supprimer le délit de solidarité." http://www.assemblee-nationale.fr/13/propositions/pion1542.asp. 2009.

Goldwater, Robert. "The Development of Ethnological Museums." In *Museum Studies: An Anthology of Contexts,* ed. Bettina Messias Carbonell, 133–138. Oxford: Blackwell Publishing, 2004.

Gomis, Alain. *L'Afrance.* Mille et une Productions, 2001.

Gondola, Didier. *L'Africanisme: la crise d'une illusion.* Paris: Editions L'Harmattan, 2007.

———. "Dream and Drama: The Search for Elegance among Congolese Youth." *African Studies Review* 42.1 (1999): 23–48.

Gonin, Patrick, ed. *Les migrations subsahariennes.* Special dossier, *Hommes et Migrations* 1286–1287 (July–October 2010): 4–278.

González, Jennifer A. *Subject to Display: Reframing Race in Contemporary Installation Art.* Boston: MIT Press, 2008.

Goumane, Dembo. *Dembo Story.* Paris: Editions Hachette, 2006.

Gourévitch, Jean-Paul. *L'Afrique, le Fric, la France. L'aide, la dette, l'immigration, l'avenir: vérités et mensonges.* Paris: Editions Le Pré aux Clercs, 1997.

Goytisolo, Juan. "Défense de l'hybridité ou La pureté, mère de tous les vices." Trans. Jean-Marie Laclavetine. In *Je est un autre. Pour une identité-monde,* eds. Michel Le Bris and Jean Rouaud, 205–218. Paris: Editions Gallimard, 2010.

Green, Nancy L. "A French Ellis Island? Museums, Memory and History in France and the United States." *History Workshop Journal* 63 (2007): 239–253.

Griffiths, Gareth. "Breaking the Chains Nominated for National Award." http://www.empiremuseum.co.uk/aboutus/relationalnews.htm. 2007.

Grognet, Fabrice. "Quand 'l'étranger' devient patrimoine français." *La Cité Nationale de l'Histoire de l'Immigration: Une collection en devenir, Hommes et Migrations* 1267 (2007): 28–37.

Guaino, Henri. "L'homme africain et l'histoire, par Henri Guaino." *Le Monde,* http://www.lemonde.fr/idees/article/2008/07/26/henri-guaino-toute-l-afrique-n-a-pas-rejete-le-discours-de-dakar_1077506_3232.html. June 28, 2008.

Guéant, Claude. "Quelle France pour demain?" *Le Monde,* May 31, 2011.

———. "Les résultats de la politique migratoire," http://www.interieur.gouv.fr/sections/le_ministre/claude-gueant/interventions/resultats-politique-migratoire/view. 10 January 10, 2012.

Guène, Faïza. Interview with Sarah Adams. "Voice of the People." *The Guardian.* http://www.guardian.co.uk/society/2006/may/10/books.socialexclusion. May 10, 2006.

———. *Dreams from the Endz.* Trans. Sarah Adams. London: Chatto & Windus, 2008.

———. *Du rêve pour les oufs.* Paris: Hachette Littératures, 2006.

———. "Je suis qui je suis." *Chroniques pour une société annoncée.* Paris: Editions Stock, 2007.

———. *Just Like Tomorrow.* Trans. Sarah Adams. London: Definitions, 2006.

———. *Kiffe kiffe demain.* Paris: Hachette Littératures, 2004.

Gugler, Joseph. *African Film: Re-Imagining a Continent.* Bloomington: Indiana University Press, 2003.

Guimont, Fabienne. *Les étudiants africains en France: 1950–1965.* Paris: Editions L'Harmattan, 1997.

Habermas, Jürgen. *Europe: The Faltering project.* Cambridge, UK: Polity Press, 2009.

Hajjat, Abdellali. *Les frontières de l'identité nationale: L'injonction à l'assimilation en France métropolitaine et coloniale.* Paris: Editions La Découverte, 2012.

Hardy, Georges. *Une conquête morale, L'enseignement en A.O.F.* Paris: Editions Armand Colin, 1917.

Harel, Xavier and Thomas Hofnung. *Le scandale des biens mal acquis. Enquête sur les milliards volés de la françafrique.* Paris: Editions La Découverte, 2011.

Hargreaves, Alec G. "Gatekeepers and Gateways: Post-colonial minorities and French television." In *Post-Colonial Cultures in France,* ed. Alec G. Hargreaves and Mark McKinney, 84–98. London: Routledge, 1997.

———. *Immigration and Identity in beur fiction: Voices from the North African Community in France.* Oxford: Berg, 1991.

———. "Minority ethnic identification and mobilization." In *Multi-Ethnic France: Immi-*

gration, Politics, Culture, and Society, ed. Alec G. Hargreaves, 75–139. London: Routledge, 2007.

———. *Multi-Ethnic France: Immigration, Politics, Culture and Society.* London: Routledge, 2007.

———. "Politics and public policy." In *Multi-Ethnic France: Immigration, Politics, Culture and Society,* ed. Alec G. Hargreaves, 165–203. London: Routledge, 2007.

———. "Testimony, Co-Authorship, and Dispossession among Women of Maghrebi Origin in France." In *Textual Ownership in Francophone African Literature,* eds. Alec G. Hargreaves, Nicki Hitchcott, and Dominic Thomas, *Research in African Literatures* 37.1 (Spring 2006): 42–54.

———. "Translator's Introduction." Azouz Begag, *Ethnicity and Equality: France in the Balance.* Lincoln: University of Nebraska Press, 2007, 7–28.

Hargreaves, Alec G., and Mark McKinney, eds. *Post-Colonial Cultures in France.* London: Routledge, 1997.

Harrow, Kenneth W. *Postcolonial African Cinema: From Political Engagement to Postmodernism.* Bloomington: Indiana University Press, 2007.

Hatzfeld, Marc. *La culture des cités: Une énergie positive.* Paris: Editions Autrement, 2006.

Hegel, Georg W. F. *Philosophy of History.* Trans. John Sibree. New York: American Dome Library Company, 1902 [first pub. 1822].

Hennebelle, Guy, and Roland Schneider, eds. *Cinémas métis: de hollywood aux films beurs. CinémAction* 56 (July 1990).

"Henri Guaino: Le gourou du Président." *Le Nouvel Observateur* 2245 (November 15–21, 2007).

Henry, Jean-Robert. "Sarkozy, the Mediterranean and the Arab Spring." *Contemporary French and Francophone Studies: Sites* 16.3 (June 2012): 405–415.

Hewitt, Nicholas, ed. *The Cambridge Companion to Modern French Culture.* Cambridge, UK: Cambridge University Press, 2003.

Hitchcott, Nicki. *Calixthe Beyala: Performances of Migration.* Liverpool: Liverpool University Press, 2006.

———. "Calixthe Beyala: Prizes, Plagiarism, and 'Authenticity'." In *Textual Ownership in Francophone African Literature,* eds. Alec G. Hargreaves, Nicki Hitchcott, and Dominic Thomas, *Research in African Literatures* 37.1 (Spring 2006): 100–109.

———. *Women Writers in Francophone Africa.* Oxford: Berg, 2000.

H-Magnum. "Plafond de verre." *Rafales.* CD.

Hofnung, Thomas. "Ouattara et Sarkozy, les copains d'abord," *Libération,* January 26, 2012, 8.

Hondo, Med. "The Cinema of Exile." In *Cinemas of the Black Diaspora: Diversity, Dependence, and Oppositionality,* ed. Michael T. Martin, 339–343. Detroit: Wayne State University Press, 1995.

———. "What Is Cinema for Us." In *African Experiences of Cinema,* ed. Imruh Bakari and Mbye B. Cham, 39–41. London: British Film Institute, 1996.

Hooper-Greenhill, Eilean. "Changing values in the Art Museum: Rethinking Communication and Learning." In *Museum Studies: An Anthology of Contexts,* ed. Bettina Messias Carbonell, 556–575. Oxford: Blackwell Publishing, 2004.

Hortefeux, Brice. "Cohérence, justice, efficacité: la nouvelle politique d'immigration de la France."

———. "Ma vision de l'identité nationale." *Libération,* July 27 2007, 20.

———. "Migrations économiques, cohésion sociale et développement: vers une approche intégrée." http://www.coe.int/t/dg3/migration/Ministerial_Conferences/8th

%20conference/Speeches/Inaugural%20Session%20-%20II%20-%20Introductory %20speech%20by%20Mr%20Hortefeux_fr.pdf. September 4–5, 2008, 1–7.
———. "Préface." *Les orientations de la politique de l'immigration.* Paris: La Documentation Française, 2007, 7–9.
Huntzinger, Jacques. "La Méditerranée d'une rive à l'autre." *Questions Internationales* 36 (2009): 6–12.
ICOM. www.icom.museum/definition.html.
"Identité nationale et passé colonial. Pour un véritable débat." http://www.achac.com/?O=204. December 24, 2009.
Iglesias, Eduardo. *Tarifa: L'auberge de l'Allemand* [Tarifa, la venta del alemán, 2004]. Trans. William Soler. Lyon: Rouge Inside, 2011.
"Images d'immigrés." In *Cinémas africains, une oasis dans le désert,* ed. Samuel Lelièvre, *CinémAction* 106 (2003): 50–55.
"Immigration, rétentions, expulsions: les étrangers indésirables." *Lignes 26* (2008).
International Convention on the Protection of the Rights of All Migrant Workers and Members of Their Families. http://www.un.org/documents/ga/res/45/a45r158.htm. 2003.
"Invitation au Jardin des Outre-mer." http://www.2011-annee-des-outre-mer.gouv.fr/actualites/345/invitation-au-jardin-des-outre-mer.html?date=20110627. April 9, 2011.
"Irregular immigration." http://ec.europa.eu/home-affairs/policies/immigration/immigration_illegal_en.htm.
Isaacs, Marc. *Calais, la dernière frontière.* Andana Films, 2003.
Iweala, Uzodinma. "Cessez de vouloir 'sauver' l'Afrique!" *Le Monde,* 29–30 July, 2007, 13.
Jarry, Grégory, and Otto T. *Petite histoire des colonies françaises. Tome 4: La Françafrique.* Poitiers: Editions Flblb, 2011.
Jay, Salim. *Tu ne traverseras pas le* détroit. Paris: Editions Fayard, 2001.
Jean-Baptiste, Lucien. *La première étoile.* Vendredi Film, France 2 Cinéma, 2009.
Jewsiewicki, Bogumil. "La mémoire est-elle soluble dans l'esthétique." *Le débat* 147 (November–December 2007): 174–177.
———. "Le refus de savoir est un refus de reconnaissance" In *Petit précis de remise à niveau sur l'histoire africaine à l'usage du président Sarkozy,* ed. Adame Ba Konaré, 139–148. Paris: Editions La Découverte, 2008
Johnson, Linton Kwesi. "New Word Hawdah, 102–3." *Selected Poems.* London: Penguin, 2006.
Jules-Rosette, Bennetta. *Black Paris: The African Writers' Landscape.* Urbana: University of Illinois Press, 1998.
Kabara, Medhi, and Régis Chaoupa. *Diaspora. La communauté noire en France.* Diaspora Communication, 2006.
Kane, Cheikh Hamidou. *Ambiguous Adventure.* Trans. Katherine Woods. Exeter: Heinemann Educational Books, Ltd., 1963.
———. *L'aventure ambiguë.* Paris: Editions Julliard, 1961.
Kaprièlian, Nelly. Dossier littéraire. "Marie Ndiaye: aux prises avec Le Monde," *Les inrockuptibles* 716 (August 18–24, 2009): 28–33.
———. Interview with Marie Ndiaye."Écris et tais-toi." *les inrockuptibles* 729 (18–24 November, 2009): 8–11.
Kapuscinski, Ryszard. *The Other.* London: Verso, 2008.
Karp, Ivan. "Culture and Representation." In *Exhibiting Cultures: The Poetics and Politics of Museum Display,* eds. Ivan Karp and Steven D. Lavine, 11–24. Washington, DC: Smithsonian, 1991.

Karp, Ivan, Corinne A. Kratz, Lynn Szwaja, and Tomás Ybarra-Frausto, eds. *Museum Frictions: Public Cultures/Global Transformations.* Durham, NC: Duke University Press, 2007.

Kassovitz, Mathieu. *La haine.* Canal +, 1995.

Keaton, Trica. *Muslim Girls and the Other France: Race, Identity Politics, and Social Exclusion.* Bloomington: Indiana University Press, 2006.

Kechiche, Abdellatif. *L'Esquive.* Lola Films and CinéCinémas, 2003.

Kelman, Gaston. *Au-delà du Noir et du Blanc.* Paris: Max Milo Editions, 2005.

———. *Les hirondelles du printemps africains.* Paris: Editions Jean-Claude Lattès, 2008.

———. *Je suis noir et je n'aime pas le manioc.* Paris: Max Milo Editions, 2003.

———. *Parlons enfants de la patrie.* Paris: Max Milo Editions, 2007.

Kemedjio, Cilas. "The Western Anticolonialist of the Postcolonial Age: The Reformist Syndrome and the Memory of Decolonization in (Post-) Imperial French Thought." *Remembering Africa,* ed. Elisabeth Mudimbe, 32–55. Portsmouth: Heinemann, 2002.

Kennedy, Roger G. "Some Thoughts about National Museums at the End of the Century." In *Museum Studies: An Anthology of Contexts,* ed. Bettina Messias Carbonell, 302–306. Oxford: Blackwell Publishing, 2004.

Khouma, Pap. *I Was an Elephant Salesman: Adventures between Dakar, Paris, and Milan.* Trans. Rebecca Hopkins. Bloomington: Indiana University Press, 2010 [first pub. 1990].

Kirshenblatt-Gimblett, Barbara. *Destination Culture: Tourism, Museums, and Heritage.* Berkeley: University of California Press, 1998.

Klein, Hilde S. *The Museum in Transition: A Philosophical Perspective.* Washington, DC: Smithsonian, 2000.

Klein, Julia M. "One Part History, Two Parts Shrine." *New York Times,* March 19, 2009.

Kobelinsky, Carolina, and Chowra Makaremi, eds. *Enfermés dehors. Enquêtes sur le confinement des* étrangers. Bellecombe-en-Bauges: Editions du Croquant, 2009.

Konaré, Adame Ba, ed. *Petit précis de remise à niveau sur l'histoire africaine à l'usage du président Sarkozy.* Paris: Editions La Découverte, 2008.

Konaté, Moussa. *L'Afrique noire est-elle maudite.* Paris: Editions Fayard, 2010.

Kotlok, Nathalie. "Une politique migratoire au service du développement des pays africains?" In *Les migrations subsahariennes,* ed. Patrick Gonin. Special dossier, *Hommes et Migrations* 1286–1287 (July-October 2010): 268–278.

Kounkou, Charles Thomas. "L'ontologie négative de l'Afrique. Remarques sur le discours de Nicolas Sarkozy à Dakar." *Cahiers d'études africaines* 50 (2–3–4): 198–199–200 (2010): 755–770.

Kramsch, Claire. "Grammar Games and Bilingual Blends." PMLA 124.3 (2009): 887–895.

Kratz, Corinne A., and Ciraj Rassool. "Remapping the Museum." In *Museum Frictions: Public Cultures/Global Transformations,* eds. Ivan Karp, Corinne A. Kratz, Lynn Szwaja, and Tomás Ybarra-Frausto, 347–356. Durham, NC: Duke University Press, 2007.

Krémer, Pascale. "Les cités s'emparent de la caméra." *Le Monde,* 2 (Supplement), 207 (February 2, 2008): 24–28.

Kréyol factory: Des artistes interrogent les identités créoles. Paris: Editions Gallimard, 2009.

Kriegel, Lara. "After the Exhibitionary Complex: Museum Histories and the Future of the Victorian Past." *Victorian Studies* 48.4 (Summer 2006): 681–704.

Krier, Jacques. *Ouvriers noirs de Paris.* Paris: Institut National de l'Audiovisuel, INA, 1964.

Krus, Patricia. "Postcolonial Performance." *Ariel: A Review of International Literature* 38.1 (2007): 121–125.

Laacher, Smaïn. *Après Sangatte . . . Nouvelles immigrations, nouveaux enjeux.* Paris: Editions La Dispute, 2002.
———. *Des étrangers en situation de «transit» au Centre d'Hébergement et d'Accueil d'Urgence Humanitaire de Sangatte.* Paris: CNRS-EHESS, 2002.
Labarthe, Gilles. "Histoires brouillées." *Le Courrier: Un quotidien suisse d'information et d'opinion* (24 June 2006). www.lecourrier.ch. Consulted March 1, 2007.
———. *Sarko l'Africain.* Paris: Editions Hugo & Cie, 2011.
Labarthe, Gilles, with Xavier-François Verschave. *L'or africain. Pillages, trafics et commerce international.* Marseille: Editions Agone, 2007.
LaCapra, Dominick. "Reconfiguring French Studies" In *History and Reading: Tocqueville, Foucault, French Studies,* 169–226. Toronto: University of Toronto Press, 2000.
Laclau, Ernesto. *La guerre des identités. Grammaire de l'émancipation.* Paris: Editions La Découverte, 2000.
Lacoste, Thomas. *Ulysse Clandestin.* www.labandepassante.org.
Laferrière, Dany. *Je suis un écrivain japonais.* Paris: Editions Grasset & Fasquelle, 2008.
———. *L'Enigme du retour.* Paris: Editions Grasset & Fasquelle, 2009.
Lafont-Couturier, Hélène. "Les coulisses d'une collection en formation." *La Cité Nationale de l'Histoire de l'Immigration: Une collection en devenir, Hommes et Migrations* 1267, 8–15.
Lalami, Laïla. *Hope and other pursuits.* Chapel Hill: Algonquin Books, 2005.
Laronde, Michel. *Autour du roman beur: Immigration et identité.* Paris: L'Harmattan, 1993.
Laroussi, Farid, and Christopher L. Miller, eds. *The Challenge of Expanding Horizons, Yale French Studies* 103 (2003).
Lask, Tomke. "Introduction." In *Museums, Collections, Interpretations: Rethinking the Construction of Meanings and Identities,* ed. Tomke Last, *Civilisations* LII.2 (2005): 7–19.
Lauwaert, Françoise. "Comme une écaille sur le mur: A propos de 'Le Dernier caravansérail (Odyssées)', un spectacle en deux parties du Théâtre du Soleil." *Civilisations* 56.1–2 (2007): 159–182.
Lebovics, Herman. *Bringing the Empire Back Home: France in the Global Age.* Durham, NC: Duke University Press, 2004.
———. *Mona Lisa's Escort: André Malraux and the Reinvention of French Culture.* Ithaca, NY: Cornell University Press, 1999.
———. "The Dance of the Museums." In *Bringing the Empire Back Home: France in the Global Age,* 143–216. Durham, NC: Duke University Press, 2004.
———. *True France: The Wars over Cultural Identity, 1900–1945.* Ithaca, NY: Cornell University Press, 1992.
Le Bris, Michel. "Lisez Rimbaud." In *Je est un autre. Pour une identité-monde,* eds. Michel Le Bris and Jean Rouaud, 11–27. Paris: Editions Gallimard, 2010.
———. "Pour une littérature-monde en français." In *Pour une littérature-monde,* eds. Michel Le Bris and Jean Rouaud, 23–53. Paris: Editions Gallimard, 2007.
Le Bris, Michel, and Jean Rouaud. "Avant-propos." In *Je est un autre. Pour une identité-monde,* eds. Michel Le Bris and Jean Rouaud, 7–9. Paris: Editions Gallimard, 2010.
———, eds. *Je est un autre. Pour une identité-monde.* Paris: Editions Gallimard, 2010.
———, eds. *Pour une littérature-monde.* Paris: Editions Gallimard, 2007.
Lecadre, Renaud. "Les grandes manœuvres de Bolloré dans le port de Conakry." *Libération,* July 29, 2011, 14.
Le Clézio, Jean-Marie Gustave. "Universalisme et Multiculturalisme dans Le Monde, francophone" [Universalism and Multiculturalism in the Francophone World].

Roundtable discussion, Hankuk University for Foreign Languages, Seoul, South Korea, December 12, 2009.

Le Cour Grandmaison, Olivier. "Apologie du colonialisme, usages de l'histoire et identité nationale: sur la rhétorique de Nicolas Sarkozy." In *Petit précis de remise à niveau sur l'histoire africaine à l'usage du président Sarkozy,* ed. Adame Ba Konaré, 163–173. Paris: Editions La Découverte, 2008.

———, ed. *Douce France: Rafles, Rétentions, Expulsions.* Paris: Editions du Seuil/RESF, 2009, 291–292.

———. *La République impériale: Politique et racisme d'état.* Paris: Editions La Découverte, 2009.

———. "Sur la réhabilitation du passé colonial de la France." In *La fracture coloniale: La société française au prisme de l'héritage colonial,* eds. Pascal Blanchard, Nicolas Bancel, and Sandrine Lemaire, 121–128. Paris: Editions La Découverte, 2005.

———. "Xénophobie d'état et politique de la peur." *Lignes 26* (May 2008): 23–38.

Le Cour Grandmaison, Olivier, Gilles Lhuilier, and Jérôme Valluy, eds. *Le retour des camps: Sangatte, Lampedusa, Guantanamo.* Paris: Editions Autrement, 2007.

Lefeuvre, Daniel. *Pour en finir avec la repentance coloniale.* Paris: Editions Flammarion, 2006.

Lefeuvre, Daniel, and Michel Renard, *Faut-il avoir honte de l'identité nationale?* Paris: Editions Larousse, 2008.

Le Fourn, Jonathan, and Andreï Schtakleff. *L'exil et le royaume.* L'Harmattan/Red Star Cinema, 2009.

Legoux, Luc. "La réorganisation mondiale de l'asile." In *L'asile au Sud,* eds. Luc Cambrézy, Smaïn Laacher, Véronique Lassailly-Jacob, and Luc Legoux, 9–22. Paris: Editions La Dispute, 2008.

Leménager, Grégoire. http://bibliobs.nouvelobs.com/20091111/15823/marie-ndiaye-en-appelle-a-mitterrand-et-maintient-ses-propos-apres-le-texte-grotesque. November 11, 2009.

Lemoine, Hervé. "La Maison de l'Histoire de France": *Pour la création d'un centre de recherche et de collections permanentes dédié à l'histoire civile et militaire de la France.* April 16, 2008.

Le Pen, Marine. "Face à l'anomie, redonner un sens." http://www.frontnational.com/?p=4143#more-4143. March 2, 2010.

"Lettre de Mission." http://www.immigration.gouv.fr/spip.php?page=dossiers_them_org&numrubrique=341. March 31, 2009.

Lequeret, Elisabeth. "Un aller simple pour Paris." In *Afrique 50: Singularités d'un cinéma pluriel,* ed. Catherine Ruelle, 215–216. Paris: Editions L'Harmattan, 2005.

Lewis, Mary Dewhurst. *The Boundaries of the Republic: Migrant Rights and the Limits of Universalism in France, 1918–1940.* Stanford: Stanford University Press, 2007.

Liagre, Romain, and Frédéric Dumont. "Sangatte: vie et mort d'un centre de réfugiés." *Annales de Géographie* 114 (2005): 93–112.

Liauzu, Claude. *Colonisation, migrations, racismes. Histoires d'une passeurs de civilisations.* Paris: Editions Syllepse, 2009.

———. "Ministère de l'hostilité." *Le Monde diplomatique,* July 2007, 28.

Lindon, Vincent. "Débat sur les migrations." http://www.paperblog.fr/2330480/sangatte-detruit-la-jungle-de-calais-aneantie-violences-arretes-deporteset-demain/. 2009.

Limet, Yun Sun. "Analyse d'une sous-texte," http://remue.net/spip.php?article3433. November 11, 2009.

Lionnet, Françoise. "The Mirror and the Tomb: Africa, Museums, and Memory." *African* Arts 54.3 (Autumn 2001): 50–59.
Lioret, Philippe. *Welcome.* Nord-Ouest Films, 2009.
Loshitzky, Josefa. *Screening Strangers: Migration and Diaspora in Contemporary European Cinema.* Bloomington: Indiana University Press, 2010.
Lozès, Patrick. *Nous les noirs de France.* Paris: Editions Danger Public, 2007.
Lüsebrink, Hans-Jürgen. "Acculturation coloniale et pédagogie interculturelle—l'œuvre de Georges Hardy." In *Sénégal-Forum: Littérature et Histoire,* ed. Papa Samba Diop, 113–122. Frankfurt, Germany: IKO Verlag, 1995.
Lyannaj kont pwofitasion. (Union Against Exploitation). *Manifeste pour les "produits" de Haute Nécessité.* Paris: Editions Galaade, 2009.
Lydie, Virginie. *Traversée interdite! Les harragas face à l'Europe forteresse.* Le Pré Saint-Gervais: Editions le passager clandestin, 2011.
Mabanckou, Alain. *Bleu-Blanc-Rouge.* Paris: Editions Présence Africaine, 1998.
———. "Le chant de l'oiseau migrateur." In *Pour une littérature-monde,* eds. Michel Le Bris and Jean Rouaud, 55–65. Paris: Editions Gallimard, 2007.
———. "La francophonie." *Balma info* 41 (April 2009): 13.
———. *Lettre à Jimmy.* Paris: Editions Fayard, 2007.
———. "Le sang, le sol, la souche." In *Je est un autre. Pour une identité-monde,* eds. Michel Le Bris and Jean Rouaud, 39–44. Paris: Editions Gallimard, 2010.
———. *Le Sanglot de l'Homme Noir.* Paris: Editions Fayard, 2012.
Mabanckou, Alain, and Christophe Merlin. *L'Europe depuis l'Afrique.* Paris: Editions Naïve, 2009.
Macé, Éric. "Postcolonialité et francité dans les imaginaires télévisuels de la nation." In *Ruptures postcoloniales: Les nouveaux visages de la société française,* eds. Nicolas Bancel, Pascal Blanchard, Françoise Vergès, Achille Mbembe, and Florence Bernault, 391–402. Paris: Editions La Découverte, 2010.
Maghraoui, Driss. "French Identity, Islam and North Africans: Colonial Legacies, Postcolonial Realities." In *French Civilization and Its Discontents: nationalism, colonialism, race,* eds. Tyler Stovall and Georges Van Den Abbeele, 213–234. Lanham: Lexington Books, 2003.
Mahany, Habiba. *Je kiffe ma race.* Paris: Editions Jean-Claude Lattès, 2008.
Maillot, Agnès. *Identité nationale et immigration: La liaison dangereuse.* Paris: Editions Les Carnets de l'Info, 2008.
Manceron, Gilles. "La loi: régulateur ou acteur des guerres de mémoires?" In *Les Guerres de mémoires: La France et son histoire. Enjeux politiques, controverses historiques, stratégies médiatiques,* eds. Pascal Blanchard and Isabelle Veyrat-Masson, 241–251. Paris: Editions La Découverte, 2008.
Mandin, Didier. *Banlieue Voltaire.* Paris: Editions Desnel, 2006.
"Manifeste par le collectif *Qui fait la France?*" *Les inrockuptibles* 614 (September 4, 2007): 18.
"Manifeste pour une littérature monde." http://www.etonnants-voyageurs.com/spip.php?article1574. *Le Monde,* March 16, 2007, 2.
Maran, René. *Batouala: véritable roman nègre.* Paris: Editions Albin Michel, 1921.
Margolis, Karen. "Missing: Germany's Immigration Museum." http://www.mut-gegen-rechte-gewalt.de/eng/news/missing-germanys-immigration-museum, April 3, 2008. Consulted April 10, 2009.
Marstine, Janet, ed. *New Museum Theory and Practice.* Oxford: Blackwell, 2006.
Martin, Michael T., ed. "Framing the 'Black' in Black Diasporic Cinemas." In *Cinemas of*

the Black Diaspora: Diversity, Dependence, and Oppositionality, ed. Michael T. Martin, 1–21. Detroit: Wayne State University Press, 1995.

Martin, Stéphane. Interview. "Un musée pas comme les autres." *Le débat* 147 (November–December 2007): 5–22.

———. *Musée du Quai Branly. Là où dialoguent les cultures.* Paris: Editions Gallimard, 2011.

Masset-Depasse, Olivier. *Illégal.* Belgium: O'Brother Distribution, 2010.

Masure, Françoise. "Des Français paradoxaux. L'expérience de la naturalisation des enfants de l'immigration maghrébine." In *Les nouvelles frontières de la société français,* ed. Didier Fassin, 565–590. Paris: Editions La Découverte, 2010.

Matha, Antoine. *Épitaphe.* Paris: Editions Gallimard, 2009.

Mbem, André Julien. *Nicolas Sarkozy à Dakar. Débats et enjeux autour d'un discours.* Paris: Editions L'Harmattan, 2007.

Mbembe, Achille. "At the Edge of the World: Boundaries, Territoriality, and Sovereignty in Africa." Trans. Steven Rendall. In *Globalization,* ed. Arjun Appadurai, 22–55. Durham, NC: Duke University Press, 2001.

———. "Enterrons la Françafrique." http://www.africapresse.com/politique/achille-mbembe-enterrons-la-francafrique/11/12/2010/. December 11, 2010.

———. "Figures du Multiple: La France peut-elle réinventer son identité?" *Le Messager* (November 2005). Article: http://www.europe-solidaire.org/spip.php?article4898.

———. "Figures of the Multiplicity: Can France Reinvent Its Identity?." Trans. Jean Marie Todd. In *Frenchness and the African Diaspora: Identity and Uprising in Contemporary France,* eds. Charles Tshimanga, Didier Gondola, and Peter J. Bloom, 55–69. Bloomington: Indiana University Press, 2009.

———. "L'intarissable puit aux fantasmes." In *L'Afrique de Sarkozy: Un déni de l'histoire,* ed. Jean-Pierre Chrétien, 91–32. Paris: Editions Karthala, 2008.

———. "Nicolas Sarkozy's Africa." Trans. Melissa Thackway. http://www.africaresource.com/index.php?option=com_content&view=article&id=376:a-critique-of-nicolas-sarkozy&catid=36:essays-a-discussions&Itemid=346. August 8, 2007.

———. *On the Postcolony.* Berkeley: University of California Press, 2001.

———. "Pièce d'identité et désirs d'apartheid." In *Je est un autre. Pour une identité-monde,* eds. Michel Le Bris and Jean Rouaud, 115–122. Paris: Editions Gallimard, 2010.

———. "Provincializing France?" Trans. Janet Roitman. *Public Culture* 23.1 (2011): 85–119.

———. "The Republic and Its Beast: On the Riots in the French *Banlieues.*" Trans. Jean Marie Todd. In *Frenchness and the African Diaspora: Identity and Uprising in Contemporary France,* eds. Charles Tshimanga, Didier Gondola, and Peter J. Bloom, 47–69. Bloomington: Indiana University Press, 2009.

———. "La république désœuvrée: La France à l'ère post-coloniale." *Le débat* 137 (November–December 2005): 159–175.

———. "La République et sa Bête: À propos des émeutes dans les banlieues de France." www.africultures.com. November 2005.

———. *Sortir de la grande nuit. Essai sur l'Afrique décolonisée.* Paris: Editions La Découverte, 2010.

Mbembe, Achille, and Nicolas Bancel. "De la pensée postcoloniale." *Cultures du Sud* 165 (April–June 2007): 83–92.

McClellan, Andrew. "Museum Studies Now." In *Spectacle and Display,* ed. Deborah Cherry and Fintan Cullen, 92–96. Oxford: Blackwell, 2008.

Meek, James. "What Is Europe?" *The Guardian,* December 17, 2004, 2.

Migration museums map. http://www.migrationmuseums.org/web/index.php?page=map.

"Migration policy from Control to Governance." http://www.opendemocracy.net/people-migrationeurope/militarising_borders_3735.jsp. July 12, 2006. Consulted May 13, 2010.
Miller, Christopher L. *Blank Darkness: Africanist Discourse in French.* Chicago: University of Chicago Press, 1985.
———. *The French Atlantic Triangle: Literature and Culture of the Slave Trade.* Durham, NC: Duke University Press, 2008.
———. *Nationalist and Nomads: Essays on Francophone African Literature and Culture.* Chicago: University of Chicago Press, 1998.
———. "The Slave Trade, *La Françafrique,* and the Globalization of French." In *French Global: A New Approach to Literary History,* eds. Christie McDonald and Susan Rubin Suleiman, 240–256. New York: Columbia University Press, 2010.
Miller, Judith G. "New Forms for New Conflicts: Thinking About Ariane Mnouchkine and Tony Kushner." *Contemporary Theatre Review* 16.2 (2006): 212–219.
Mills-Affif, Édouard. *Filmer les immigrés, les représentations audiovisuelles de l'immigration à la télévision française (1960–1986).* Brussels, Belgium: De Boeck, 2004.
"Missions and Role." http://www.immigration.gouv.fr/spip.php?page=dossiers_det_org&numrubrique=311&numarticle=1331.
Mitterrand, François. "Discours de La Baule." http://www.rfi.fr/actufr/articles/037/article_20103.asp. June 20, 1990.
Mitterrand, Frédéric. "Frédéric Mitterrand ne souhaite pas 'arbitrer' la polémique NDiaye-Raoult," http://www.lemonde.fr/politique/article/2009/11/12/frederic-mitterrand-ne-souhaite-pas-arbitrer-la-polemique-ndiaye-raoult_1266002_823448.html. November 12, 2009.
Mnouchkine, Ariane. *Le Dernier Caravansérail* (Odyssées). Théâtre du Soleil, Bel Air Media, Arte video/Bel Air Classiques, 2006.
Mo, V. "Sa banlieue de A à Z." *Le Parisien,* August 23, 2006: 10.
Mohammadi, Wali. *De Kaboul à Calais. L'incroyable périple d'un jeune Afghan.* Paris: Editions Robert Laffont, 2009.
Mohen, Jean-Pierre. "Musée du Quai Branly: actualité et devenir: entretien croisé avec Jean-Pierre Mohen et Dominic Thomas." In *Le retour du colonial,* ed. Nicolas Bancel, *Cultures du Sud* (May–July 2007): 41–46.
Moï, Anna. *Espéranto, désespéranto. La francophonie sans les français.* Paris: Editions Gallimard, 2006.
Morrison, Donald. "The Death of French Culture." *Time Magazine.* November 21, 2007.
Moudileno, Lydie. "Fame, Celebrity, and the Conditions of Visibility of the Postcolonial Writer." In *Francophone sub-Saharan African Literature in Global Contexts,* eds. Alain Mabanckou and Dominic Thomas, *Yale French Studies* 120 (2011): 62–74.
———."La fiction de la migration: manipulation des corps et des récits dans *Bleu blanc rouge* d'Alain Mabanckou." *Présence Africaine* 163–164 (2001): 182–89.
———. "Magical Realism: "Arme miraculeuse' for the African Novel?" In *Textual Ownership in Francophone African Literature,* eds. Alec G. Hargreaves, Nicki Hitchcott, and Dominic Thomas, *Research in African Literatures* 37.1 (Spring 2006): 28–41.
Moura, Jean-Marc. "Les influences et permanences coloniales dans le domaine littéraire." In *Culture post-coloniale 1961–2006: Traces et mémoires coloniales en France,* eds. Pascal Blanchard and Nicolas Bancel, 166–175. Paris: Editions Autrement, 2006.
———. *Littératures francophones et théorie postcoloniale.* Paris: Presses Universitaires de France, 2007.
Mongaillard, Vincent. "Faïza Guène, plume du bitume." Sa banlieue de A à Z." *Le Parisien,* August 23, 2006, 10.

Moulier Boutang, Yann. *La révolte des banlieues ou les habits nus de la République.* Paris: Editions Amsterdam, 2005.

Mucchielli, Laurent. "Les émeutes de novembre 2005: les raisons de La colère." In *Quand les banlieues brûlent… Retour sue les émeutes de novembre 2005,* eds. Laurent Mucchielli and Véronique Le Goaziou, 11–35. Paris: Editions La Découverte, 2006.

———. "Faire du chiffre: le 'nouveau management de la sécurité.'" In *La frénésie sécuritaire. Retour à l'ordre et nouveau contrôle social,* ed. Laurent Mucchielli, 99–112. Paris: Editions La Découverte, 2008.

———. ed., *La frénésie sécuritaire. Retour à l'ordre et nouveau contrôle social.* Paris: Editions La Découverte, 2008.

———. *L'invention de la violence. Des peurs, des chiffres et des faits.* Paris: Editions La Découverte, 2011.

Mudimbe, V. Y., eds. *The Surreptitious Speech:* Présence Africaine *and the Politics of Otherness, 1947–1987.* Chicago: Chicago University Press, 1992.

———. *The Idea of Africa.* Bloomington: Indiana University Press, 1994.

Müller, Bernard. "Faut-il restituer les butins des expéditions coloniales." *Le Monde Diplomatique,* July 2007, 20–21.

Multiple discrimination, Roma Rights. Journal of the European Roma Rights Centre, Number 2, 2009.

Murphy, David, and Patrick Williams. *Postcolonial African Cinema: Ten Directors,* Manchester: Manchester University Press, 2007.

Murphy, Maureen. "Le CNHI au Palais de la Porte Dorée." *La Cité Nationale de l'Histoire de l'Immigration: Une collection en devenir, Hommes et Migrations* 1267 (2007): 44–55.

———. *Un Palais pour une cité: Du musée des colonies à la Cité nationale de l'histoire de l'immigration.* Paris: Réunion des musées nationaux 2007.

Nancy, Jean-Luc. *Identités.* Editions Galilée, 2010.

National Assembly. file:///Users/cdhuser/Desktop/French%20history/Assemblee.Debate.webarchive.

Naudillon, Françoise, and Jean Ouédraogo, eds. *Images et mirages des migrations dans les littératures et les cinémas d'Afrique francophone.* Montréal, Québéc: Mémoire d'encrier, 2011.

Ndaywel È Nziem, Isidore. "L'Union pour la Méditerranée: un projet pour diviser l'Afrique et tourner le dos à la Francophonie." In *Petit précis de remise à niveau sur l'histoire africaine à l'usage du président Sarkozy,* ed. Adame Ba Konaré, 268–280. Paris: Editions La Découverte, 2008.

NDiaye, Marie. "Les sœurs." In Pap Ndiaye, *La condition noire: Essai sur une minorité ethnique française,* 9–15. Paris: Editions Calmann-Lévy, 2008.

———. *Trois femmes puissantes.* Paris: Editions Gallimard, 2009.

Ndiaye, Pap. *La condition noire: Essai sur une minorité ethnique française.* Paris: Editions Calmann-Lévy, 2008.

Ndione, Abasse. *Mbëkë mi: A l'assaut des vagues de l'Atlantique.* Paris: Editions Gallimard, 2008.

Nesbitt, Nick. *Voicing Memory: History and Subjectivity in French Caribbean Literature.* Charlottesville: University of Virginia Press, 2003.

A New Framework Strategy for Multilingualism. http://ec.europa.eu/education/policies/lang/doc/com596_en.pdf. November 22, 2005.

"A New Framework Strategy for Multilingualism." http://ec.europa.eu/education/languages/eu-language-policy/doc99_en.htm. August 19, 2009, 1–30.

Newman, Andrew, and Fiona McLean. "Architectures of inclusion: museums, galleries and inclusive communities." In *Museums, Society, Equality,* ed. Richard Sandell, 56–68. London: Routledge, 2002.

Ngalasso, Mwatha Musanji. "*Je suis venu vous dire*... Anatomie d'un discours néocolonial en langue de caoutchouc." In *L'Afrique répond à Sarkozy: Contre le discours de Dakar,* ed. Makhily Gassama, 297–340. Paris: Editions Philippe Rey, 2008.

Ngatcha, Arnaud, and Jérôme Sesquin. *Noirs, l'identité au coeur de la question noire.* Jackie Bastide Production, France 5, France 3, Tabo Films, Arno Production, 2006.

Ngùgì wa Thiong'o. *Decolonizing the Mind: The Politics of Language in African Literature.* London: Heinemann, 1986.

———. *Something Torn and New: An African Renaissance.* New York: Basic Civitas Books, 2009.

Niney, François. *Le documentaire et ses faux-semblants.* Paris: Editions Klincksieck, 2009.

Nini, Soraya. *Ils disent que je suis une beurette*... Paris: Editions Fixot, 1993.

Nnaemeka, Obioma. "Nego-Feminism: Theorizing, Practicing, and Pruning Africa's Way." *Signs: Journal of Women in Culture and Society* 29.2 (Winter 2004): 357–385.

Noiriel, Gérard. *Immigrations, antisémitisme et racisme en France (XIXe–XXe siècles).* Paris: Editions Fayard, 2007.

———. "Venus d'ailleurs." *Textes et Documents pour la Classe* 936 (2007): 6–13.

———. *A quoi sert "l'identité nationale."* Marseille: Editions Agone, 2007.

Nora, Pierre, ed. *Realms of Memory: Rethinking the French Past.* Trans. Arthur Goldhammer. New York: Columbia University Press, 1996.

———. *Les lieux de mémoire.* Paris: Editions Gallimard, 1984–1992.

Norindr, Panivong, "*La Plus Grande France:* French Cultural Identity and Nation Building under Mitterrand." In *Identity Papers Contested Nationhood in Twentieth-Century France,* eds. Steven Ungar and Tom Conley, 233–258. Minneapolis: University of Minnesota Press, 1996.

"Nous exigeons la suppression du ministère de l'Identité nationale et de l'Immigration." http://www.liberation.fr/societe/0101606559-nous-exigeons-la-suppression-du-ministere-de-l-identite-nationale-et-de-l-immigration. December 4, 2009.

N'Sondé, Wilfried. "Ethnidentité." In *Je est un autre. Pour une identité-monde,* eds. Michel Le Bris and Jean Rouaud, 95–100. Paris: Editions Gallimard, 2010.

Odenbach, Marcel. "Im schiffbruch nicht schwimmen können." Video installation. 2011.

Onana, Jean-Baptiste. *Sois-nègre et tais-toi.* Nantes: Editions du Temps, 2007.

"On ne s'improvise pas en diplomate." http://www.lemonde.fr/idees/article/2011/02/22/on-ne-s-improvise-pas-diplomate_1483517_3232.html. February 23, 2011, 7. Consulted February 24, 2011.

O'Neill, Mark. "The good enough visitor." In *Museums, Society, Equality,* ed. Richard Sandell, 24–40. London: Routledge, 2002.

Orisha, Ifé. "Sony Labou Tansi face à douze mots." *Equateur* 1 (October–November 1986): 29–32.

Les Orientations de la politique de l'immigration. Paris: La Documentation Française, 2007.

Ormerod, Beverley, and Jean-Marie Volet. *Romancières africaines d'expression française: le sud du Sahara.* Paris: Editions L'Harmattan, 2004.

Osouf, Valérie. *L'identité nationale.* Granit Films, 2012.

Paglen, Trevor. *Blank Spots on the Map.* New York: Dutton, 2009.

Palcy, Euzhan. *Rue cases-nègres.* NEF Diffusion/Orca Productions, 1983.

Pamuk, Orhan. *The Museum of Innocence.* Trans. Maureen Freely. New York: Alfred A. Knopf, 2009.

Patricot, Aymeric. *Azima la rouge.* Paris: Editions Flammarion, 2006.

Peabody, Susan, and Tyler Stovall, eds. *The Color of Liberty: Histories of Race in France.* Durham, NC: Duke University Press, 2003.

Péan, Pierre. *L'argent noir. Corruption et sous-développement.* Paris: Editions Fayard, 1988.

———. *L'Homme de l'Ombre.* Paris: Editions Fayard, 1990.

Perreau, Yann, and Thomas Dutter. *Clandestin, mon semblable, mon frère.* France Culture, 2003.

Petty, Sheila. "Postcolonial geographies: Landscape and Alienation in *Clando.*" In *Cinema and Social Discourse in Cameroon,* ed. Alexie Tcheuyap, *Bayreuth African Studies* 69 (2005): 159–171.

Pfaff, Françoise. "Africa from Within: The Films of Gaston Kaboré and Idrissa Ouedraogo as Anthropological Sources." In *African Experiences of Cinema,* eds. Imruh Bakari & Mbye B. Cham, 223–238. London: British Film Institute, 1996.

———. "The Films of Med Hondo An African filmmaker in Paris." *Jump Cut: A Review of Contemporary Media* 31 (1986): 44–46.

Phillips, Caryl. *Color Me English: Migration and Belonging Before and After 9/11.* New York: The New Press, 2011.

———. "Strangers in a Strange Land." *Color Me English: Migration and Belonging Before and After 9/11,* 281–288. New York: The New Press, 2011.

Pinçon, Michel, and Monique Pinçon-Charlot. *Le président des riches. Enquête sur l'oligarchie dans la France de Nicolas Sarkozy.* Paris: Editions La Découverte, 2010.

Plumelle-Uribe, Rosa Amelia. "Vous avez dit indépendance." In *L'Afrique répond à Sarkozy: Contre le discours de Dakar,* ed. Makhily Gassama, 483–507. Paris: Editions Philippe Rey, 2008.

Poli, Alexandra, Jonna Louvrier, and Michel Wieviorka. "Introduction." *La Cité Nationale de l'Histoire de l'Immigration: Quels publics? Hommes et Migrations* 1267 (2007): 10–25.

Polloni, Camille, and Pierre Siankowski. "Éric Raoult s'attaque à Marie Ndiaye et invente un 'devoir de réserve' pour les prix Goncourt." http://www.lesinrocks.com/actualite/actu-article/article/eric-raoult-sattaque-a-marie-ndiaye-et-invente-un-devoir-de-reserve-pour-les-prix-goncourt/. November 10, 2009.

Poinsot, Marie. "Convaincre tous les publics." *La Cité Nationale de l'Histoire de l'Immigration: Quels publics? Hommes et Migrations* 1207 (2007): 1.

"Pour une 'littérature-monde' en français." *Le Monde,* March 16, 2007, 1–3.

"Pour un véritable débat: Identité nationale et histoire coloniale." http://www.achac.com/?O=204, 1–5. Consulted February 14, 2010.

Prencipe, Lorenzo. "Médias et immigration: un rapport difficile." *Migrations Société* 14.81–82 (May–August 2002): 139–156.

Press Dossier. http://www.histoire-immigration.fr/upload/file/ext_media_fichier_342_dossier_presse.pdf.

Preziosi, Donald, and Claire Farago, eds. *Grasping the World: The Idea of the Museum.* Aldershot, UK: Ashgate Publishing Limited, 2004.

Price, Sally. *Paris Primitive: Jacques Chirac's Museum on the Quai Branly.* Chicago: Chicago University Press, 2007.

"Projet de loi relatif à la maîtrise de l'immigration, à l'intégration et à l'asile." http://www.assemblee-nationale.fr/13/ta/ta0026.asp. September 19, 2007.

"Projet de loi relatif à l'immigration, à l'intégration et à la nationalité." http://www.immigration.gouv.fr/IMG/pdf/DP20100401ProjLoi.pdf. April 1, 2010.

Provost, Nicolas. *L'Envahisseur.* Belgium, O'Brother Distribution, 2011.
Purtschert, Patricia. "On the limit of spirit: Hegel's racism revisited." *Philosophy & Social Criticism* 36 (November 2010): 1039–1051.
Quétel, Claude. *Murs. Une Autre histoire des hommes.* Paris: Editions Perrin, 2012.
Rachedi, Mabrouk. *Le poids d'une âme.* Paris: Editions Jean-Claude Lattès, 2006.
Rambaud, Patrick. *Chronique du règne de Nicolas Ier.* Paris: Editions Grasset & Fasquelle, 2008.
Rao, Sathya. "Mythologies et mythoscopies de l'exil dans les cinémas africain francophone et de la postcolonie." In *Images et mirages des migrations dans les littératures et les cinémas d'Afrique francophone,* eds. Françoise Naudillon and Jean Ouédraogo, 103–117. Montréal, Québéc: Mémoire d'encrier, 2011.
Raoult, Eric. www.youtube.com/watch?v=lN_Yh4AHB5I. November 10, 2009.
Ravanello, Olivier. "Interview with Costa-Gavras." http://www.musiquesdumonde.fr/COSTA-GAVRAS-EDEN-A-L-OUEST,1781. Consulted May 12, 2010.
Razane, Mohamed. *Dit violent.* Paris: Editions Gallimard, 2006.
Rea, Andrea. "Laisser circuler, laisser enfermer: les orientations paradoxales d'une politique migratoire débridée en Europe." In *Enfermés dehors. Enquêtes sur le confinement des étrangers,* eds. Carolina Kobelinsky and Chowra Makaremi, 265–280. Bellecombe-en-Bauges: Editions du Croquant, 2009.
Redouane, Najib. *Clandestins dans le texte maghrébin de langue française.* Paris: Editions L'Harmattan, 2008.
Reichenbach, François. *Un Coeur gros comme ça.* Production Pierre Braunberger, 1962.
Reid, Mark A. "Producing African Cinema in Paris." In *Cinemas of the Black Diaspora: Diversity, Dependence, and Oppositionality,* ed. Michael T. Martin, 346–353. Detroit: Wayne State University Press, 1995.
Rémy, Jacqueline, ed. *Comment je suis devenu français.* Paris: Editions du Seuil, 2007.
Renard, Isabelle. "Lorsque l'art contemporain interroge l'histoire." *La Cité Nationale de l'Histoire de l'Immigration: Une collection en devenir, Hommes et Migrations* 1267 (2007), 16–27.
Reynié, Dominique. *Populismes: la pente fatale.* Paris: Editions Plon, 2011.
Ribert, Evelyne. *Liberté, égalité, carte d'identité: les jeunes issus de l'immigration et l'appartenace nationale.* Paris: Editions La Découverte, 2006.
Ribbe, Claude. *Les Nègres de la République.* Monaco: Editions Alphée, 2007.
Rice, Danielle. "Museums: Theory, Practice, and Illusion." In *Art and its Publics: Museum Studies at the Millennium,* ed. Andrew McClellan, 77–95. Oxford: Blackwell Publishing, 2003.
Riding, Alan. "Neocolonialists Seize the French Language: An Invading Legion of Foreign Writers Is Snapping Up the Medals." *New York Times,* 8 October 1997.
Rigaud, Jacques, and Olivier Duhamel. "De l'utilité d'un ministre pour la culture, l'exemple de Jacques Duhamel." *débat* 164 (March–April 2011): 27–36.
Rigouste, Mathieu. *L'ennemi intérieur. La généalogie coloniale et militaire de l'ordre sécuritaire dans la France métropolitaine.* Paris: Editions La Découverte, 2009.
Ritaine, Évelyne. "Des migrants face aux murs d'un monde frontière." In *L'enjeu mondial. Les migrations,* eds. Christophe Jaffrelot and Christian Lequesne, 157–164. Paris: Presses de la Fondation Nationale des Sciences Politiques, 2009.
Rivera, Annamaria. *Les dérives de l'universalisme. Ethnocentrisme et islamophobie en France et en Italie.* Trans. Michaël Gasperoni. Paris: Editions La Découverte, 2010.
Rivet, Jean-François. *Ma 6-T va crack-er.* Actes prolétériens, 1997.
Rodier, Claire. "Aux marges de l'Europe: la construction de l'inacceptable." In *Le retour*

des camps: Sangatte, Lampedusa, Guantanamo, eds. Olivier Le Cour Grandmaison, Gilles Lhuilier, and Jérôme Valluy, 130–138. Paris: Editions Autrement, 2007.

———. "Europe et migrations: la gestion de l'inquiétude. L'exemple de la directive 'retour.'" In *Douce France. Rafles, rétentions, expulsions,* ed. Olivier Le Cour Grandmaison, 259–282. Paris: Editions du Seuil, 2009.

Rolin, Jean. *Terminal Frigo.* Paris: P.O.L, 2005.

Roman, Joël. "La question de l'identité nationale n'est pas taboue!" *Diasporiques* 2 (2008): 24–27.

Rosello, Mireille. *Postcolonial Hospitality: The Immigrant as Guest.* Stanford: Stanford University Press, 2001.

———. "Representing Illegal Immigrants in France: From *clandestins* to *l'affaire des sans-papiers de Saint-Bernard.*" *Journal of European Studies* 38 (1998): 137–151.

Ross, Kristin. *Fast Cars, Clean Bodies: Decolonization and the Reordering of French Culture.* Boston: MIT Press, 1996.

Rouane, Houda. *Pieds-blancs.* Paris: Editions Philippe Rey, 2006.

Ruscio, Alain. *Y'a bon les colonies? La France sarkozyste face à l'histoire coloniale, à l'identité nationale et à l'immigration.* Paris: Le Temps des Cerises, 2011.

Ryam, Thomté. *Banlieue noire.* Paris: Editions Présence Africaine, 2006.

Saada, Emmanuelle. "Un racisme de l'expansion. Les discriminations raciales au regard des situations coloniales." In *De la question sociale à la question raciale. Représenter la société francaise,* eds. Didier Fassin and Éric Fassin, 55–71. Paris: Editions La Découverte, 2006.

Sagan, Françoise. *Bonjour tristesse.* Paris: Editions Julliard, 1954.

Said, Edward W. *Culture and Imperialism.* New York: Alfred A. Knopf, 1993.

Sané, Insa. *Sarcelles-Dakar.* Paris: Editions Sarbacane, 2006.

Sapega, Ellen W. "Remembering Empire/Forgetting the Colonies: Accretions of Memory and the Limits of Commemoration in a Lisbon Neighborhood." *History & Memory* 20.2 (2008): 18–38.

Sarkozy, Nicolas. "Address at the University Cheikh Anta Diop." http://www.africaresource.com/index.php?option=com_content&view=article&id=437%3Athe-unofficial-english-translation-of-sarkozys-speech&catid=36%3Aessays-a-discussions&Itemid=346. July 26, 2007.

———. "Discours à l'Université de Dakar." http://www.elysee.fr/president/root/bank/pdf/president-8264.pdf. July 26, 2007.

———. "Discours à Toulon." http://mouveuropeprovence.free.fr/serendipity/index.php?/archives/17http://www.google.com/search?client=safari&rls=en&q=http://mouveuropeprovence.free.fr/serendipity/index.php%3F/archives/17-Discours-Nicolas-Sarkozy-a-Toulon,-Mercredi-7-fevrier-2007.html.&ie=UTF-8&oe=UTF-8-Discours-Nicolas-Sarkozy-a-Toulon,-Mercredi-7-fevrier-2007.html. February 7, 2007.

———. "Discours au Cap." http://www.cellulefrancafrique.org/Le-discours-de-Sarkozy-au-Cap.html. February 28, 2008.

———. "Discours: Cérémonie d'hommage solennel de la Nation à Aimé Césaire." http://www.elysee.fr/president/les-actualites/discours/2011/discours-ceremonie-d-hommage-solennel-de-la.11063.html. April 6, 2011.

———. "Discours de Cotonou." http://discours.vie-publique.fr/notices/063001811.html. May 19, 2006.

———. "Discours de Grenoble sur la sécurité et l'immigration." http://www.elysee.fr/president/les-actualites/discours/2010/discours-de-m-le-president-de-la-republique-a.9399.html. July 30, 2010.

———. "Discours de Tanger sur le projet de l'Union de la Méditerranée." http://www.ambafrance-uk.org/Discours-du-President-Sarkozy-sur.html. October 23, 2007.
———. "Discours du Président de la République à Toulon," http://www.elysee.fr/president/les-actualites/discours/2011/discours-du-president-de-la-republique-a-toulon.12553.html. December 1, 2012.
———. "Discours sur la nation." http://www.gauchemip.org/spip.php?article2702. March 9, 2007.
———. "Diversity Speech." http://www.elysee.fr/documents/index.php?mode=cview&cat_id=7&press_id=2142&lang=fr. December 17, 2007.
———. "Un nouvel avenir pour notre agriculture." http://www.elysee.fr/president/mediatheque/videos/2009/octobre/un-nouvel-avenir-pour-notre-agriculture.4967.html. October 27, 2009.
———. "Opening Speech. 25th Africa-France summit." https://pastel.diplomatie.gouv.fr/editorial/actual/ae12/bulletin.asp?liste=20100601.html. May 31, 2010.
———. "Vœux aux acteurs de la Culture." http://www.culture.gouv.fr/culture/actualites/conferen/albanel/prculture09.pdf. January 13, 2009, 1–24.
Sarkozy, Nicolas, with Thibauld Collin and Philipe Verdin. *La République, les religions, l'espérance.* Paris: Éditions du Cerf, 2004.
Sarrazin, Thilo. *Deutschland Schafft Sich Ab: Wie wir unser Land aufs Spiel setzen.* Munich, Germany: DVA, 2010.
Sassen, Saskia. *Globalization and Its Discontents: Essays on the New Mobility of People and Money.* New York: The New Press, 1998.
"The Schengen *acquis.*" Official Journal of the European Communities. http://eur-lex.europa.eu/LexUriServ/LexUriServ.do?uri=OJ:L:2000:239:0001:0473:EN:PDF. 2000.
Sciolino, Elaine. "From Paris Suburbs, a Different Voice." *New York Times,* October 26, 2004.
Sebbar, Leïla. *Parle mon fils, parle à ta mère.* Paris: Editions Stock, 1984.
Secrétariat général du comité interministériel de contrôle de l'immigation. *Rapport annuel: Les orientations de la politique de l'immigration et de l'intégration.* Paris: Direction de l'information légale et administrative, 2011.
Sembene, Ousmane. "Black Girl." Trans. Ellen Conroy Kennedy. In *Under African Skies: Modern African Stories,* ed. Charles R. Larson, 42–54. New York: The Noonday Press, 1997.
———. *Le docker noir.* Paris: Editions Présence Africaine, 1956.
"Seminar on 'The Role of the African Film-Maker in Rousing an Awareness of Black Civilization,' Ouagadougou, April 8–13, 1974." In *Cinemas of the Black Diaspora: Diversity, Dependence, and Oppositionality,* ed. Michael T. Martin, 473–497. Detroit: Wayne State University Press, 1995.
Schäfer, Isabel. "Politiques migratoires et identitaires de l'"Union européenne dans l'espace euro-méditerranéen." Hybrid European-Muslim Identity-Models (HEYMAT), *Heymat Working Paper Nr. 01/2010.* http://www.heymat.hu-berlin.de/heymat-workingpaper. December 2010.
Schoendoerffer, Pierre. *Diên Biên Phú.* AMLF, 1992.
Shaka, Femi Okiremuete. "Film Production Structures and Sponsorship Policies in Francophone Africa." In *Modernity and the African Cinema: A Study in Colonialist Discourse, Postcoloniality, and Modern African Identities,* 301–328. Trenton: Africa World Press, 2004.
Sherzer, Dina. "Introduction." In *Cinema, Colonialism, Postcolonialism: Perspectives from the French and Francophone Worlds,* ed. Dina Sherzer, 1–19. Austin: University of Texas Press, 1996.

Signaté, Ibrahima. *Med Hondo: Un cinéaste rebelle.* Paris: Editions Présence Africaine, 1994.

Silverman, Maxim. *Deconstructing the Nation: Immigration, Racism and Citizenship in Modern France.* London: Routledge, 1992.

Simon, Patrick. "Nationalité et sentiment national." In *Trajectoires et origines. Enquête sur la diversité des populations en France,* eds. Cris Beauchemin, Christelle Hamel, and Patrick Simon, 117–122. Documents de travail 168: http://www.ined.fr/fichier/t_telechargement/35196/telechargement_fichier_fr_dt168.13janvier11.pdf. October 2010.

———. "La République face à la diversité: comment décoloniser les imaginaires." In *La fracture coloniale: La société française au prisme de l'héritage colonial,* eds. Pascal Blanchard, Nicolas Bancel, and Sandrine Lemaire, 237–254. Paris: Editions La Découverte, 2005.

Slama, Serge. "Politique d'immigration: un laboratoire de la frénésie sécuritaire." In *La frénésie sécuritaire. Retour à l'ordre et nouveau contrôle social,* ed. Laurent Mucchielli, 64–76. Paris: Editions La Découverte, 2008.

Smaïl, Paul. *Vivre me tue.* Paris: Editions Balland, 1997.

Smith, Stephen. *Négrologie: pourquoi l'Afrique meurt.* Paris: Editions Calmann-Lévy, 2003.

Smouts, Marie-Claude, ed. *La Situation postcoloniale: Les* postcolonial studies *dans le débat français.* Paris: Presses de Sciences Po, 2007.

Socé, Ousmane. *Mirages de Paris.* Paris: Nouvelles Editions Latines, 1937.

Sontag, Susan. *Regarding the Pain of Others.* New York: Penguin, 2003.

Souad, and Marie-Thérèse Cuny. *Brûlée vive.* Paris: Oh! Editions, 2003.

Soudan, François. "Rama Yade: 'Sarkozy, les Africains et moi.'" *Jeune Afrique* http://www.jeuneafrique.com/Article/ARTJAJA2511p022-029-bis.xm10/france-interview-rama-yade-secretaire-d-etatrama-yade-sarkozy-les-africains-et-moi.html. February 25, 2009.

Soullez, Christophe. *Les violences urbaines.* Toulouse: Les Editions Milan, 2006.

Spaas, Lieve. *The Francophone Film: A Struggle for Identity.* Manchester: Manchester University Press, 2001.

Spire, Alexis. *Accueillir ou reconduire. Enquête sur les guichets de l'immigration.* Paris: Editions Raison d'Agir, 2008.

Stassen, Jean-Philippe. "Les visiteurs de Gibraltar." *XXI* (January–March 2008): 156–185.

Steketee, Lionel. *Case départ.* Légende Films, 2011.

Stephanou, Constantin. "'Union européenne' et 'Union pour la Méditerranée': Des projets politiques concurrents ou complémentaires?" In *Euro-Méditerranée: Histoire d'un futur,* ed. Ali Sedjari, 131–136. Paris: Editions L'Harmattan, 2010.

Stevens, Mary. "Designing Diversity: The Visual Identity of the *Cité nationale de l'histoire de l'immigration* (National Museum of Immigration)," http://www.susdiv.org/uploadfiles/ED2007-056.pdf. December 2007, 1–16.

———. "Still the Family Secret? The Representation of Colonialism in the *Cité nationale de l'histoire de l'immigration.*" *African and Black Diaspora: An International Journal* 2 (July 2009): 245–255.

Stora, Benjamin. *La gangrène et l'oubli. La mémoire de la guerre d'Algérie.* Paris: Editions La Découverte, 1992.

Stovall, Tyler. *Paris Noir: African Americans in the City of Lights.* New York: Houghton Mifflin Company, 1996.

———. "From Red Belt to Black Belt: Race, Class, and Urban Marginality in Twentieth-Century Paris." In *The Color of Liberty: Histories of Race in France,* eds. Susan Peabody and Tyler Stovall, 351–369. Durham, NC: Duke University Press, 2003.

Stovall, Tyler, and Georges Van Den Abbeele, eds. *French Civilization and Its Discontents: Nationalism, Colonialism, Race.* Lanham: Lexington Books, 2003.
Tadjer, Akli. *Bel-Avenir.* Paris: Editions Flammarion, 2006.
Tapsoda, Clément. "Portrait de Paulin S. Vieyra (1925–1987): *l'homme à la casquette.*" In *Afrique 50: Singularités d'un cinéma pluriel.*, ed. Catherine Ruelle, 293–295. Paris: Editions L'Harmattan, 2005.
Tarr, Carrie. "French Cinema and Post-Colonial Minorities." In *Post-Colonial Cultures in France,* eds. Alec G. Hargreaves and Mark McKinney, 59–83. London: Routledge, 1997.
———. *Reframing Difference: 'Beur' and 'Banlieue' Filmmaking in France.* Manchester: Manchester University Press, 2005.
Taubira, Christiane. *Egalité pour les exclus: La politique face à l'histoire et à la mémoire coloniales.* Paris: Editions du Temps Présent, 2009.
Taylor, Anne-Christine. "Les vies d'un objet de musée." TDC, *Le musée du quai Branly* 918 (June 15, 2006): 6–13.
Taylor, Ian. *International Relations of Sub-Saharan Africa.* New York: Continuum, 2010.
Taylor, Saul. "Barriers and Barrios: Melilla." *Monocle* 28.3 (2009): 55–59.
Tcheuyap, Alexie, ed. *Cinema and Social Discourse in* Cameroon. *Bayreuth African Studies* 69 (2005).
"Textes de lois relatifs à la mémoire et à l'histoire." In *La colonisation, la loi et l'histoire,* eds. Claude Liauzu and Gilles Manceron, 161–167. Paris: Editions Syllepse, 2006.
"Textes de référence." http://www.debatidentitenationale.fr/bibliotheque/. Consulted January 12, 2010.
Tevanian, Pierre. "Le legs colonial." In *Une mauvaise décolonisation: La France: de l'Empire aux émeutes des quartiers populaires,* eds. Georges Labica, Francis Arzalier, Olivier Le Cour Grandmaison, Pierre Tevanian, and Saïd Bouamama, 59–74. Paris: Le Temps des Cerises, 2008.
———. *Le ministère de la peur. Réflexions sur le nouvel ordre sécuritaire.* Paris: Editions L'Esprit frappeur, 2003.
———. *La République du mépris. Les métamorphoses du racisme dans la France des années Sarkozy.* Paris: Editions La Découverte, 2007.
Tevanian, Pierre, and Sylvie Tissot. *Dictionnaire de la lepénisation des esprits.* Paris: Editions L'Esprit frappeur, 2002.
Thackway, Melissa. *Africa Shoots Back: Alternative Perspectives in Sub-Saharan Francophone: Alternative Perspectives.* Bloomington: Indiana University Press, 2003.
———. "Filming the Immigrant Experience: Francophone African cinema in Europe." In *Africa Shoots Back: Alternative Perspectives in Sub-Saharan Francophone: Alternative Perspectives,* 120–146. Bloomington: Indiana University Press, 2003.
Le Théâtre du Soleil. http://www.theatre-du-soleil.fr/caravan/index.shtml.
Thiesse, Anne-Marie. *La création des identités nationales. Europe XVIIIe–XXe.* Paris: Editions du Seuil, 2001.
"Third Annual Report on Migration and Integration." http://europa.eu/rapid/pressReleasesAction.do?reference=MEMO/07/351&format=HTML&aged=1&language=EN&guiLanguage=en. September 11, 2007.
Thomas, Dominic. *Black France: Colonialism, Immigration, and Transnatinalism.* Bloomington: Indiana University Press, 2007.
———, ed. *Museums in Postcolonial Europe.* London: Routledge, 2009.
Thuram, Lilian, et al. *Appel pour une République multiculturelle et postraciale. Respect Mag* 10 (January–March 2010).

Tiberj, Vincent. *La crispation hexagonale. France fermée contre France plurielle, 2001–2007.* Paris: Collection Fondation Jean Jaurès/ Editions Plon, 2008.

Tobner, Odile. "Préface." In Mongo Béti, *La France contre l'Afrique. Retour au Cameroon.* Paris: Editions La Découverte, 2006, 205–217.

———. "La vision de l'Afrique chez les présidents de la Cinquième République française." In *L'Afrique répond à Sarkozy: Contre le discours de Dakar,* ed. Makhily Gassama, 509–523. Paris: Editions Philippe Rey, 2008.

Todorov, Tzvetan. "A bas le multiculturalisme!" *Télérama horizons* 4 (April 2011): 46–53.

Touati, Sylvain. "French Foreign Policy in Africa: Between *pré-carré* and Multilaterialism." The Royal Institute of International Affairs. http://www.chathamhouse.org/sites/default/files/public/Research/Africa/bnafrica0207.pdf. 2007, 1–22.

Toubon, Jacques. *Mission de préfiguration du Centre de ressources et de mémoires de l'immigration.* Paris: La Documentation Française, 2004.

———. "La place des immigrés dans la construction de la France." Jacques Toubon, *Mission de préfiguration du Centre de ressources et de mémoires de l'immigration.* Paris: La Documentation Française, 2004, 9–11.

"Toward a World Literature in French." Trans. Daniel Simon. *World Literature Today* 83.2 (March–April 2009): 54–56.

"Towards a Common European Union Migration Policy." http://ec.europa.eu/justice_home/fsj/immigration/integration/fsj_immigration_integration_en.htm. September 2007.

"Towards a Real Debate: National Identity and Colonial History." Trans. Dominic Thomas. http://www.achac.com/?O=204, 1–7. Consulted February 14, 2010.

Traoré, Aminata. *L'Afrique dans un monde sans frontières.* Arles: Actes Sud, 1999.

———. *Lettre au Président des Français à propos de la Côte d'Ivoire et de l'Afrique en général.* Paris: Editions Fayard, 2005.

———. *Le viol de l'imaginaire.* Paris: Actes Sud/Editions Fayard, 2002.

Tribalat, Michèle. *Les Yeux grands fermés. L'immigration en France.* Paris: Editions Denöel, 2010.

Truchot, Claude. "Le régime linguistique des institutions de l'Union européenne: le droit . . . et la pratique." *Questions Internationales* 36 (2009): 94–101.

———. *Europe: l'enjeu linguistique.* Paris: La Documentation Française, 2009.

Tshimanga, Charles, Didier Gondola, and Peter J. Bloom eds. *Frenchness and the African Diaspora: Identity and Uprising in Contemporary France.* Bloomington: Indiana University Press, 2009.

United Nations High Commissioner for Refugees (UNHCR). www.unhcr.org/cgi-bin/texis/vtx/asylum?page=home.

United Nations Convention on Human Rights. http://portal.unesco.org/shs/en/files/2874/11163348401InfoKit_en.pdf/InfoKit%2Ben.pdf.

Ukadike, Nwachukwu Frank. *Black African Cinema.* Berkeley: University of California Press, 1994.

UNESCO-IOM Migration Museums Initiative. http://www.migrationmuseums.org/web/.

Valluy, Jérôme. "L'Empire du rejet: xénophobie de gouvernement et politiques antimigratoires entre Europe et Afrique." In *Douce France. Rafles, rétentions, expulsion,* ed. Olivier Le Cour Grandmaison, 121–143. Paris: Editions du Seuil, 2009.

———. *Rejet des exilés. Le grand retournement du droit d'asile.* Bellecombe-en-Bauges: Editions du Croquant, 2009.

Van Eeckhout, Laetitia. "Brice Hortefeux à la tête d'un grand ministère de l'immigration incluant l'identité nationale." *Le Monde,* May 19, 2007.

Veil, Simone. Comité de reflexion sur le préambule de la Constitution: Rapport au Président de la République. December 2008.
Ventura, Rafaelle, and Samir Abdallah. *La Ballade des sans-papiers.* Agence IM'media/Les Yeux ouverts, 1996.
Vergès, Françoise. "La mémoire de l'esclavage et la loi." *La mémoire enchaînée: Questions sur l'esclavage,* 105–148. Paris: Editions Albin Michel, 2006.
———. Rapport de la mission sur la mémoire des expositions ethnographiques et coloniales. http://www.ladocumentationfrancaise.fr/rapports-publics/114000663/index.shtml. Consulted May 9, 2012.
Verschave, François-Xavier. *De la Françafrique à la Mafiafrique.* Brussels, Belgium: Editions Tribord, 2004.
———. *La Françafrique. Le plus long scandale de la République.* Paris: Editions Stock, 1998.
———. *Noir silence: Qui arrêtera la Françafrique.* Paris: Editions des Arènes, 2000.
———. *Noir Chirac. Secret et impunité.* Paris: Editions des Arènes, 2002.
Verschave, François-Xavier, and Philippe Hauser. *Au mépris des peuples: Le néocolonialisme franco-africain.* Paris: La Fabrique Editions, 2004.
Vieyra, Paulin S. *Le cinéma africain.* Paris: Editions Présence Africaine, 1969.
———. "Propos sur le cinéma africain." *Présence Africaine* 22 (1958): 106–117.
———. "Quand le cinéma français parle au nom de l'Afrique noire." *Présence Africaine* 11 (1956–1957): 142–145.
———. "Responsabilités du cinéma dans la formation d'une conscience nationale." *Présence africaine* 27–28 (1959): 303–313.
Vogel, Susan. "Always True to the Object, in Our Fashion." In *Exhibiting Cultures: The Poetics and Politics of Museum Display,* eds. Ivan Karp and Steven S. Lavine, 191–203. Washington, DC: Smithsonian, 1991.
———. "Des ombres sur la Seine: L'art africain, l'obscurité et le musée du quai Branly." *Le débat* 147 (2007): 178–192.
Waberi, Abdourahman A. *Aux États-Unis d'Afrique.* Paris: Editions Jean-Claude Lattès, 2006.
———. "Le blues de Moussa l'Africain." In *Culture post-coloniale 1961–2006: Traces et mémoires coloniales en France,* eds. Pascal Blanchard and Nicolas Bancel, 268–273. Paris: Editions Autrement, 2006.
———. "Ecrivains en position d'entraver." In *Pour une littérature-monde,* eds. Michel Le Bris and Jean Rouaud, 67–75. Paris: Editions Gallimard, 2007.
———. *In the United States of Africa.* Trans. David and Nicole Ball. Lincoln: University of Nebraska Press, 2009.
———. *Transit.* Paris: Editions Gallimard, 2003.
Wacquant, Loïc. Banlieues françaises et ghettos noir américain: de l'amalgame à la comparaison." *French Politics and Society* 10.4 (1992): 81–103.
———. *Punir les pauvres. Le nouveau gouvernement de l'insécurité sociale.* Marseille: Editions Agone, 2004.
———. *Parias urbains: Ghetto, banlieues, état.* Paris: Editions La Découverte, 2006.
———, ed. *Pierre Bourdieu and Democratic Politics: The Mystery of Ministry.* Cambridge, UK: Polity Press, 2005.
Wagener, Albin. *Le débat sur "l'identité nationale." Essai à propos d'un fantôme.* Paris: Editions L'Harmattan, 2010.
Walcott, Derek. "The Lost Empire" *White Egrets,* 37–38. London: Faber and Faber, 2010.
Walkowitz, Daniel J., and Lisa Maya Knauer, eds. *Contested Histories in Public Space.* Durham, NC: Duke University Press, 2009.

Wane, Fatimata, and Didier Gondola. *Transient Citizens* (*Les citoyens de l'avion*). DVD documentary, 2006.

Wargnier, Régis. *Indochine*. Bac Films, 1992.

Wauthier, Claude. *Quatre Présidents et l'Afrique. De Gaulle, Pompidou, Giscard d'Estaing, Mitterrand*. Paris: Editions du Seuil, 1995.

Weber, Eugen. *Peasants into Frenchmen: The Modernization of France*. Cambridge: Harvard University Press, 1977.

Weil, Patrick. *How to Be French: Nationality in the Making Since 1789*. Trans. Catherine Porter. Durham, NC: Duke University Press, 2008.

———. "Politique de la mémoire: l'interdit de la commémoration." *Liberté, égalité, discriminations: 'l'identité nationale' au regard de l'histoire*, 165–209. Paris: Editions Grasset & Fasquelle, 2008.

———. *Qu'est-ce qu'un francais? Histoire de la nationalité française depuis la Révolution* Paris: Editions Grasset & Fasquelle, 2002.

Wieviorka, Michel. *La diversité: Rapport à la Ministre de l'Enseignement supérieur et de la Recherche*. Paris: Editions Robert Laffont, 2009.

———. Inscrire l'immigration dans le récit national." *La Cité Nationale de l'Histoire de l'Immigration: Quels publics? Hommes et Migrations* (2007): 8–9.

Whiteman, Kaye. "The Man Who Ran Françafrique." *National Interest* 49 (Fall 1997).

Wihtol de Wenden, Catherine. "La crise de l'asile." In *Allers-Retour*, eds. Abdellatif Chaouite and Marie Virolle, 159–165. Paris: Téraèdre Publishing /Revues Plurielles, 2008.

———. *L'Immigration en Europe*. Paris: La Documentation Française, 1997.

———. "Immigration: une politique contradictoire." *Esprit* 11 339 (2007): 83–87.

Wilder, Gary. *The French Imperial Nation State: Negritude and Colonial Humanism between the Two World Wars*. Chicago: University of Chicago Press, 2005.

Williams, Patrick. "Roads to Freedom: Jean-Paul Sartre and Anti-Colonialism." In *Postcolonial Thought in the French-Speaking World*, eds. Charles Forsdick and David Murphy, 147–156. Liverpool: Liverpool University Press, 2009.

Yade-Zimet, Rama. *Noirs de France*. Paris: Editions Calmann-Lévy, 2007.

Yahi, Naïma. "L'immigré dans la fiction, des années soixante à nos jours." In *Immigrances: L'immigration en France au XXème siècle*, eds. Benjamin Stora and Emile Temine, 275–298. Paris: Editions Hachette, 2007.

Yaméogo, S. Pierre. *Moi et mon blanc*. Dunia Productions/Les films de l'espoir, 2003.

Websites

www.africamuseum.be.
www.arretezcedebat.com.
www.bundesregierung.de.
www.cimade.org.
www.citeart.free.fr.
www.culture.gouv.fr.
www.debatidentitenationale.fr.
www.debatidentitenationale.fr/bibliotheque/.
www.ehess.fr/cena/membres/ndiaye.html.
www.empiremuseum.co.uk.
www.enattendantdemain.org.

www.francophonie.org.
www.frontex.europa.eu.
www.histoire-immigration.fr.
www.icetream.com.
www.indigenes-republique.fr.www.olympedegouges.wordpress.com/qui-sommes-nous/.
www.immigration.gouv.fr.
www.kit.nl.
www.kreyolfactory.com/exposition/parcours_de_l_exposition.html.
www.les-engraineurs.org.
www.lkp-gwa.org.
www.mediapart.fr.
www.prix-litteraires.net/goncourt_liste.php.
www.prix-litteraires.net/renaudot_liste.php.
www.quaibranly.fr.
www.quaibranly.fr/en/programmation/exhibitions/last-exhibitions/planete-metisse-to-mix-or-not-to-mix.html.
www.quaibranly.fr/index.php?id=diaspora.
www.quifaitlafrance.com.
www.regards@banlieue.org.
www.svr-migration.de.

INDEX

DOMINIC THOMAS is Professor of Comparative Literature and French and Francophone Studies at the University of California, Los Angeles. He is the author of *Nation-Building, Propaganda and Literature in Francophone Africa* (IUP, 2002) and *Black France: Colonialism, Immigration and Transnationalism* (IUP, 2007). He is also the editor of the series Global African Voices at Indiana University Press.